STUDY GUIDE

Frederic S. Mishkin
Columbia University

Apostolos Serletis
University of Calgary

Saad Kiryakos
University of Ottawa

The Economics of Money, Banking, and Financial Markets

Third Canadian Edition

Frederic S. Mishkin
Apostolos Serletis

Toronto

ISBN-13: 978-0-321-42394-8
ISBN-10: 0-321-42394-1

Acquisitions Editor: Don Thompson
Developmental Editor: Lisa Cicinelli
Production Editor: Mary Ann Field
Production Coordinator: Avinash Chandra

1 2 3 4 5   11 10 09 08 07

Printed and bound in Canada.

Contents

CHAPTER 1

Why Study Money, Banking, and Financial Markets?

CHAPTER SYNOPSIS/COMPLETIONS

The study of money is an extremely important part of both economics and finance. Research has found money to play an important role in the determination of aggregate output, the aggregate price level, the rate of inflation, and the level of interest rates.

Without the services provided in (1) ________________ markets such as the bond market, the stock market, and foreign exchange market, Canadians could not enjoy the present high standard of living to which they have become accustomed. These markets have become increasingly important areas of study. Small movements in bond and stock prices can have significant effects, and changes in (2)________________ ________________ (the price of one country's currency in terms of another's) not only affect those individuals involved in international trade, but all consumers and producers.

The bond market is important since interest rates are determined in this market, while the (3)________________ ________________ is the most widely followed financial market in Canada.

Exchange rates are determined in foreign currency markets and have important effects on international trade. For example, a (4)________________ dollar means that the value of the dollar rises relative to foreign currencies and foreign goods become less expensive to Canadians—good news for consumers. Unfortunately, a stronger dollar means that goods produced in Canada become more (5)________________ to foreign purchasers, who are now likely to purchase fewer Canadian goods—bad news for producers. Thus we see that a stronger dollar is a double-edged sword.

Another major area of study in this course is the business of banking. Banks play an important role in determining the quantity of money in an economy. At one time, banks were unique among financial institutions in their roles as monetary policy players. Now a large number of (6)________________ ________________ can have important effects on the nation's money supply. However, since the financial intermediary that people deal with most frequently is a commercial (7)________________, that will be the institution most discussed throughout the book.

Financial intermediaries are an important part of a modern industrial economy. They play an important role in transferring funds from those who wish to save to those who wish to (8)________________, thereby ensuring that resources are put to more productive uses. This process of channelling funds by way of an intermediary or middleman is known as (9)________________ ________________.

The upward and downward movements in economic activity, commonly referred to as the (10)____________________, also have exhibited a close relationship to money growth. Indeed, every recession in Canada in the twentieth century has been preceded by a decline in the rate of money growth.

(11)__________________, the condition of a continually rising price level, has exhibited a close relation to the money supply over so many countries and so many time periods that Nobel Laureate Milton Friedman has stated that "Inflation is always and everywhere a monetary phenomenon." Evidence indicates that those countries with the highest rates of inflation are also the ones with the highest money growth rates.

Moreover, economic theory suggests, and historical evidence indicates, that money has an important influence on the level of interest rates. Since interest rates play such an important role in people's (12)__________________ and (13)__________________ decisions, it should not be surprising that this has been one of the more intensively studied relationships in economics. For example, (14)__________________ interest rates are typically blamed for the depressed conditions experienced by the housing industry from time to time. Thus, high interest rates may cause people to put off buying a house, but it may encourage them to save in hopes of buying one in the future.

Also of concern to economists has been the recent volatility of interest rates. Concern that these substantial fluctuations might reduce investment has led to additional research of this relationship. A related area concerns the interconnection between (15)__________________ growth, interest rates, and fiscal policy. Clearly, the study of money is diverse and intimately related to many important economic events.

EXERCISES

EXERCISE 1: Bond, Stock, and Foreign Exchange Markets

Some of the most important financial markets are discussed briefly in Chapter 1. The statements below refer to three of these markets in Canada: the bond market, the stock market, and the foreign exchange market. Indicate to which of the three markets the statement refers. Let B = bond market, S = stock market, and F = foreign exchange market.

_____ 1. The market where interest rates are determined.

_____ 2. The market where claims on the earnings of corporations are traded.

_____ 3. The market that made major news when the S&P/TSX Composite fell by more than 400 points on October 19, 1987.

_____ 4. Individuals trying to decide whether to vacation in British Columbia or France might be influenced by the outcomes in this market.

_____ 5. The most widely followed financial market in Canada.

_____ 6. The prices of Japanese video cassette recorders sold in Canada are affected by trading in this market.

EXERCISE 2: Pawnbrokers and Financial Intermediation

A pawnshop is a retail store that sells used goods such as jewelry, clothing, and electronic equipment. The pawnbroker obtains these used goods from individuals who borrow from the pawnbroker. The pawnbroker promises to return the used goods to the individual once the loan and interest charges are paid. However, if the individual does not bring in the pawn receipt by the agreed date, then the pawnbroker sells the goods. Are pawnbrokers financial intermediaries? How are they similar to banks? In what ways do they differ?

____

____

____

EXERCISE 3: Money and Inflation

Money growth and inflation rates are reported for a number of selected countries in the table below. Graph the money growth-inflation coordinate for each country, creating a scatter diagram in Figure 1A. Sketch a single line to illustrate the general relationship between money growth and inflation depicted in the scatter diagram. Does the line slope upward to the right?

Country	Average Annual Rate of Money Growth (1975–1984)	Average Annual Rate of Inflation (1975–1984)
Chile	59.4	54.4
Ecuador	24.5	19.0
France	11.9	10.5
Germany	6.3	4.2
Italy	17.3	16.1
Mexico	39.2	40.1
Portugal	15.3	22.8
Turkey	39.5	45.3
United Kingdom	13.0	11.4
United States	7.5	7.6

Source: *International Financial Statistics*

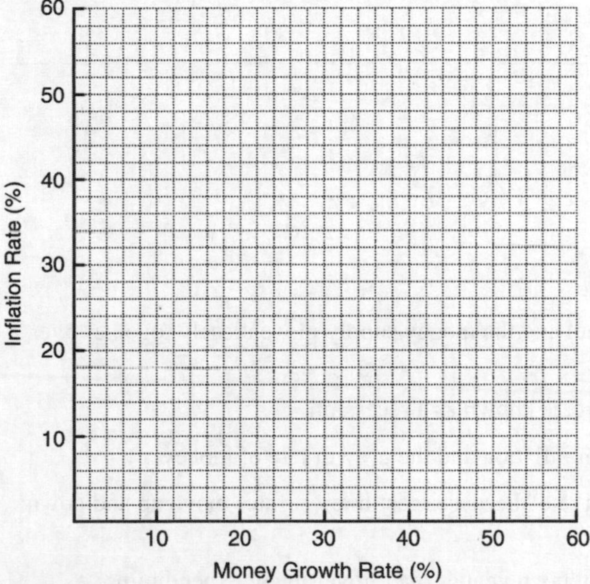

Figure 1A

EXERCISE 4: Money and Business Cycles

On the eve of the Great Depression in 1929, the money supply (M2) in Canada was approximately $2.2 billion. By 1933, the money supply had fallen to $1.9 billion. Predict what happened to the price level and economic activity in Canada during the period 1929 to 1933.

EXERCISE 5: The Foreign Exchange Market

For each of the following cases, indicate whether it represents depreciation or an appreciation of Canadian dollar, by writing in the space provided a D for depreciation and an A for appreciation.

_____ 1. Canadian goods become more expensive in other countries.

_____ 2. It becomes cheaper to travel to other countries.

_____ 3. Imported cars become more expensive in Canada.

_____ 4. Canadian exported goods cost less in foreign countries.

_____ 5. Canadians will prefer to buy imported jeans, not Canadian-made jeans.

_____ 6. The value of each euro in terms of a Canadian dollar decreases.

EXERCISE 6: Aggregate Price Level

A. Suppose that the real GDP and the GDP deflator of a country in 2007 are 11 and 180, respectively. Calculate the nominal GDP of this country in 2007.

____

____

B. Assume that the cost of a basket of goods and services in 2006 was $1200, and the CPI of this country in 2007 is 35%. Find the cost of the same basket in 2007.

____

____

SELF-TEST

PART A: True-False Questions

Circle whether the following statements are true (T) or false (F).

T F 1. Empirical evidence suggests that the price level and the money supply move closely together over long periods of time.

T F 2. The condition of a continually rising price level is known as a recession.

T F 3. There is a strong negative association between inflation and the growth rate of money.

T F 4. Economists frequently talk about "the interest rate" because most interest rates move up and down together.

T F 5. The budget deficit is the excess of government tax revenues over government expenditures.

T F 6. Monetary policy is defined as the management of money and interest rates.

T F 7. Some economists express concern that huge government budget deficits cause the money supply to grow more rapidly, causing inflation.

T F 8. One can reasonably assume that financial intermediaries would not exist unless they provided services that people valued.

T F 9. Economists tend to disregard events in the stock market since stock prices tend to be extremely stable and are therefore of little interest.

T F 10. A stronger dollar means that Canadian goods become more expensive in foreign countries and so foreigners will buy fewer of them.

T F 11. A decline in the exchange rate is associated with the appreciation of the domestic currency.

T F 12. A once and for all increase in the general price level does not constitute inflation.

T F 13. The interest rate on long-term corporate bonds is lower, on average, than the other interest rates.

PART B: Multiple-Choice Questions

Circle the appropriate answer.

1. Why do poorly performing financial markets in a country contribute to poverty?
   a. Credit is difficult to obtain and therefore there is less spending.
   b. Funds are not channelled from savers to spenders.
   c. There are too many opportunities to borrow funds.
   d. only (a) and (b) of the above.
   e. only (a) and (c) of the above.
2. The process of channelling funds from individuals with surplus funds to those desiring additional funds in which the security issued by the borrower is not purchased by the saver is known as
   a. theft.
   b. redistribution.
   c. barter.
   d. financial intermediation.
3. An increase in interest rates is likely to cause spending on houses to
   a. fall.
   b. rise.
   c. rise in the short run if interest rates are expected to fall in the future.
   d. remain unchanged.
4. Lower interest rates may lead to
   a. more spending on automobiles by households.
   b. less saving by households.
   c. more investment spending on new equipment by firms.
   d. all of the above.
   e. only (a) and (b) of the above.
5. A _____ is an example of a security, which is a claim on future income or _____.
   a. bond; interest rate
   b. bond; debt.
   c. stock; assets.
   d. stock; debt.
   e. bank; assets.
6. Which of the following statements regarding stock prices are false?
   a. The worst single-day drop in stock prices was in 2000.
   b. Stock prices may affect household spending.
   c. When stock prices rise, it is more difficult for firms to raise funds.
   d. only (a) and (b) of the above.
   e. only (a) and (c) of the above.

7. Assume that large budget deficits have significant impacts on the level of interest rates. In which market will budget deficits have their biggest impact directly?
   a. The stock market
   b. The bond market
   c. The wheat market
   d. The gold market

8. An increase in the value of the dollar relative to all foreign currencies means that the price of foreign goods purchased by Canadians
   a. increases.
   b. falls.
   c. remains unchanged.
   d. There is not enough information to answer.

9. Which of the following is most likely to result from a stronger yen?
   a. Canadian goods exported abroad will cost less in Japan, and so Japanese will buy more of them.
   b. Canadian goods exported abroad will cost more in Japan, and so Japanese will buy more of them.
   c. Canadian goods exported abroad will cost more in Japan, and so Japanese will buy fewer of them.
   d. Canadians will purchase more foreign goods.

10. From 1985 to 1992 the Canadian dollar depreciated in value, thereby benefiting _____ and harming _____.
    a. Canadian businesses; Canadian consumers
    b. Canadian businesses; foreign consumers
    c. foreign consumers; Canadian businesses
    d. foreign businesses; Canadian consumers

11. Banks are an important part of the study of how money affects the economy since
    a. banks play a critical role in the creation of money.
    b. banks have been important in the rapid pace of financial innovation.
    c. both (a) and (b) are correct.
    d. neither (a) nor (b) are correct.

12. Financial innovation
    a. proceeds at a slow pace.
    b. makes use of computers and the Internet.
    c. demonstrates a lack of creativity.
    d. does not lead to higher profits.
    e. all of the above.

13. Which of the following provides financial intermediation?
    a. A financial self-help book.
    b. An insurance company.
    c. A credit union.
    d. only (a) and (b) of the above.
    e. only (b) and (c) of the above.

14. Suppose that due to a fear that Canada is about to enter a long period of stagnant growth, stock prices fall by 50% on average. Predict what would happen to spending by consumers.
    a. Spending would probably increase.
    b. Spending would probably fall.
    c. Spending would probably be unaffected.
    d. The change in spending would be ambiguous.
15. The expansion of the Canadian economy from 1991 to 2003
    a. was the longest in Canadian history.
    b. was accompanied by a drop in the unemployment rate.
    c. was accompanied by a drop in aggregate output.
    d. only (a) and (b) of the above.
    e. only (b) and (c) of the above.
16. Money appears to have a major influence on
    a. inflation.
    b. the business cycle.
    c. interest rates.
    d. each of the above.
    e. only (a) and (c) of the above.
17. An increase in the growth rate of the money supply is most likely to be followed by
    a. a recession.
    b. a decline in economic activity.
    c. inflation.
    d. all of the above.
18. A sharp decrease in the growth rate of the money supply is most likely to be followed by
    a. a decline in economic activity.
    b. an upswing in the business cycle.
    c. inflation.
    d. all of the above.
19. Which of the following are true statements?
    a. Inflation is defined as a continual increase in the money supply.
    b. Inflation is a condition of a continually rising price level.
    c. The inflation rate is measured as the rate of change in the aggregate price level.
    d. All of the above are true statements.
    e. Only (b) and (c) of the above are true statements.
20. If France experiences higher inflation than Thailand, then
    a. the percentage change of the price level is greater in France.
    b. the percentage change of the price level is greater in Thailand.
    c. the growth rate of the money supply is likely higher in Thailand.
    d. only (a) and (c) of the above.
    e. none of the above.

21. Monetary policy, which involves the setting of interest rates, is usually conducted by a
    a. commercial bank.
    b. national bank.
    c. central bank.
    d. presidential bank.
    e. foreign bank.
22. Budget deficits are important to study in a money and banking class because
    a. budget deficits cause banks to fail.
    b. without budget deficits banks would not exist.
    c. budget deficits may influence the conduct of monetary policy.
    d. of each of the above.
    e. of none of the above.
23. Budget deficits can be a concern because they might
    a. ultimately lead to lower inflation.
    b. lead to lower interest rates.
    c. lead to a higher rate of money growth.
    d. cause all of the above to occur.
    e. cause both (a) and (b) of the above to occur.
24. Fiscal policy includes government spending and taxation and
    a. therefore determines the budget deficit.
    b. therefore determines the budget surplus.
    c. led to budget surpluses from 1999 to 2001.
    d. may affect the inflation rate and the interest rate.
    e. all of the above.
25. Past evidence from Canada shows that
    a. there is a negative relationship between general economic activity and money growth.
    b. recessions have followed declines in share prices on the stock exchange.
    c. recessions have followed a depreciation of the dollar.
    d. recessions have followed a decline in the growth rate of money.
26. The high rates of inflation experienced in many Latin American economies is likely the result of
    a. relatively slow money supply growth rates in these countries.
    b. relatively rapid money supply growth rates in these countries.
    c. a fall in the prices of commodities in these countries.
    d. none of the above.
27. The Canadian dollar appreciated against the U.S. dollar from 1985 to 1992. Compared to 1985, one would expect that
    a. there were fewer Americans travelling to Canada in 1992.
    b. the Americans imported more ice wine from Canada in 1992.
    c. Canadians exported more wheat to the United States in 1992.
    d. there were more Americans travelling to Canada in 1992.

28. Interest rates are determined in the ________.
    a. bond market
    b. stock market
    c. foreign exchange market
    d. central bank
29. An increase in the value of the Canadian dollar in terms of Euros is called ________.
    a. an appreciation
    b. a depreciation
    c. inflation
    d. disinflation
30. Which of the following items is part of Canada's GDP in 2007?
    a. David purchases 100 existing shares of Nortel.
    b. 100 cars produced in 2006 but sold in 2007.
    c. 100 tires used to produce 25 cars in 2007.
    d. 100 tires are sold at Canadian Tire.
31. The Canadian economic experience in the twentieth century shows that every recession has been preceded by
    a. a decline in the rate of money growth.
    b. a rise in the rate of money growth.
    c. a rise in government spending.
    d. a rise in the level of exports.

CHAPTER 2

An Overview of the Financial System

CHAPTER SYNOPSIS/COMPLETIONS

The financial system is a critical element in a well-functioning economy. Chapter 2 examines the general structure and operation of financial markets and institutions.

Financial markets perform the essential function of channelling funds from savers who have excess funds to spenders who have insufficient funds. In (1)_______________ finance, borrowers obtain funds directly from lenders in financial markets through the sale of securities. In indirect finance, funds move from lenders to borrowers with the help of middlemen called (2)_______________ _______________. Financial markets improve the economic welfare of the society because they move funds from those without productive investment opportunities to those with such opportunities. They also directly improve the well-being of consumers by allowing them to make their purchases when they desire them most. When the financial system breaks down, as it did recently in East Asia, severe economic hardship results.

Financial markets can be classified as debt or (3)_______________ markets, primary or secondary markets, organized exchanges or (4)_______________-_______________-_______________ markets, and money or (5)_______________ markets.

A debt instrument is a contractual agreement by the borrower to pay the holder of the instrument fixed dollar amounts at regular intervals. A debt instrument is (6)_______________ term if its maturity is a year or less, is intermediate term if its maturity is from one to 10 years, and is long term if its maturity exceeds 10 years. An (7)_______________ is a claim to share in the net income and the assets of a business firm.

A primary market is a financial market in which new issues of a security are sold to initial buyers by the corporation or government agency borrowing the funds. A secondary market is a financial market in which the securities that have been previously issued can be resold. Secondary markets can be organized in two ways. One is to organize (8)_______________, where buyers and sellers of securities meet in one central location to conduct trades. The other is to have an over-the-counter market, in which dealers at different locations buy and sell securities. The (9)_______________ market is a financial market in which only short-term debt instruments are traded, while the capital market is the market in which longer-term debt and equity instruments are traded.

In the 1960s, 1970s, and 1980s, volatile interest rates made for dynamic financial markets as new types of financial instruments emerged in response to investor demands. Change in the financial markets since the early 1980s has come primarily from a different source: the internationalization of financial markets. The traditional instruments in the international bond market are foreign (10)______________, which are bonds that are sold in another country and that are denominated in that country's currency. A recent innovation is the (11)______________, which is a U.S. dollar deposit that is in a bank outside of the United States. Growth in Eurobonds has been so strong that the Eurobond market exceeds the U.S. corporate bond market as a source of new funds.

Interest in foreign stocks has increased greatly in recent years. For instance, until quite recently, the stock market in the United States was by far the largest in the world. Beginning in the mid-1980s, however, the value of stocks traded in Japan has at times exceeded the value of stocks traded in the United States. Importantly, the internationalization of financial markets has facilitated the financing of domestic corporate and government debt; without these funds, the Canadian economy would be far less healthy.

Financial intermediaries are financial institutions that acquire funds from lenders-savers by issuing (12)______________ and then, in turn, use the funds to make loans to borrowers-spenders. Financial intermediaries allow small savers and borrowers to benefit from the existence of financial markets, thus extending the benefits of these markets to nearly everyone in the economy.

Two factors help to explain the dominant role played by financial intermediaries in our financial structure: transactions costs and problems that arise from information asymmetries. Banks reduce transactions costs by bundling the funds they attract from small savers into loans large enough to finance business undertakings. The bargaining, contracting, and administrative costs (that is, transaction costs) decline as a percentage of the loan amount as the size of the loan increases. Therefore, the administration of loans is subject to economies of scale.

Financial intermediaries engage in (13)______________ ______________by selling low-risk assets and then purchasing high-risk assets. They also lower risk through (14)______________, which entails investing in a portfolio of assets whose returns do not always move together.

Because borrowers know better the potential returns and associated risks of their investment alternatives than do lenders, financial markets are characterized by asymmetries of information. This informational disadvantage can create problems both before and after the financial transaction is made. (15)______________ ______________ is the problem created by asymmetric information before the transaction occurs; moral hazard is the problem created by asymmetric information after the deal has been made.

Adverse selection in financial markets occurs when bad credit risks are the ones who most actively seek financing and are thus the ones most likely to be financed. Moral hazard occurs when borrowers have incentives to engage in activities that are undesirable (i.e., immoral) from the lenders' point of view.

The principal financial intermediaries fall into three categories: depository institutions (banks), contractual savings institutions, and investment intermediaries. (16)______________ institutions are financial intermediaries that accept deposits from individuals and institutions and use the acquired funds to make loans. They include commercial banks, trust and mortgage loan companies, and credit unions and *caisses populaires*. Contractual savings institutions (life insurance companies, property and casualty insurance companies, and pension funds) are financial intermediaries that acquire funds at periodic intervals on a contractual basis. Investment intermediaries include finance companies, mutual funds, and money market mutual funds.

The financial system is among the most heavily regulated sectors of the Canadian economy. A combination of economic and political forces have shaped past and current government regulatory policy, explaining governments' active role in: (a) providing information to investors, (b) ensuring the soundness of the financial system, (c) improving control of monetary policy, and (d) encouraging home ownership. Regulations include: requiring disclosure of information to the public, restrictions on who can set up a financial intermediary, restrictions on what assets financial intermediaries can hold, the provision of deposit insurance, and the requirement that depository institutions maintain minimum levels of capital.

EXERCISES

EXERCISE 1: Direct versus Indirect Finance

For each of the following financial transactions indicate whether it involves direct finance or indirect finance by writing in the space provided a D for direct finance and an I for indirect finance.

_____ 1. You take out a car loan from a finance company.

_____ 2. You buy a Canada bond.

_____ 3. You buy a share of Nortel stock.

_____ 4. You buy a share of a mutual fund.

_____ 5. You borrow $1000 from your father.

_____ 6. You obtain a $50,000 mortgage from your local credit union.

_____ 7. You buy a life insurance policy.

_____ 8. Nortel sells a share of its stock to IBM.

_____ 9. Chase Manhattan Bank issues commercial paper to AT&T.

_____ 10. AT&T issues commercial paper to Mobil Oil Corp.

EXERCISE 2: Financial Intermediaries

A. Next to each of the following financial intermediaries, write the letter(s) corresponding to its primary assets.

		Intermediary		Primary Assets
_____	1.	Commercial banks	a.	mortgages
_____	2.	Trust and mortgage loan companies	b.	consumer loans
_____	3.	*Caisses populaires*	c.	money market instruments
_____	4.	Credit unions	d.	business loans
_____	5.	Life insurance companies	e.	corporate bonds
_____	6.	Pension funds	f.	Canada bonds
_____	7.	Property and casualty insurance companies	g.	corporate stock
_____	8.	Mutual funds	h.	municipal bonds
_____	9.	Money market mutual funds		
_____	10.	Finance companies		

B. Next to each of the following financial intermediaries, write the letter(s) corresponding to its primary liabilities.

		Intermediary	**Primary Liabilities**
_____	1.	Commercial banks	a. deposits
_____	2.	Trust and mortgage loan companies	b. premiums from policies
_____	3.	*Caisses populaires*	c. savings deposits
_____	4.	Credit unions	d. employee contributions
_____	5.	Life insurance companies	e. corporate bonds
_____	6.	Pension funds	f. shares
_____	7.	Property and casualty insurance companies	g. corporate stock
_____	8.	Mutual funds	h. commercial paper
_____	9.	Money market mutual funds	
_____	10.	Finance companies	

EXERCISE 3: Lending and Transaction Costs

Suppose that Julie has $15,000 to invest and that she learns that banks typically charge an interest rate of 8% on a car loan. Thinking that this is a good rate of return, she decides to issue a car loan with the funds that she has. Describe some of the transaction costs that Julie will face, as the lender, if she decides to loan $15,000 to someone in order for him or her to purchase a car.

____

____

____

EXERCISE 4: Financial Regulation

Match the regulatory agency to whom it regulates. Remember that some financial institutions are regulated by more than one agency.

		Regulatory Agency	**Whom It Regulates**
_____	1.	Office of the Superintendent of Financial Institutions Canada (OSFI)	
_____	2.	Quebec Deposit Insurance Board	a. Commercial banks
_____	3.	CompCorp	b. Organized exchanges
_____	4.	Bank of Canada	c. TMLs
_____	5.	Canada Deposit Insurance Corporation (CDIC)	d. CUCPs
_____	6.	PACIC	e. Life insurance companies
_____	7.	Ontario Securities Commission (OSC)	f. Futures market traders
			g. P&C insurance companies

EXERCISE 5: Money Market Instruments

List the six types of money market instruments.

1. ______________________________
2. ______________________________
3. ______________________________
4. ______________________________
5. ______________________________
6. ______________________________

SELF-TEST

PART A: True-False Questions

Circle whether the following statements are true (T) or false (F).

T F 1. When financial markets enable a consumer to buy a refrigerator before she has saved up enough funds to buy it, they are helping to increase economic welfare.

T F 2. Direct finance does not involve the activities of financial intermediaries.

T F 3. The difference between a primary and a secondary market is that in a primary market new issues of a security are sold, while in a secondary market previously issued securities are sold.

T F 4. An over-the-counter market has the characteristic that dealers in securities conduct their trades in one central location.

T F 5. Financial intermediaries only exist because there are substantial information and transactions costs in the economy.

T F 6. Liquidity of assets is as important a consideration for contractual savings institutions as it is for depository institutions.

T F 7. Money market mutual funds to some extent function as depository institutions.

T F 8. The volume of new corporate bonds issued in Canada is substantially greater than the volume of new stock issues.

T F 9. The Ontario Securities Commission is the chartering agency for all commercial banks in Ontario.

T F 10. The primary role of the Ontario Securities Commission is to make sure that adequate and accurate information can be obtained by investors.

T F 11. An over-the-counter market is less competitive than a market with an organized exchange.

T F 12. The money market has fewer price fluctuations compared to the capital market.

T F 13. A well-functioning financial market has negative effects on the wellbeing of consumers.

T F 14. The main disadvantage of owning a corporation's equities rather than its debt is that an equity holder is a residual claimant.

T F 15. Treasury bills are the most liquid of all the money market instruments because they are the least actively traded.

PART B: Multiple-Choice Questions

Circle the appropriate answer.

1. Which of the following cannot be described as indirect finance?
   a. You take out a mortgage from your local bank.
   b. An insurance company lends money to General Motors Corporation.
   c. You borrow $1000 from your best friend.
   d. You buy shares in a mutual fund.
   e. None of the above.
2. Which of the following statements regarding direct finance is false?
   a. An investor with funds lends directly to the borrower in direct finance.
   b. Financial intermediaries are not used in direct finance.
   c. Financial markets are not used in direct finance.
   d. Liabilities are created in direct finance.
3. Which of the following is a short-term financial instrument?
   a. Government of Canada treasury bill.
   b. Share of Air Canada stock.
   c. Municipal bond with a maturity of 2 years.
   d. Residential mortgage.
4. If you want to invest funds for a period greater than one year, you would most likely invest in which market?
   a. A primary market.
   b. A capital market.
   c. A money market.
   d. An over-the-counter market.
   e. None of the above.
5. As compared to capital markets, money markets
   a. are usually more widely traded.
   b. trade debt instruments with shorter terms.
   c. have smaller fluctuations in price.
   d. all of the above.
   e. none of the above.
6. Which of the following statements about the characteristics of debt and equity is true?
   a. They can both be short-term financial instruments.
   b. Bondholders are a residual claimant.
   c. The income from bonds is typically more variable than that from equities.
   d. Bonds pay dividends.
   e. None of the above.
7. Which of the following markets in Canada is never set up as an organized exchange?
   a. Stock market.
   b. Corporate bond market.
   c. Canadian government bond market.
   d. Futures market.

8. Which of the following statements regarding equities is true?
   a. Equities often pay dividends.
   b. Equities are debt instruments.
   c. The equity owner is the residual claimant.
   d. only (a) and (b) of the above.
   e. only (a) and (c) of the above.

9. A bond denominated in a currency other than that of the country in which it is sold is called a(n)
   a. foreign bond.
   b. Eurobond.
   c. equity bond.
   d. currency bond.

10. If a bond is sold in India but it is denominated in British pounds, then that financial instrument is called
    a. a Eurodollar.
    b. a euro.
    c. a Eurobond.
    d. a Europe.
    e. none of the above.

11. Financial intermediaries promote efficiency and thereby increase people's wealth
    a. by reducing the transaction costs of linking together lenders and borrowers.
    b. to the extent that they help solve problems created by adverse selection and moral hazard.
    c. by providing additional jobs.
    d. because of all of the above.
    e. because of only (a) and (b) of the above.

12. Which of the following can reduce the amount of financial risk for a group of investors?
    a. A credit union.
    b. An insurance company.
    c. An investment bank.
    d. All of the above.
    e. None of the above.

13. Banks engage in asset transformation in order to
    a. decrease their liabilities.
    b. lower transaction costs.
    c. create less risky assets.
    d. provide liquidity services.
    e. none of the above.

14. Typically, lenders have inferior information relative to borrowers about the potential returns and risks associated with any investment project. This difference in information is called _______________, and it gives rise to the _______________ problem.
    a. asymmetric information; moral hazard
    b. asymmetric information; adverse selection
    c. adverse selection; moral hazard
    d. adverse selection; asymmetric information

15. Contractual savings institutions include:
    a. commercial banks and TMLs.
    b. life insurance companies and pension funds.
    c. finance companies and mutual funds.
    d. all of the above.
    e. only (a) and (b) of the above.
16. TMLs and CUCPs
    a. are not depository institutions.
    b. primarily hold business loans as assets.
    c. are not currently regulated by the government.
    d. have become more like banks over time.
    e. none of the above.
17. Which of the following is a depository institution?
    a. Life insurance company.
    b. Credit union.
    c. Pension fund.
    d. Finance company.
18. The primary assets of TMLs and CUCPs are
    a. money market instruments.
    b. corporate bonds and stock.
    c. consumer and business loans.
    d. mortgages.
19. The primary liabilities of TMLs are
    a. bonds.
    b. mortgages.
    c. deposits.
    d. commercial paper.
20. TMLs and CUCPs are regulated by
    a. the Bank of Canada.
    b. the Office of the Superintendent of Financial Institutions Canada (OSFI).
    c. the Canada Deposit Insurance Corporation (CDIC).
    d. all of the above.
21. The Canada Deposit Insurance Corporation (CDIC) was created
    a. in order to provide life insurance to all households.
    b. in order to limit interest rates that are paid on deposits.
    c. in order to protect depositors from bank failure.
    d. only (a) and (b) of the above.
    e. only (b) and (c) of the above.
22. Financial panics generally occur when
    a. depositors cannot determine which banks are sound and which are unsound.
    b. interest rates are too low.
    c. deposit insurance is created.
    d. the government regulates the banking sector.

23. Which of the following is a transaction involving indirect finance?
    a. New shares of stock are issued by a corporation.
    b. One corporation buys a bond issued by another corporation.
    c. A pension fund manager buys a bond in the secondary market.
    d. Both (a) and (b) of the above.
24. Which of the following are the primary liabilities of property and casualty insurance companies?
    a. stocks and bonds.
    b. premiums from policies.
    c. chequing accounts.
    d. all of the above.
25. Lenders usually have inferior information, as compared to borrowers, about potential risks associated with an investment project. The difference in information is known as
    a. relative informational disadvantage.
    b. asymmetric information.
    c. variable information.
    d. caveat venditor.
26. Treasury bills are the ________ liquid of all money market instruments and they have (a) ________ possibility of default.
    a. least; high
    b. least; no
    c. most; high
    d. most; no
27. Which of the following is true?
    a. Treasury bills earn more interest than certificates of deposit.
    b. Treasury bills and certificates of deposit are long term.
    c. Overnight funds are the loans made by the Bank of Canada to other banks.
    d. none of the above.
28. A bond denominated in Euros is called a ________ only if it is sold ________ the countries that have adopted the euro.
    a. Eurobond, outside
    b. Eurobond, inside
    c. foreign bond, outside
    d. foreign bond, inside
29. Chartered banks, TMLs, and CUCPs are regulated by ________ and ________.
    a. the Bank of Canada, the Office of the Superintendent of Financial Institutions Canada
    b. the Bank of Canada, Canada Deposit Insurance Corporation
    c. the Office of the Superintendent of Financial Institutions Canada, Provincial Securities and Exchange Commission
    d. both (b) and (c) of the above
30. All deposits under ________ at member deposit-taking financial institutions are insured by CDIC.
    a. $10 000
    b. $50 000
    c. $100 000
    d. $1 000 000

31. Money market securities are usually:
    a. more widely traded than long-term securities and so tend to be more liquid.
    b. more widely traded than long-term securities and so tend to be less liquid.
    c. less widely traded than long-term securities and so tend to be more liquid.
    d. less widely traded than long-term securities and so tend to be less liquid.

CHAPTER 3

What Is Money?

CHAPTER SYNOPSIS/COMPLETIONS

Chapter 3 deals with a problem that has received increased attention among economists since the mid-1970s: just what is money or the money supply? This topic is given expanded treatment in a later chapter, but raising the issue here allows us to consider the importance of money, discovering why it evolves in all but the most primitive societies.

Economists define (1)______________ as anything that is generally accepted in payment for goods and services or in the repayment of debts. This usually means currency to most people, but to economists this definition is far too narrow. Economists include chequing account deposits and travellers' cheques with currency to come up with a narrow definition of the (2)______________ called M1.

Before discussing the significance of money, it is important that one distinguish money from income. Money is a stock; that is, it represents a measure at a point in time. Income is a (3)______________ of earnings per unit of time. Money serves a purpose, or in economists' jargon, it is productive. If money was not productive, we would abandon its use. Money's productivity results largely from its ability to reduce transaction costs and encourage (4)______________ and the division of labour.

Money has three primary functions: It is a medium of exchange, unit of account, and (5)______________ ______________, which all act to reduce transaction costs and encourage specialization. Generally regarded as its most important function, money's ability to serve as a medium of exchange is what distinguishes it from other assets, both financial and physical. Without money, exchanges would be strictly (6)______________ transactions. And while barter can be an efficient system for small groups of people, transaction costs rise significantly as the population grows because people find it increasingly difficult to satisfy a double coincidence of wants. Money reduces the high search costs that are characteristic of barter exchanges.

Money also lowers information and exchange costs by serving as a unit of account. Comparison shopping is extremely time-consuming and costly when goods are not priced in a common unit, whether the units be dollars, cigarettes, or beaver pelts.

Finally, money serves as a store of value. This function of money facilitates the exchange of goods over (7)______________. Although money is not unique as a store of value, it is the most (8)______________ of all assets, and thus it tends to be the preferred store of value for most people most of the time. To illustrate just how strong this tendency is, consider that people did not completely abandon the use of German currency even during the hyperinflationary 1920s, though barter did become much more prevalent.

Money's evolution over time has been driven by efforts designed to reduce transaction costs further. The introduction and subsequent acceptance of (9)_______________ _______________ and cheques greatly reduced transportation costs and the loss from theft, respectively. More recently, there has been progression toward a chequeless society. Although concerns about fraud have slowed development of (10)_______________ - _______________ such as debit cards, one continues to observe movements in this direction.

Because it is not clear what assets should be considered money, the Bank of Canada monitors closely the movements of several (11)_______________ _______________. Most important are the two narrowest definitions, M1B and M2. If both measures moved together and exhibited a high degree of correlation with economic activity, the Bank's job would be much easier. Such is not the case, however, and there seems little optimism among economists that a solution will be found soon to the measurement problem.

Further complicating matters is the unreliability of (12)_______________ money statistics. Given all these problems, it is no wonder that some commentators refer to monetary policymaking as an art rather than a science. At the same time, it is this kind of controversy and uncertainty that makes the study of money and banking so interesting.

EXERCISES

EXERCISE 1: Medium of Exchange

Assume that there are three students on campus named Allen (A), Barbi (B), and Clyde (C). They live in the same dorm and know each other well. Allen owns a CD by R.E.M. (R), Barbi owns a Sugar Ray (S) CD, and Clyde has a CD by Shania Twain (T). Further assume that Allen prefers the Sugar Ray CD to the one by R.E.M. and that he prefers the R.E.M. CD to the one by Shania Twain. Barbi prefers the Shania Twain CD to her Sugar Ray CD, but likes R.E.M. the least. Clyde prefers the R.E.M. CD to his Shania Twain CD, liking the Sugar Ray CD the least. If we rank each student's preferences for the CDs, representing preference with the ">" symbol, we get the following table:

Individual	Preferences	Initial CD
A	S > R > T	R
B	T > S > R	S
C	R > T > S	T

Now assume an economy with no money, so that all trades are barter transactions. Note that when Allen (because he likes Sugar Ray better than R.E.M.) approaches Barbi about trading CDs, Barbi will be unwilling to trade since she will be worse off (she prefers Sugar Ray to R.E.M.). The same happens when any two individuals try to trade directly. Allen will be unwilling to give R.E.M. for Shania Twain in a trade with Clyde, and Clyde will be unwilling to trade away Shania Twain in an exchange with Barbi.

Thus we see from this example that barter between any two individuals (because there is not a double coincidence of wants) prevents the three individuals from getting their most preferred musical artist.

However, if we assume that Barbi is aware of Clyde's willingness to trade his Shania Twain for the R.E.M. CD, then Barbi will be willing to accept the R.E.M. CD in exchange for her Sugar Ray since she knows that she will be able to exchange with Clyde at a later date.

Finish filling in the table below showing the movement of the CDs among Allen, Barbi, and Clyde.

Individual	Initial CD	Intermediate CD	Final CD
A	R	______	______
B	S	______	______
C	T	______	______

What has the R.E.M. CD functioned as?

____.

EXERCISE 2: The Functions of Money

Money has three primary functions: It is a medium of exchange, a store of value, and a unit of account. The statements below provide examples of these three functions. Indicate which of the three primary functions of money is illustrated by each statement. Let M = medium of exchange, S = store of value, and U = unit of account.

_____ 1. Erin purchases tickets to the Pearl Jam concert by writing a cheque.

_____ 2. Christopher drops the change from his pocket into the wine bottle bank on his study desk.

_____ 3. So that they might avoid calculating relative prices of goods in terms of all other goods, the traders at the trading post agreed to value their wares in terms of beaver pelts.

_____ 4. Everyone understood, including nonsmokers, that the prices of commodities traded in the prisoner-of-war camp were to be stated in terms of cigarettes.

_____ 5. Although he loved to smoke, Andrew saved cigarettes for he would be able to purchase chocolate bars on more favourable terms as the supply of cigarettes dwindled in the POW camp.

_____ 6. Anthony calculates that the opportunity cost of his time is $15.00 per hour.

_____ 7. Meghan purchases for $9.95 the videotape she plans to give to her parents for Christmas.

_____ 8. This function of money is important if people are to specialize at what they do best.

_____ 9. Function of money that reduces transaction costs in an economy by reducing the number of prices that need to be considered.

_____ 10. The role of money that would not be provided if bananas were to serve as money.

EXERCISE 3: Functions of Money—Unit of Account

The price of one good in terms of another is referred to as the barter price or exchange rate. The benefits of using money are best appreciated by thinking of a barter economy. Between any two goods there is one barter price or exchange rate. But as the number of goods increases, the number of barter prices or exchange rates grows more rapidly. Complete the following table which dramatically illustrates the virtues of a unit of account.

Number of Prices in a Barter Versus a Money Economy

Number of Goods	Number of Prices in a Barter Economy	Number of Prices in a Money Economy
5	_______	5
25	_______	25
50	_______	_______
500	124,750	_______
5000	_______	_______

EXERCISE 4: Fiat Money, Universal Acceptance, and Expectations

People accept fiat money because they expect that they will be able to trade the money for goods and services today and in the future. The government plays a large role in maintaining universal acceptance of a currency by promoting expectations that the currency will continue to be used in the future. Suppose that you learn that the government is issuing a new currency tomorrow and that, after today, no one will be legally required to accept dollars. Explain why your reaction will likely be to spend all of your dollars today. Now suppose that you learn that the new currency will be issued next week rather than tomorrow. Explain why your reaction continues to be to spend all of your dollars today, as long as you think that other people have the same expectations that you do regarding the new currency.

____

____

____

____

EXERCISE 5: UNIT OF ACCOUNT AND MEASURING MONEY

A. In a barter economy with 30 goods, how many prices are needed to be known by people?

____

A. Match the following terms on the right with the definition or description on the left. Place the letter of the term in the blank provided next to the appropriate definition.

_____	1. The narrowest measure of money.	a. M1+
_____	2. M1B plus the chequable deposits at TML's and CUCPs.	b. M2++
_____	3. Includes non-money-market mutual funds.	c. M1+ and M1++
_____	4. The measure of money that is good at capturing the changes in savings behaviour.	d. M1B
_____	5. The measure of money that is good at capturing the changes in expectations of the household sector of economy.	

SELF-TEST

PART A: True-False Questions

Circle whether the following statements are true (T) or false (F).

T F 1. Since cheques are accepted as payment for purchases of goods and services, economists consider chequing account deposits as money.

T F 2. Of its three functions, it is as a unit of account that distinguishes money from other assets.

T F 3. Money is a unique store of value, since physical goods depreciate over time.

T F 4. Money can be traded for other goods quickly and easily compared to all other assets. Thus money is said to be liquid.

T F 5. Money proves to be a good store of value during inflationary episodes, since the value of money is positively related to the price level.

T F 6. Paper currency evolved because it is less costly to transport than is commodity money.

T F 7. Inflation may reduce economic efficiency if it induces people to resort to barter.

T F 8. The major impetus behind the move to expand electronic payment systems is the relatively high cost of transporting and processing cheques.

T F 9. In times past when only currency functioned as money, measuring money would have been conceptually much easier.

T F 10. The past behaviour of M1B and M2 indicates that using only one monetary aggregate to guide policy is sufficient, since they move together very closely.

T F 11. For economists, money, income, and wealth have the same meaning.

T F 12. Fiat money is a paper currency decreed by governments and is convertible into coins and precious metals.

T F 13. M2++ equals M2+ plus the Canada Savings Bonds and non-money-market mutual funds.

T F 14. Money has an advantage as a store of value over all other types of assets.

T F 15. The M2 monetary aggregate includes M1B plus nonpersonal term deposits at chartered banks.

PART B: Multiple-Choice Questions

Circle the appropriate answer.

1. Money is measured as a ______________ of dollars, while income is measured as a ______________ of dollars.
   a. medium; stock
   b. flow; stock
   c. liquidity; flow
   d. stock; payment
   e. stock; flow

2. When an economist talks about the impossibility of barter, she really is not saying that barter is impossible. Rather, she means to imply that
   a. barter transactions are relatively costly.
   b. barter has no useful place in today's world.
   c. it is impossible for barter transactions to leave the parties to an exchange better off.
   d. each of the above is true.

3. The resources expended trying to find potential buyers or sellers and negotiating over price and terms are called
   a. barter costs.
   b. transaction costs.
   c. information costs.
   d. enforcement costs.

4. If cigarettes serve as a medium of exchange, a unit of account, and a store of wealth, cigarettes are said to function as
   a. bank deposits.
   b. reserves.
   c. money.
   d. loanable funds.

5. Because money reduces both the time it takes to make exchanges and the necessity of a double coincidence of wants, people will find that they can more easily pursue their individual comparative advantages. Thus money
   a. encourages nonproductive pursuits.
   b. encourages specialization.
   c. forces people to become too specialized.
   d. causes a waste of resources due to the duplication of many activities.

6. As the transaction costs of selling an asset rise, the asset is said to become
   a. more valuable.
   b. more liquid.
   c. less liquid.
   d. more moneylike.

7. The conversion of a barter economy to one that uses money
   a. increases efficiency by reducing the need to exchange goods.
   b. increases efficiency by reducing transaction costs.
   c. has no effect on economic efficiency since efficiency is a production concept, not an exchange concept.
   d. decreases efficiency by reducing the need to specialize.

8. Which of the following is an example of fiat money?
   a. Cigarettes traded in a prisoner-of-war camp.
   b. Canadian paper currency that is not redeemable in gold.
   c. Canadian paper currency that is redeemable in gold.
   d. Silver coins.
   e. only (a) and (d) of the above.

9. Which of the following is not a desirable characteristic of money?
   a. Money must be difficult to counterfeit.
   b. Money must be difficult to carry.
   c. Money must not deteriorate quickly.
   d. Money must be recognizable.
   e. Money must be divisible into small units.

10. During the Depression, the government stopped redeeming paper currency for gold. When this happened,
    a. paper currency became fiat money.
    b. the money supply fell to zero.
    c. the dollar was no longer a unit of account.
    d. the dollar was no longer a store of value.
    e. all of the above.

11. At many colleges students can use their identification card to pay for copies and meals, with the balance remaining on the card reduced after each purchase. These cards function as
    a. credit cards.
    b. commodity money.
    c. stored-value cards.
    d. M2.

12. Metal tokens can be used to play games at the video arcade but cannot be used for purchases at other stores. Why do tokens, unlike Canadian coins, not function as money everywhere?
    a. Tokens are too large to transport.
    b. Tokens are easily stolen.
    c. Tokens are not widely accepted by merchants.
    d. Tokens are not a good store of value.

13. During a period of hyperinflation
    a. money is a poor store of value.
    b. the inflation rate is very high.
    c. money may stop being used as a medium of exchange.
    d. all of the above.
    e. only (a) and (b) of the above.
14. Which of the following are problems with a payments system based largely on cheques?
    a. Cheques are costly to process.
    b. Cheques are costly to transport.
    c. Cheques take time to move through the cheque-clearing system.
    d. All of the above.
    e. Only (a) and (b) of the above.
15. Starting January 1, 1999
    a. the exchange rates of countries entering the European Union were fixed permanently to the euro.
    b. the European Central Bank took over monetary policy from the individual national central banks.
    c. the governments of the member countries began issuing debt in euros.
    d. all of the above occurred.
    e. only (a) and (b) of the above occurred.
16. Which of the following are true about the evolution of the payments system?
    a. The evolution of the payments system from barter to precious metals, then to fiat money, then to cheques can best be understood as a consequence of innovations that allowed traders to more easily escape oppressive taxes on exchange.
    b. Precious metals had the advantage of being widely accepted, being divisible into relatively small units, and being durable, but had the disadvantage of being difficult to carry and transport from one place to another.
    c. Paper money has the advantage of being easy to transport, but has the disadvantage of being less accepted than cheques.
    d. Only (a) and (b) of the above are true.
17. In Europe, individual currencies, such as the German mark, were recently replaced by a common currency called the euro. The anticipated effect was to
    a. reduce the need for money.
    b. change the unit of account.
    c. increase transaction costs.
    d. promote barter.
    e. make currency less liquid.
18. Generally, the problem of defining money becomes _______________ troublesome as the pace of financial innovation _______________.
    a. less; quickens
    b. more; quickens
    c. more; slows
    d. more; stops

19. If an individual "cashes in" a Canada Savings Bond for currency,
   a. M1B increases and M2 stays the same.
   b. M1B stays the same and M2 increases.
   c. M1B stays the same and M2 stays the same.
   d. M1B increases and M2++ decreases.
20. The narrowest measure of money, called M1B, consists of
   a. currency and chequing account deposits.
   b. currency, chequing account deposits, and money market mutual funds.
   c. currency, chequing account deposits, and money market deposit account funds.
   d. currency, chequing account deposits, and traveller's cheques.
21. Which of the following is not included in the money aggregate M2?
   a. Currency.
   b. Personal savings deposits at chartered banks.
   c. Overnight repurchase agreements.
   d. Current accounts.
22. Which of the following best describes the behaviour of the money aggregates M1B and M2?
   a. While both M1B and M2 tend to rise and fall together, they often grow at very different rates.
   b. M1B tends to grow at a much faster rate than M2.
   c. While both M1B and M2 tend to move closely together over periods as short as a year, in the long run they tend to move in opposite directions.
   d. While both M1B and M2 tend to move closely together over periods as short as a year, in the long run their growth rates are vastly different.
23. Economists do not define money as the sum of all currency because
   a. it is impossible to adequately measure currency.
   b. currency is sometimes stolen.
   c. other items besides currency function as money.
   d. currency is fiat money.
   e. e-cash is stored on computers.
24. Which of the following statements regarding monetary aggregates is true?
   a. M1B is always greater than M2.
   b. The growth rate of M2 is always greater than the growth rate of M1B.
   c. The Bank of Canada rarely revises estimates of M1B and M2.
   d. The Bank of Canada is concerned mainly with longer-run, rather than short-run, movements in money aggregates.
   e. None of the above.
25. Generally speaking, the initial data on the monetary aggregates reported by the Bank of Canada are
   a. not a reliable guide to the short-run behaviour of the money supply.
   b. a reliable guide to the long-run behaviour of the money supply.
   c. a reliable guide to the short-run behaviour of the money supply.
   d. both (a) and (b) of the above.
   e. both (b) and (c) of the above.

26. When prices are rising rapidly
    a. money is not a good store of value.
    b. money fails as a good unit of account.
    c. money fails as a good medium of exchange.
    d. money fails as a good standard of value.

27. Money is a medium of exchange because it
    a. eliminates the need for a double coincidence of wants.
    b. encourages specialization.
    c. lowers transaction costs.
    d. does all of the above.
    e. does only (a) and (b) of the above.

28. Hyperinflation refers to inflation rates higher than ______ per ________.
    a. 100%, month
    b. 50%, month
    c. 50%, year
    d. 100%, year

29. ______ and ________ show the most liquid and the largest measures of monetary aggregates in Canada, respectively.
    a. M1B, M3
    b. M2++, M3
    c. M1B, M2++
    d. M2++, M1B

30. If John, who is Canadian, transfers $1000 from his US dollar account to his Canadian dollar account,
    a. M2++ increases and M2+ stays the same.
    b. M3 increases and M1B decreases.
    c. M3 decreases and M1B increases.
    d. M2++ stays the same and M1B decreases.

31. Which of the following is not part of M2+:
    a. Deposits at trust and mortgage loan companies.
    b. Non-money-market mutual funds.
    c. Life insurance company individual annuities.
    d. Money market mutual funds.

32. What is hyperinflation?
    a. A rapid increase in the price level, money loses value rapidly, individuals are reluctant to hold money.
    b. A rapid decrease in the price level, money gains value rapidly, individuals want to hold as much money as possible.
    c. An inflation where the inflation rate exceeds 50% per month.
    d. An inflation where the inflation rate exceeds 100% per month.
    e. An inflation where the inflation rate exceeds 50-100% per year.

33. The primary objective of what invention was to reduce the problem of transporting paper currency and coins?
   a. E-money.
   b. Electronic payment.
   c. Cheques.
   d. E-Cash.

34. Which of the following assets is most appropriately associated with the potential use as a medium of exchange?
   a. A Jackson Pollock painting.
   b. A notice deposit account with a trust company.
   c. A 90-day Canadian Treasury Bill.
   d. One share of Nortel stock.
   e. All of the above.

CHAPTER 4

Understanding Interest Rates

CHAPTER SYNOPSIS/COMPLETIONS

Interest rates are among the most important variables in the economy. This chapter explains how interest rates are measured and shows that the interest rate on a bond is not always an accurate measure of how good an investment it will be.

The concept of (1)______________ ______________ tells us that a dollar in the future is not as valuable as a dollar today; that is, a dollar received *n* years from now is worth $\$1/(1 + i)^n$ today. The yield to maturity, the economists' preferred measure of the interest rate, is the interest rate that equates the present value of future payments of a debt instrument with its value (or price) today. Applications of this principle reveal that bond prices and interest rates are (2)______________ related; when the interest rate rises, the price of the bond falls, and vice versa.

Credit market instruments generally fall into four types: a simple loan, a fixed-payment loan, a coupon bond, and a discount bond. A simple loan provides the borrower with an amount of funds that must be repaid at the maturity date along with an interest payment. A (3)______________-______________ loan requires the borrower to make the same payment every period until the maturity date. A coupon bond pays the owner a fixed coupon payment every year until the maturity date when the face value is repaid. Its (4)______________ ______________ equals the coupon payment expressed as a percentage of the face value of the bond. A (5)______________ bond is bought at a price below its face value, but the face value is repaid at the maturity date.

There are two less accurate measures of interest rates that are commonly used to quote interest rates. One is the current yield, which equals the (6)______________ payment divided by the price of the coupon bond. The other is the yield on a discount basis (also called a discount yield) which is used in the case of (7)______________ bonds. Even when either of these measures is a misleading guide to the level of the interest rate, a rise in either of these rates signals a (8)______________ in the yield to maturity, and a fall signals a fall in the yield to maturity.

How well you have done by holding a security over a period of time is measured by the security's (9)______________ —the payments to the owner plus the change in its value, expressed as a percentage of the purchase price. The return is equal to the yield to maturity in only one special case: when the holding period is equal to the (10)______________ of the bond. For bonds with maturities greater than the holding period, capital gains and losses can be substantial when (11)______________ ______________ change. Returns can therefore differ greatly from the yield to maturity. This is why long-term bonds are not considered to be safe assets with a certain return over short holding periods. The real interest rate is defined as the nominal interest rate minus the expected rate of inflation. It is a better measure of the incentives to borrow and lend than is the nominal interest rate, making it a better indicator of the tightness of (12)______________ ______________ conditions than is the nominal interest rate.

EXERCISES

EXERCISE 1: Present Value and Future Value

The formula $PV = FV/(1 + i)^n$ (or $FV = PV * (1 + i)^n$) allows one to determine equivalent values in different time periods. Obviously, fifty dollars received in the year 2004 has a value of fifty dollars in the year 2004. However, in the year 2004 the value (PV) of fifty dollars received in the year 2005 is $50/(1 + i). Likewise, in the year 2004 the value (FV) of fifty dollars received in the year 2003 is $50 ∗ (1 + i). This simply illustrates the principle that dollars received in the future are worth less today while dollars received in the past are worth more today. Complete the following table by calculating the value in the Year Payment Valued of receiving fifty dollars in the Year Payment Received.

Year	Year Payment Received		
Payment Valued	2003	2004	2005
2003	$50	(a) _____	(b) _____
2004	$50 ∗ (1 + i)	$50	$50/(1 + i)
2005	(c) _____	(d) _____	$50

EXERCISE 2: Present Value

Calculate the present value for the following payments:

1. $500 two years from now when the interest rate is 5%. _____
2. $500 two years from now when the interest rate is 10%. _____
3. $500 four years from now when the interest rate is 10%. _____
4. What do the calculations indicate about the present value of a payment as the interest rate rises?

   _____

5. What do the calculations indicate about the present value of a payment as it is paid further in the future?

   _____

EXERCISE 3: Yield to Maturity

A. Suppose you are offered a $1000 fixed-payment car loan that requires you to make payments of $600 a year for the next two years.

   1. Write down the equation that can be solved for the yield to maturity on this loan: that is, the equation that equates the present value of the payments on the loan to the amount of the loan.

      _____

   2. Calculate the present value of the loan payments when the interest rate is 10%.

      _____

   3. Must the yield to maturity be above or below 10%? _____
   4. Calculate the present value of the loan payments when the interest rate is 15%.

      _____

   5. Must the yield to maturity be above or below 15%? _____

   Verify that the present value of the loan payments is approximately $1000 when the interest rate is 13%, indicating that this is the yield to maturity.

B. Suppose you are thinking of buying a $1000 face-value coupon bond with a coupon rate of 10%, a maturity of 3 years, and a price of $1079.

1. Is the yield to maturity going to be above or below 10%? ______________ Why?

____

2. Write down the equation that can be solved for the yield to maturity of this bond: that is, the equation that equates the present value of the bond payments to the price of the bond.

____

3. Calculate the present value of the bond when the interest rate is 8%.

____

4. Must the yield to maturity be above or below 8%? ______________

5. Calculate the present value of the bond when the interest rate is 5%.

____

6. Must the yield to maturity be above or below 5%? ______________

Verify that the present value of the loan payments is approximately $1079 when the interest rate is 7%, indicating that this is the yield to maturity.

EXERCISE 4: Yield to Maturity and Yield on a Discount Basis

For discount bonds with a face value of $1000, fill in the yield to maturity (annual rate) and the yield on a discount basis in the following table.

Price of the Discount Bond	Maturity	Yield on a Discount Basis	Yield to Maturity
$900	1 year (365 days)		
$950	6 months (182 days)		
$975	3 months (91 days)		

Note: For bonds with a maturity of 6 months, the yield to maturity at an annual rate equals $[(1 + i_6)^2 - 1]$, where i_6 is the return over 6 months; for bonds with a maturity of 3 months, the yield to maturity at an annual rate equals $[(1 + i_3)^4 - 1]$, where i_3 is the return over 3 months.

EXERCISE 5: Current Yield

For the five Canada bonds on May 16, 2000, fill in the value of the current yield in the following table:

Coupon Rate	Maturity Date	Price	Yield to Maturity	Current Yield
10 3/4	May 2003	110 11/32	6.87%	
12 3/8	May 2004	118 31/32	6.86%	
6 3/4	May 2005	100 5/32	6.71%	
6 1/2	Nov 2026	101 12/32	6.39%	
6 1/4	May 2030	101 26/32	6.12%	

For which of these bonds is the current yield a good measure of the interest rate? Why?

____

____

EXERCISE 6: The Rate of Return

A. For a consol with a yearly payment of $100, calculate the return for the year if its yield to maturity at the beginning of the year is 10% and at the end of the year is 5%. (Hint: Calculate the initial price and end-of-year price first; then calculate the return.)

____

B. For a 10% coupon bond selling at par with 2 years to maturity, calculate the return for the year if its yield to maturity at the beginning of the year is 10% and at the end of the year is 5%. (Hint: Calculate the initial price and end-of-year price first; then calculate the return.)

____

Which of the bonds is a better investment? ____________________

Why do you think that this has happened? ____________________

____

EXERCISE 7: Real Interest Rates

Calculate the real interest rate in the following situations:

A. The interest rate is 3% and the expected inflation rate is –3%. ____________

B. The interest rate is 10% and the expected inflation rate is 20%. ____________

C. The interest rate is 6% and the expected inflation rate is 3%. ____________

D. The interest rate is 15% and the expected inflation rate is 15%. ____________

In which of these situations would you prefer (everything else equal) to be a lender?

____________________ A borrower? ____________________

EXERCISE 8: Fixed-Payment Loan

Assume that Tara wants to buy a new car and needs to borrow $10,000 from the Bank of Montreal. Calculate the annual payment to the bank for each of the following cases.

1. If she wants to pay off the loan in 15 years and the interest rate is 5%.

____

2. She wants to pay off the loan in 10 years and the interest rate is 4%.

____

3. She wants to pay off the loan in 20 years and the interest rate is 10%.

____

4. She wants to pay off the loan in 10 years and the interest rate is 5%.

____

SELF-TEST

PART A: True-False Questions

Circle whether the following statements are true (T) or false (F).

T F 1. A bond that pays the bondholder the face value at the maturity date and makes no interest payments is called a discount bond.

T F 2. The yield to maturity of a coupon bond that is selling for less than its face value is less than the coupon rate.

T F 3. You would prefer to own a security that pays you $1000 at the end of 10 years than a security that pays you $100 every year for 10 years.

T F 4. The yield to maturity on a coupon bond can always be calculated as long as the coupon rate and the price of the bond are known.

T F 5. The current yield is the most accurate measure of interest rates, and it is what economists mean when they use the term interest rates.

T F 6. You would prefer to hold a 1-year Canada bond with a yield on a discount basis of 10% to a 1-year Canada bond with a yield to maturity of 9.9%.

T F 7. A 5-year $1000 coupon bond selling for $1008 with a 9% current yield has a higher yield to maturity than a 1-year discount bond with a yield on a discount basis of 8.9%.

T F 8. When interest rates rise from 4 to 5%, bondholders are made better off.

T F 9. If interest rates on all bonds fall from 8 to 6% over the course of the year, you would rather have been holding a long-term bond than a short-term bond.

T F 10. Business firms are more likely to borrow when the interest rate is 2% and the price level is stable than when the interest rate is 15% and the expected inflation rate is 14%.

T F 11. When the yield to maturity falls, the price of bonds falls too.

T F 12. For simple loans, the simple interest rate is greater than the yield to maturity.

T F 13. Price and returns for long-term bonds are more volatile than those for shorter-term bonds.

T F 14. When the coupon bond is priced at its face value, the yield to maturity is greater than the coupon rate.

PART B: Multiple-Choice Questions

Circle the appropriate answer.

1. With an interest rate of 5%, the present value of a security that pays $52.50 next year and $110.25 two years from now is
   a. $162.50.
   b. $50.
   c. $100.
   d. $150.

2. The present value of a security that pays you $55 next year and $133 three years from now is $150 if the interest rate is
   a. 10%.
   b. 5%.
   c. 15%.
   d. 20%.

3. Which of the following payment terms should a professional athlete prefer in his "ten million dollar" contract if he wants to obtain the greatest present value of income?
   a. Receive $2 million in each of the next five years.
   b. Receive $6 million next year and then receive $1million in each of the subsequent four years.
   c. Receive $1 million in each of the next four years and then receive $6 million in the subsequent year.
   d. All of the above have the same present value of income.

4. The present value of A plus B is
   a. the present value of A multiplied by B.
   b. the present value of A plus B divided by the future value.
   c. the present value of A plus the present value of B.
   d. the present value of A multiplied by the present value of B.

5. A $5000 coupon bond with a coupon rate of 5% has a coupon payment every year of
   a. $50.
   b. $500.
   c. $250.
   d. $100.
   e. none of the above.

6. If a security pays you $105 next year and $110.25 the year after that, what is its yield to maturity if it sells for $200?
   a. 4%
   b. 5%
   c. 6%
   d. 7%

7. The yield to maturity on a $20,000 face value discount bond that matures in one year's time and currently sells for $15,000 is
   a. 20%.
   b. 25%.
   c. 33 1/3 %.
   d. 66 2/3 %.

8. Which of the following $1000 face value securities has the lowest yield to maturity?
   a. 5% coupon bond selling for $1000
   b. 5% coupon bond selling for $1200
   c. 5% coupon bond selling for $900
   d. 10% coupon bond selling for $1000
   e. 10% coupon bond selling for $900

9. Which of the following $1000 face value securities has the highest yield to maturity?
   a. 5% coupon bond selling for $1000
   b. 5% coupon bond selling for $1200
   c. 5% coupon bond selling for $900
   d. 10% coupon bond selling for $1000
   e. 10% coupon bond selling for $900
10. If a $5000 face value discount bond maturing in 1 year is selling for $4000, its yield to maturity is
    a. 5%.
    b. 10%.
    c. 25%.
    d. 50%.
11. People who own a bond do not like to read that the interest rate increased because
    a. their coupon payments will fall.
    b. their return will rise.
    c. the yield to maturity on their bond will fall.
    d. the price of their bonds has fallen.
12. A bond that makes a fixed coupon payment forever is known as a
    a. Real Return Bond.
    b. discount bond.
    c. nominal bond.
    d. present bond.
    e. consol.
13. A discount bond
    a. pays the bondholder the same amount every period until the maturity date.
    b. at the maturity date pays the bondholder the face value of the bond plus an interest payment.
    c. pays the bondholder a fixed interest payment every period and repays the face value at the maturity date.
    d. pays the bondholder the face value at the maturity date.
14. The current yield on a $5000 10% coupon bond selling for $4000 is
    a. 5%.
    b. 10%.
    c. 12.5%.
    d. 15%.
15. The yield on a discount basis
    a. always moves in the same direction as the yield to maturity.
    b. is a somewhat misleading measure of the interest rate.
    c. understates the interest rate as measured by the yield to maturity.
    d. all of the above.

16. The current yield is a
    a. more accurate approximation of the yield to maturity, the nearer the bond's price is to the par value and the shorter the maturity of the bond.
    b. less accurate approximation of the yield to maturity, the nearer the bond's price is to the par value and the longer the maturity of the bond.
    c. more accurate approximation of the yield to maturity, the nearer the bond's price is to the par value and the longer the maturity of the bond.
    d. more accurate approximation of the yield to maturity, the farther the bond's price is to the par value and the shorter the maturity of the bond.
17. The yield on a discount basis of a 180-day $1000 treasury bill selling for $975 is
    a. 5.2%.
    b. 10.5%.
    c. 20.5%.
    d. 50%.
18. Today, Canadian government treasury bill dealers report the yield on a discount basis because
    a. dealers historically reported the discount yield.
    b. the discount yield is the interest rate that is most preferred by economists.
    c. the discount yield is difficult to calculate.
    d. the yield to maturity cannot be calculated for treasury bills.
19. If it is reported that the interest rate rose by six basis points, then the interest rate rose by
    a. .06%.
    b. 6%.
    c. 6 cents.
    d. $6.00
    e. none of the above.
20. If you buy a discount bond for $980 with 90 days until maturity and a face value of $1000, then the yield on a discount basis is
    a. 9.5%.
    b. 8.3%.
    c. 7.5%.
    d. 6.3%.
    e. 5.5%.
21. What is the return on a 15% coupon bond that initially sells for $1000 and sells for $700 next year?
    a. 15%
    b. 10%
    c. −5%
    d. −15%
22. If a discount bond, which matures in one year, is purchased and held until it matures, then the yield to maturity and ______________ are identical.
    a. the coupon rate
    b. the discount yield
    c. the capital gain
    d. the return
    e. current yield

23. Which of the following cannot be calculated at the time that a bond is purchased?
    a. The current yield.
    b. The return.
    c. The yield to maturity.
    d. only (a) and (b) of the above.
    e. only (b) and (c) of the above.
24. If Edmund pays $900 for a bond with a $1000 face value and a coupon payment of $70, and if he sells the bond next year for $936, then Edmund's rate of capital gain is
    a. 2%.
    b. 3%.
    c. 4%.
    d. 5%.
    e. 6%.
25. In which of the following situations would you rather be borrowing?
    a. The interest rate is 20% and expected inflation rate is 15%.
    b. The interest rate is 4% and expected inflation rate is 1%.
    c. The interest rate is 13% and expected inflation rate is 15%.
    d. The interest rate is 10% and expected inflation rate is 15%.
26. If a bond has a coupon rate of 4% and a face value of $20,000, then the yearly coupon payment is
    a. $40.
    b. $80
    c. $400.
    d. $800.
27. Which of the following says that the nominal interest rate equals the real interest rate plus the expected rate of inflation?
    a. The Fisher equation.
    b. The Keynesian equation
    c. The Marshall equation.
    d. The multiplier equation.
28. The price of a consol is $5000 which pays $150 annually. What is the yield to maturity on this consol?
    a. 5%
    b. 3%
    c. 4%
    d. 2%
29. What is the discount yield of a 30-day treasury bill that is selling for $490 and has a face value of $500?
    a. 2.04%
    b. 10%
    c. 24.48%
    d. 24.83%

30. What is the internal rate of return for a machine that costs $7000 and has $2000 revenue per year for 5 years?
    a. 15%
    b. 10%
    c. 13.2%
    d. 42.8%

31. When the real interest rate is low, then
    a. there are greater incentives to borrow and greater incentives to lend.
    b. there are fewer incentives to borrow and fewer incentives to lend.
    c. there are greater incentives to borrow and fewer incentives to lend.
    d. there are fewer incentives to borrow and greater incentives to lend.

32. The yield to maturity is greater than the coupon rate when
    a. the bond price is below its face value.
    b. the bond price is above its face value.
    c. the bond price is below its yield to discount rate.
    d. the bond price is above its yield to discount rate.

33. When the yield to maturity rises, what happens to the price of the bond?
    a. Price rises above face value.
    b. Price falls below face value.
    c. Price rises above yield to maturity.
    d. Price falls below yield to maturity.
    e. Price stays the same.

34. What 3 equal payments 3, 5, and 9 years from now would be equal to $125,000 today if the rate of interest is 6% per year? (Answers are rounded to nearest dollar).
    a. $57 372
    b. $353 048
    c. $49 626
    d. $55 760
    e. $29 630

CHAPTER 5

The Behaviour of Interest Rates

CHAPTER SYNOPSIS/COMPLETIONS

Chapter 5 examines how interest rates are determined and the factors that influence their behaviour. The supply and demand analysis developed here explains why interest rates have had such substantial fluctuations in recent years. The supply and demand analysis for bonds provides one theory of how interest rates are determined. The (1)_______________ for bonds is the relationship between the quantity demanded and the bond price (which is (2)_______________ related to the interest rate) when all other economic variables are held constant.

With the bond price plotted on the left-hand vertical axis, the demand curve is downward sloping because a lower bond price means a (3)_______________ interest rate, thereby causing the expected return on bonds to rise, resulting in an increase in the quantity of bonds demanded. If the interest rate is plotted on the right-hand vertical axis, the interest rate decreases as one moves (4)_______________ the axis because of the inverse relationship between bond prices and interest rates.

The supply curve for bonds is upward sloping because a rising bond price means a (5)___________ interest rate, thereby reducing the cost of borrowing funds (issuing bonds), resulting in an increase in the quantity of bonds supplied. The market interest rate is the market (6)_______________, which occurs when the quantity of bonds demanded equals the quantity supplied; that is, at the intersection of the supply and the demand curves.

The theory of asset demand portfolio choice indicates that there are four factors that cause the demand curve for bonds to shift. Specifically, the demand curve shifts to the right when wealth (7)_______________, when the expected return on bonds relative to alternative assets (8)_______________, when the riskiness of bonds relative to alternative assets (9)_______________ or when the liquidity of bonds relative to alternative assets (10)_______________.

There are three factors that cause the supply curve for bonds to shift. Specifically, the supply curve shifts to the right when the expected profitability of investment opportunities increases, as in a business cycle boom, when expected inflation (11)_______________, or when the government increases the supply of debt by running high budget deficits. Changes in any of these factors cause interest rates to change. This supply and demand analysis indicates, for example, that a rise in expected inflation leads to a rise in interest rates, a phenomenon known as the (12)_______________ effect.

An alternative theory of how interest rates are determined is provided by the liquidity preference framework, which analyzes the supply and demand for money. The demand curve for money slopes downward because, with a lower interest rate, the expected return on bonds falls relative to the expected return on money. According to the theory of asset demand, this causes the quantity of money demanded to (13)______________. The demand curve for money shifts to the right when income (14)______________, when the price level increases, or when inflation is expected to increase.

The central bank is assumed to control the quantity of money supplied at a fixed amount, meaning that the supply curve for money is a vertical line. The equilibrium interest rate occurs at the intersection of the supply and demand curves for money. The supply and demand analysis of the money market indicates that the interest rate rises when either income or the price level rises, or when the money supply (15)______________.

The liquidity preference framework indicates that there are four possible effects of an increase in the rate of money supply growth on interest rates: (a) the liquidity effect, (b) the income effect, (c) the price-level effect, and (d) the expected inflation effect. The liquidity effect indicates that higher money supply growth leads to a (16)______________ in interest rates; the other effects work in the (17)______________ direction. The evidence seems to indicate that the income, price-level, and expected inflation effects dominate the liquidity effect, implying that an increase in money supply growth leads to permanently (18)______________ interest rates. Whether interest rates initially fall rather than rise when money growth is increased depends critically on how fast people's expectations about inflation adjust.

EXERCISES

EXERCISE 1: Theory of Asset Demand

In the third column of the following table indicate with an arrow whether the quantity demanded of the asset will increase (↑) or decrease (↓):

Variable	Change in Variable	Change in Quantity Demanded
Wealth	↓	
Liquidity of asset	↓	
Riskiness of asset	↓	
Expected return of asset	↓	
Riskiness of other assets	↓	
Liquidity of other assets	↓	
Expected return of other assets	↓	

EXERCISE 2: Factors That Shift Supply and Demand Curves for Bonds

For each of the following situations (holding everything else constant), indicate in the space provided how the supply and demand curves for bonds shift: D → for demand curve to the right, ← D for demand curve to the left, S → for supply curve to the right, and ← S for supply curve to the left.

_____ 1. A decline in brokerage commission on bonds.

_____ 2. Expected inflation rises.

_____ 3. There is a new tax on purchases and sales of gold.

_____ 4. There is a large federal budget deficit.

_____ 5. Businessmen become more optimistic about the success of their investments in new plant and equipment.

_____ 6. Bond prices become more volatile.

_____ 7. The economy booms and wealth rises.

_____ 8. Stock prices become more volatile.

_____ 9. People suddenly expect a bear market (a decline in prices) for stocks.

_____ 10. People suddenly expect interest rates to rise.

EXERCISE 3: Analyzing a Change in the Equilibrium Interest Rate

Suppose the supply and the demand for long-term bonds are as marked in Figure 5A and market equilibrium is at point 1. Suppose that the federal government begins to run a large budget deficit and at the same time the volatility of interest rates increases. Draw in the new supply and demand curves in Figure 5A.

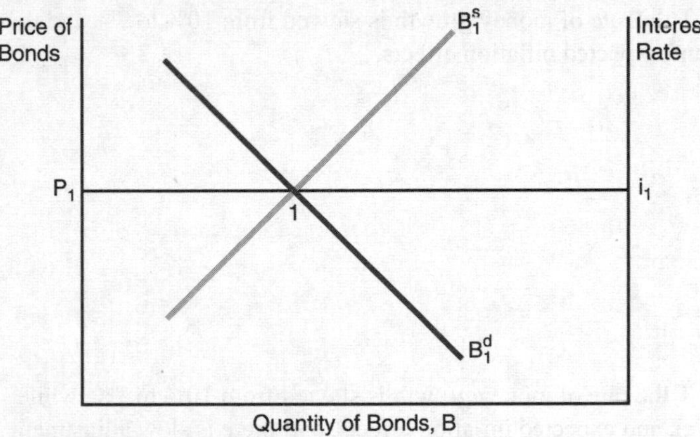

Figure 5A

What happens to the interest rate? ______________________________

EXERCISE 4: Orange County and Municipal Bonds in the United States

Orange County, California, defaulted on over $1 billion of debt when it declared bankruptcy in 1994. Local governments throughout the United States, however, felt the effects as plans for many long-term projects such as schools, jails, and parks were cancelled. These projects are often paid for through funds that are raised when local governments sell municipal bonds. Explain the effect of Orange County's bankruptcy on the U.S. municipal bond market and indicate whether bond supply or bond demand is affected. Then explain why project costs rose for local governments in the United States.

____

____

____

____

EXERCISE 5: Supply and Demand Analysis of the Money Market

Suppose the supply and the demand for money are as drawn in Figure 5B. Now the Bank of Canada decreases the money supply and as a result income falls. Draw the new supply and demand curves in Figure 5B.

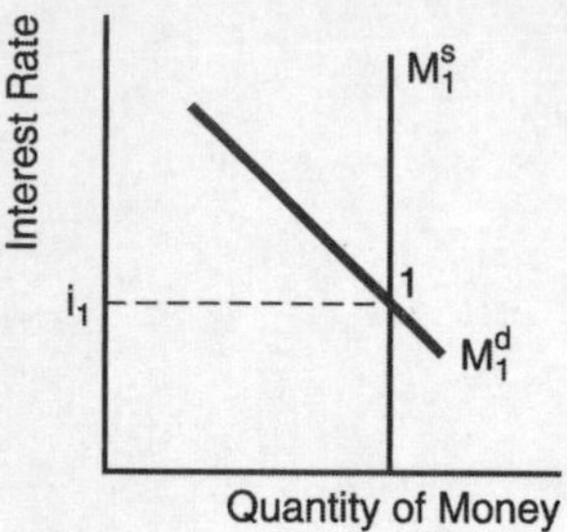

Figure 5B

What happens to the interest rate? ____

EXERCISE 6: Money Growth and Interest Rates

Plot in Figure 5C the path of the interest rate, if at time T the rate of money growth is slowed from 10% to 7% and the liquidity effect is greater than the income, price-level, and expected inflation effects.

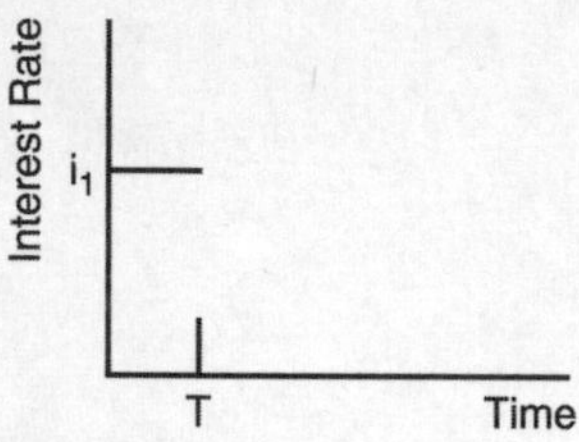

Figure 5C

Plot in Figure 5D the path of the interest rate, if at time T the rate of money growth is slowed from 10% to 7%, while the liquidity effect is smaller than the income, price-level, and expected inflation effects, and there is slow adjustment of inflation expectations.

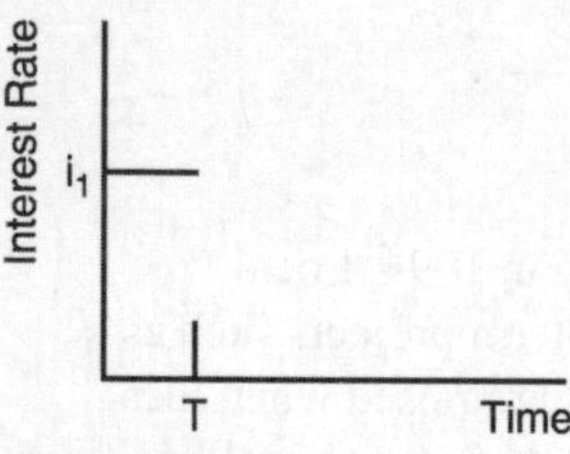

Figure 5D

EXERCISE 7: Liquidity Preference Framework

A. Assume that money and bonds are the only categories of assets that people use to store their wealth, and the quantity of money and bonds that people want to hold is 150 and 120, respectively. Given that the supply of money is 200, find the quantity of bonds that has to be supplied to create equilibrium in the asset market.

____

____

B. Suppose that the bond market is in equilibrium and the demand for money is 100. Find the quantity of money supply that creates equilibrium in the asset market.

____

____

EXERCISE 8: The Behaviour of Interest Rates

A. Define the 4 determinants of asset demand and indicate the relationship between each determinant with the quantity demanded.

1. ______
2. ______
3. ______
4. ______

B. How do these asset demand factors affect the demand curve? Are there any shifts and if so, specify.

______

______

C. Identify the factors that shift the supply of bonds and explain the correlation between the factors and the supply curve shift.

______

______

D. The Bank of Canada used the open market operation function to conduct monetary policy. Initially:

$Supply: 2x+1$

$Demand: -x+1$

Determine the initial equilibrium.

______

______

E. The supply has now shifted due to expected inflation but we are not sure where it has shifted. All we have is a new equation for the supply curve. Determine where it has shifted. $Supply: 2x+3$. Determine the new equilibrium and where the supply curve has shifted.

______

______

SELF-TEST

PART A: True-False Questions

Circle whether the following statements are true (T) or false (F).

T F 1. The demand curve for bonds slopes downward because at a lower bond price, the expected return on the bonds is higher and the quantity demanded is higher.

T F 2. When the interest rate rises, the bond price rises too.

T F 3. A rise in the price of a bond shifts the demand curve for bonds to the left.

T F 4. When businessmen become optimistic about the future health of the economy, the supply curve for bonds shifts to the left.

T F 5. A rise in the expected future price of long-term bonds shifts the demand curve for long-term bonds to the right.

T F 6. A federal budget surplus will shift the supply curve for bonds to the right.

T F 7. The Fisher effect suggests that periods of high interest rates will also tend to be periods of high inflation.

T F 8. In Keynes's view of the world in which there are only two assets, an excess demand in the money market implies that there is an excess demand in the bond market.

T F 9. If the stock market becomes riskier, the demand curve for money shifts to the right.

T F 10. The reason that Milton Friedman is unwilling to accept the view that lower interest rates will result from higher money growth is that he disagrees with Keynes's liquidity preference analysis.

T F 11. A decline in the expected return on the stock market will cause the demand for bonds to shift to the left.

T F 12. An increase in the money supply will always decrease the interest rates.

T F 13. Holding everything else constant, an increase in wealth raises the quantity demanded of an asset.

PART B: Multiple-Choice Questions

Circle the appropriate answer.

1. Which of the following assets is the least liquid?
   a. Currency.
   b. Automobile.
   c. Canada bond.
   d. Savings account.
2. When the interest rate is below the equilibrium interest rate, there is an excess ____________ for (of) bonds and the interest rate will ____________.
   a. supply; fall
   b. supply; rise
   c. demand; rise
   d. demand; fall
3. When brokerage commissions in the housing market are raised from 6 to 7% of the sales price, the ____________ curve for bonds shifts to the ____________.
   a. demand; right
   b. demand; left
   c. supply; left
   d. supply; right
4. When rare coin prices become less volatile, the ____________ curve for bonds shifts to the ____________.
   a. demand; right
   b. demand; left
   c. supply; left
   d. supply; right
5. When the expected inflation rate decreases, the demand for bonds shifts to the ____________, the supply of bonds shifts to the ____________, and the interest rate ____________.
   a. right; right; rises
   b. right; left; falls
   c. left; left; falls
   d. left; right; rises

6. When people revise downward their expectations of next year's short-term interest rate, the demand for long-term bonds shifts to the _______________ and their interest rates _______________.
   a. right; rise
   b. right; fall
   c. left; fall
   d. left; rise
7. In a recession, normally, the demand for bonds shifts to the _______________, the supply of bonds shifts to the _______________ and the interest rate _______________.
   a. right; right; rises
   b. right; left; falls
   c. left; left; falls
   d. left; right; rises
8. When the interest rate on a bond is _______________ the equilibrium interest rate, in the bond market there is excess _______________ and the price of bonds will _______________.
   a. below; demand; rise
   b. above; demand; fall
   c. below; supply; fall
   d. above; supply; rise
9. If the government decides to exclude the interest earned on bonds from income taxation, then bond _______________ will likely _______________, and the interest rate will _______________.
   a. demand; rise; fall
   b. supply; rise; fall
   c. demand; fall; rise
   d. supply; fall; rise
10. Since it has become easier in recent years to buy and sell stocks on the Internet, one expects that bond _______________ has fallen since bonds are _______________ liquid relative to stocks.
    a. demand; more
    b. supply; less
    c. demand; less
    d. supply; more
11. When equilibrium in the bond market changes, then
    a. the quantity of bonds bought and sold always increases.
    b. the equilibrium price and interest rate always move in opposite directions.
    c. either bond demand or bond supply or both curves have shifted.
    d. only (a) and (b) of the above.
    e. only (b) and (c) of the above.
12. The bond demand curve is downward sloping because
    a. the quantity demanded of bonds rises when the expected return on bonds rises.
    b. the expected return on bonds rises when the price of bonds rises.
    c. the expected return on bonds rises when the interest rate falls.
    d. only (a) and (b) of the above.
    e. only (a) and (c) of the above.

13. Which of the following will lead to an interest rate increase in the bond market?
    a. The riskiness of stocks rises.
    b. The expected inflation rate rises.
    c. The government deficit falls.
    d. The expected interest rate falls.
    e. none of the above.

14. As the interest rate on bonds ______________, the opportunity cost of holding money ______________, and the quantity of money demanded ______________.
    a. rises; rises; rises
    b. rises; falls; falls
    c. falls; rises; falls
    d. falls; falls; rises
    e. falls; falls; falls

15. If interest rates are predicted to rise in the future, then bond ______________ will ______________.
    a. demand; fall
    b. supply; fall
    c. demand; rise
    d. supply; rise

16. The bond supply curve is upward sloping because
    a. the quantity supplied of bonds rises when the cost to borrow by issuing bonds falls.
    b. the cost to borrow by issuing bonds falls when the price of bonds rises.
    c. the cost to borrow by issuing bonds falls when the interest rate rises.
    d. only (a) and (b) of the above.
    e. only (a) and (c) of the above.

17. In the money market, when the interest rate is below the equilibrium interest rate, there is an excess ______________ for (of) money, people will try to sell bonds, and the interest rate will ______________.
    a. demand; rise
    b. demand; fall
    c. supply; fall
    d. supply; rise

18. If the price level falls, the demand curve for money will shift to the ______________ and the interest rate will ______________.
    a. right; rise
    b. right; fall
    c. left; rise
    d. left; fall

19. In the Keynesian liquidity preference framework, when income is ______________ during a business cycle contraction, interest rates will ______________.
    a. rising, rise
    b. rising, fall
    c. falling, rise
    d. falling, fall

20. In the liquidity preference framework, the price level effect of a one-time increase in the money supply will have its maximum impact on interest rates
    a. at the moment the price level hits its peak (stops rising) because both the price level and expected inflation effects are at work.
    b. immediately after the price level begins to rise, because both the price level and expected inflation effects are at work.
    c. at the moment the expected inflation rate hits its peak.
    d. at the moment the inflation rate hits its peak.
21. The demanded quantity of an asset ________ as the risk of its return falls, and it ________ as the asset gets more liquid.
    a. decreases, decreases
    b. increases, decreases
    c. decreases, increases
    d. increases, increases
22. If the Bank of Canada wants to permanently lower interest rates, then it should raise the rate of money growth if
    a. there is a fast adjustment of expected inflation.
    b. there is slow adjustment of expected inflation.
    c. the liquidity effect is smaller than the expected inflation effect.
    d. the liquidity effect is larger than the other effects.
23. When the growth rate of the money supply is increased, interest rates will rise immediately if the liquidity effect is ____________ than the other money supply effects and there is ____________ adjustment of expected inflation.
    a. larger; fast
    b. larger; slow
    c. smaller; slow
    d. smaller; fast
24. In the liquidity preference framework, the difference between the price level and expected inflation effects of a one-time increase in the money supply can be stated as follows:
    a. the increase in the interest rate caused by the rise in the price level remains once the price level has stopped rising, but the increase in the interest rate caused by expected inflation will be reversed once the price level stops rising.
    b. the increase in the interest rate caused by the rise in the expected inflation rate remains once the price level has stopped rising, but the increase in the interest rate caused by the rise in the price level will be reversed once the price level stops rising.
    c. once the price level stops rising, the interest rate declines because of the price level effect, but the expected inflation effect remains after the price level has stopped rising.
    d. there is no difference, as both effects cause the interest rate to rise.
25. The most plausible explanation for why interest rates rose in the 1970s is
    a. the contractionary monetary policy pursued by the Bank of Canada.
    b. the decline in the money supply caused by the many failures of commercial banks.
    c. the rapidly rising level of income.
    d. the continual increase in expected inflation.
    e. the steady increase in the price level.

26. If prices in the market for fine art become less uncertain, then
    a. the demand curve for bonds shifts to the left and the interest rate rises.
    b. the demand curve for bonds shifts to the left and the interest rate falls.
    c. the demand curve for bonds shifts to the right and the interest rate falls.
    d. the supply curve for bonds shifts to the right and the interest rate falls.
27. If the expected inflation rate increases, then the ______________ for (of) bonds increases while the ______________ curve shifts to the left.
    a. demand; demand
    b. demand; supply
    c. supply; demand
    d. supply; supply
28. When the bond market becomes less volatile, the _________ for (of) bonds shifts to the right, and when the expected inflation increases, the _________ curve shifts to the _________.
    a. supply, demand, right
    b. supply, demand, left
    c. demand, supply, right
    d. demand, supply, left
29. In the late 1990s, Japan experienced a recession and deflation. Deflation caused the demand for bonds to _________ and the supply of bonds to _________. The outcome was a ________ in bond price and a _________ in the interest rate.
    a. fall, rise, fall, rise
    b. rise, fall, rise, fall
    c. fall, fall, rise, rise
    d. rise, rise, fall, fall
30. The income effect and the expected inflation effect of a decrease in the money supply are a _________ and a _________ in the interest rate, respectively.
    a. rise, rise
    b. fall, fall
    c. rise, fall
    d. fall, rise
31. An increase in expected inflation causes
    a. the supply of bonds to increase and the supply curve to shift to the right.
    b. the supply of bonds to decrease and the supply curve to shift to the left.
    c. the supply of bonds to increase and the supply curve to shift to the left.
    d. the supply of bonds to decrease and the supply curve to shift to the right.
32. A rise in the price level causes
    a. the demand for money at each interest rate to decrease.
    b. the supply of money at each interest rate to increase.
    c. a simultaneous increase in demand for and supply of money at each interest rate to increase.
    d. the demand for money at each interest rate to increase.
33. According to Keynes's liquidity preference analysis, the two factors that cause the demand curve for money to shift are
    a. production level and price level.
    b. income and production.
    c. income and price level.
    d. income and interest rate.

CHAPTER 6

The Risk and Term Structure of Interest Rates

CHAPTER SYNOPSIS/COMPLETIONS

The supply and demand analysis of interest rate behaviour in Chapter 5 examined the determination of just one interest rate, even though there are many different interest rates in the economy. This chapter completes the interest rate picture by examining the relationship among interest rates on securities that differ in their riskiness, liquidity, income tax treatment, and term to maturity.

The relationship among interest rates on different securities with the same term to maturity is called the (1)______________ structure of interest rates. One attribute of a bond that influences its interest rate is its (2)______________ ______________, the chance that the issuer of the bond will default, that is, be unable to make interest payments or pay the face value when the bond matures. When default risk on a bond increases, the demand curve for this bond shifts to the left and the demand curve for default-free bonds shifts to the right. The result is that as default risk increases, the (3)______________ premium (the spread between this bond's interest rate and the interest rate on a default-free bond) rises.

Another attribute of a bond that influences its interest rate is its (4)______________, that is, how quickly and cheaply it can be converted into cash if the need arises. Supply and demand analysis reveals that the less liquid a bond is, the higher its interest rate will be relative to more liquid securities. Therefore, the lower liquidity of corporate bonds relative to Canada bonds (5)______________ the spread between the interest rates on these two bonds and thereby contributes to the risk premium of corporate bonds.

Income tax rules also have an impact on the risk structure of interest rates. For example, the tax exemption of municipal bonds in the United States (6)______________ their interest rate relative to U.S. Treasury securities; notice that municipal bonds in Canada are not tax-exempt. The risk structure of interest rates is, therefore, explained by three factors: default risk, liquidity, and the income tax treatment of the bond.

The relationship among interest rates on bonds with different terms to maturity is called the (7)______________ structure of interest rates. It is graphed as the (8)______________ ______________, a plot of the yields on default-free government bonds with differing terms to maturity. Three theories have been proposed to explain the term structure of interest rates. The first theory, the expectations theory, is derived using the assumption that bonds of different maturities are perfect substitutes, implying that their expected returns must be equal. It indicates, therefore, that the interest rate on a long-term bond will equal an average of short-term interest rates that people expect to occur over the life of the long-term bond. Although the expectations theory can explain the empirical fact that interest rates on bonds of different maturities tend to move together over time, it is unable to explain the fact that yield curves are usually (9)______________ sloping.

The (10)______________ ______________ theory of the term structure sees markets as completely separated or segmented. It assumes that bonds of different maturities are not substitutes at all. Hence, the interest rate for each maturity bond is determined by the supply and demand for that maturity with no effects from expected returns on bonds with either shorter or longer maturities. Although this theory can explain why yield curves usually slope upward, it cannot explain the empirical fact that interest rates on bonds of different maturities move together.

The liquidity premium theory of the term structure states the following: the interest rate on a long-term bond will equal an average of short-term interest rates expected to occur over the life of the long-term bond, plus a (11)______________ or term premium that responds to supply and demand conditions for that bond. The theory takes the view that bonds of different maturities are (12)______________, so that the expected return on a bond of one maturity does influence the expected return of a bond with a different maturity, but it also allows investors to prefer one bond maturity over another.

The liquidity premium theory, and a closely related theory called the preferred habitat theory, are able to explain the two empirical facts discussed above. It explains why interest rates on different maturity bonds move together over time. If short-term interest rates are expected, on average, to be (13)______________ in the future, then long-term interest rates will rise along with them. Moreover, it explains why yield curves are usually upward-sloping, suggesting that the liquidity premium is (14)______________ because of people's preference for short-term bonds. Also, the theory explains a third empirical fact: when short-term interest rates are low, yield curves are more likely to have a steep upward slope; when short-term interest rates are high, yield curves are more likely to slope downward.

The liquidity premium theory has the additional attractive feature that it permits one to infer what the market is predicting for the movement of short-term interest rates in the future. A steep upward slope of the yield curve means that short-term rates are expected to (15)______________; a mild upward slope means that short-term rates are expected to remain the same; a flat slope means that short-term rates are expected to fall moderately; and a downward slope means that short-term rates are expected to fall sharply.

EXERCISES

EXERCISE 1: Default Risk and Liquidity Effects on the Risk Structure

Consider the loanable funds framework and plot the supply and demand curves in the corporate bond market and the Canada bond markets. If the health of the economy improves so that the probability of bankruptcy decreases, draw the new supply and demand curves.

A. What happens to the interest rate on corporate bonds? ______________

B. What happens to the interest rate on Canada bonds? ______________

C. What happens to the size of the risk premium? ______________

EXERCISE 2: Tax Effects on the Risk Structure

Suppose your income tax bracket is 25%.

A. What is your after-tax return from holding a 1-year tax-exempt bond with an 8% yield to maturity?

____

B. What is your after-tax return from holding a 1-year corporate bond with a 10% yield to maturity?

____

C. If both these securities have the same amount of risk and liquidity, then which one of them would you prefer to own?

____

D. What does this example suggest about the relationship found in the bond market between interest rates on tax exempt securities and those on other securities?

____

EXERCISE 3: Deriving a Yield Curve

Given that the expectations theory of the term structure is correct, plot in Figure 6A the yield curve when the expected path of 1-year interest rates over the next 10 years is the following: 1%, 2%, 3%, 4%, 5%, 5%, 4%, 3%, 2%, 1%.

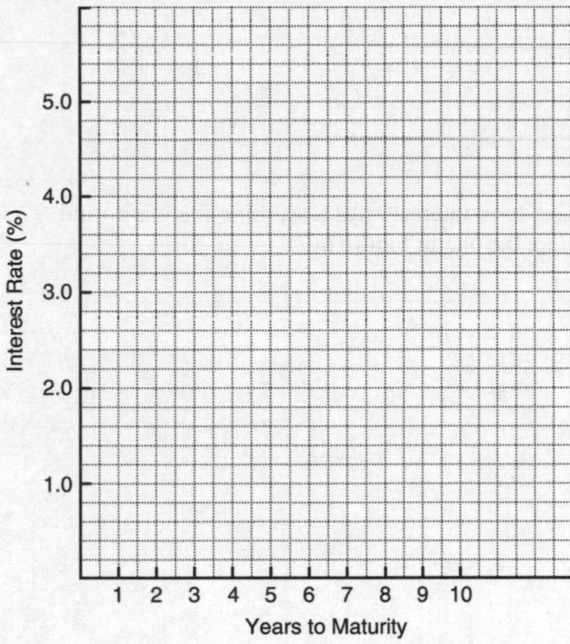

Figure 6A

EXERCISE 4: Expectations Theory of the Term Structure

An investor is presented with the following two alternative investment strategies: Purchase a 3-year bond with an interest rate of 6% and hold it until maturity, or purchase a 1-year bond with an interest rate of 7%, and when it matures, purchase another 1-year bond with an expected interest rate of 6%, and when it matures, purchase another 1-year bond with an interest rate of 5%.

A. What is the expected return for the first strategy?

____

B. What is the expected average return over the 3 years for the second strategy?

____

C. What is the relationship between the expected returns of the two strategies?

____

D. Why does our analysis of the expectations theory indicate that this is exactly what you should expect to find?

____

EXERCISE 5: Inferring Market Predictions of Future Interest Rates

A. What is the market predicting about the movement of future short-term interest rates (assuming there is a mild preference for shorter maturity bonds) if the yield curve looks like the one in Figure 6B?

____

____

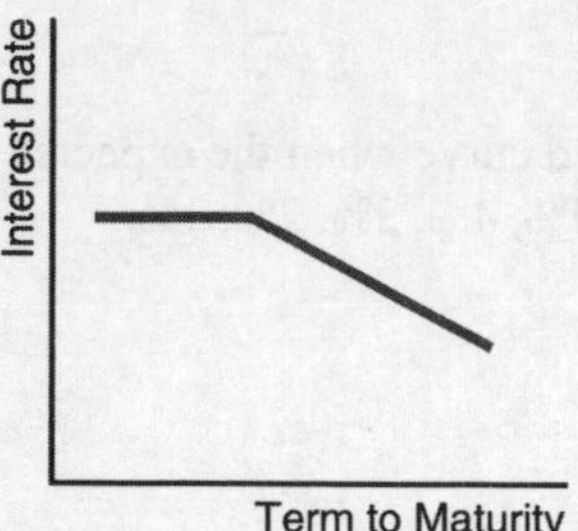

Figure 6B

B. What is the market predicting about the movement of future short-term interest rates (assuming there is a mild preference for shorter maturity bonds) if the yield curve looks like the one in Figure 6C?

____

____

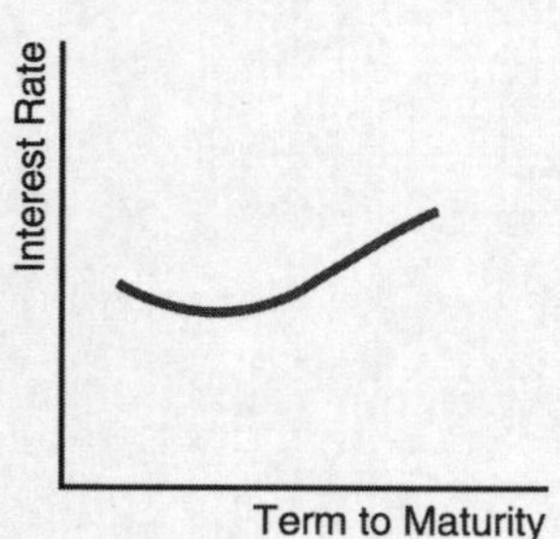

Figure 6C

EXERCISE 6: Changing Yield Curve

Suppose that over the course of one year, the Bank of Canada lowers interest rates and the yield curve shifts downward as shown in Figure 6D.

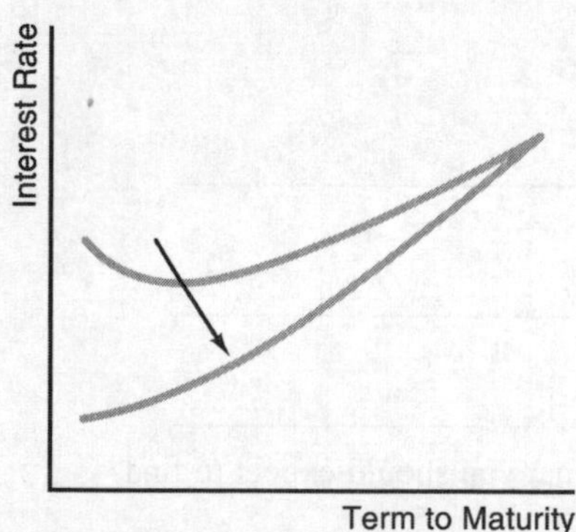

Figure 6D

A. If there are mild preferences for shorter maturity bonds, and if the liquidity premium theory is correct, then does the first yield curve indicate that the Bank of Canada's actions were expected?

____

B. If there are mild preferences for shorter maturity bonds, and if the liquidity premium theory is correct, does the second yield curve indicate that the Bank's actions are expected to be permanent?

____

EXERCISE 7: Expectations Theory

Suppose that the one-year interest rate over the next four years is expected to be 2%, 4%, 5%, and 6%.

A. Find the interest rate on the three-year bond.

B. Find the interest rate on the four-year bond.

C. Find the interest rate on the three-year bond when the liquidity premium of the investor to hold a three-year bond is 2.25%.

EXERCISE 8: The Risk and the Term Structure of Interest Rates

A. Define junk bonds and fallen angels.

B. Why are Canadian bonds the most liquid of all long-term bonds? Why are corporate bonds are not easily traded?

C. Why does the yield curve slope upward most of the time?

D. What are the 4 theories that have been put forward to explain the relationship among interest rates on bonds of different maturities reflected in yield curve patterns?

E. Suppose that the one-year interest rate over the next 8 years is expected to be 4%, 4.5%, 4.75%, 3%, 5%, 4.25%, 6%, 5.5% and the liquidity premium for the 2nd year is 2%, the 4th 2.1%,the 6th 2.2% and the 8th 1.8%, respectively. What is the interest rate on a 3-year bond?

SELF-TEST

PART A: True-False Questions

Circle whether the following statements are true (T) or false (F).

T F 1. The term structure of interest rates is the relationship among interest rates of bonds with the same maturity.

T F 2. The greater a bond's default risk, the higher is its interest rate.

T F 3. The expected returns on perfect substitute bonds are equal.

T F 4. The risk premium on a bond only reflects the amount of risk this bond has relative to a default-free bond.

T F 5. A plot of the interest rates on default-free government bonds with different terms to maturity is called a term structure curve.

T F 6. The difference between the expectations theory of the term structure and the liquidity premium theory is that the liquidity premium theory allows for a risk premium while the expectations theory does not.

T F 7. The expectations theory of the term structure assumes that bonds of different maturities are perfect substitutes.

T F 8. The segmented markets theory of the term structure is unable to explain why yield curves usually slope upward.

T F 9. The liquidity premium theory combines elements of both the segmented markets theory and the expectations theory.

T F 10. The liquidity premium theory assumes that bonds of different maturities are not substitutes.

T F 11. The relationship among interest rates on bonds with different terms to maturity is called the term structure of interest rates.

T F 12. The bond price is positively related to the interest rates and when the price rises, the interest rates rise too.

T F 13. The higher the default risk is, the larger the risk premium will be.

T F 14. The interest rate on bonds of different maturities differ, because the short-term interest rates are expected to have different values at future dates.

T F 15. An inverted yield curve means that short-term interest rates are expected to fall moderately.

PART B: Multiple-Choice Questions

Circle the appropriate answer.

1. Which of the following long-term bonds tend to have the highest interest rate?
   a. corporate BBB bonds.
   b. Canada bonds.
   c. corporate CCC bonds.
   d. municipal bonds.

2. When the default risk on corporate bonds increases, other things equal, the demand curve for corporate bonds shifts to the ______________ and the demand curve for Canada bonds shifts to the ______________.
   a. right; right
   b. right; left
   c. left; right
   d. left; left

3. When the corporate bond market becomes less liquid, other things being equal, the demand curve for corporate bonds shifts to the ______________ and the demand curve for Canada bonds shifts to the ______________.
   a. right; right
   b. right; left
   c. left; left
   d. left; right

4. The risk premium on corporate bonds falls when
   a. brokerage commissions fall in the corporate bond market.
   b. a flurry of major corporate bankruptcies occurs.
   c. the Canada bond market becomes more liquid.
   d. both (b) and (c) of the above occur.

5. The interest rate on tax-exempt municipal bonds in the United States rises relative to the interest rate on U.S. corporate bonds when
   a. there is a major default in the municipal bond market in the United States.
   b. income tax rates are raised.
   c. U.S. Treasury securities become more widely traded.
   d. U.S. corporate bonds become riskier.

6. Because municipal bonds in the United States bear substantial default risk, their interest rates
   a. tend to be higher than interest rates on default-free U.S. Treasury bonds indicating that the default premium exceeds the tax advantages of municipal bonds.
   b. tend to be higher than interest rates on default-free U.S. Treasury bonds indicating that the default premium falls short of the tax advantages of municipal bonds.
   c. tend to be lower than interest rates on default-free U.S. Treasury bonds indicating that the default premium exceeds the tax advantages of municipal bonds.
   d. tend to be lower than interest rates on default-free U.S. Treasury bonds indicating that the default premium falls short of the tax advantages of municipal bonds.

7. When income tax rates are ________________, the interest rates on taxable bonds ________________ relative to the interest rate on tax-exempt bonds.
   a. lowered; fall
   b. lowered; rise
   c. raised; fall
   d. raised; do not change

8. The risk structure of interest rates is explained by three factors:
   a. risk of default, liquidity, and the income tax treatment of the security.
   b. risk of default, maturity, and the income tax treatment of the security.
   c. liquidity, maturity, and the income tax treatment of the security.
   d. risk of default, maturity, and the liquidity of the security.

9. Why does the interest rate on junk bonds rise relative to the interest rate on Canadian treasury bills after a big drop in the stock market?
   a. Income tax rates rise.
   b. The risk of default for Canadian treasury bills rises.
   c. The risk of default for junk bonds rises.
   d. The term premium for Canadian treasury bills falls.

10. Bonds with a low risk of default are labelled ________________ while bonds with a high risk of default are labelled ________________.
    a. corporate; Canada
    b. junk; corporate
    c. investment-grade; high-yield
    d. risky; safe

11. If the interest rates of corporate bonds and government bonds are the same in a country, then it is likely that
    a. there is no term premium.
    b. government bonds are not default-free bonds.
    c. the liquidity premium has disappeared.
    d. bonds of different maturities are perfect substitutes.
12. Which of the following theories of the term structure is able to explain the fact that when short-term interest rates are low, yield curves are more likely to slope upward?
    a. expectations theory.
    b. segmented markets theory.
    c. liquidity premium theory.
    d. both (b) and (c) of the above.
    e. both (a) and (c) of the above.
13. If the expected path of 1-year interest rates over the next 3 years is 4%, 1%, and 1% then the expectations theory predicts that today's interest rate on the 3-year bond is
    a. 1%.
    b. 2%.
    c. 3%.
    d. 4%.
    e. none of the above.
14. If the expected path of 1-year interest rates over the next 5 years is 2%, 2%, 4%, 3%, and 1%, the expectations theory predicts that the bond with the highest interest rate today is the one with a maturity of
    a. 1 year.
    b. 2 years.
    c. 3 years.
    d. 4 years.
    e. 5 years.
15. According to the liquidity premium theory
    a. a steeply rising yield curve indicates that short-term interest rates are expected to rise in the future.
    b. a moderately rising yield curve indicates that short-term interest rates are expected to decline in the future.
    c. interest rates on bonds of different maturities need not move together over time.
    d. only (a) and (b) of the above.
16. The ____________ of the term structure states the following: the interest rate on a long-term bond will equal an average of short-term interest rates expected to occur over the life of the long-term bond but investors do not prefer short-term over long-term bonds.
    a. segmented markets theory
    b. expectations theory
    c. liquidity premium theory
    d. liquidity preference theory.
17. Why, according to the expectations theory, does the interest rate on a long-term bond equal the average of expected short-term interest rates over the life of the long-term bond?
    a. Because only then will the public hold both long- and short-term bonds.
    b. Because long- and short-term bonds are not perfect substitutes.
    c. Because people prefer short-term bonds.
    d. None of the above.

18. The segmented markets theory assumes that
    a. long-term bonds are preferred to short-term bonds.
    b. people are not rational.
    c. bonds of different maturities are not substitutes.
    d. the risk of default does not influence bond demand.
    e. none of the above.
19. Which of the following is an empirical fact regarding the term structure of interest rates?
    a. Interest rates on bonds of different maturities move together.
    b. When short-term interest rates are low, yield curves are likely to slope upward.
    c. Yield curves usually slope upward.
    d. All of the above.
    e. None of the above.
20. People prefer shorter-term bonds to longer-term bonds because
    a. the maturity length is longer for shorter-term bonds.
    b. the risk of default is greater for shorter-term bonds.
    c. the interest rate risk is greater for longer-term bonds.
    d. only (a) and (b) of the above.
    e. only (b) and (c) of the above.
21. According to the expectations theory of the term structure, if people expect that the short-term interest rate will be 6% on average over the coming three years, then the interest rate on a bond with three years to maturity will be
    a. less than 6%.
    b. greater than 6%.
    c. exactly 6%.
    d. exactly 2%.
    e. less than 2%.
22. According to the liquidity premium and preferred habitat theory, a flat yield curve indicates that
    a. future short-term interest rates are expected to rise.
    b. future short-term interest rates are expected to remain constant.
    c. the liquidity premium has disappeared.
    d. the liquidity premium has risen.
    e. future short-term interest rates are expected to fall.
23. If the yield curve slopes upward mildly for short maturities and then slopes sharply upward for longer maturities, the liquidity premium theory (assuming a mild preference for short-term bonds) indicates that the market is predicting
    a. a rise in short-term interest rates in the near future and a decline further out in the future.
    b. constant short-term interest rates in the near future and a rise further out in the future.
    c. a decline in short-term interest rates in the near future and a rise further out in the future.
    d. a decline in short-term interest rates in the near future which levels off further out in the future.
24. An inverted yield curve signals that the market expects interest rates to
    a. fall in the future.
    b. rise in the future.
    c. remain constant in the future.
    d. be random in the future.

25. During the Great Depression, the difference between interest rates on low-quality corporate bonds and Canada bonds
    a. increased significantly.
    b. decreased significantly.
    c. decreased moderately.
    d. did not change.

26. In reality, short-term interest rates are just as likely to fall as to rise; this is the major shortcoming of the
    a. segmented markets theory.
    b. expectations theory.
    c. liquidity premium theory.
    d. separable markets theory.

27. When yield curves slope upward, the long-term interest rates are __________ the short-term interest rates; when yield curves are __________, short- and long-term interest rates are the same.
    a. above, flat
    b. above, downward-sloping
    c. below, downward-sloping
    d. below, flat

28. If the expected path of 1-year interest rates over the next 4 years is 4%, 3%, 2%, and 1%, the expectations theory predicts that interest rates on 3-year and 4-year bonds are ______ and ______ and the yield curve is __________.
    a. 2%, 1%, flat
    b. 2%, 2.5%, upward sloping
    c. 3%, 2.5%, downward sloping
    d. 3%, 2.5%, upward sloping

29. In the expectations theory and in the segmented markets theory, bonds with different maturities are __________ and __________, respectively.
    a. perfect substitutes, not substitutes at all
    b. perfect substitutes, substitutes
    c. substitutes, perfect substitutes
    d. not substitutes at all, perfect substitutes

30. Suppose that the one-year interest rates over the next six years are expected to be 2%, 4%, 5%, 6%, 7%, and 9%. In addition, the liquidity premiums for holding short-term bonds for one-year to six-year bonds are 0%, 0.5%, 1%, 1.5%, 2%, and 2.5%, respectively. What is the interest rate on a three-year bond and five-year bond?
    a. 6.8%, 4.67%
    b. 5%, 7%
    c. 6%, 9%
    d. 4.67%, 6.8%

31. Risk default occurs
    a. when the issuer of the bond is unable to make interest payments at the maturity date.
    b. when the issuer of the bond is unable to make interest payments and the face value at the maturity date.
    c. when the issuer of the bond is unable to repay the face value at the maturity date.
    d. when the issuer of the bond is unable or unwilling to make interest payments at the maturity date.

32. A bond with default risk will always have a positive risk premium, therefore:
    a. an increase in its default risk will decrease the risk premium.
    b. a decrease in its default risk will raise the risk premium.
    c. a decrease in its default risk will decrease the risk premium.
    d. an increase in its default risk will raise the risk premium.

CHAPTER 7

The Stock Market, the Theory of Rational Expectations, and the Efficient Markets Hypothesis

CHAPTER SYNOPSIS/COMPLETIONS

Chapter 7 discusses theories that explain changes in the stock market. First, fundamental theories of stock valuation are developed. Second, the theory of rational expectations is introduced, along with the implications of this theory as applied to financial markets, where it is known as the efficient market hypothesis. Recently, expectations theory has received great attention as economists have searched for more adequate explanations of the observed behaviour of economic variables such as unemployment, interest rates, and asset prices.

Stockholders are the residual claimants of all (1)________________________________ flowing into a firm. The cash flows from stocks are dividends and the sales price. The (2)____________________________________ valuation model states that the value of stock is the present value of all future cash flows. If the stock is not sold until far into the future, then the sales price does not affect the current value of the stock. Therefore, the generalized dividend model implies that the value of a stock is the present value of the future stream of dividends. If dividends are assumed to grow at a (3)____________________________ rate forever, and if that growth rate is assumed to be less than the required return on equity, then the Gordon growth model states that the value of a stock depends on next year's dividend, the expected dividend growth rate, and the required return on equity.

The stock market is much like any other market in that the market price is set by the buyer willing to pay the highest price and who can best take advantage of the stock. Superior (4)_______________________________ can raise the value of a stock.

Prior to the rational expectations revolution, economists tended to model expectations as if they were formed (5)_____________________________, meaning that people adjusted slowly over time in response to changes in economic variables. Adaptive expectations imply that people look only at current and (6)____________________________ behaviour of an economic variable in forming expectations of it, never adjusting to predicted changes in economic variables.

Beginning in the 1960s a number of economists began to question the desirability of adaptive expectations models, since they imply that people never learn from their past mistakes. They suggested an alternative to adaptive expectations known as (7)______________ ______________. As the name implies, this theory assumes that people behave rationally when faced with new information, adjusting their expectations quickly. For example, if people believe that the Bank of Canada is about to embark on an expansionary monetary policy to reduce unemployment, people will revise their estimates of inflation upward. The possibility of this result is ignored in adaptive expectation models because people are assumed to respond only to past events; that is, people do not respond to predicted future actions.

Rational expectationists contend that individuals make (8)______________ (formulate expectations) about the future course of an economic variable based on its past behaviour and on their assessment of future policies that affect the variable. These predictions (known as (9)______________ ______________) will be correct on average, although they will not always be perfectly accurate. Individuals make mistakes, but they will not be persistently wrong in any one direction. Alternatively, forecast errors of expectations will not be biased.

The theory of rational expectations contends that people have a strong incentive to form rational expectations since failing to do so is costly. This is especially true in financial markets.

The (10)______________ ______________ ______________ is the application of rational expectations to the pricing of securities in financial markets. The efficient markets hypothesis suggests that security (11)______________ reflect all available information at that time. If this were not the case, an unexploited profit opportunity would exist giving individuals with superior information an incentive to capture profits by either buying (they expect a higher price) or selling (they expect a lower price) the security.

Importantly, their actions quickly eliminate the profits. If, for example, the price of IBM common stock is expected to rise because a new invention makes IBM computers more valuable to own, then those individuals with this information will attempt to buy more shares of IBM common stock before its price rises. But their actions increase the demand for IBM stock, raising its price. The price of IBM common stock will continue to rise until the optimal forecast of the rate of return falls to the (12)______________ return. At this price, all unexploited profit opportunities are eliminated. This result does not depend on everyone being well informed.

The (13)______________ ______________ hypothesis contends that future changes in stock prices should for all practical purposes be unpredictable. This implication follows from efficient markets theory, since any new information that might create an unexploited profit opportunity will be quickly eliminated through the adjustment in the stock's price.

The evidence on efficient markets theory is mixed. Although evidence on the performance of investment advisors and mutual funds tends to support the random walk hypothesis for stock prices, in recent years anomalies to efficient markets indicates that the theory may not be correct. For example, the small-firm effect, the January effect, the Value Line survey, market overreaction, excessive volatility, and mean reversion indicate that efficient markets theory may not be able to generalize (generalizable) to all behaviour in financial markets.

Efficient markets theory suggests that individuals ought to be skeptical of stock brokers' hot tips and the recommendations found in the published reports of (14)______________ ______________. By the time you acquire the information, others are likely to have already used it to their benefit. Thus acting on this information will not yield abnormally high returns on average because market prices already reflect this information. Many studies confirm the proposition that published recommendations cannot allow you to outperform the overall market. Even when economists select analysts who have done well in the past, the evidence indicates that financial analysts do not consistently outperform the overall market.

Interestingly, efficient markets theory also explains why a stock's price sometimes falls when good news about the stock is announced. This occurs when announced earnings fall short of those (15)______________ by market participants. The lower earnings mean a lower rate of return at the current price. Consequently, the stock's price must fall to bring the rate of return into conformity with the rest of the market.

So how can one get rich by investing in the stock market? The efficient markets theory suggests that relying on the published reports of financial analysts and the hot tips given to you by your broker is probably an inferior strategy when compared to the "buy and hold strategy." This strategy will on average give the investor the same return (exclusive of transactions costs), but her net profits will be higher because she pays fewer (16)______________ commissions.

The stock market crash of 1987 has convinced many that the strong version of efficient markets theory (asset prices reflect the true fundamental value of securities) is not correct. Whether or not the stock market crash proves rational expectations theory is incorrect is of some dispute. To the extent that the crash could not have been predicted, rational expectations theory would seem to hold.

EXERCISES

EXERCISE 1: Definitions and Terminology

Match the following terms on the right with the definition or description on the left. Place the letter of the term in the blank provided next to the appropriate definition. Terms may be used more than once.

	Definition		Term
_____	1. Price of a security is such that optimal forecast of its return exceeds the equilibrium return.	a.	Efficient markets theory
_____	2. Expectations that are formed from past data on a single variable.	b.	Random walk
_____	3. Information not available to the public, but only to those who have close contact with a company.	c.	Unexploited profit opportunity
_____	4. Past movements of stock prices are of no use in predicting the future movement of stock prices.	d.	Insider information
_____	5. A method for predicting future stock prices using past price data.	e.	Technical analysis
_____	6. Expectations that are formed using optimal predictions of future movements in relevant variables.	f.	Adaptive expectations
_____	7. The best guess of the future using all available information.	g.	Rational expectations
_____	8. Theory that indicates that hot tips, financial analysts' published recommendations, and technical analysis cannot help the investor to outperform the market.	h.	Optimal forecast
_____	9. The application of rational expectations to the pricing of securities in financial markets.		
_____	10. A situation in which someone can earn a higher than normal return.		

EXERCISE 2: Interest Rates and Rational Expectations—Efficient Markets

Recall from Chapter 5 that there are three different outcomes for long-term interest rates when the Bank of Canada slows the growth of the money supply. Describe the interest rate outcome for each of the following conditions listed below.

A. The Bank of Canada action was widely anticipated.

____

____

____

B. The Bank of Canada action was unanticipated and people expect that the slower growth of money will be permanent.

C. The Bank of Canada action was unanticipated and people do not expect that the inflation rate will be lower.

D. What does the example here suggest about the difficulty of conducting monetary policy when expectations are rational?

EXERCISE 3: Stock Prices and Dividends

A. Suppose that a stock is expected to pay a dividend of $1 each year and that your required return on equity investments is nine percent. If you plan to purchase the stock today and expect to sell it in three years for $20, what are you willing to pay for the stock? Assume that you receive three dividend payments and that the first comes next year.

B. Suppose that the government taxes dividends at a rate of 27 percent. That means that the after-tax dividend is now 0.73 (= 1 – 0.27). Calculate the after-tax value of the stock to you if the sales price of the stock remains at $20. Does the value of the stock rise or fall if it is taxed?

EXERCISE 4: Stock Valuation

A. Assume that each share of Nortel pays $2 per year in dividends for five years, its price after five years is $100, and your required rate of return on equities is 10%. Find the current market price of the Nortel stock.

B. Suppose that the most current dividend paid per share (D0) of Coca-Cola is $2, your required return on stocks is 20%, and the dividends grow at a constant rate. Calculate the growth rate of these dividends given that the current market price of Coca-Cola stock is $94.

EXERCISE 5: Efficient Markets Hypothesis

A. Suppose that a share of Microsoft had a closing price yesterday of $115, but new information was announced after the market closed, causing a revision in the forecast of next year's price to go to $100. If the annual equilibrium return on Microsoft is 17%, what will the price be when the market opens today.

B. The annual equilibrium return on Microsoft is 17%. What would happen if the optimal forecast of the return is an annual rate of 45%?

C. Could this situation be maintained under the efficient markets condition?

SELF-TEST

PART A: True-False Questions

Circle whether the following statements are true (T) or false (F).

T F 1. Technical analysis is the only method that beats the market and creates higher returns on stocks.

T F 2. Expectations that are formed solely on the basis of past information are known as rational expectations.

T F 3. The theory of rational expectations argues that optimal forecasts need not be perfectly accurate.

T F 4. An important implication of rational expectations theory is that when there is a change in the way a variable behaves, the way expectations of this variable are formed will change as well.

T F 5. If the optimal forecast of a return on a financial asset exceeds its equilibrium return, the situation is called an unexploited profit opportunity.

T F 6. In an efficient market, all unexploited profit opportunities will be eliminated.

T F 7. Everyone in a financial market must be well informed about a security if the market is to be considered efficient.

T F 8. The efficient markets theory suggests that published reports of financial analysts can guarantee that individuals who use this information will outperform the market.

T F 9. The overwhelming majority of statistical studies indicate that financial analysts do indeed pick financial portfolios that outperform the market average.

T F 10. According to the efficient markets hypothesis, picking stocks by throwing darts at the financial page is an inferior strategy compared to employing the advice of financial analysts.

T F 11. The Black Monday crash of 1987 and the Tech crash of 2000 show that expectations in the financial markets are not rational.

T F 12. As long as stock market crashes are unpredictable, the rational expectation theory holds.

T F 13. The forecast errors of expectations will on average be greater than zero and can be predicted ahead of time.

T F 14. In efficient markets, all unexploited profit opportunities will be eliminated.

T F 15. The random-walk theory implies that the future changes in stock prices should, for all practical purposes, be predictable.

PART B: Multiple-Choice Questions

Circle the appropriate answer.

1. Suppose you read a story in the financial section of the local newspaper that announces the proposed merger of Dell Computer and Gateway. The announcement is expected to greatly increase the profitability of Gateway. If you should now decide to invest in Gateway stock, you can expect to earn
   a. above average returns since you will get to share in the higher profits.
   b. above average returns since your stock will definitely appreciate as the profits are earned.
   c. a normal return since stock prices adjust to reflect changed profit expectations almost immediately.
   d. none of the above.
2. Evidence of chaotic dynamics in stock prices
   a. implies that prediction is possible over short periods of time.
   b. implies that prediction is possible over both short and long periods of time.
   c. is questionable because of the reliability of the existing chaos tests.
   d. all of the above.
   e. only (a) and (b) of the above.
3. In countries experiencing rapid rates of inflation, announcements of money supply increases are often followed by immediate increases in interest rates. Such behaviour is consistent with which of the following?
   a. Rational expectations.
   b. Expectations of higher inflation in the near future.
   c. A tight current monetary policy.
   d. Both (a) and (b) of the above.
   e. Both (a) and (c) of the above.
4. The efficient markets hypothesis suggests that purchasing the published reports of financial analysts
   a. is likely to increase one's returns by an average of 10%.
   b. is likely to increase one's returns by an average of about 3 to 5%.
   c. is not likely to be an effective strategy for increasing financial returns.
   d. is likely to increase one's returns by an average of about 2 to 3%.
5. After the announcement of higher quarterly profits, the price of a stock falls. Such an occurrence is
   a. clearly inconsistent with the efficient markets hypothesis.
   b. possible if market participants expected lower profits.
   c. consistent with the efficient markets hypothesis.
   d. not possible.
6. Since a change in regulations permitting their existence in the mid-1970s and the explosive growth in the number of people who surf the internet, discount brokers have grown rapidly. Efficient markets theory would seem to suggest that people who use discount brokers
   a. will likely earn lower returns than those who use full-service brokers.
   b. will likely earn about the same as those who use full-service brokers, but will net more after brokerage commissions.
   c. are going against evidence that suggests that the financial analysis provided by full-service brokers can help one outperform the overall market.
   d. are likely to be poor.

7. The efficient markets hypothesis suggests that stock prices tend to follow a "random walk." Thus the best strategy for investing is
   a. a "churning strategy" of buying and selling often to catch the market swings.
   b. turning over your stock portfolio each month, selecting stocks by throwing darts at the stock page.
   c. a "buy and hold strategy" of holding onto stocks to avoid brokerage commissions.
   d. to do none of the above.
8. Rational expectations theory suggests that forecast errors of expectations
   a. tend to be persistently high or low.
   b. are unpredictable.
   c. are more likely to be negative than positive.
   d. are more likely to be positive than negative.
9. Unexploited opportunities are quickly eliminated in financial markets through
   a. changes in asset prices.
   b. changes in dividend payments.
   c. accounting conventions.
   d. exchange-rate translations.
10. Stockbrokers have at times paid newspaper reporters for information about articles to be published in future editions. This suggests that
    a. your stockbroker's hot tips will help you outperform the overall market.
    b. financial analysts' reports contain information that will help you earn a return that exceeds the market average.
    c. insider information may help ensure returns that exceed the market average.
    d. each of the above is true.
11. If expectations are formed rationally, forecast errors of expectations will on average be ____________ and therefore ____________ be predicted ahead of time.
    a. positive; can
    b. positive; cannot
    c. zero; cannot
    d. zero; can
12. That stock prices do not always rise when favourable earnings reports are released suggests that
    a. the stock market is not efficient.
    b. people trading in stocks sometimes incorrectly estimate companies' earnings.
    c. stock prices tend to be biased measures of future corporate earnings.
    d. all of the above are true.
13. According to the theory of efficient capital markets since all relevant, publicly available information is discounted in asset prices as soon as it becomes available,
    a. investors cannot construct systematically profitable trading rules based only on this information.
    b. investors have no incentive to buy stock based on favourable information, since the market will have already discounted it.
    c. investors have an incentive to buy stock based on favourable information, since the market takes time to discount it.
    d. both (a) and (b) of the above.

14. Mutual funds that outperform the market in one period are
    a. highly likely to consistently outperform the market in subsequent periods due to their superior investment strategies.
    b. likely to underperform the market in subsequent periods to average the funds' returns.
    c. not likely to consistently outperform the market in subsequent periods.
    d. not likely to outperform the market in any subsequent periods.
15. According to the theory of efficient capital markets
    a. incorrectly valued assets are quickly discovered and bought or sold until their prices are brought into line with their correct underlying value.
    b. most investors will not earn excess returns from spending resources on technical market analysis.
    c. the best strategy for most investors is to buy and hold a well-diversified portfolio of securities.
    d. all of the above are true.
16. The stockholders are residual claimants to all _______________ of the firm.
    a. cash flows
    b. expenses
    c. fundamentals
    d. liabilities
17. According to the one-period valuation model, which of the following is not important to the value of a stock?
    a. The stock dividend.
    b. The stock purchase price this period.
    c. The stock sales price next period.
    d. The required return on equity investments.
18. According to the generalized dividend valuation model, if the required return on equity investments rises, then the stock price
    a. rises.
    b. falls.
    c. remains constant.
    d. does not change in a predictable manner.
19. Even if company XYZ does not routinely pay dividends on its stock, the generalized dividend model predicts that company XYZ stock has value because
    a. company XYZ paid dividends in the past.
    b. the required return on equity investment is never zero.
    c. buyers expect company XYZ to pay dividends in the future.
    d. all companies must legally pay dividends.
20. According to the Gordon growth model, as the _______________ rises, the value of a stock _______________.
    a. required return on equity investments; rises
    b. expected growth rate of dividends; rises
    c. the most recent dividend paid; falls
    d. All of the above.
    e. None of the above.

21. If the required return on equity investments is 8%, then according to the one-period dividend model, what is the value of a stock that will pay a dividend of $0.50 next year and that is expected to sell for $30 next year?
    a. $28.24.
    b. $27.18.
    c. $10.00.
    d. $3.81.

22. If the required return on equity investments is 11% and if the expected constant growth rate of dividends is 6%, then according to the Gordon growth model, what is the value of a stock that will pay a dividend of $0.61 next year?
    a. $57.55.
    b. $12.20.
    c. $3.59.
    d. $0.55.

23. New information may lead to an immediate change in the price of a stock because
    a. the required return on this equity investment may change.
    b. the expected constant growth rate in dividends may change.
    c. the forecast of the future sales price of the stock may change.
    d. all of the above.
    e. only (a) and (c) of the above.

24. If uncertainty about the future cash flow of a stock rises, then the price of the stock falls because
    a. the amount of future dividends falls.
    b. the amount of future dividends rises.
    c. the required return on the stock falls.
    d. the required return on the stock rises.
    e. none of the above.

25. The value of a company's stock may fall when the economy enters a recession because
    a. the value of expected future dividends falls.
    b. the required return on equity investments falls.
    c. the expected growth rate of dividends falls.
    d. only (a) and (b) of the above.
    e. only (a) and (c) of the above.

26. The term "optimal forecast" in rational expectations theory is best defined as the
    a. correct forecast.
    b. correct guess.
    c. actual outcome.
    d. best guess.

27. If stock prices follow a "random walk," then stock prices
    a. will rise, then fall, then rise again.
    b. will rise and fall in a predictable manner.
    c. tend to follow trends.
    d. cannot be predicted based on past trends.

28. The average industry PE ratio for firm X is 41. What is the current price of firm X's stock if earnings per share is projected to be 1.22?
    a. $50
    b. $33.61
    c. $9
    d. $41

29. The optimal forecast of return and the equilibrium return for a given security are -10% and 5%, respectively. In such a case, based on the efficient markets hypothesis, the current price of this security will _______ and its R^{of} will _______.
    a. fall, fall
    b. rise, rise
    c. fall, rise
    d. rise, fall

30. The value of a firm's stock can be obtained by:
    a. multiplying the firm's price earnings ratio by the expected earnings per share.
    b. dividing the average industry price earnings ratio by the expected earnings per share.
    c. multiplying the average industry price earnings ratio by the expected earnings per share.
    d. none of the above

31. The efficient markets hypothesis views expectations of future prices as
    a. equal to optimal forecasts using all available information.
    b. equal to optimal forecasts using only the last period prices information.
    c. equal to optimal forecasts using the information related to the next period prices only.
    d. equal to optimal forecasts using only the information related to the rate of return.

CHAPTER 8

An Economic Analysis of Financial Structure

CHAPTER SYNOPSIS/COMPLETIONS

Lending is risky. Borrowers with ill intentions may choose to skip town and fail to leave a forwarding address, and even those with honest intentions may undertake actions that increase the probability that they will be unable to meet their payment obligations. Given these hazards, individuals may be understandably reluctant to lend. Although lending is risky for the lender, the channelling of funds from individuals with savings to others with productive investment opportunities is essential for economic growth. Channelling funds from savers to investors is beneficial for the economy and the parties to the exchange, but only if investors have incentives to honour their promises and pay back the borrowed funds. The key to understanding the structure of financial markets is to ask how the observed financial arrangements (e.g., the dominance of financial (1)____________ and complicated loan contracts) help to reduce the risk of loan defaults and the uncertainty of lending, thereby encouraging the financing of worthwhile business activities.

Although our financial system is complex in both structure and function, a few simple but powerful economic concepts provide the key insights necessary to understand its complexity. A careful examination of financial markets and institutions reveals that eight basic puzzles require explaining. Economic analysis of the eight puzzles indicates that our financial structure is best understood as a response to the problems of (2)____________ ____________ and (3)____________ ____________.

The eight basic puzzles of financial markets throughout the world include:

1. Stocks are not the most important source of finance for businesses. Between 1970 and 1985, the stock market accounted for only a very small fraction of the financing of businesses.
2. Issuing marketable securities is not the primary way businesses finance their operations. In Canada, (4)____________ are a more important source of finance than are stocks, but, combined, bonds and stocks supply less than (5)____________-____________ of the external funds corporations use to finance their activities.
3. Indirect finance, which involves the activities of (6)____________ intermediaries, is many times more important than direct finance. If direct finance is defined as the sale to households of marketable securities such as stocks and bonds, then direct finance accounts for a small fraction of the external financing of Canadian business.

4. Banks are the most important source of (7)______________ funds to finance businesses. Indeed, in most countries (but not in Canada) bank loans provide over four times more financing of corporate activities than does the stock market. Although banks remain important, their share of external funds has been declining in recent years.
5. The financial system is among the most heavily regulated sectors of the economy.
6. Only large, well-established corporations have easy access to securities markets to finance their activities.
7. Collateral is a prevalent feature of debt contracts for both households and businesses.
8. Debt contracts are typically (8)______________ legal documents that place substantial restrictions on the behaviour of the borrower.

Two factors help to explain the dominant role played by financial intermediaries in our financial structure: transaction costs and problems that arise from asymmetric (9)______________. Banks reduce transaction costs by bundling the funds they attract from small savers into loans large enough to finance business undertakings. The bargaining, contracting, and administrative costs (that is, transaction costs) decline as the size of the loan increases. Therefore, the administration of loans is subject to economies of scale. Economies of scale in financial markets also helps to explain the popularity of mutual funds.

Financial intermediaries further reduce transaction costs through their expertise in computer technology so that they can make it easier for customers to conduct transactions.

Because borrowers know better the potential returns and associated risks of their investment alternatives than do lenders, financial markets are characterized by asymmetries of information. This informational disadvantage can create problems both before and after the financial transaction is made. (10)______________ ______________ is the problem created by asymmetric information before the transaction occurs; moral hazard is the problem created by asymmetric information after the deal has been made.

Adverse selection in financial markets occurs when bad credit risks are the ones who most actively seek financing. Moral hazard in financial markets occurs when borrowers have incentives to engage in activities that are undesirable from the lenders' point of view. The analysis of how asymmetric information problems affect economic behaviour is called (11)______________ ______________.

Tools to help solve adverse selection include: the private production and sale of information (e.g., bond rating services), government regulation to increase information in securities markets, financial intermediation, requirements that collateral be pledged in loan contracts, and requirements that borrowers have sufficient net worth.

The concept of adverse selection explains the first seven of the eight puzzles about financial structure. The first four puzzles emphasize the importance of financial intermediaries. Financial intermediaries, because they have expertise in evaluating credit (12)______________ are better able to identify and screen potential bad risks. Moreover, since financial intermediaries such as banks hold mostly non-traded bank loans, they are better able to avoid the free-rider problem that would otherwise reduce their incentives to produce such information. Puzzle five, that financial markets are heavily regulated, is explained by the problem of asymmetric information. Puzzles six and seven can be understood as mechanisms by which lenders (1) screen on the basis of net worth, and (2) reduce their risk exposure by asking that collateral be pledged. Borrowers who are good risks will neither want to lose their collateral nor have their net worth diminished, thus these requirements discourage bad risks from asking for loans and thereby reduce the "lemons problem" in financial markets.

Moral hazard in (13)______________ contracts is known as the principal-agent problem because the manager (the agent) has less incentive to maximize profits than do the stockholders (the principals). Because principals have an incentive to free-ride on others' information gathering efforts, it is likely that too few resources will be devoted to monitoring the agent. Government regulations that force firms to adhere to standard accounting principles, venture capital firms, and debt contracts are financial market mechanisms that reduce principal-agent problems.

The prevalence of debt contracts, relative to equity contracts, does not, however, imply that the use of debt is the sole solution to moral hazard problems. High net worth can reduce moral hazard problems in debt contracts by making them incentive compatible. Lenders further reduce their risks by requiring that borrowers comply with a (sometimes lengthy) list of conditions called (14)______________ ______________. Finally, because of free-rider problems, financial intermediaries have a comparative advantage in reducing or avoiding moral hazard problems.

Although means have been devised for reducing adverse selection and moral hazard problems, (15)_____________ _____________ remind us that financial markets are not immune to the disruptions caused by the failure of a major financial or non-financial firm. Financial crises occur when rising adverse selection and moral hazard problems prevent financial markets from channelling funds to those with productive investment opportunities, hastening the decline in economic activity. There are four factors that lead to financial crises: (1) increases in interest rates, (2) increases in uncertainty, (3) stock market declines, and (4) deterioration of banks' balance sheets.

The important economic concepts of adverse selection and moral hazard help us to better understand the structure of our financial system. In the next five chapters, we find that these two important concepts contribute additional insights to workings in financial markets and the behaviour of financial market participants.

EXERCISES

EXERCISE 1: Adverse Selection and Moral Hazard

The eight basic puzzles of financial markets are listed below. For each of the following puzzles indicate whether the puzzle is explained by adverse selection (A), moral hazard (M), or both (B).

_____ 1. Stocks are not the most important source of finance for businesses.

_____ 2. Issuing marketable securities is not the primary way businesses finance their operations.

_____ 3. Indirect finance, which involves the activities of financial intermediaries, is more important than direct finance, in which businesses raise funds directly from lenders in financial markets.

_____ 4. Banks are the most important source of external funds to finance businesses.

_____ 5. The financial system is among the most heavily regulated sectors of the economy.

_____ 6. Only large, well-established corporations have easy access to securities markets to finance their activities.

_____ 7. Collateral is a prevalent feature of debt contracts for both households and businesses.

_____ 8. Debt contracts are typically extremely complicated legal documents that place substantial restrictions on the behaviour of the borrower.

EXERCISE 2: Financial Structure Definitions and Terminology

Match the terms on the right with the definition or description on the left. Place the letter of the term in the blank provided next to the appropriate definition or description.

_____ 1. Problem of too little information gathering and monitoring activity because the person undertaking the activity cannot prevent others from benefiting from the information and monitoring.	a. Adverse selection
_____ 2. Another term for equity capital, the difference between a firm's assets and its liabilities.	b. Moral hazard
_____ 3. Problem that results when the manager behaves contrary to the wishes of stockholders due to the separation of ownership and control.	c. Collateralized debt

_____	4. Term describing the solution that high net worth provides to the moral hazard problem in debt contracts by aligning the incentives of the borrower to that of the lender.	d.	Restrictive covenants
_____	5. Major disruptions in financial markets characterized by sharp declines in asset prices and the failures of many financial and nonfinancial firms.	e.	Collateral
_____	6. Property that is pledged to the lender if a borrower cannot make his or her debt payments.	f.	Financial crises
_____	7. Clauses in bond and loan contracts that either proscribe certain activities that borrowers may have incentive to undertake, or require certain activities that borrowers may not have incentive to undertake.	g.	Incentive compatible
_____	8. The predominant form of household debt contract, accounting for the majority of household debt.	h.	Principal-agent problem
_____	9. The problem in which borrowers have incentives to use funds obtained from external sources to finance riskier projects than originally envisioned by the lender.	i.	Net worth
_____	10. The lemons problem.	j.	Free-rider problem
_____	11. The decline in firms' net worth because of the increased burden of indebtedness due to a substantial decline in the price level.	k.	Debt deflation

EXERCISE 3: Financial Crises and Aggregate Economic Activity

A. Asset Market Effects on Balance Sheets

List the four factors in the economic environment that can lead to a substantial deterioration of firms' balance sheets that can worsen adverse selection and moral hazard problems in financial markets, eventually leading to a financial crisis.

1. ________________________________
2. ________________________________
3. ________________________________
4. ________________________________

B. Most financial crises in Canada have begun with the following four factors:

1. ________________________________
2. ________________________________
3. ________________________________
4. ________________________________

EXERCISE 4: Asymmetric Information and Royalty Sales

Recently the performer David Bowie raised over $55 million by issuing personal bonds, which he agreed to pay off when they mature in ten years. As collateral, Bowie offered royalty sales from his past albums. Which asymmetric information problem would exist if Bowie offered royalty sales from future albums as collateral?

____

____

____

EXERCISE 5: Conflicts of Interest

A. List two major types of financial service activities that have created conflicts of interest in financial institutions.

1. ____
2. ____

B. List the policy measures that have been introduced in the United States and Ontario to deal with conflicts of interest.

1. ____
2. ____
3. ____

SELF-TEST

PART A: True-False Questions

Circle whether the following statements are true (T) or false (F).

T F 1. Stocks are the most important source of external finance for businesses.

T F 2. In Canada, bonds are a more important source of external finance for business than are stocks.

T F 3. Most Canadian households own financial market securities.

T F 4. Financial intermediaries benefit savers by reducing transaction costs.

T F 5. Banks avoid the free-rider problem by primarily making private loans rather than purchasing securities that are traded in financial markets.

T F 6. Collateral, which is property promised to the lender if the borrower defaults, reduces the consequences of adverse selection because it reduces the lender's losses in the case of default.

T F 7. Firms with higher net worth are the ones most likely to default.

T F 8. Venture capitalists, unlike banks, are able to reduce moral hazard problems by placing individuals on the board of directors of the firm receiving the loan.

T F 9. One way of describing the solution that high net worth provides to the moral hazard problem is to say that it makes the debt contract incentive compatible.

T F 10. The requirement that the borrower keep her collateral in good condition, as one of the conditions to receiving a loan, is called a restrictive covenant.

T F 11. Moral hazard arises before transactions, and adverse selection is an asymmetric information problem that occurs after transactions.

T F 12. Conflict of interest is defined as a situation in which the professional and personal interests of an individual are competing with each other.

T F 13. Only large, well-established corporations have easy access to securities markets to finance their activities.

PART B: Multiple-Choice Questions

Circle the appropriate answer.

1. The recovery process from an economic downturn can be short-circuited by a substantial decline in the price level that reduces firms' net worth, a process called
   a. adverse selection.
   b. moral hazard.
   c. debt deflation.
   d. insolvency.
2. Which of the following statements concerning external sources of financing for nonfinancial businesses in Canada are true?
   a. Issuing marketable securities is not the primary way businesses finance their operations.
   b. Direct finance is many times more important than indirect finance as a source of external funds.
   c. Banks are not the most important source of external funds used to finance businesses.
   d. All of the above.
3. Poor people have difficulty getting loans because
   a. they typically have little collateral.
   b. they are less likely to benefit from access to financial markets.
   c. of both (a) and (b) of the above.
   d. of neither (a) nor (b) of the above.
4. Financial intermediaries provide their customers with
   a. reduced transaction costs.
   b. increased diversification.
   c. reduced risk.
   d. all of the above.
   e. only (b) and (c) of the above.
5. Because of the adverse selection problem,
   a. lenders are reluctant to make loans that are not secured by collateral.
   b. lenders may choose to lend only to those who "do not need the money."
   c. Lenders may refuse loans to individuals with high net worth.
   d. all of the above.
   e. only (a) and (b) of the above.

6. That most used cars are sold by intermediaries (i.e., used car dealers) provides evidence that these intermediaries
   a. help solve the adverse selection problem in this market.
   b. profit by becoming experts in determining whether an automobile is of good-quality or a lemon.
   c. are unable to prevent purchasers from free-riding off the information they provide.
   d. do all of the above.
   e. do only (a) and (b) of the above.
7. Mishkin's analysis of adverse selection indicates that financial intermediaries in general, and banks in particular, because they hold a large fraction of non-traded loans ________.
   a. play a greater role in moving funds to corporations than do securities markets as a result of their ability to overcome the free-rider problem.
   b. provide better-known and larger corporations a higher percentage of their external funds than they do to newer and smaller corporations, which tend to rely on the new issues market for funds.
   c. both (a) and (b) of the above.
   d. neither (a) nor (b) of the above.
8. The principal-agent problem arises because
   a. principals find it difficult and costly to monitor agents' activities.
   b. agents' incentives are not always compatible with those of the principals.
   c. principals have incentives to free-ride off the monitoring expenditures of other principals.
   d. of all of the above.
   e. of only (a) and (b) of the above.
9. Equity contracts
   a. are agreements by the borrowers to pay the lenders fixed dollar amounts at periodic intervals.
   b. have the advantage over debt contracts of a lower costly state verification.
   c. are used much more frequently to raise capital than are debt contracts.
   d. are none of the above.
10. Factors that lead to worsening conditions in financial markets include
    a. declining interest rates.
    b. declining stock prices.
    c. unanticipated increases in the price level.
    d. only (a) and (c) of the above.
    e. only (b) and (c) of the above.
11. The "lemons problem" is a term used to describe the
    a. moral hazard problem.
    b. adverse selection problem.
    c. free-rider problem.
    d. principal-agent problem.
12. The ______________ problem helps to explain why ______________ cannot be eliminated solely by the private production and sale of information.
    a. free-rider; adverse selection
    b. free-rider; moral hazard
    c. principal-agent; adverse selection
    d. principal-agent; moral hazard

13. Equity contracts are subject to a particular example of ____________ called the ____________ problem.
    a. adverse selection; principal-agent
    b. moral hazard; principal-agent
    c. adverse selection; free-rider
    d. moral hazard; free-rider
14. Debt-deflation occurs when the price level ____________, reducing the value of business firms' ____________.
    a. rises; net worth
    b. rises; collateral
    c. falls; net worth
    d. falls; collateral
15. Important factors leading up to the financial crises in both Mexico and East Asia in the mid- to late 1990s include
    a. weak supervision of banks by regulators.
    b. lack of expertise in screening and monitoring borrowers at banking institutions.
    c. an increase in indebtedness due to depreciation of their currencies.
    d. all of the above.
    e. only (a) and (b) of the above.
16. The largest source of external funds for businesses is ____________ while the smallest source is ____________.
    a. stock; bonds
    b. bank loans; stock
    c. bonds; stock
    d. bank loans; nonbank loans
    e. bonds; bank loans
17. Small investors cannot easily purchase financial instruments because
    a. transaction costs are too small.
    b. the minimum purchase price is often too small.
    c. brokerage fees may be a small part of the purchase price.
    d. all of the above.
    e. none of the above.
18. Compared to large companies, small companies are less likely to borrow funds through issuing
    a. debt.
    b. equity.
    c. collateral.
    d. only (a) and (b) of the above.
    e. only (a) and (c) of the above.
19. Adverse selection problems in financial markets can often be reduced by
    a. providing collateral.
    b. monitoring borrower behaviour.
    c. enforcement of restrictive covenants.
    d. all of the above.
    e. only (b) and (c) of the above.

20. Accurate accounting information
    a. reduces problems from adverse selection and moral hazard.
    b. is generally required of publicly traded firms by the Ontario Securities Commission.
    c. is subject to the free-rider problem.
    d. all of the above.
    e. none of the above.
21. Government fiscal imbalances in emerging market countries may lead to a contraction in economic activity because
    a. the government may default on its debt, which lowers bank assets.
    b. the government is issuing too little debt.
    c. the value of the currency may rise.
    d. bank lending may rise.
    e. all of the above.
22. The financial crisis in Argentina in 2001 was accompanied by
    a. large government surpluses.
    b. a banking panic.
    c. a rise in the value of Argentina's currency.
    d. only (a) and (b) of the above.
    e. only (b) and (c) of the above.
23. A venture capital firm avoids the free-rider problem in the face of moral hazard by
    a. acquiring equity in the start-up firm.
    b. placing its own people on the board of directors of the start-up firm.
    c. requiring collateral for loans.
    d. investing in costly state verification.
    e. not allowing others to purchase start-up firm equity shares.
24. Types of restrictive covenants that reduce moral hazard in debt contracts include
    a. covenants to keep collateral valuable.
    b. covenants to discourage desirable behaviour.
    c. covenants to provide information.
    d. both (a) and (b) of the above.
    e. both (a) and (c) of the above.
25. The pecking order hypothesis
    a. claims that small firms can more easily issue securities.
    b. claims that lesser known firms can more easily issue securities.
    c. claims that information about the quality of a firm does not influence whether or not it can issue securities.
    d. none of the above.
26. High net worth solves the moral hazard problem because it
    a. makes the debt contract incentive compatible.
    b. collateralizes the debt contract.
    c. state verifies the debt contract.
    d. does none of the above.

27. Which of the following events would be least likely to cause a financial crisis?
    a. Increase in interest rates
    b. Bank panic
    c. Increase in uncertainty
    d. Stock market decline

28. ________ keeps security markets such as the stock markets and bond markets from being effective in channelling funds from savers to borrowers.
    a. Transaction costs
    b. Economies of scale
    c. Lemons problem
    d. Lack of expertise

29. Four categories of factors can trigger financial crises:
    a. decrease in interest rates, increase in uncertainty, adverse selection, conflict of interests.
    b. decrease in interest rates, increase in uncertainty, moral hazard, conflict of interests.
    c. decrease in interest rates, decrease in uncertainty, moral hazard, conflict of interests.
    d. increase in interest rates, increase in uncertainty, asset market effects on balance sheets, and problems in the banking sector.

30. A sharp ________ in the stock market is one factor that can cause a serious deterioration in a firm's balance sheet, which in turn ________ adverse selection and moral hazard problems and can provoke financial crises.
    a. decline, decreases
    b. decline, increases
    c. increase, decreases
    d. increase, increases

31. Direct finance involves a process wherein:
    a. A business raises funds directly from lenders in domestic financial markets.
    b. A business raises funds directly from lenders in foreign financial markets.
    c. A business raises funds directly from lenders in financial markets.
    d. none of the above.

32. The costly state verification makes the equity contract:
    a. more desirable; it explains why equity is not a more important factor in the Canadian financial sector.
    b. less desirable; it explains why equity is not a more important factor in the Canadian financial sector.
    c. more desirable; it explains why equity is a more important factor in the Canadian financial sector.
    d. less desirable; it explains why equity is the most important factor in the Canadian financial sector.

CHAPTER 9

Banking and the Management of Financial Institutions

CHAPTER SYNOPSIS/COMPLETIONS

Banks are the most important financial intermediaries in Canada. In this chapter we examine the bank balance sheet and the basic principles of bank management in order to improve our understanding of how banks operate in our economy.

The bank balance sheet, which lists assets and liabilities, can be thought of as a list of the sources and uses of bank funds. It has the characteristic that total assets equal total liabilities plus bank equity (1)______________. The bank's liabilities are its (2)______________ of funds, which include: demand deposits, chequable deposits, borrowings, and bank equity capital. The bank's assets are its uses of funds, and include: reserves, cash items in process of collection, deposits at other banks, securities, loans, and other assets (mostly physical capital). Reserves are either settlement balances held at the Bank of Canada or currency that is physically held by banks (called (3)______________ ______________). Reserves are held for two reasons. First, banks keep a certain fraction of deposits as reserves, called (4)______________ ______________. Additional reserves, called excess reserves, can be used by a bank to meet obligations to depositors. Banks also hold Canadian government securities, sometimes referred to as secondary (5)______________ because of their high liquidity.

The basic operation of a bank is to make profits by engaging in the process of asset transformation. Banks issue liabilities such as deposits and use the proceeds to acquire income earning assets such as loans. An important consideration for a bank engaged in this process is that when it receives additional deposits it gains an equal amount of reserves, but when it loses deposits, it loses an equal amount of reserves.

Banks must ensure that they have enough ready cash to pay their depositors in the event of deposit (6)______________. To keep enough cash on hand, the bank must engage in (7)______________ management, the acquisition of sufficiently liquid assets to meet the obligations of the bank to depositors. Specifically, banks hold excess reserves to escape the costs of (a) borrowing from other banks in the overnight funds market, (b) selling securities, (c) borrowing from the Bank of Canada, and (d) calling in or selling loans—the latter being the costliest way of acquiring reserves when there is a deposit outflow. Excess reserves are insurance against the cost of deposit outflows. Hence, the higher the cost, the more excess reserves banks will want to hold.

Banks manage their assets using the following four principles. First, they try to find borrowers who will pay high interest rates and are unlikely to (8)______________ on their loans. Second, banks try to purchase securities with high expected returns and low risk. Third, banks attempt to minimize risk by (9)______________ their holdings of both loans and securities. Fourth, banks must manage the liquidity of their assets so they can satisfy reserve requirements without incurring huge costs. This means that banks hold liquid assets even if they earn a somewhat lower return than other assets.

Before the 1960s, liability management was a staid affair. For the most part, banks took their liabilities as fixed and spent their time trying to achieve an optimal mix of assets. Starting in the 1960s, large banks in key financial centers began to explore ways in which liabilities on their balance sheets could provide them with reserves and liquidity. This led to an expansion of overnight loan markets, such as the (10)______________________________ market, and the development of new financial instruments such as negotiable CDs (introduced in 1961). Large banks no longer took their sources of funds (liabilities) as given; instead, they aggressively set target goals for asset growth, acquiring funds by issuing liabilities as they were needed.

A bank must manage capital to reduce the chance that it will become insolvent and then fail, assure an adequate return to its shareholders, and satisfy minimum capital requirements. A bank can raise capital by issuing equity or reducing its (11) _______________ to shareholders. Alternatively, a bank can respond to a shortage of capital by restraining asset growth.

Another important banking development to emerge in recent years has been the growth in off-balance-sheet activities. Off-balance-sheet activities consist of trading financial instruments and the generation of income from fees, both of which affect bank profits but are not visible on bank balance sheets. Although these activities can increase bank profitability, many believe that they expose banks to increased risk.

EXERCISES

EXERCISE 1: Definitions and Terminology

Match the terms on the right with the definition or description on the left. Place the letter of the term in the blank provided next to the appropriate definition.

____	1.	The ratio of after-tax net profits to total assets.	a.	Bank liabilities
____	2.	The riskiness of earnings and returns that is associated with changes in interest rates.	b.	Deposits
____	3.	Trading financial instruments and the generation of fee income, for example.	c.	Interest-rate risk
____	4.	Commercial banks' sources of funds.	d.	Negotiable CDs
____	5.	Commercial banks' uses of funds.	e.	Off-balance-sheet activities
____	6.	The primary source of bank funds.	f.	Bank assets
____	7.	A simplified balance sheet that lists the changes that occur in balance sheet items.	g.	Liquidity management
____	8.	The acquisition of sufficiently liquid assets to meet the obligations of the bank to depositors.	h.	T-account
____	9.	Financial instruments developed in the early 1960s that enabled money center banks to quickly acquire funds.	i.	Return on assets

EXERCISE 2: T-Accounts, and Deposits and Withdrawals

A. Fill in the T-account of the First Bank if Shirley Student deposits $2000 in cash into her chequing account at this bank.

First Bank

Assets	Liabilities

B. Fill in the T-accounts of the First Bank and the Second Bank when Shirley writes a $1000 cheque written on her account at the First Bank to pay her tuition at the University of Toronto, which in turn deposits the cheque in its accounts at the Second Bank.

First Bank

Asset	Liabilities

Second Bank

Assets	Liabilities

C. What is the net effect of the transactions in A and B on the reserve position at the two banks?

____

EXERCISE 3: Bank Response to Deposit Outflows and Liquidity Management

Suppose that the First Bank has the following balance-sheet position and that the desired reserve ratio on deposits is 20% (in millions of dollars).

Assets		Liabilities	
Reserves	$25	Deposits	$100
Loans	75	Bank capital	10
Securities	10		

A. If the bank suffers a deposit outflow of $6 million, what will its balance sheet now look like? Show this by filling in the amounts in the following balance sheet.

Assets		Liabilities	
Reserves		Deposits	
Loans		Bank capital	
Securities			

Must the bank make any adjustment in its balance sheet? ______________________

Why? ____

B. Suppose the bank is hit by another $4 million deposit outflow. What will its balance-sheet position look like now? Show this by filling in the amounts in the following balance sheet.

Assets		Liabilities	
Reserves		Deposits	
Loans		Bank capital	
Securities			

Must the bank make any adjustment in its balance sheet? ______________________

Why? ____

C. If the bank satisfies its reserve requirements by selling off securities, how much will it have to sell?

____

Why? ______________________________

D. After selling off the securities to meet its reserve requirements, what will its balance sheet look like? Show this by filling in the amounts in the following balance sheet:

Assets		Liabilities	
Reserves		Deposits	
Loans		Bank capital	
Securities			

E. If after selling off the securities the bank is hit by another $10 million of withdrawals of deposits and it sells off all its securities to obtain reserves, what will its balance sheet look like? Again show this by filling in the amounts in the following balance sheet:

Assets		Liabilities	
Reserves		Deposits	
Loans		Bank capital	
Securities			

If the bank is now unable to call in or sell any of its loans and no one is willing to lend funds to this bank, then what will happen to the bank and why?

____

____

EXERCISE 4: Asset Management

List the four main concerns of bank asset management.

1. ______________________________
2. ______________________________
3. ______________________________
4. ______________________________

EXERCISE 5: Liability Management

List three of the changes in the way banks operate as a result of the flexibility in liability management that occurred after 1960.

1. ______________________________
2. ______________________________
3. ______________________________

EXERCISE 6: Return on Equity and Assets

Suppose that the First Bank has the following balance sheet (in millions of dollars):

Assets		Liabilities	
Reserves	$5	Deposits	$35
Loans	40	Capital	10

A. If net profit after taxes for this bank is $0.9 million dollars, then what is the return on assets (ROA) and the return on equity (ROE)?

ROA = (net profit after taxes) / (assets) = 0.9 / 45 = 2%

ROE = 0.9 / 10 = 9%

B. Suppose that the bank wants to increase ROE by increasing deposits from $35 million to $50 million. If the desired reserve ratio is ten percent, and if the bank holds only desired reserves and loans out all excess reserves, then how much in reserves will the bank have? How much in loans will the bank have?

C. If the ROA is unchanged, what is the net profit after taxes that the bank earns?

D. What is the new ROE?

EXERCISE 7: Measuring Bank Performance

Suppose that the assets and equity capital of XYZ Bank are 2500 and 110, respectively. In addition, the total operating income of this bank is 100, its no interest and interest incomes are 40 and 25, respectively, and its net income is 18.

A. What are the return on assets (ROA) and the return on equity (ROE)?

B. What is the net interest margin (NIM) and the equity multiplier (EM)?

C. Show that ROE=ROA × EM.

EXERCISE 8: Measuring Bank Performance

Suppose there are two banks in the economy, the Bretton Woods Bank and the Doha Development Bank. Both banks have a return on assets (ROA) of 1.5%, and their balance sheets are:

Bretton Woods Bank

Asset	Liabilities
Reserves: $45,000	Deposits: $296,000
Loans: $255,000	Bank Capital: $4,000

Second Bank

Assets	Liabilities
Reserves: $52,500	Deposits: $343,000
Loans: $297,500	Bank Capital: $7,000

A. What is the equity multiplier for the Bretton Woods Bank and the Doha Development Bank?

B. What is the return on equity for the Bretton Woods Bank and the Doha Development Bank?

C. Equity holders of which bank will be the more satisfied with their returns?

EXERCISE 9: Bank Response to Deposit Outflows and Reserve Ratios

On July 1, 1935, S.D.K deposited $200 dollars into the Bank of Cambridge. The bank requires that its deposits have a reserve ratio of 25%. At this point the bank's balance sheet is:

Assets		Liabilities	
Reserves	$50	Deposits	$180
Loans	130	Bank capital	20
Securities	20		

A. On July 2, 1935, the government withdraws $50 from the Bank of Cambridge to finance its expenditure. What changes occur in the bank's balance sheet?

Assets		Liabilities	
Reserves		Deposits	
Loans		Bank capital	
Securities			

B. What does the new bank balance sheet say about the initial level of reserves that the bank holds?

____

____

C. What four actions could be taken to restore the reserve ratio?

____

____

D. Why is it important for banks to hold excess reserves? What is the downfall of holding a very large amount of excess reserves?

____

____

SELF-TEST

PART A: True-False Questions

Circle whether the following statements are true (T) or false (F).

T F 1. A bank's assets are its sources of funds.

T F 2. Bank capital equals the total assets of the bank minus the total liabilities.

T F 3. Savings accounts are the most common type of chequable deposit.

T F 4. Chequable deposits are usually the lowest-cost source of bank funds.

T F 5. Chequable deposits are the primary source of bank funds.

T F 6. Interest paid on deposits makes up over half of total bank operating expenses.

T F 7. Banks are only able to borrow reserves from the Bank of Canada.

T F 8. Loans provide banks with most of their revenue.

T F 9. Providing backup line of credit is an off-balance-sheet activity.

T F 10. Off-balance-sheet activities have declined in importance for banks over the past two decades.

T F 11. The currency that is physically held by banks is called vault cash.

T F 12. Canadian banks are required to hold cash reserves.

T F 13. Opening a savings account leads to an increase in the bank's reserves equal to the increase in savings deposits.

T F 14. A bank will maximize its profits by issuing loans to a limited number of specific sectors in the economy.

PART B: Multiple-Choice Questions

Circle the appropriate answer.

1. Which of the following bank assets is the most liquid?
   a. Consumer loans
   b. Provincial and local government securities
   c. Physical capital
   d. Canadian government securities
2. Reserves
   a. equal the deposits banks hold at the Bank of Canada.
   b. include bank holdings of Canadian government securities.
   c. can be divided up into desired reserves plus excess reserves.
   d. equal both (a) and (c) of the above.
3. When a $1000 cheque written on the Bank of Montreal is deposited in an account at the Royal Bank, then
   a. the liabilities of the Bank of Montreal increase by $1000.
   b. the reserves of the Bank of Montreal increase by $1000.
   c. the liabilities of the Royal Bank fall by $1000.
   d. the reserves of the Royal Bank increase by $1000.
4. When you deposit a $100 cheque in your bank account at the First Bank of Calgary and you withdraw $50 in cash, then
   a. the liabilities of First Bank rise by $100.
   b. the reserves of First Bank rise by $100.
   c. the assets of the First Bank rise by $100.
   d. the liabilities of the First Bank rise by $50.
   e. none of the above occurs.
5. If a bank has $1 million of deposits and a desired reserve ratio of 5%, and it holds $100,000 in reserves, then it must rearrange its balance sheet if there is a deposit outflow of
   a. $51,000.
   b. $20,000.
   c. $30,000.
   d. $40,000.

(e.) none of the above.

6. A bank will want to hold less excess reserves (everything else equal) when
   (a.) it expects to have deposit inflows in the near future.
   b. brokerage commissions on selling bonds rise.
   c. both (a) and (b) of the above occur.
   d. neither (a) nor (b) of the above occurs.
7. When a bank faces a reserve deficiency because of a deposit outflow, it will try to do which of the following first?
   a. Call in loans.
   b. Borrow from the Bank of Canada.
   c. Sell securities.
   (d.) Borrow from other banks.
8. A bank failure is more likely to occur when
   a. a bank holds more Canadian government securities.
   (b.) a bank suffers large deposit outflows.
   c. a bank holds more excess reserves.
   d. a bank has more bank capital.
9. When interest rates are expected to fall in the future, a banker is likely to
   a. make short-term rather than long-term loans.
   b. buy short-term rather than long-term bonds.
   (c.) buy long-term rather than short-term bonds.
   d. do both (a) and (b) of the above.
10. Banks want to hold ________ as an insurance against the costs associated with deposit outflows.
    a. interbank deposits
    (b.) excess reserves
    c. securities
    d. both (a) and (b)
11. Items listed on the liability side of banks' balance sheets include
    (a.) bank capital.
    b. loans.
    c. reserves.
    d. all of the above.
    e. only (a) and (b) of the above.
12. Collectively, reserves, cash items in process of collection, and deposits at other banks, are referred to as ______________ in a bank balance sheet.
    a. secondary reserves
    (b.) total cash reserves
    c. liquid items
    d. compensating balances
13. In less uncertain times, bank managers might want to hold _______ capital, have a _______ equity multiplier, and thereby ________ the return on equity.
    (a.) less, high, increase
    b. more, high, decrease
    c. less, low, increase

d. more, high, increase

14. For a given return on _____________, the _____________ is bank capital, the _____________ is the return for the owners of the bank.
    a. liabilities; lower; lower
    (b.) assets; lower; higher
    c. assets; higher; higher
    d. liabilities; lower; higher
15. Chequable deposits
    a. include time deposits.
    b. are the most expensive way for banks to acquire funds.
    c. are an asset for the bank.
    d. have become a larger share of bank liabilities over time.
    (e.) none of the above.
16. Which of the following financial instruments are commercial banks legally not allowed to hold?
    a. Bonds issued by a local government.
    b. Stock issued by a foreign company.
    c. Stock issued by a domestic company.
    d. only (a) and (b) of the above.
    (e.) only (b) and (c) of the above.
17. Banks generally earn the highest rate of return on which of their assets?
    a. Reserves.
    b. Certificates of deposit.
    c. Canadian government securities.
    (d.) Loans.
    e. Deposits at other banks.
18. If Steve writes a cheque for $200 to Beth that she deposits into her account, and if Steve and Beth use the same bank, then
    a. thc bank eventually loses reserves equal to $200.
    b. total liabilities of the bank rise by $200.
    c. total assets of the bank fall by $200.
    d. excess reserves increase by $200.
    (e.) none of the above.
19. In order to reduce excess reserves after a deposit inflow, a bank can
    (a.) purchase loans from another bank.
    b. borrow from the Bank of Canada.
    c. call in loans.
    d. sell securities.
20. For a given return on assets, a bank with more capital has a _____________ risk of insolvency and a _____________ return on equity.
    a. lower; higher
    (b.) lower; lower
    c. higher; lower

d. higher; higher

21. If the equity multiplier for a bank is 10, and if the return on assets is 2%, then the return on equity is
    a. 50%.
    b. 20%.
    c. 10%.
    d. 2%.
    e. 1%.

22. If a bank wants to increase the equity multiplier in order to raise the return on equity, then it can
    a. sell securities.
    b. call in loans.
    c. use reserves to purchase securities.
    d. borrow in the overnight funds market and issue loans.

23. Banks often specialize in providing loans to firms in a common industry because this
    a. allows the banks to increase portfolio diversification.
    b. is required by law.
    c. reduces the costs of acquiring information.
    d. decreases profitability.

24. When a bank sells a loan to another financial institution
    a. the loan does not remain on the bank's balance sheet.
    b. the bank receives another asset in return for selling the loan.
    c. liabilities of the bank rise.
    d. only (a) and (b) of the above.
    e. only (b) and (c) of the above.

25. When you deposit a $50 bill in the Pacific Coast Bank,
    a. its liabilities decrease by $50.
    b. its reserves decrease by $50.
    c. its assets increase by $50.
    d. only (b) and (c) of the above occur.

26. Which of the following will concern bank management?
    a. acquiring funds at low cost.
    b. having cash to meet deposit outflows.
    c. minimizing risk by diversifying asset holdings.
    d. all of the above.

27. _________, _________, and _________ are off-balance-sheet activities.
    a. Interest rate swaps, interbank deposits, trading in financial futures
    b. Interest rate swaps, interbank deposits, loan sale
    c. Loan sale, providing backup lines of credit, interbank deposits
    d. Loan sale, providing backup lines of credit, trading in financial futures

28. _________, _________, ROE, and _________ are measures that can be used to measure bank performance.
    a. Net income, ROA, net interest margin
    b. Bank capital, ROA, net interest margin
    c. Bank capital, net interest margin, deposits
    d. Net income, equity multiplier, bank capital

29. If the XYZ Bank decreases its capital from 500 to 100 and ROA stays constant, given that its ROE was 1, what will be its new ROE?
    a. 5
    b. 0.2
    c. 0.25
    d. 1

30. When the interest income, interest expenses, and assets of a bank are 20, 15, 20, respectively, the ________ is 0.25.
    a. ROA
    b. ROE
    c. NIM
    d. EM

31. The higher the costs associated with deposit outflows,
    a. the less excess reserves banks will want to hold.
    b. the more excess reserves banks will want to hold.
    c. the less desired reserves banks will want to hold.
    d. the more desired reserves banks will want to hold.

32. Equity multiplier is defined as
    a. the amount of net profit divided by equity capital.
    b. the amount of assets divided by net profit after taxes.
    c. the amount of assets divided by equity capital.
    d. the equity capital divided by net profit after taxes.

CHAPTER 10

Banking Industry: Structure and Competition

CHAPTER SYNOPSIS/COMPLETIONS

See the appendix on the website for a brief introduction to the history of banking in Canada. It then examines how financial innovations have increased the competitive environment in banking, fundamentally changing this industry. The chapter next describes the commercial banking industry and goes on to look at the near banking industry in Canada. Lastly, the chapter examines the forces behind the growth in international banking with special emphasis on developments that have affected us in Canada.

Modern commercial banking in Canada dates to 1817 when the Bank of Montreal was created in Montreal. Initially, the Bank of Montreal was without statutory authority, but a charter was approved by the legislature of Lower Canada and confirmed by royal assent in 1822. At that time, other banks opened for business, such as for example the Bank of New Brunswick and the Bank of Upper Canada. There were some differences between the charters of these banks. For example, the terms of the charter of the Bank of New Brunswick followed the banking tradition of New England whereas the charter of the Bank of Montreal almost duplicated the terms governing the Bank of the United States.

By 1867, when Canada was created by the (1)_______________, there were 34 chartered banks in Canada with a total of 127 branches. No national currency existed at that time in Canada and the chartered banks were issuing (2)_______________ on their own credit. It was the Provincial Notes Act of 1866 that authorized the issue of provincial notes and the Dominion Notes Act of 1870 that gave the government a monopoly over small-denomination notes, the (3)_______________, by restricting the ability of banks to issue only large denomination notes (over $5). Both banknotes and Dominion notes were superseded by Bank of Canada notes right after the creation of the (4)_______________ in 1935.

Financial innovation was little discussed only 30 years ago. Since then it has received increasing attention from economists as they have come to realize that the financial structure of the economy and its institutions respond in ways that may nullify the intended effects of regulations and blur the distinctions among financial institutions. For example, lenders discovered that adjustable-rate (5)_______________ reduced interest-rate risk to the benefit of both lender and borrower. Borrowers were able to get adjustable-rate mortgages at lower interest rates than fixed-rate mortgages, while lenders reduced their exposure to interest-rate risk.

Changes in information technology have stimulated innovations by lowering the cost of supplying financial services. Examples include the expansion of credit and debit cards, and the rapid growth of electronic banking.

Ironically, government financial regulations have spurred financial innovations designed to avoid the regulations, a process Edward Kane calls (6)_______________ _______________. For example, nonuniform reserve requirements and Regulation Q ceilings in the United States gave U.S. banks a strong incentive to create new accounts free of the requirements and ceilings in order to prevent (7)_______________ when market interest rates rose above regulated ceilings. Money market mutual funds and sweep accounts are two of the innovations either created or expanded in response to regulations that prevented an orderly adjustment to rising interest rates. The traditional role of the banking industry has been in decline for thirty years.

The decline in the relative importance of banks and near banks (trust and mortgage loan companies and credit unions and *caisses populaires*) in the provision of financial services began when inflation of the late 1960s and early 1970s eroded their (8)_______________ advantage in acquiring funds. Regulations, that had once virtually assured bank profitability, hindered their efforts to acquire funds by limiting what banks could pay for deposits. Disintermediation (the net withdrawal of deposits from financial intermediaries) crimped bank loan growth and profitability.

Compounding the loss of cost advantages, banks and near banks have realized an erosion of their income advantages in financial markets. The growth of the (9)_______________ paper market, the (10)_______________ bond market, and securitization are the three most important developments that have eroded banks' income advantage over their competitors. The process of financial innovation that has eroded banks' cost advantages in acquiring funds and income advantages in making loans is the source of the decline in the industry's traditional banking business. Although it is of no consolation to Canadian bankers, banks in other industrialized countries have seen the similar declines in their market shares as financial deregulation and innovations have allowed firms direct access to securities markets.

The U.S. banking industry until a few years ago was characterized by many (11)_______________ banks. This structure was best explained by the restrictions of both the federal government and many state governments to open bank (12)_______________. In Canada, as of March 2003, there were 68 chartered banks with over 8000 branches. Sixteen of these banks were Schedule I banks, 31 were Schedule II banks, and the remaining were (13)_______________ banks.

The rapid expansion in international trade has spurred the growth of (14)_______________ banking. Contributing to this growth has been banks' desire to escape burdensome regulations, and to tap into the large pool of dollar-denominated deposits in foreign countries known as (15)_______________.

The growth of international trade has increased the presence of foreign banks in Canada. Foreign banks now hold more than 15% of total bank assets in Canada.

EXERCISES

EXERCISE 1: Definitions and Terminology

Match the terms on the right with the definition or description on the left. Place the letter of the term in the blank provided next to the appropriate definition.

_____	1. Deposits in banks outside the United States denominated in dollars.	a.	The Finance Act (of 1914)
_____	2. Until 1981, they were not allowed to operate in Canada.	b.	OSFI
_____	3. Canadian legislation that allowed the Department of Finance to act a lender of last resort (that is, to provide Dominion notes to banks).	c.	superregional banks
_____	4. Cannot make loans to domestic residents but can make loans to foreigners and accept their deposits.	d.	foreign banks
_____	5. Bank holding companies that rival money center banks in size.	e.	Eurodollars
_____	6. Regulatory body that supervises banks.	f.	central bank
_____	7. Government institution responsible for supplying money and credit in economy.	g.	international banking facilities

EXERCISE 2: Costs of Reserve Requirements

Suppose that the interest rate that banks charge for loans is 8% and that banks keep 10% of deposits as reserves.

A. For every $1000 in deposits, how much do banks lose in foregone interest because of the reserve requirement?

____

B. Interest rates fell to forty-year lows by 2002. Does the banking industry have more or less incentive to develop financial innovations? Explain.

____

____

EXERCISE 3: The Decline of Traditional Banking

A. List the financial innovations that have contributed to the decline in traditional banking.

1. ____
2. ____
3. ____
4. ____

B. Explain why the rise of the junk bond market reduced the demand for bank loans.

____

____

EXERCISE 4: Responses to Branching Restrictions in the United States

List the two financial innovations that U.S. banks have used to get around the restrictions to branch banking.

1. ____
2. ____

EXERCISE 5: Fixed-Rate Mortgage

In January the market interest rate was 7%. In April, it increased to 13%. In September it then increased to 15%.

A. Would it be more profitable for a household to borrow from a financial institution using an adjustable-rate mortgage or a fixed-rate mortgage?

____

____

B. Would it be more profitable for a financial institution to lend to a household using an adjustable-rate mortgage or a fixed-rate mortgage?

____

____

SELF-TEST

PART A: True-False Questions

Circle whether the following statements are true (T) or false (F).

T F 1. Economic analysis suggests that banks will devise ways around regulations which restrict certain banking activities.

T F 2. Noting the lack of strong regulation, many economists argue that bank failures in the first half of the nineteenth century resulted from fraudulent practices.

T F 3. The Canada Deposit Insurance Corporation (CDIC) has been granted the sole responsibility for supervising bank holding companies in Canada.

T F 4. Regulations that restrict competition in the banking industry are often justified by the desire to prevent bank failures.

T F 5. Periodic examinations of banks help regulators identify problems at banks before they have a detrimental effect on the financial soundness of the economy.

T F 6. It has been argued that the small number of commercial banks in Canada—about 68 in late 2005—can be seen as an indication of the absence of competition rather than the presence of competition.

T F 7. One impetus in the early 1980s leading to an increase in the number of foreign banks in Canada was the absence of competition in the Canadian financial services industry.

T F 8. Information technology has lowered the costs of processing financial transactions.

T F 9. The rise of the junk bond market has contributed to the decline in banking.

T F 10. The same technological forces that have hurt the competitiveness of banks in Canada also seem to be at work abroad, helping to explain the decline of banking in other nations.

T F 11. Two sets of regulations that restricted the ability of the U.S. banks to make profits are: reserve requirements and restriction on interest paid on deposits.

T F 12. The simultaneous rise of cost and income advantages has resulted in reduced profitability of the traditional banking system.

T F 13. A change in the financial environment will stimulate a search by financial institutions for innovations that are likely to be less profitable.

T F 14. High volatility of interest rates leads to a higher level of interest-rate risk.

T F 15. During the 1970s and early 1980s, a large proportion of the bank's foreign lending was in sovereign loans.

PART B: Multiple-Choice Questions

Circle the appropriate answer.

1. Which of the following is a bank regulatory agency?
   a. Office of the Superintendent of Financial Institutions Canada.
   b. Bank of Canada.
   c. Canada Deposit Insurance Corporation.
   d. All of the above.

2. The bundling of a portfolio of mortgage or auto loans into a marketable capital market instrument is known as
   a. "fastbacking."
   b. arbitrage.
   c. computerization.

d. securitization.
e. optioning the portfolio.

3. Near banks (TMLs and CUCPs) are regulated by
   a. the Bank of Canada.
   b. the CDIC.
   c. the Office of the Superintendent of Financial Institutions Canada.
   d. all of the above.
   e. only (b) and (c) of the above.
4. Which of the following factors explain the rapid growth in international banking in the past 25 years?
   a. Rapid growth of world trade in this period
   b. Decline in world trade since 1960
   c. Creation of the League of Nations
   d. None of the above
5. When economists argue that banking regulations have been a mixed blessing, they are referring to the fact that
   a. bank regulations foster competition at the expense of banking system safety.
   b. bank regulations foster banking system safety at the expense of competition.
   c. branch banking, while desired by consumers, leads to less competition.
   d. bank regulations foster competition by limiting branching.
6. The U.S. banking system has been labeled a dual system because
   a. banks offer both chequing and savings accounts.
   b. it actually includes both banks and thrift institutions.
   c. it is regulated by both federal and state governments.
   d. it was established during the Civil War, thus making it necessary to create separate regulatory bodies for the North and South.
7. A *caisse populaire* is usually
   a. regulated by the provincial government.
   b. an investor in mortgage loans.
   c. linked to the Canadian Payments System through a *Centrale*.
   d. all of the above.
8. A *caisse populaire* is usually
   a. more profitable than a Schedule I bank.
   b. regulated by the OSFI.
   c. regulated by a *Centrale*.
   d. an investor in mortgage loans.
9. Credit unions are usually
   a. regulated by the provincial government.
   b. regulated by the Bank of Canada.
   c. regulated by a *Centrale*.
   d. investors in mortgage loans.
   e. both (a) and (d) of the above.

10. Credit unions and *caisses populaires*
    a. are funded almost entirely by deposits.
    b. are regulated and supervised by the OSFI.
    c. are investors in commercial loans.
    d. none of the above.

11. Trust and mortgage loan companies outside Quebec
    a. are funded almost entirely by deposits, guaranteed investment certificates, and debentures.
    b. are directly covered by the CDIC.
    c. are bigger than TMLs in Quebec.
    d. both (a) and (b) of the above.

12. Financial innovation has caused banks' cost advantages to ____________, and their income advantages to ____________.
    a. increase; increase
    b. increase; decrease
    c. decrease; increase
    d. decrease; decrease

13. The most important developments that have reduced banks' cost advantages in the past thirty years include:
    a. the elimination of Regulation Q ceilings in the United States.
    b. the competition from money market mutual funds.
    c. the competition from junk bonds.
    d. all of the above.
    e. only (a) and (b) of the above.

14. The most important developments that have reduced banks' income advantages in the past thirty years include:
    a. the growth of the junk bond market.
    b. the competition from money market mutual funds.
    c. the growth of securitization.
    d. only (a) and (b) of the above.
    e. only (a) and (c) of the above.

15. Schedule II banks are
    a. regulated by the OSFI.
    b. more profitable than Schedule I banks.
    c. small, universal, and domestic.
    d. all of the above.

16. An improvement in technology stimulates financial innovations by
    a. lowering the cost of providing new services.
    b. raising the demand of providing new services.
    c. reducing the competition from those providing financial services.
    d. doing all of the above.

17. Adjustable-rate mortgages are offered by banks because these mortgages
    a. lower interest rate risk for banks.
    b. guarantee the maximum monthly payment from borrowers.
    c. are the only mortgages that households desire.
    d. have a payment that remains fixed over the life of the loan.

18. A large number of banks started providing credit card services
    a. before World War II.
    b. after computer technology reduced transaction costs of these services.
    c. in order to earn profit from loan defaults.
    d. despite the fact that these services are generally not profitable.

19. Financial derivatives were created by the Chicago Board of Trade in the 1970s and they
    a. are essentially a futures contract in financial instruments.
    b. protect institutions from interest-rate risk.
    c. have a payoff that is linked to previously issued financial securities.
    d. all of the above.
    e. only (a) and (b) of the above.

20. A bank bundling together a collection of student loans and selling claims to principal and interest payments to a third party is known as
    a. collateralization.
    b. selling junk bonds.
    c. securitization.
    d. selling commercial paper.
    e. modernization.

21. The Four Pillars refers to
    a. banks, life insurance companies, P&C insurance companies, and pension funds.
    b. the Bank of Canada, the Big Six, the OSFI, and the CDIC.
    c. banks, insurance companies, finance companies, and merchant banks.
    d. banks, insurance companies, trust companies, and mutual funds.

22. Sweep accounts, which transform corporate chequing accounts into overnight securities, has which advantage for banks?
    a. Sweep accounts reduce costs since they require few transactions.
    b. Sweep accounts are not subject to corporate income taxation.
    c. Sweep accounts reduce costs since they are not subject to reserve requirements.
    d. None of the above.

23. The possible benefits of larger banking institutions and nation-wide banking include
    a. raising the efficiency of the banking sector through more competition.
    b. an increase in lending to small businesses.
    c. decreased diversification of banks' loan portfolios.
    d. only (a) and (b) of the above.

24. As compared to banks, credit unions
    a. have customers that share a common bond.
    b. tend to be larger.
    c. are only provincially chartered.
    d. have no deposit insurance.

25. Economies of scope refers to the idea that
    a. larger banks are more efficient than smaller banks.
    b. taxes are reduced for banks that consolidate.
    c. one resource can be used to provide many products and services.

d. international banking is generally more profitable than domestic banking.

26. Which of the following are true statements?
   a. Schedule I and Schedule II banks have identical powers.
   b. widely held foreign banks can own 100% of a Canadian bank subsidiary.
   c. a Schedule II bank may have a significant shareholder (more than 10%) for up to 10 years after chartering.
   d. all of the above.

27. Bank holding companies
   a. own almost all large banks.
   b. are largely not restricted in branch banking.
   c. have grown tremendously in the past decade.
   d. All of the above are true.
   e. Only (a) and (c) are true.

28. A foreign bank can enter the Canadian banking industry as either a Schedule _______ or as a Schedule _______ bank. In the former case, it will be a Canadian subsidiary of a foreign bank, whereas in the latter case, it is allowed to branch directly into Canada.
   a. I, II b. I, III c. II, III d. III, II

29. The near-banks in Canada are
   a. trust and mortgage loan companies.
   b. Ontario saving office and credit unions.
   c. credit unions and *caisses populaires*.
   d. both (a) and (c).

30. According to the three-tiered ownership regime, small, medium-size, and large banks have __________, __________, and __________ billion dollars of equity capital, respectively.
   a. under 5, between 5 and 20, more than 20
   b. under 5, between 5 and 10, more than 10
   c. under 1, between 1 and 5, more than 5
   d. under 1, between 1 and 10, more than 10

31. Debt-equity swaps are a form of
   a. futures contracts.
   b. financial derivatives.
   c. financial engineering.
   d. debt conversion.

32. Which members of the Big Six have the largest percent of international assets in total assets?
   a. Bank of Montreal, Bank of Nova Scotia
   b. Toronto Dominion, National Bank
   c. CIBC, Royal Bank
   d. Toronto Dominion, Royal Bank

33. Venezuela borrowed $500 million from Canadian financial institutions. Unable to repay the loans, Venezuela became indebted to Canada. To alleviate the debt, the debt denominated in Venezuelan currency was converted into Canadian currency. This form of debt conversion is called
   a. debt-debt swaps.
   b. debt-currency swaps.
   c. debt-equality swaps.
   d. none of the above.

CHAPTER 11

Economic Analysis of Banking Regulation

CHAPTER SYNOPSIS/COMPLETIONS

This chapter develops an economic analysis of how banking regulation affects the behaviour of banking institutions. This analysis explains why banking is among the most heavily regulated sectors of the economy, why the banking crisis occurred in the 1980s, and whether recent banking legislation or other proposed reforms are likely to ensure that future financial crises can be avoided.

In Canada, most depositors hold their funds in accounts insured by the CDIC. Deposit insurance has been a politically popular program since its introduction in 1967. Unfortunately, deposit insurance makes it necessary that bank and near bank regulators be particularly diligent. Because deposits up to $100,000 are completely insured, depositors lose their incentives to (1)________________ their funds when they suspect that the bank is taking on too much risk. The attenuation of depositors' incentives exacerbates adverse selection and (2)________________ ________________ problems, encouraging bank and near bank managers to take on excessive risk.

Because deposit insurance gives financial institutions greater incentives to take on additional risk, regulators must devise methods to discipline managers of banks and near banks to reduce excessive risk taking. For example, chartering regulations reduce (3)________________ ________________ problems by preventing undesirable people (e.g., crooks) from gaining control of financial institutions. Restrictions that prevent banks from holding risky assets such as common stocks and junk bonds, and requirements that banks hold minimum levels of capital reduce (4)________________ ________________ by increasing the cost to owners of bank failures. Regular bank (5)________________ help to ensure that banks and thrifts comply with these requirements.

In the early-1990s, the CDIC came under increasing criticism for its "too-big-to-fail" policy. Under this policy, the CDIC uses the purchase and assumption method to resolve the failure of a big bank, in effect guaranteeing all deposits. The rationale for this policy is that the failure of a large bank increases the likelihood that a major (6)________________ disruption will occur. This policy, however, reduces the incentives of depositors at big banks to monitor the riskiness of bank assets, thereby encouraging moral hazard. Moreover, critics complain that the CDIC's policy discriminates against small banks as they find it more difficult to attract large depositors.

In today's world, financial innovation has made it easier for banks and their employees to make huge bets easily and quickly (as demonstrated by the failure of Barrings in 1995). This change in the financial environment has fostered new approaches to bank supervision. Bank examiners now place greater emphasis on evaluating risk management systems. Indeed, bank examiners now give a separate risk management rating as part of the CAMELS system.

Other requirements that regulators impose on banks include: adherence to standard accounting principles, mandates to protect consumer borrowers through "truth in lending," restrictions on asset holdings, and limits on off-balance-sheet activities.

Canadian banks have been experiencing increasing competition for funds from money market mutual funds, and a loss of lending business to the commercial paper market and securitization. As earnings from these traditional activities declined, banks and near banks sought other, but riskier, business to raise profits. Innovation produced new financial instruments that widened the scope for risk taking. Moreover, legislation that deregulated banks and near banks expanded their ability to engage in risky activities, further increasing moral hazard.

Regulatory reforms that may make banking more sound include: limiting the too-big-to-fail doctrine, prompt corrective action, and risk-based insurance premiums. Until recently, CDIC premium revenue was not tied to the risk profile of the financial institutions. On March 31, 1999, however, the CDIC developed the (7)__________ __________ __________ that requires the CDIC to intervene early when a deposit-based financial institution gets into trouble. Member deposit-taking institutions are now classified into (8)__________ groups based on their risk profile. Another interesting CDIC development that came into effect on October 15, 1999 is the (9)__________ __________ that allows Schedule III banks to opt out of CDIC. These recent CDIC provisions are designed to reduce the (10)__________ __________ option for regulators and reduce (11)__________ __________.

An examination of recent banking crises in other countries indicates that the economic and political forces are strikingly similar to those we experienced in the 1980s.

EXERCISES

EXERCISE 1: Problems of Deposit Insurance

Ironically, the existence of deposit insurance increases the likelihood that depositors will require deposit protection, because the threat of withdrawals no longer constrains the managers of banks and thrifts from taking on too much risk. List some of the problems that deposit insurance creates or makes worse.

1. ______________________________
2. ______________________________
3. ______________________________

EXERCISE 2: Bank Regulation—Reducing Adverse Selection and Moral Hazard

A. List the several ways that bank regulations reduce the adverse selection and moral hazard problems in banking.

1. ______________________________
____
2. ______________________________
____
3. ______________________________
____
4. ______________________________
____

B. Explain how regulations specifically designed to reduce moral hazard produce the additional benefit of reducing adverse selection.

____
____
____

EXERCISE 3: The "Too-Big-To-Fail" Policy

Describe the intended purpose of the "too-big-to-fail" policy.

EXERCISE 4: The 1980s: A Rocky Decade for Bank Regulators

A. In the banking industry, moral hazard and adverse selection problems increased in prominence in the 1980s. List the factors that contributed to worsening conditions in the banking industry in the early 1980s.

1. __________
2. __________
3. __________

B. How did regulators respond to worsening bank performance in the 1980s?

C. Explain why regulators pursued this course of action.

1. __________
2. __________

EXERCISE 5: Bank Act Reform of 2001

List the major provisions of the 2001 Bank Act Reform.

1. __________
2. __________
3. __________
4. __________
5. __________

EXERCISE 6: The Political Economy of the 1980s Canadian Banking Crisis

That taxpayers were poorly served by bank regulators in the 1980s is now quite clear. An analysis of the political economy of the banking crisis helps one to understand this poor performance, and explains why elected agents of the taxpayers failed to faithfully serve their constituents by directing regulators to do their job. Explain why both politicians and bank regulators shirked their responsibilities to the taxpayers in the 1980s.

EXERCISE 7: Recent CDIC Legislation

Recent CDIC legislation includes reforms for the deposit insurance system to protect depositors from bank insolvency, thereby ensuring financial stability. List three major changes in the deposit insurance system in the last 5 years.

1. ______________________________
2. ______________________________
3. ______________________________

EXERCISE 8: Bank Failure

John Smith has the following deposits with XYZ Bank, a CDIC member bank (all funds CAD except where noted):

Chequing Account:	$5,000
Savings Account:	$25,000
USD Term Deposit:	$15,000
3-Year GIC:	$50,000
7-Year GIC:	$20,000

A. In the event of a bank failure, how much of John Smith's deposits is insured by the CDIC?

____

____

B. If the CDIC decides XYZ Bank is too big to fail, what will happen? What method will they use to handle the bank?

____

____

C. Why might the CDIC declare XYZ Bank too big to fail?

____

____

SELF-TEST

PART A: True-False Questions

Circle whether the following statements are true (T) or false (F).

T F 1. Actions taken by regulators to reduce moral hazard by preventing banks from taking on too much risk (such as regular bank examinations) also help to reduce adverse selection problems by discouraging risk-prone entrepreneurs from entering the banking industry.

T F 2. The CDIC argues that the too-big-to-fail policy protects the soundness of the banking system, since the failure of a very large bank makes it more likely that a major financial disruption will occur.

T F 3. Large banks are actually put at a competitive disadvantage relative to small banks as a result of the CDIC's too-big-to-fail policy.

T F 4. A financial innovation that widened the scope for risk taking was junk bonds.

T F 5. Part of the policy of regulatory forbearance pursued by thrift regulators in the United States in the 1980s included allowing S&Ls to include in their capital calculations a high value for tangible capital called "goodwill."

T F 6. In the 1980s, regulators pursued a policy of regulatory forbearance in hopes that the problems of banks and near banks would go away.

T F 7. The policy of regulatory forbearance was effective in reducing the risks that banking institutions took on in the 1980s.

T F 8. The moral hazard associated with a government safety net discourages too much risk taking on the part of banks.

T F 9. The leverage ratio is defined as the amount of equity capital divided by the bank's liabilities.

T F 10. Term deposits with an initial maturity date of more than five years, treasury bills, and bonds issued by governments are insured by CDIC.

T F 11. The collapse of real estate prices in the late 1980s was the main cause of the banking crises in Scandinavian countries.

T F 12. Banks with a government safety net have less incentive to take on greater risks than they would otherwise.

T F 13. One problem with the too-big-to-fail policy is that it increases the moral hazard incentive for large banks.

T F 14. Schedule II and Schedule III banks are permitted to opt out of CDIC membership.

PART B: Multiple-Choice Questions

Circle the appropriate answer.

1. Moral hazard is an important feature of insurance arrangements because the existence of insurance
   a. reduces the incentives for risk taking.
   b. is a hinderance to efficient risk taking.
   c. causes the private cost of the insured activity to increase.
   d. does all of the above.
   e. does none of the above.

2. Deposit insurance
   a. attracts risk-prone entrepreneurs to the banking industry.
   b. encourages bank managers to take on greater risks than they otherwise would.
   c. increases the incentives of depositors to monitor the riskiness of their banks' asset portfolios.
   d. does all of the above.
   e. does only (a) and (b) of the above.

3. Regular bank examinations help to reduce the ______________ problem, but also help to indirectly reduce the ______________ problem because, given fewer opportunities to take on risk, risk-prone entrepreneurs will be discouraged from entering the banking industry.
   a. adverse selection; adverse selection
   b. adverse selection; moral hazard

c. moral hazard; adverse selection

d. moral hazard; moral hazard

4. If the CDIC decides that a bank is too big to fail, it will use the

a. payoff method, effectively covering all deposits—even those that exceed the $100,000 ceiling.

b. payoff method, covering only those deposits that do not exceed the $100,000 ceiling.

c. purchase and assumption method, effectively covering all deposits—even those that exceed the $100,000 ceiling.

d. purchase and assumption method, covering only those deposits that do not exceed the $100,000 ceiling.

5. The too-big-to-fail policy

a. puts small banks at a competitive disadvantage relative to large banks in attracting large depositors.

b. treats large depositors of small banks inequitably when compared to depositors of large banks.

c. ameliorates moral hazard problems.

d. does all of the above.

e. does only (a) and (b) of the above.

6. The Bank Act of 1992

a. allowed chartered banks to own trust companies.

b. allowed trust companies to make commercial loans.

c. made provisions for increases in reserve requirements.

d. only (a) and (b) of the above.

7. The Differential Premiums By-law that came into effect on March 31, 1999

a. reduces the moral hazard incentives of banks to take on higher risk.

b. encourages banks to hold more capital.

c. increases the incentives of uninsured depositors to monitor the risk-taking activities of banks.

d. permits chartered banks to opt out of CDIC membership and therefore to operate without deposit insurance.

e. only (a) and (b) of the above.

8. The CDIC insures

a. only deposits in Canadian currency and payable in Canada.

b. term deposits with an initial maturity date of more than five years.

c. government of Canada t-bills and bonds.

d. debentures issued by governments and corporations, investments in stocks, mutual funds, and mortgages.

e. all of the above.

9. Which of the following statements are true?

a. the primary rationale for deposit insurance is protecting depositors from bank insolvency and thus ensuring financial stability.

b. by insuring deposits at deposit-taking financial institutions, the CDIC effectively removes barriers to entry for new deposit takers.

c. in the absence of deposit insurance, it is difficult for new banks to attract deposits.

d. all of the above are true.

10. Eliminating deposit insurance has the disadvantage of

a. reducing the stability of the banking system due to an increase in the likelihood of bank runs.

b. not being a politically feasible strategy.

c. encouraging banks to engage in excessive risk taking.

d. all of the above.

e. only (a) and (b) of the above.

11. When a bank is well-capitalized, the bank has ______________ to lose if it fails and is thus ______________ likely to pursue risky activities.
    a. more; more
    b. more; less
    c. less; more
    d. less; less
12. One problem with the too-big-to-fail policy is that it ______________ the incentives for ______________ by big banks.
    a. increases; moral hazard
    b. decreases; moral hazard
    c. increases; adverse selection
    d. decreases; adverse selection
13. The premium rates for CDIC member institutions in Canada depend on which of the following criteria?
    a. Capital adequacy.
    b. Profitability.
    c. Asset concentration.
    d. All of the above.
14. Banking crises in other countries indicate that
    a. deposit insurance is to blame in each country.
    b. a government safety net for depositors need not increase moral hazard.
    c. expertise in screening borrowers cannot prevent loan losses.
    d. deregulation combined with poor regulatory supervision raises moral hazard incentives.
15. Which of the following contributed to the savings and loan crisis in the United States?
    a. Interest rates fell in the late 1970s and early 1980s.
    b. Savings and loans held predominately long-term assets such as mortgages.
    c. Federal deposit insurance levels were lowered.
    d. Regulators began to restrict the activities of savings and loans.
16. The ______________ effect states that with uncertainty about the health of the banking system, the failure of one bank can lead to a failure of many banks.
    a. failure
    b. contagion
    c. adverse
    d. reciprocating
    e. stampede
17. The central bank is often referred to as the "lender of last resort" because it
    a. offers the lowest interest rates on loans.
    b. will lend to customers even if banks will not.
    c. will lend to financially troubled banks.
    d. regulates lending by banks.
    e. none of the above.
18. The Basel Accord, which was originally agreed upon in 1988,
    a. has been adopted by only a handful of countries.
    b. requires banks to hold at least half of their assets in the form of loans.

c. regulates only foreign banks in a country.
d. implements a system of risk-based capital requirements.

19. Governments in many countries, including Canada, have protected banks from competition through legislation because
    a. banks will respond by lowering charges to consumers.
    b. competition may decrease the efficiency of banking institutions.
    c. competition may increase the moral hazard incentives for banks to take on risk.
    d. all of the above.
    e. none of the above.
20. The Opting-Out By-law that came into effect on October 15, 1999 permits
    a. chartered banks to opt out of CDIC membership and therefore to operate without deposit insurance.
    b. Schedule II banks to opt out of CDIC membership and therefore to operate without deposit insurance.
    c. Schedule III banks to opt out of CDIC membership and therefore to operate without deposit insurance.
    d. all of the above.
21. The Differential Premiums By-law that came into effect on March 31, 1999
    a. reduces the moral hazard incentives of banks to take on higher risk.
    b. encourages banks to hold more capital.
    c. increases the incentives of uninsured depositors to monitor the risk-taking activities of banks.
    d. only (a) and (b) of the above.
22. The Insurance Companies Act of 1992
    a. replaced the Canadian and British Insurance Companies Act and the Foreign Insurance Companies Act.
    b. set rules for life insurers and P&C insurers.
    c. allowed insurance companies to own Schedule II chartered banks.
    d. followed the same format as the Bank Act.
    e. all of the above.
23. The Trust and Loan Companies Act of 1992
    a. replaced the Trust Companies Act and the Loan Companies Act, both passed in 1914.
    b. set rules for TMLs reporting to the OSFI.
    c. required large, formerly closely held TMLs to become 35% widely held.
    d. all of the above.
24. The Argentine banking crisis of 2001
    a. included a banking panic in which customers rushed to withdraw their deposits.
    b. was fueled by the rise in the value of the Argentine peso.
    c. will not cost much relative to GDP.
    d. began despite low levels of Argentine government debt.
25. A large amount of bank capital helps to prevent bank failures because it
    a. is useful in absorbing deposit outflow losses.
    b. means that the bank has a higher income.
    c. allows loans to be more easily sold.
    d. makes it easier to call in loans.

26. Financial consolidation poses two challenges to banking regulation. First, it increases the _______ problem and second, it __________.
    a. moral hazard, creates adverse selection
    b. too-big-to-fail, increases the government's safety net
    c. moral hazard, increases the possibility of bank panics
    d. adverse selection, increases the government's safety net
27. Which of the following can be used by regulators to make banks avoid too much risk?
    a. Restricting banks from holding common stocks.
    b. Promoting diversification in assets and loans.
    c. Forcing the banks to hold large amounts of equity capital.
    d. All of the above.
28. ________ and ________ of the banking system have triggered banking crises in most countries.
    a. Adverse selection, privatization
    b. Real estate boom, privatization
    c. Adverse selection, deregulation
    d. Collapse of real estate, deregulation
29. The 1980s' Canadian banking crisis was the result of
    a. the sharp increases in interest rates from 1979 to 1981.
    b. the severe recession in 1981-1982.
    c. the collapse in the price of energy and agriculture products.
    d. all of the above.
30. In Canada, a chartered bank obtains a charter through either an Act of Parliament or through
    a. an application to the Governor of the Bank of Canada.
    b. an application to the Minister of Finance.
    c. an application to the President of the Treasury Board.
    d. all of the above.

CHAPTER **12**

Risk Management in Financial Institutions

CHAPTER SYNOPSIS/COMPLETIONS

This chapter introduces the student to risk management tools. There are several methods to measure and reduce the risks in financial institutions. Credit risk and interest-rate risk are two types of risks that students learn to measure.

Banks attempt to reduce their exposure to credit risk by (a) screening good from bad credit risks; (b) specializing in lending to particular firms; (c) monitoring and enforcing restrictive covenants; (d) fostering long-term relationships with loan customers; (e) requiring collateral and compensating balances; and (f) rationing credit.

With the increased volatility of interest rates that occurred in the 1980s, banks have become more concerned about their exposure to interest-rate risk—the riskiness of earnings and returns that is associated with changes in interest rates. Interest rate fluctuations can have a significant impact on bank profits. For example, if a bank has (1)_______________ rate-sensitive liabilities than assets, a rise in interest rates will reduce bank profits, while a decline in interest rates will raise bank profits.

Bank managers can measure the sensitivity of bank profits to changes in interest rates using two techniques. Under (2)_______________ analysis, the difference of rate-sensitive assets and rate-sensitive liabilities (that is, the gap) is multiplied by the change in the interest rate to obtain the effect on bank profits. Alternatively, (3)_______________ analysis is based on Macaulay's concept of duration, which measures the average lifetime of a security's stream of payments. If the average duration of a bank's assets exceeds the average duration of its liabilities, then rising interest rates will reduce the bank's net worth.

EXERCISES

EXERCISE 1: Risk Management

List six management methods that banks use to reduce their exposure to credit risk.

1. ______________________________
2. ______________________________
3. ______________________________
4. ______________________________

5. ______________________________

6. ______________________________

EXERCISE 2: Gap Analysis

Suppose that the First Bank has the following balance sheet (in millions of dollars):

Assets		Liabilities	
Variable-Rate Loans	20	Variable-Rate CDs	30
Short-Term Securities	10	Money Market Deposits	15
Reserves	10	Overnight Funds	5
Long-Term Loans	40	Chequable and Savings Deposits	30
Long-Term Securities	10	Long-Term CDs	20

A. Calculate the gap by subtracting the amount of rate-sensitive liabilities from rate-sensitive assets.
Gap = ______________________________

B. If interest rates suddenly increase by two percentage points, will First Bank's profits increase or decrease?
____

C. By how much do profits change? ______________________________

D. If, instead, interest rates were to drop by three percentage points, what will be the change in First Bank's profits?
____

EXERCISE 3: Duration Gap

XYZ Bank has total asset value of $200 million, and total liability value of $180 million. The average duration of assets is 2.50, and the average duration of liabilities is 1.10.

A. What is the duration gap for XYZ Bank?

____

____

B. What is the change in the market value of net worth as a percentage of assets if interest rates fall from 6% to 5%?

____

____

C. What is the change in the market value of net worth?

____

____

SELF-TEST

PART A: True-False Questions

Circle whether the following statements are true (T) or false (F).

T F 1. If a bank has more rate-sensitive assets than liabilities, a rise in interest rates will reduce bank profits.

T F 2. Money loans are a major part of the business of financial institutions.

T F 3. Financial institutions can reduce asymmetric information by establishing long-term customer relationships.

T F 4. Establishing a long-term customer relationship reduces the cost of screening and monitoring.

T F 5. Collateral and credit rationing can be used to manage the interest-rate risk.

T F 6. Chequable accounts are not rate-sensitive.

T F 7. Income gap can be calculated by subtracting rate-sensitive assets from rate-sensitive liabilities.

T F 8. Basic gap analysis allows managers to figure out the changes in income over several years due to changes in interest rates.

T F 9. The duration of a securities portfolio is the simple average of the durations of the individual securities.

T F 10. Compensating balances are a form of collateral that is required when a bank makes commercial loans.

Part B: Multiple-Choice Questions

Circle the appropriate answer.

1. Managing financial institutions is a difficult task because of __________.
   a. changes in interest rates
   b. uncertainty in the economic environment
   c. credit risks
   d. both (a) and (c) of the above

2. ______________ states that borrowers may have incentives to engage in activities that are undesirable from the lender's point of view, and ____________ indicates that individuals with higher risk are the ones who have a higher probability of getting loans.
   a. Moral hazard, default
   b. Adverse selection, risk
   c. Adverse selection, moral hazard
   d. Moral hazard, adverse selection

3. __________ can be used to control adverse selection, and __________ can be used to control moral hazard.
   a. Monitoring, collateral
   b. Monitoring, loan commitments
   c. Monitoring, screening
   d. Screening, monitoring

4. __________ and __________ reduce the bank's costs for screening and information collecting.
   a. Long-term customer relationship, collateral
   b. Long-term customer relationship, loan commitment
   c. Loan commitment, compensating balances
   d. both (a) and (b) of the above

5. Which of the following is rate-sensitive?
   a. Securities with maturity of less than one year.
   b. Commercial loans with maturity of two years.
   c. Money market deposit accounts.
   d. both (a) and (c) of the above.

6. When a financial institution has __________ rate-sensitive liabilities than assets, a __________ in interest rates will __________ the net interest margin and income.

   a. more, fall, raise
   b. more, rise, raise
   c. fewer, rise, reduce
   d. fewer, fall, raise

7. If Bruce the Bank Manager determines that his bank's gap is a positive \$20 million, then a five percentage point increase in interest rates will cause bank profits to

   a. increase by \$1 million.
   b. decrease by \$1 million.
   c. increase by \$10 million.
   d. decrease by \$10 million.

8. Credit risk management tools include:

   a. credit rationing.
   b. collateral.
   c. compensating balances.
   d. all of the above.

9. Assume that the rate-sensitive assets and liabilities of First Bank are 40 million and 25 million dollars, respectively. What is the change in income if the interest rate falls by 2%?

   a. \$-300 000
   b. \$300 000
   c. \$800 000
   d. \$500 000

10. __________ examines the sensitivity of the market value of the financial institution's net worth to changes in interest rates.

    a. Basic gap analysis
    b. Maturity bucket approach
    c. Duration gap analysis
    d. both (b) and (c) of the above

11. Assume that the assets and liabilities of Bank XYZ are \$150 and \$120, respectively, and their durations are 3 and 4. What will be the effect of a fall in interest rate from 15% to 10% on the net worth of the bank?

    a. -\$10.4
    b. -\$1.3
    c. \$10.4
    d. \$1.3

12. A __________ income gap shows that the bank has __________ rate-sensitive assets than liabilities, and it will suffer from an increase in the interest rate.

    a. negative, more
    b. negative, less
    c. positive, more
    d. positive, less

13. When Bank XYZ has a negative income gap, it will benefit from interest rate ___________, and the bank can increase its rate-sensitivity by purchasing assets of ___________ maturity.
    a. declines, shorter
    b. declines, longer
    c. rises, shorter
    d. rises, longer

14. Assume that the market value of liabilities and assets of First Bank are 200 and 350, and average duration of assets is 4. Find the average duration of liabilities that eliminates the interest-rate risk for this bank.
    a. 6
    b. 3
    c. 7
    d. 4

15. Assume that the market value of liabilities and assets of First Bank are 400 and 310, and their average durations are 2 and 1.8. Find the new market value of assets that eliminates the interest-rate risk for this bank.
    a. 444.44
    b. 400
    c. 180
    d. 200

CHAPTER 13

Hedging With Financial Derivatives

CHAPTER SYNOPSIS/COMPLETIONS

Beginning in the 1970s and continuing into the 1980s and 1990s, interest rates and foreign exchange rates became more volatile, increasing the risk to financial institutions. To combat this, managers of financial institutions have demanded financial instruments to better manage risk. These instruments called *financial derivatives* have become an important source of profits for financial institutions, particularly larger banks. In this chapter, we investigate the use of forward contracts, financial futures, options, and swaps to reduce risk.

When financial institutions (1)_____, they write a financial contract that reduces or eliminates risk. A long contract means that the holder agrees to buy the asset in the future while the (2)________________ contract holder agrees to sell the asset. The principle of hedging risk involves offsetting a long position by taking an additional short position, or offsetting a short position by taking an additional long position.

A forward contract is an agreement for the exchange of assets in the future. An *interest-rate forward contract* exchanges debt instruments such as bonds. The price and date of the exchange are agreed upon up front. Forward contracts have the advantage of being as flexible as the parties want them to be, but they have the disadvantages of lacking liquidity (finding a counterparty may be difficult) and being subject to default (3)_____________, if one or the other party chooses not to complete their end of the bargain.

An *interest-rate futures contract* reduces risk because when the price of the underlying asset moves one way, the price of the futures contract will move by the same amount in the (4)________________ direction, effectively cancelling any gains or losses due to unanticipated movements in interest rates. An interest-rate futures contract is similar to an interest-rate forward contract, but differs in ways that overcome liquidity and default problems of forward contracts. For example, the quantities delivered and the delivery dates of interest-rate futures are (5)_____________________ so that it is easier to find a counterparty. Moreover, interest-rate futures contracts can be traded again at any time until the delivery date, and, in the case of a Canada bond futures contract, any Canada bond that neither matures nor is callable for 15 years can be deliverable on the delivery date. These three features increase the liquidity of interest-rate futures.

A micro hedge occurs when a futures contract is purchased or sold to hedge one particular security. Macro hedges occur when futures contracts are purchased or sold to offset an entire portfolio. A clearinghouse for the exchange requires that both buyers and sellers must make a *margin requirement* into a margin account at their brokerage firm. This feature of financial futures contracts (6)________________ the risk of default. Additionally, to protect the exchange from loss, they are *marked to market* every day. This means that at the end of every trading day, the change in the value of the futures contract is added or subtracted from a margin account. If the margin account falls too low, the investor must replenish it.

A final advantage that futures have over forward contracts is that most futures contracts do not result in delivery of the underlying asset on the expiration date, (7)_______________ transaction costs compared to forward contracts that do require delivery. A trader who sells short a futures contract can avoid making delivery on the expiration date by making an offsetting purchase of a long futures contract.

Alternatives to using forward and futures contracts to hedge risk are options and swaps. Options are contracts that give the purchaser the option, or (8)_____________, to buy or sell the underlying financial instrument at the (9)_____________ (exercise) price. Although the seller of an option is obligated to buy or sell, the owner (buyer) need not exercise the option. Because the right to buy a financial instrument at a specified price has value, one must pay a *premium* to buy an option. American options can be exercised at any time up to the expiration date; (10)_______________ options can be exercised only on the expiration date.

Options on individual stocks are called stock options. Options on financial futures, commonly called futures options, were developed in 1982 and have become the most widely traded option contracts. A call option is a contract that gives the owner the right to buy a financial instrument at the exercise price. A put option gives the owner the right to (11)___________ a financial instrument at the strike price.

Interest-rate swaps are an important tool for controlling interest-rate risk. In a simple swap, called the *plain vanilla swap*, one firm agrees to pay a fixed rate of interest on a stated sum and another firm agrees to pay a floating interest rate on the same sum. The advantage of this arrangement is that it effectively converts fixed-rate assets into floating rate assets and vice versa. A bank that finds that it has more interest rate-sensitive liabilities than assets can protect itself (hedge) from an increase in interest rates by agreeing to pay a fixed rate on a swap in exchange for receiving floating rate payments. What this does is convert fixed rate assets into floating-rate assets.

The use of swaps to eliminate interest-rate risk can be cheaper than rearranging a bank's balance sheet. Swaps have an advantage over futures because swaps can be written for (12)____________ periods of time. The disadvantage of swaps is that they suffer from the liquidity and default risk that plague the forward market. Intermediaries have set up markets in swaps that help alleviate these problems. For example, Citicorp will match firms together and each firm will deal exclusively with the bank.

EXERCISES

EXERCISE 1: Forward Contracts and Financial Futures Contracts

List four features that distinguish futures contracts from forward contracts.

1. ____
2. ____
3. ____
4. ____

EXERCISE 2: Definitions and Terminology

Match the following terms in the column on the right with the definition or description in the column on the left. Place the letter of the term in the blank provided next to the appropriate definition. Terms may be used once, more than once, or not at all.

_____	1. A security that is derived from another security.	a. Micro hedge
_____	2. A non-standardized agreement where one party agrees to sell an asset and another party agrees to buy the asset in the future.	b. Lack of liquidity
_____	3. A standardized agreement where one party agrees to sell an asset and another party agrees to buy the asset in the future.	c. Hedge

_____	4. A method of reducing risk where the change in contract value just offsets the change in asset value.	d. Derivative
_____	5. The contract holder agrees to buy the asset in the future.	e. Macro hedge
_____	6. The contract holder agrees to sell the asset in the future.	f. Futures contract
_____	7. The change in the value of the futures contract is added or subtracted from a margin account.	g. Long contract
_____	8. A futures contract designed to hedge one particular asset.	h. Forward contract
_____	9. A futures contract designed to hedge an entire portfolio.	i. Short contract
_____	10. A disadvantage of interest-rate forward contract is that it may be difficult to make or that it will have to be made at a disadvantageous price.	j. Marked to market

EXERCISE 3: More Definitions and Terminology

Match the following terms in the column on the right with the definition or description in the column on the left. Place the letter of the term in the blank provided next to the appropriate definition. Terms may be used once, more than once, or not at all.

_____	1. An option that gives the holder the right to sell an asset in the future.	a. Option
_____	2. An option that gives the holder the right to buy an asset in the future.	b. Premium
_____	3. The price an option permits the holder to buy or sell an asset.	c. European option
_____	4. The price of an option.	d. Call option
_____	5. An arrangement where one party pays a fixed interest rate and another pays a floating interest rate.	e. Notional principal
_____	6. An option that can be exercised any time up to maturity.	f. Strike price
_____	7. An option that can be exercised only at maturity.	g. Arbitrage
_____	8. The amount of funds on which the interest is being paid.	h. Swap
_____	9. A contract that gives the purchaser the right to buy or sell an underlying security.	i. American option
_____	10. The elimination of riskless profit opportunities in the futures market.	j. Put option

EXERCISE 4: Forwards and Futures

Fill in the Blank

1. A firm with a portfolio of Canada bonds may hedge by ____________ futures contracts.
2. A ___________ contract is where the investor agrees to sell an asset at some time in the future at an agreed upon price.
3. Forward contracts are subject to ____________ risk since the counterparty could go bankrupt.
4. The elimination of riskless profit opportunities in the futures markets is referred to as ____________, and it guarantees that the price of the futures contract at expiration equals the price of the underlying asset to be delivered.
5. Because futures contracts are ___________________ it is easier for an investor to find a counterparty.
6. Each day futures contracts are marked to market, helping to ___________ the chance of losses to the exchange.

EXERCISE 5: Options and Swaps

Fill in the Blank

1. A contract that gives the purchaser the right to buy or sell an asset is a(n) ____________.
2. A __________ option gives the holder the right to buy an underlying asset.
3. A __________ option gives the holder the right to sell an underlying asset.
4. The price that the holder of a call option can demand from exercising the option is the ____________ price.
5. An option that cannot be exercised until maturity is called an ____________ option.
6. An option that can be exercised any time up until maturity is called an ____________ option.
7. A ___________ can be used to reduce interest-rate risk without requiring the firm to restructure its balance sheet.

EXERCISE 6: Hedging with Futures and Options

Suppose that in January you purchase $100,000 face value Canada bonds for a price of $95,000. Assume that the bonds mature in fifteen years and that you plan to sell the bonds at the end of March.

A. In Table 13.A, calculate the gain or loss (indicate loss with a negative) of the March sale that you incur for each potential bond selling price.

Table 13.A Gain or Loss

			Price of Asset		
	$85,000	**$90,000**	**$95,000**	**$100,000**	**$105,000**
.Selling Canada bonds					
Selling Futures contract					
Purchasing Put option					

B. Suppose that you want to hedge your long position by selling a futures contract for Canada bonds for $95,000 (95 points). Thus, at the end of March, the buyer of the futures contract agrees to buy from you Canada bonds for $95,000. In Table 13.A, calculate the gain or loss (indicate loss with a negative) that you incur from selling the futures contract for each potential bond selling price.

C. Suppose instead that you want to hedge your long position by purchasing a put option on a Canada bond futures contract with a strike price of $95,000 (95 points) and a premium of $2,000. Thus, at the end of March, you have the option of selling a futures contract for $95,000. In Table 13.A, calculate the gain or loss (indicate loss with a negative) that you incur from exercising (if profitable to do so) the put option for each potential futures contract price. Be sure to include the option premium in your gain or loss. If it is not profitable to exercise the put option, show the loss incurred from the premium.

EXERCISE 7: Interest-Rate Swap

A. The most common type of interest-rate swap is called the __________ __________, which specifies:

1. ______________________________
2. ______________________________
3. ______________________________
4. ______________________________

B. List two advantages of interest-rate swaps:

1. ______________________________
2. ______________________________

C. List three disadvantages of interest-rate swaps:

1. ______________________________
2. ______________________________
3. ______________________________

SELF-TEST

PART A: True-False Questions

Circle whether the following statements are true (T) or false (F).

T F 1. Interest-rate futures can be used to reduce the risk of selling goods overseas.

T F 2. Forward contracts are more flexible than futures contracts because they are not standardized.

T F 3. To hedge against interest rate increases, a bank with a portfolio of Canada securities could sell futures contracts.

T F 4. A serious problem for the market in financial futures contracts is that it may be difficult to make the financial transaction or that it will have to be made at a disadvantageous price; in the parlance of financial economists, this market suffers from a lack of liquidity.

T F 5. To corner a market means that someone has purchased the bulk of a particular asset so that high prices can be charged when contracts are settled.

T F 6. Open interest refers to the number of futures contracts that have not been settled.

T F 7. Option premiums are generally higher the greater the exercise price.

T F 8. Option premiums are higher the greater the volatility of the underlying asset.

T F 9. A call option gives the holder the right to buy the underlying asset.

T F 10. A swap is a financial contract that obligates one party to exchange a set of payments it owns for another set of payments owned by another party.

T F 11. An interest-rate future contract and an interest-rate forward contract have the same meaning.

T F 12. A call with asset price equal to the exercise price is said to be in the money.

T F 13. At the expiration date of a futures contract, the price of the contract is higher than the price of the underlying asset to be delivered.

T F 14. A put option is a contract that gives the owner the right to buy a stock at the exercise price within a specific period of time.

T F 15. The greater the term to expiration, everything else being equal, the higher the premiums for both call and put options.

T F 16. The greater the volatility of the price of underlying assets, the higher the premiums for both call and put option.

PART B: Multiple-Choice Questions

Circle the appropriate answer.

1. An investor who chooses to hedge in the futures market
   a. gives up the opportunity for gains.
   b. reduces the opportunity for losses.
   c. increases her earnings potential.
   d. does both (a) and (b) of the above.
2. A portfolio manager with $100 million in Canada securities could reduce interest-rate risk by
   a. selling financial futures.
   b. going long on financial futures.
   c. buying financial futures.
   d. both (b) and (c) are true.
3. A bank sold a futures contract that perfectly hedges its portfolio of Canada securities; if interest rates fall,
   a. the bank suffers a loss.
   b. the bank has a gain.
   c. the bank income is unchanged.
   d. none of the above.
4. When an investor agrees to buy an asset at some time in the future he is said to have gone
   a. long.
   b. short.
   c. ahead.
   d. back.
5. The main advantage of a forward contract is that it
   a. is standardized, thereby reducing the cost of finding a counterparty.
   b. is default risk free since the contract is between the exchange and the investor.
   c. is flexible because it can be written any way the parties desire.
   d. both (a) and (b) are true.
6. At the expiration date of a futures contract, the price of the contract is
   a. equal to the price of the underlying asset to be delivered.
   b. equal to the price of the counterparty.
   c. equal to the hedge position.
   d. equal to the value of the hedged asset.
7. Futures markets have been successful and have grown rapidly because
   a. of standardization of the futures contract.
   b. of the ability to buy or sell the contract up to the maturity.
   c. of the reduced risk of default in the futures market.
   d. all of the above.
8. When compared to forward contracts, financial futures have the advantage that
   a. they are standardized, making it more likely that different parties can be matched, thereby increasing liquidity in the market.

b. they specify that more than one bond is eligible for delivery, to reduce the possibility that someone might corner the market and "squeeze" traders who have sold contracts.
c. they cannot be traded at any time before the delivery date, thereby increasing liquidity in the market.
d. all of the above are true.
e. only (a) and (b) of the above are true.

9. Option premiums are increased when
   a. time to maturity increases.
   b. volatility is lower on the underlying asset.
   c. strike price is lower.
   d. both (b) and (c) are true.
10. An option that lets the holder buy an asset in the future is a
    a. put option.
    b. call option.
    c. swap.
    d. premium.
11. An option that lets the holder sell an asset in the future is a
    a. put option.
    b. call option.
    c. swap.
    d. premium.
12. The holder of an option
    a. limits his gains.
    b. limits his losses.
    c. limits both his gains and his losses.
    d. has no limits on his gains and losses.
13. An important tool for managing interest-rate risk that requires the exchange of payment streams on assets is a
    a. futures contract.
    b. forward contract.
    c. swap.
    d. micro hedge.
14. Which of the following is a disadvantage of the swap as a method for controlling interest-rate risk?
    a. Swaps, unlike forward contracts, are not subject to default risk.
    b. Swaps are more expensive than simply restructuring the balance sheet.
    c. Swaps, like forward contracts, lack liquidity.
    d. All of the above are disadvantages of swaps.
    e. Only (a) and (b) of the above are disadvantages of swaps.
15. Which of the following is an advantage of interest-rate swaps?
    a. Swaps lower interest-rate risk more cheaply than simply restructuring the balance sheet.
    b. Swaps, unlike forward contracts, are quite liquid.
    c. Swaps, unlike forward contracts, are not subject to default risk.
    d. All of the above are advantages of swaps.
    e. Only (a) and (b) of the above are advantages of swaps.
16. The principle of hedging risk involves offsetting a _____ position by taking an additional _____ position.
    a. risky; risk-free

b. long; future
c. short; long
d. put; call
e. risky; short

17. Arbitrage is best defined as
a. the pricing of options.
b. the pricing of futures.
c. the elimination of riskless profit opportunities.
d. the right to buy or sell a security.
e. none of the above.

18. At the expiration date of a futures contract, the price of the contract is _____ the price of the underlying asset to be delivered.
a. the same as
b. less than
c. greater than
d. unrelated to

19. A _____ hedges the interest-rate risk for a specific asset that a financial institution is holding.
a. put
b. stock
c. micro hedge
d. none of the above

20. If you want to hedge $4 million worth of Canada bonds, and if the contract size is $50,000, then how many bond futures contracts must you sell?
a. 4000.
b. 540.
c. 400.
d. 100.
e. 80.

21. The likelihood that someone will corner a bond market, and therefore discourage futures contract trading, is reduced because
a. the size of futures contracts is standardized.
b. more than one bond is eligible for delivery in a futures contract.
c. futures contracts can be traded before the delivery date.
d. clearinghouses usually have margin requirements.

22. Financial futures options
a. are more common than options on bonds.
b. are not very common.
c. are the same as stock options.
d. only (a) and (c) of the above.
e. none of the above.

23. A call option on a futures contract will be exercised if
a. the strike price is below the premium.
b. the option is "out of the money."
c. the current futures contract price is below the strike price.

d. it is profitable to exercise a put option on the same futures contract.

e. none of the above.

24. Which of the following is an example of a long position?

a. A bank purchases $10 million in mortgage-backed securities.

b. A financial institution purchases financial futures put options.

c. An investment bank sells $10 euro in the forward currency market.

d. only (a) and (b) of the above.

e. only (b) and (c) of the above.

25. As compared to financial futures contracts, options on financial futures contracts

a. usually require delivery of the underlying financial asset.

b. are usually subject to greater potential loss.

c. can provide greater potential gains.

d. only (a) and (c) of the above.

e. none of the above.

26. If interest rates ______ in the future then you will profit if you sold a short futures contract.

a. rise

b. fall

c. remain the same

d. fluctuate

27. Which type of option gives the owner the right to sell a financial instrument at the exercise price within a specified period of time?

a. A call option

b. A put option

c. A specified option

d. A European option

e. A class option

28. At the expiration date of a futures contract, the price of the contract is ________ the price of the underlying assets to be delivered.

a. the same as

b. lower than

c. higher than

d. larger than or equal to

29. A call is said to be in the money when _______, and the net profit of exercising this call is _______.

a. $C<X$, $C-\alpha$

b. $C<X$, C

c. $C>X$, $C-\alpha$

d. $C>X$, C

30. Which of the following financial instruments is not considered a derivative financial instrument?

a. Bonds

b. Interest-rate future contracts

c. Stock index options

d. Swaps

31. Options are contracts that give the purchaser the option to
    a. buy the underlying asset at a specified price.
    b. sell the underlying asset at a specified price.
    c. buy or sell the underlying asset at a specified price.
    d. buy or sell the underlying asset at an unspecified price.

32. A call option is a contract that gives
    a. the owner the right to sell a stock at the exercise price.
    b. the owner the right to buy a stock at the exercise price.
    c. the owner the right to buy and sell a stock at the exercise price.
    d. none of the above.

CHAPTER 14

Structure of Central Banks and the Bank of Canada

CHAPTER SYNOPSIS/COMPLETIONS

Chapter 14 describes the unique structure of the Bank of Canada and its evolution since 1934. Although the Bank of Canada has been granted a high degree of independence, a clearer understanding of its decisions requires that one acknowledge the political and bureaucratic forces influencing its behaviour.

The overall responsibility for the operation of the Bank of Canada rests with a (1)_______________ _______________. The Board consists of fifteen members: the governor, the senior deputy governor, the deputy minister of finance, and twelve outside directors. The Board appoints the governor and senior deputy governor with the government's approval, for a renewable term of seven years. The outside directors are appointed by the minister of finance, with cabinet approval, for a three-year term and they are required to come from all regions of Canada representing a variety of occupations with the exception of banking.

The governor of the Bank (currently David Dodge) is the chief executive officer and chairman of the Board of Directors. In 1994 the Board of Directors made some changes in the internal organization of the Bank. It established a new senior decision-making authority within the Bank, called the (2)_______________ _______________. The Council is chaired by the governor and is composed of the senior deputy governor and the four deputy governors. Since this change, the Governing Council assumes responsibility for the Bank's policy. This system of 'collective responsibility' ensures that the governor of the Bank of Canada is not personally identified with the Bank's policy.

The European Central Bank (ECB) was created on January 1, 1999 and is based in Frankfurt, Germany. It is the central bank of the euro area, currently consisting of 12 countries. The Eurosystem is the term used to refer to the ECB and the 12 national banks of the countries that have adopted the euro. The European System of Central Banks is the term used to refer to the ECB, the 12 national banks of the countries that have adopted the euro, and the national central banks of the 3 European Union countries (Denmark, Sweden, and the United Kingdom) that have not yet adopted the euro.

Of all the central banks in the world, the Federal Reserve System in the United States has the most unusual structure, reflecting Americans' distrust of the concentration of power in banking. Although responsibility is formally shared across separate, cooperating entities, the Federal Reserve is fundamentally a hierarchical organization. At the top is the (3)______________________________—a group of seven members appointed to lengthy terms by the president of the United States and confirmed by the Senate. One member is chosen as chairman (currently, Ben Bernanke) who serves a four-year term and may be reappointed. The chairman of the Board of Governors wields great power in Washington, D.C.

In the United States, monetary policy decisions are determined by a majority vote of the twelve-member Federal Open Market Committee or FOMC. The voting members of the committee consist of the seven members of the Board of Governors, the president of the Federal Reserve Bank of (4)____________________, and four presidents from other Federal Reserve banks.

While the Bank of Canada retains a relatively high degree of independence, it is not free from political pressure. Politicians need favourable economic conditions to help them win reelection, while lenders and the housing industry want low (5)________________ rates, and still other groups (such as those who have retired on fixed incomes) want low inflation. Given these pressures, the theory of (6)________________ behaviour suggests that the Bank of Canada will do best for itself by avoiding conflict with these groups.

A short survey of the structure and independence of the central banks in Canada, the United States, England, Japan, and the new European Central Bank indicates that we have been seeing a remarkable trend toward greater (7)____________________. Both theory and evidence suggest that more independent central banks produce better monetary policy, thus providing an impetus for this trend.

Good arguments have been made both for retaining the Bank of Canada's independence and for restricting it. The strongest argument to be made for an independent Bank of Canada rests on the belief that subjecting the Bank to more political pressure would impart an (8)________________ bias to monetary policy. However, critics of an independent central bank contend that it is (9)____________________ to have monetary policy controlled by a group that is not directly responsive to the electorate. The jury is still out on how best to improve monetary policy (see Chapter 21 on recent research), but recognition that the Bank of Canada is subject to political and bureaucratic forces helps one to better understand current and past monetary policy and helps one to predict how the Bank of Canada will respond to future events.

EXERCISES

EXERCISE 1: Structure of the Bank of Canada

The Bank of Canada (founded in 1934) is the federal government's fiscal agent and is responsible for monetary policy in the country. Match the Bank of Canada entity to its responsibilities and duties given on the left by placing the appropriate letter in the space provided.

	Responsibilities and Duties	Bank of Canada Entity
_____	1. *Monetary Policy Report*	a. Board of Directors
_____	2. Overall operation of the Bank of Canada	
_____	3. *Monetary Policy Report Update*	
_____	4. Appointed by the Board of Directors of the Bank of Canada	
_____	5. Serves a renewable 7-year term	b. Governor of the Bank of Canada
_____	6. Chairman of the Board of Directors	

_____ 7. Appoints the Senior Deputy Governor

_____ 8. Monetary policy

_____ 9. Sets the operating band of the overnight rate c. Governing Council

EXERCISE 2: Should the Bank of Canada be Independent?

A. List three arguments made by those who support a Bank of Canada that is independent of direct control from either the executive or legislative branches of government.

1. ______________________________
2. ______________________________
3. ______________________________

B. List three arguments that favour a Bank of Canada that is brought under the control of the government.

1. ______________________________
2. ______________________________
3. ______________________________

EXERCISE 3: The Functions of the Bank of Canada

A. List four functions of the Bank of Canada that are mentioned in the Bank's web page.

1. ______________________________
2. ______________________________
3. ______________________________
4. ______________________________

B. List the entities of the Federal Reserve System of the United States.

1. ______________________________
2. ______________________________
3. ______________________________
4. ______________________________
5. ______________________________

EXERCISE 4: Role of the Bank of Canada

Fill in the blanks.

A. Systematic and permanent differences in macroeconomic outcomes that differ by political party are known as ______________________.

B. Over the past decade, the Bank of Canada has rejected multiple policy instruments by adopting the ______________________ as the centerpiece of its monetary policy implementation and by focusing on ______________________.

C. The Bank of Canada employs such tools as open market operations defined as ____ ____.

D. The Bank of Canada also plays a central role in Canada's national payments system which is an electronic system that ____, currently handling ______________________.

E. In its role as provider of paper money, the Bank's overall objective is to ____.

F. In its role as the federal government's fiscal agent, the Bank of Canada provides ______________________ such as ______________________, ______________________, and ______________________.

G. Unlike the US Federal Reserve and the European Central Banks that have both instrument independence and goal independence, and are remarkably free of political pressures that influence other government agencies, the Bank of Canada has ______________________, but not ______________________.

H. The most important task of the Bank of Canada's economists is to ____ and ____.

I. The legislation governing the Bank of Canada's responsibility for monetary policy has ______________________ since the Bank Act of 1967.

J. The argument supporting Bank of Canada independence is that the ______________ problem is worse for ______________ than for ______________ because ______________ incentives to act in the public interest.

SELF-TEST

PART A: True-False Questions

Circle whether the following statements are true (T) or false (F).

T F 1. The Bank of Canada was created by the Bank of Canada Act in 1934.

T F 2. The Bank of Canada is not responsible for monetary policy.

T F 3. Base money consists of currency in circulation and bank deposits.

T F 4. It would be accurate to say that the European Central Bank was modeled after the U.S. Federal Reserve System.

T F 5. In the United States, district Federal Reserve Banks essentially have no input regarding monetary policy decisions, since the Board of Governors has sole responsibility for monetary policy.

T F 6. Open-market operations, believe it or not, were not envisioned as a monetary policy tool when the Bank of Canada was created.

T F 7. The theory of bureaucratic behaviour may help explain why the Bank of Canada seems to be so preoccupied with the level of short-term interest rates.

T F 8. Although all 12 Federal Reserve Bank presidents attend the FOMC meetings, only those five presidents who have a vote actively participate in the deliberations.

T F 9. Placing the Bank of Canada under the control of the government may lead to a monetary policy that is more responsive to political pressures.

T F 10. Supporters of placing the Bank of Canada under control of the government believe that the electorate should have more control over monetary policy.

T F 11. A change in the monetary base has no impact on the money supply.

T F 12. Central Banks' actions affect interest rates and the money supply, but have no effect on the aggregate output and inflation.

T F 13. The Central Bank goal of low inflation is directly linked to the objective of stable economic growth.

PART B: Multiple-Choice Questions

Circle the appropriate answer.

1. The main motivation for the formation of the Bank of Canada in 1934 was
   a. political.
   b. the need for Canada to reflect its growing political independence from Britain.
   c. the need for Canada to coordinate its international economic policy.
   d. all of the above.

2. The theory of bureaucratic behaviour indicates that
   a. government agencies attempt to increase their power and prestige.
   b. government agencies attempt to avoid conflicts with the legislative and executive branches of government.
   c. both (a) and (b) of the above are true.
   d. neither (a) nor (b) of the above are true.

3. Which of the following are entities of the Bank of Canada?
   a. The Board of Directors
   b. The Governing Council
   c. The Canada Deposit Insurance Corporation (CDIC)
   d. Both (a) and (b) of the above

4. While the regional Federal Reserve banks in the United States "establish" the discount rate, in truth, the discount rate is determined by
   a. Congress.
   b. the President of the United States.
   c. the Board of Governors.
   d. the Federal Reserve Advisory Council.

5. A majority of the Federal Open Market Committee is comprised of
   a. the 12 Federal Reserve bank presidents.
   b. the five voting Federal Reserve bank presidents.
   c. the seven members of the Board of Governors.
   d. none of the above.

6. Which of the following is an element of the Bank of Canada?
   a. The Office of the Superintendent of Financial Institutions Canada (OSFI)
   b. The Governing Council
   c. The Federal Open Market Committee
   d. The Federal Reserve Advisory Council
7. Power within the U.S. Federal Reserve is essentially located in
   a. New York.
   b. Washington, D.C.
   c. Boston.
   d. San Francisco.
8. While the Fed enjoys a relatively high degree of independence for a government agency, it feels political pressure from the President and Congress because
   a. Fed members desire reappointment every 3 years.
   b. the Fed must go to Congress each year for operating revenues.
   c. Congress could limit Fed power through legislation.
   d. of all of the above.
   e. of only (b) and (c) of the above.
9. Which of the following functions are not performed by the Bank of Canada?
   a. Cheque clearing
   b. Conducting economic research
   c. Setting interest rates payable on time deposits.
   d. Issuing new currency
10. Supporters of keeping the Bank of Canada independent from both the executive and legislative branches of government believe that a less independent Bank of Canada would
    a. pursue overly expansionary monetary policies.
    b. be more likely to pursue policies consistent with the political business cycle.
    c. ignore short-run problems in favour of longer-run concerns.
    d. do only (a) and (b) of the above.
11. In its role as the federal government's fiscal agent, the Bank of Canada provides debt management services for the federal government such as
    a. advising on federal government borrowings.
    b. managing new debt offerings by the federal government.
    c. servicing the federal government's outstanding debt.
    d. all of the above.

12. Although the Bank of Japan has new powers and greater autonomy under 1998 legislation, critics
   a. contend that the central bank's independence is limited because the Ministry of Finance has veto power over a portion of the bank's budget.
   b. contend that the central bank's independence is too great because the central bank need not pursue a policy of price stability even if that is the popular will of the people.
   c. contend that the central bank's independence is too great because the central bank can now ignore concerns of the Ministry of Finance since it no longer has veto power over the bank's budget.
   d. contend that the central bank's independence is limited because the Ministry of Finance retained the power to dismiss senior bank officials.
13. In its role as provider of banking services, the Bank of Canada
   a. serves as a lender of last resort if a deposit-taking institution faces a liquidity crisis.
   b. plays a central role in Canada's national payments system.
   c. is responsible for the government's operating accounts and for managing the government's foreign exchange reserves.
   d. all of the above.
14. Under the current "joint responsibility system,"
   a. the Bank of Canada and the minister of finance consult regularly.
   b. in the event of a serious policy conflict the minister of finance can issue a directive that the Bank of Canada must follow.
   c. the government accepts full responsibility for monetary policy.
   d. the Bank of Canada has considerable autonomy in the conduct of day-to-day monetary policy.
   e. all of the above.
15. The ability of a central bank to set reserve requirements is an example of
   a. goal independence.
   b. the theory of bureaucratic behaviour.
   c. independent review.
   d. instrument independence.
   e. the public interest view.
16. Which of the following statements concerning the 14-year term for members of the Board of Governors is *false*?
   a. The 14-year term is nonrenewable.
   b. The 14-year term allows great independence from political considerations.
   c. Most governors serve out the entire 14-year term.
   d. The President of the United States appoints governors to a 14-year term.
17. Which of the following are entities of the Eurosystem?
   a. The European Central Bank
   b. The Executive Board of the European Central Bank
   c. The Governing Council of the European Central Bank
   d. all of the above

18. Which of the following is an example of the U.S. Fed becoming more transparent?
   a. Since 1994, the results of the FOMC meetings are immediately released.
   b. The Board of Governors does not release its "blue" and "green" books.
   c. The Chairman of the Board of Governors is appointed to a 4-year term.
   d. all of the above.
   e. none of the above.
19. A political business cycle is ________ likely to be caused by a more independent central bank as compared to a less independent central bank.
   a. less
   b. more
   c. just as
   d. none of the above
20. The principal-agent problem is ________ for an independent Bank of Canada than for politicians, because it has ________ incentives to act against the interests of the public.
   a. greater; more
   b. less; more
   c. greater; fewer
   d. less; fewer
21. Worldwide data show that a more independent central bank leads to
   a. a higher inflation rate.
   b. a higher unemployment rate.
   c. greater output fluctuations.
   d. none of the above.
22. Central banks' actions are capable of affecting __________.
   a. money supply
   b. interest rates
   c. the amount of credit
   d. all of the above
23. During the Great Depression, from 1929 to 1933, Canadian real GDP fell by almost ______ and the unemployment rate increased _______.
   a. 5%, twofold
   b. 30%, twofold
   c. 5%, sevenfold
   d. 30%, sevenfold
24. The president of the Federal Reserve Bank of ________ is the only permanent member of the FOMC among the Federal Reserve bank presidents.
   a. Chicago
   b. San Francisco
   c. New York
   d. Atlanta

25. The Bank of England has ________ goal independence as the Bank of Canada, but ________ goal independence than the Fed.
    a. the same, less
    b. the same, more
    c. less, less
    d. more, more
26. Political business cycle means that just before an election, ________ policies are pursued to ________ the unemployment rate and interest rates.
    a. expansionary, raise
    b. contractionary, lower
    c. expansionary, lower
    d. monetary, control
27. ________ determines monetary policy, and the responsibility for policy rests with ________.
    a. The Bank of Canada, the government
    b. The Bank of Canada, the Bank of Canada
    c. The government, the Bank of Canada
    d. The government, the government
28. The ultimate goal of the Bank of Canada is to
    a. keep the unemployment rate low
    b. control the money supply
    c. keep inflation low
    d. both (a) and (c) of the above
29. Recent research shows that inflation performance is the best for countries with the ________ independent central banks, and these countries are ________ likely to have high unemployment.
    a. least, less
    b. least, no more
    c. most, less
    d. most, no more
30. The overall responsibility for the operation of the Bank of Canada rests with the________, which consists of ________ members.
    a. Board of Directors, 15
    b. Board of Directors, 17
    c. Governing Council, 15
    d. Governing Council, 17
31. ________ consists of the monetary liabilities of the central bank; it is ________ the money supply.
    a. Base money, larger than
    b. Monetary base, larger than
    c. Monetary base, equal to
    d. Base money, less than

32. Instrument independence of the central bank is defined as
    a. the ability of the central bank to choose the instrument to use to achieve the goals of monetary policy
    b. the ability of the central bank to set the goals of monetary policy
    c. the ability of the central bank to determine government spending
    d. the ability of the central bank to change the tax structure

33. Central banks' actions affect all but one of the following:
    a. interest rates
    b. government spending
    c. money supply
    d. amount of credit

34. A cohesive program that will promote economic stability can be achieved by:
    a. monetary policy.
    b. fiscal policy.
    c. a substantial tax cut.
    d. a mixed monetary–fiscal policy.

CHAPTER 15

Multiple Deposit Creation and the Money Supply Process

CHAPTER SYNOPSIS/COMPLETIONS

Movements in the money supply influence us all by affecting the health of the economy; thus it is important to understand how the money supply is determined. Since deposits at banks (and other depository institutions) comprise the largest component of the money supply, understanding how these deposits are created is the first step in understanding the money supply process. In this and the next chapter we discover how the actions of the four players in the money supply process (the (1)_______________ bank, (2)_______________, depositors, and borrowers from banks) cause changes in the money supply. Of the four players, the (3)_______________ _______________, the central bank of Canada, is the most important and therefore receives the most attention.

Examination of the Bank of Canada's balance sheet provides us with a framework for understanding the money supply process. An increase in the Bank's monetary liabilities (currency in circulation and (4)_______________) leads to an increase in the money supply. The sum of currency in circulation (coins and Bank of Canada notes) and Bank of Canada liabilities is called the (5)_______________ _______________, or high-powered money.

The primary method used by the Bank of Canada for changing the monetary base is through an (6)_______________ _______________ operation, the purchase or sale of a government bond. Open market purchases or sales may involve banks or the nonbank public. Open-market purchases from banks increase reserves and the monetary base by the amount of the purchase. If the open market purchase is from a member of the nonbank public who deposits the cheque, the purchase has an effect on reserves and the monetary base that is (7)_______________ to the open market purchase from a bank. Thus the distinction between reserves and the monetary base is not important for these two transactions.

It is when a member of the nonbank public cashes the Bank of Canada's cheque (causing currency in circulation to increase) that a distinction between the effect on the monetary base and reserves needs to be made. The effect of an open market purchase on the monetary base, however, is always the same, whether the proceeds are held as deposits or as (8)_______________.

An open market sale will have a predictable impact on the monetary base. The decline in reserves will equal the decline in the monetary base if the sale is to the bank or if a cheque is drawn to pay for the security. If the security is purchased with currency, reserves remain unchanged, but the monetary base (9)_______________. Thus the Bank of Canada is more certain about the effect of open market operations on the monetary base than on reserves.

There is an additional reason why the Bank of Canada has greater control over the monetary base than over reserves. Shifts from (10)_______________ to currency affect the volume of reserves in the banking system, but such shifts have no impact on the level of the monetary base, making it a more stable variable.

Although the preceding discussion indicates that the Bank of Canada has far better control over the monetary base than it does over reserves, factors other than Bank of Canada actions seemingly could thwart the Bank's ability to control the monetary base. As the Bank's balance sheet indicates, factors other than Bank actions (for example, float and government of Canada deposits) can and do affect the monetary base. Nevertheless, even these substantial *short-run* fluctuations do not prevent the Bank from accurately controlling the monetary base, as changes in government deposits and float are often predictable and easily offset.

While an individual bank can lend and create deposits of an amount equal to its excess reserves, the banking system can generate a (11)________________ expansion of deposits when reserves in the system increase. When the Bank of Canada provides additional reserves to the banking system, chequable deposits and, therefore, the money supply increase by an amount that exceeds the initial change in reserves. This expansion occurs whether a bank chooses to use its excess reserves to purchase securities or make loans. The expression describing the multiple increase in deposits generated from an increase in reserves is called the (12)________________ ________________ ________________ and is equal to the reciprocal of the desired reserve ratio. A decline in reserves will cause a multiple contraction of deposits.

The simple deposit expansion model indicates that the Bank of Canada is able to exercise complete control over the level of deposits by setting the level of reserves, but a realistic approach recognizes that the behaviour of banks and depositors influences the level of deposits and hence the money supply. If depositors choose to hold more currency as deposits increase, or if banks choose to hold (13)________________ reserves, then the actual deposit expansion multiplier will be (14)________________ than the simple deposit expansion multiplier.

The next chapter presents a more accurate picture of the deposit-expansion process; still, the main findings of this chapter are retained: The Bank of Canada changes the money supply through its influence on the level of reserves, and a change in reserves leads to either a multiple expansion or contraction in deposits.

EXERCISES

EXERCISE 1: Open Market Operations, Reserves, and the Monetary Base

A. How will a Bank of Canada sale of $100 of government bonds to banks affect the monetary base and reserves? Fill in the following T-accounts in arriving at your answers:

Banking System

Assets	Liabilities

The Bank of Canada

Assets	Liabilities

Change in the monetary base = ________

Change in reserves = ________

B. How will a Bank of Canada sale of $100 of government bonds to the nonbank public affect the monetary base and reserves if the nonbank public pays for the bonds with cheques? Fill in the following T-accounts in arriving at your answers:

Nonbank Public

Assets	Liabilities

Banking System

Assets	Liabilities

The Bank of Canada

Assets	Liabilities

Change in the monetary base = ___________

Change in reserves = ___________

C. How will a Bank of Canada sale of $100 of government bonds to the nonbank public affect the monetary base and reserves if the nonbank public pay for the bonds with currency? Fill in the following T-accounts in arriving at your answer:

Nonbank Public

Assets	Liabilities

The Bank of Canada

Assets	Liabilities

Change in the monetary base = ___________

Change in reserves = ___________

How do these answers differ from those in parts A and B? ____________________

____

EXERCISE 2: How the Bank of Canada Provides Reserves to the Banking System

A. Fill in the entries in the following T-accounts when the Bank of Canada sells $100,000 of T-bills to the First Bank.

First Bank

Assets	Liabilities

The Bank of Canada

Assets	Liabilities

What has happened to reserves in the banking system? ____________________

B. If, instead, the First Bank pays off a $100,000 Bank of Canada advance what will be the entries in the T-accounts below?

First Bank

Assets	Liabilities

The Bank of Canada

Assets	Liabilities

What has happened to reserves in the banking system? ____________________

EXERCISE 3: Deposit Creation—The Single Bank

Suppose that the balance sheet of Panther Bank is currently as follows:

Panther Bank

Assets		Liabilities	
Vault cash	$ 100		
On deposit with Bank of Canada	900	Chequable Deposits	$9,000
Loans	8,000		

A. Calculate the level of excess reserves held by Panther Bank if the desired reserve ratio is 10%.

____

B. How much can Panther Bank lend? ____________________

C. Complete the following T-account showing the changes in assets resulting when Panther Bank lends the amount you answered to Part B, assuming the deposits created by the bank are deposited with another bank.

Panther Bank

Assets	Liabilities

EXERCISE 4: Deposit Creation: The Banking System

A. Assume that the desired reserve ratio is 0.20 and that the Bank of Canada purchases $1000 in government bonds from the First Bank of Toronto, which, in turn, lends the $1000 of reserves it has just acquired to a customer for the purchase of a used car. If the used car dealer deposits the proceeds from the sale in Bank A, how much in additional loans can Bank A make?

B. Suppose that this loan is used to purchase a computer, and that the computer store deposits the proceeds into Bank B. What has been the total change in chequable deposits at Bank A?

C. Assume a similar process occurs for Bank B, Bank C, and Bank D. Complete the following table for these banks (see Table 15-1 in the text for an example) and the totals for all banks.

Bank	Change in Deposits	Change in Loans	Change in Reserves
First Bank of Toronto	+$0.00	+$1000.00	+$0.00
A	+1000.00	+800.00	+200.00
B	+800.00	+640.00	+160.00
C	______	______	______
D	______	______	______
•	•	•	•
•	•	•	•
•	•	•	•
Total All Banks	______	______	______

EXERCISE 5: The Simple Deposit Multiplier

A. Write down the formula for the simple deposit multiplier.

B. Assuming that the desired reserve ratio is 0.20, what is the change in reserves when the Bank of Canada sells $10 billion of government bonds and extends advances of $5 billion to commercial banks?

C. Using the simple deposit multiplier formula, calculate the resulting change in chequable deposits.

EXERCISE 6: Cheque Writing and Multiple Deposit Creation

A. Suppose that Mark writes a cheque to Lisa for $50 and it is deposited in Lisa's bank. Show the effect of this transaction on the T-account of each bank.

Mark's Bank

Assets	Liabilities

Lisa's Bank

Assets	Liabilities

B. Assume that the desired reserve ratio is 10% and that before the cheque was deposited neither bank held excess reserves. After the deposit, by how much is Mark's bank below its desired reserve amount? By how much is Lisa's bank above its desired reserve amount?

C. Explain why chequable deposits in the banking system will not increase when Mark writes Lisa a cheque.

Exercise 7: Control of the Monetary Base

The Bank of Canada can cause changes in the monetary base through open market operations. Suppose the Bank of Canada purchases $5000 of bonds from a bank and there is no change in currency circulation.

A. What happens to the T-account for the banking system?

B. What happens to the T-account for the Bank of Canada?

C. What is the net result of the open market purchase?

SELF-TEST

PART A: True-False Questions

Circle whether the following statements are true (T) or false (F).

T F 1. The government of Canada functions as the country's central bank.

T F 2. Currency held by depository institutions (banks) is added to currency circulating in the hands of the public to get total currency in circulation.

T F 3. The Bank of Canada's buying and selling of bonds in the open market is referred to as widening the market.

T F 4. If the First Security Bank of Calgary has $50 in excess reserves, it will be able to lend more than an additional $50 as long as the desired reserve ratio is below 100%.

T F 5. Assuming that the desired reserve ratio is 20%, an open market sale of $100 in government bonds by the Bank of Canada will cause chequable deposits to fall by $500 in the simple deposit expansion model.

T F 6. When a bank chooses to purchase securities instead of making loans, deposit expansion is diminished.

T F 7. In the simple model, deposits in the banking system contract by a multiple of the loss in reserves caused by a Bank of Canada sale of government bonds.

T F 8. A rise in government deposits at the Bank of Canada increases the monetary base.

T F 9. Government securities and reserves are two assets of the Bank of Canada.

T F 10. Because many factors beyond the direct control of the Bank of Canada affect the monetary base, it is unreasonable to expect the Bank to have any meaningful control over the monetary base.

T F 11. Overnight interest rates are determined by the Bank of Canada.

T F 12. The Bank of Canada has more control over reserves than over the monetary base.

T F 13. High-powered money equals currency in circulation plus the total reserves in the banking system.

T F 14. The banking system will be in equilibrium when the total amount of desired reserves equals the total amount of reserves.

T F 15. Whether a bank chooses to use its excess reserves to make loans or to purchase securities, the effect on deposit expansion is the same.

T F 16. A bank can make loans for an amount greater than the excess reserves it has before it makes the loan.

T F 17. The effect of open market operations on the monetary base is much more certain than its effect on reserves.

PART B: Multiple-Choice Questions

Circle the appropriate answer.

1. The monetary base is comprised of
   a. currency in circulation and Bank of Canada notes.
   b. currency in circulation and government securities.
   c. currency in circulation and reserves.
   d. reserves and government securities.
2. The sum of vault cash and bank deposits with the Bank of Canada minus desired reserves is called
   a. the monetary base.
   b. the money supply.
   c. excess reserves.
   d. total reserves.
3. When the Bank of Canada simultaneously purchases government bonds and extends advances to banks,
   a. chequable deposits unambiguously fall.
   b. chequable deposits unambiguously rise.
   c. the net effect on chequable deposits cannot be determined because the two Bank of Canada actions counteract each other.
   d. the Bank of Canada action has no effect on chequable deposits.
4. When the Bank of Canada simultaneously extends advances to banks and sells government bonds,
   a. chequable deposits unambiguously increase.
   b. chequable deposits unambiguously fall.
   c. the net effect on chequable deposits cannot be determined without further information because the two Bank of Canada actions counteract each other.
   d. the Bank of Canada action has no effect on chequable deposits.
5. When the Bank of Canada wants to reduce reserves in the banking system, it will
   a. purchase government bonds.
   b. extend advances to banks.
   c. print more currency.
   d. sell government bonds.
6. The simple deposit multiplier is equal to 4 when the desired reserve ratio is equal to
   a. 0.25.
   b. 0.40.
   c. 0.05.
   d. 0.15.
7. The First Bank of London has $150 in excess reserves. If the desired reserve ratio is 10%, how much extra can the First Bank lend?
   a. $1500
   b. $750
   c. $150
   d. $0

8. If excess reserves in the banking system amount to $75 and the desired reserve ratio is 0.20, chequable deposits could potentially expand by
   a. $75.
   b. $750.
   c. $37.50.
   d. $375.

9. A sale of government bonds by the Bank of Canada
   a. is called an open market sale.
   b. reduces the monetary base, all else the same.
   c. increases currency in circulation, all else the same.
   d. does all of the above.
   e. does only (a) and (b) of the above.

10. If a member of the nonbank public purchases a government bond from the Bank of Canada with currency, then
   a. both the monetary base and reserves will fall.
   b. both the monetary base and reserves will rise.
   c. the monetary base will fall, but reserves will remain unchanged.
   d. the monetary base will fall, but currency in circulation will remain unchanged.
   e. none of the above will occur.

11. Which of the following are found on the asset side of the Bank of Canada's balance sheet?
   a. Government securities
   b. Government deposits
   c. Advances to banks
   d. Only (a) and (b) of the above
   e. Only (a) and (c) of the above

12. Which of the following are found on the liability side of the Bank of Canada's balance sheet?
   a. Advances to banks
   b. Reserves
   c. Government securities
   d. All of the above
   e. Only (b) and (c) of the above

13. When float increases,
   a. currency in circulation falls.
   b. the monetary base falls.
   c. the monetary base rises.
   d. the monetary supply falls.
   e. none of the above occurs.

14. A reduction in which of the following leads to an increase in the monetary base?
   a. Government deposits
   b. Float
   c. Advances to banks
   d. All of the above

15. Commercial banks create money whenever they
    a. issue loans.
    b. buy government securities.
    c. create chequable deposits.
    d. only (a) and (b) of the above.
    e. only (a) and (c) of the above.
16. When the Bank of Canada purchases Canadian government securities, the amount of chequable deposits in the banking sector rises because
    a. the Bank of Canada typically purchases securities from many banks.
    b. banks gain excess reserves and increase loans.
    c. the government has deposits at the Bank of Canada.
    d. all of the above.
    e. none of the above.
17. If banks hold excess reserves, then the simple deposit multiplier _____ the impact of an increase in reserves on the increase in chequable deposits.
    a. overstates
    b. understates
    c. is unrelated to
    d. perfectly describes
18. If Victor withdraws $400 in cash from his chequing account, then
    a. vault cash rises by $400 at his bank.
    b. desired reserves fall by $400 at his bank.
    c. chequable deposits will rise at his bank.
    d. desired reserves rise by $400 at his bank.
    e. none of the above.
19. When the Bank of Canada issues advances to banks, Bank assets _____ and the monetary base _____.
    a. rise; rises
    b. fall; rises
    c. rise; falls
    d. fall; falls
20. If a bank robber steals $20,000 in cash from a bank, and if the desired reserve ratio is 20%, then
    a. desired reserves have fallen by $4,000.
    b. excess reserves have fallen by $16,000.
    c. reserves have fallen by $5,000.
    d. vault cash has fallen by $20,000.
    e. none of the above.
21. All else the same, the monetary base, also known as high-powered money, will fall when the Bank of Canada
    a. increases bank reserves.
    b. decreases currency in circulation.
    c. increases the amount of government securities that it holds.
    d. decreases the desired reserve ratio.
    e. only (b) and (d) of the above.

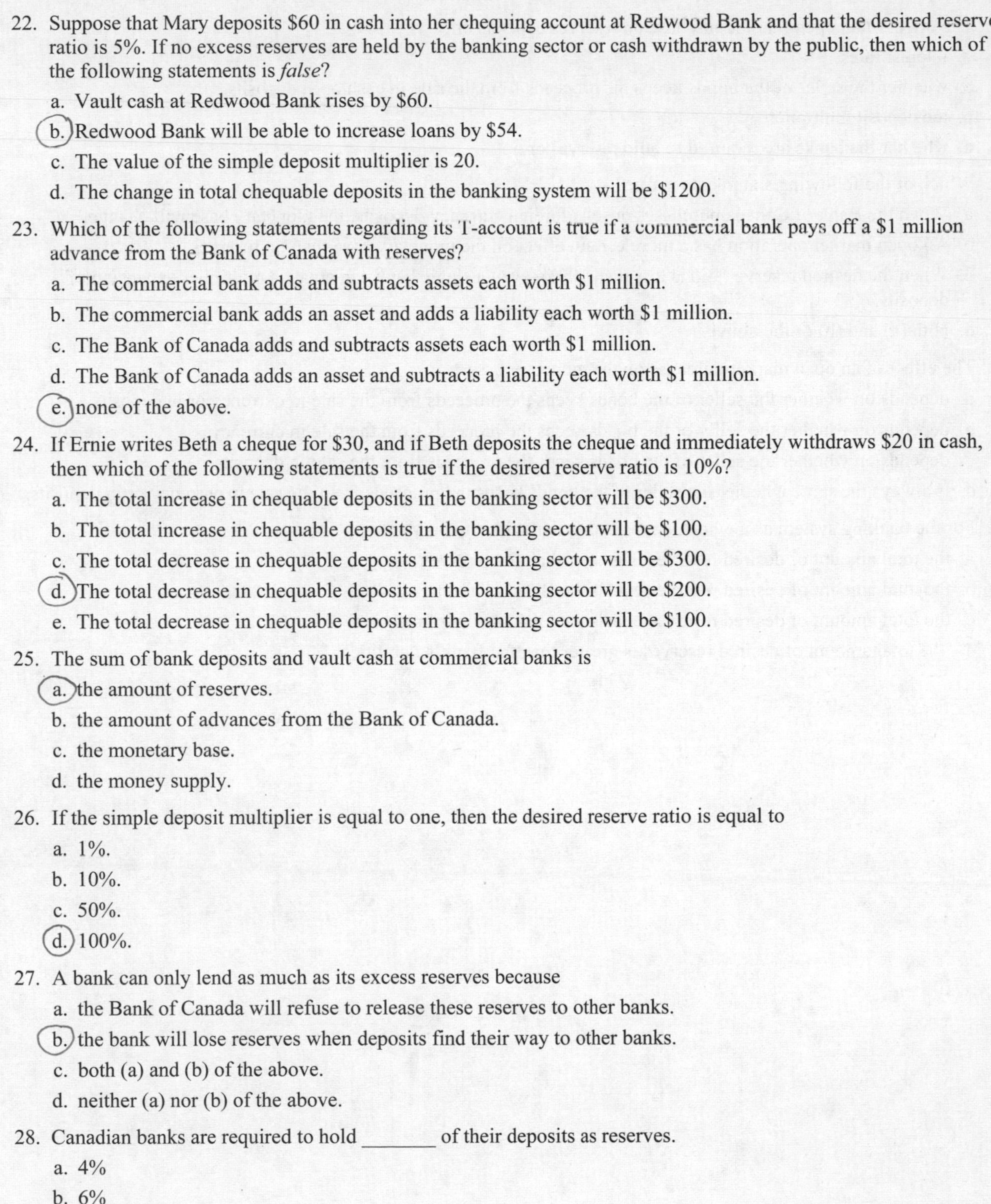

22. Suppose that Mary deposits $60 in cash into her chequing account at Redwood Bank and that the desired reserve ratio is 5%. If no excess reserves are held by the banking sector or cash withdrawn by the public, then which of the following statements is *false*?
    a. Vault cash at Redwood Bank rises by $60.
    b. Redwood Bank will be able to increase loans by $54.
    c. The value of the simple deposit multiplier is 20.
    d. The change in total chequable deposits in the banking system will be $1200.

23. Which of the following statements regarding its T-account is true if a commercial bank pays off a $1 million advance from the Bank of Canada with reserves?
    a. The commercial bank adds and subtracts assets each worth $1 million.
    b. The commercial bank adds an asset and adds a liability each worth $1 million.
    c. The Bank of Canada adds and subtracts assets each worth $1 million.
    d. The Bank of Canada adds an asset and subtracts a liability each worth $1 million.
    e. none of the above.

24. If Ernie writes Beth a cheque for $30, and if Beth deposits the cheque and immediately withdraws $20 in cash, then which of the following statements is true if the desired reserve ratio is 10%?
    a. The total increase in chequable deposits in the banking sector will be $300.
    b. The total increase in chequable deposits in the banking sector will be $100.
    c. The total decrease in chequable deposits in the banking sector will be $300.
    d. The total decrease in chequable deposits in the banking sector will be $200.
    e. The total decrease in chequable deposits in the banking sector will be $100.

25. The sum of bank deposits and vault cash at commercial banks is
    a. the amount of reserves.
    b. the amount of advances from the Bank of Canada.
    c. the monetary base.
    d. the money supply.

26. If the simple deposit multiplier is equal to one, then the desired reserve ratio is equal to
    a. 1%.
    b. 10%.
    c. 50%.
    d. 100%.

27. A bank can only lend as much as its excess reserves because
    a. the Bank of Canada will refuse to release these reserves to other banks.
    b. the bank will lose reserves when deposits find their way to other banks.
    c. both (a) and (b) of the above.
    d. neither (a) nor (b) of the above.

28. Canadian banks are required to hold _______ of their deposits as reserves.
    a. 4%
    b. 6%
    c. 10%
    d. none of the above.

29. The effect of an open market purchase on reserves depends on
   a. interest rates.
   b. whether the seller of the bonds keeps the proceeds from the sale in cash or in deposits.
   c. the deposit multiplier.
   d. whether the banks are required to hold reserves or not.

30. Which of the following statements is true?
   a. When the Bank of Canada purchases or sells foreign currency deposits, the monetary base will change.
   b. An open market operation has a more certain effect on the monetary base than on reserves.
   c. When the desired reserve ratio is less than 100%, even a single bank can create a multiplier expansion of deposits.
   d. both (a) and (b) of the above.

31. The effect of an open market purchase on the monetary base
   a. depends on whether the seller of the bonds keeps the proceeds from the sale in currency or in deposits.
   b. depends on whether the seller of the bonds keeps the proceeds from the sale in currency.
   c. depends on whether the seller of the bonds keeps the proceeds from the sale in deposits.
   d. is always the same whether the seller of the bonds keeps the proceeds from the sale in currency or in deposits.

32. For the banking system as a whole, deposits creation will stop only when
   a. the total amount of desired reserves is greater than the reserve ratio.
   b. the total amount of desired reserves equals the Bank's liabilities.
   c. the total amount of desired reserves equals the total amount of reserves.
   d. the total amount of desired reserves is greater than the Bank's liabilities.

CHAPTER 16

Determinants of the Money Supply

CHAPTER SYNOPSIS/COMPLETIONS

This chapter incorporates depositor and bank behaviour into the monetary process, presenting a more realistic model of the money supply process. The analysis is separated into three steps. First, because the Bank of Canada's control of the monetary base is more precise than its control over reserves, the model links changes in the money supply to changes in the monetary base. Next, the money multiplier, a ratio that relates the change in the money supply to a given change in the monetary base, is derived. Third, factors determining the money multiplier are examined.

The sum of currency in circulation and total reserves is called the monetary base or high-powered money. Because Bank of Canada actions have a more predictable effect on the monetary base than on (1)_______________, money supply models typically focus on the Bank of Canada's control over high-powered money.

In our model of multiple deposit creation in Chapter 15, we ignored the effects on deposit creation of changes in the public's holdings of (2)_________________ and banks' holdings of excess reserves. We incorporate these changes into the deposit expansion model by assuming that the desired levels of currency and reserves grow proportionally with (3)_______________ _______________. That is, the currency and desired reserves ratios are constants.

The money multiplier is the key factor separating the Bank of Canada's control of the money supply from its ability to affect the (4)_______________ _______________. An important characteristic of the money multiplier is that it is less than the simple deposit multiplier found in Chapter 15.

Inclusion of depositor behaviour into the money supply model reveals that the money multiplier depends on depositor preferences for currency relative to chequable deposits. A numerical example that accounts for currency withdrawals reveals that the simple deposit multiplier greatly (5)__________________ the expansion in deposits. The key to understanding this result is that although there is multiple expansion of deposits, there is no such expansion for currency. Since an (6)_________________ in the monetary base will mean an increase in currency in circulation, only part of any increase in the monetary base will be available for deposit expansion. Because reserves leave the bank as currency in circulation, the money supply will not increase as much for a given change in the monetary base, meaning a smaller money multiplier.

When banks increase their holdings of reserves, their volume of loans contracts for a given level of the monetary base, thereby causing a (7)_______________ in the money multiplier. The banking system's desired reserves ratio is negatively related to the market (8)_______________ __________, but (9)_______________ related to expected deposit outflows.

Changes in the desired reserve ratio and the currency ratio alter the value of the money (10)______________________. Increases in any of these ratios (because they reduce the reserves available for lending and deposit expansion) reduce the money multiplier.

Also, banks' decisions to borrow reserves from the Bank of Canada affect the money supply. If banks seek additional advances from the Bank of Canada, the money supply (11)______________________, if the Bank of Canada does not act to offset the increase in reserves. Alternatively, if banks choose to reduce their borrowing from the Bank of Canada, the money supply contracts.

EXERCISES

EXERCISE 1: The Money Multiplier

A. Write the formula for the money multiplier.

____

B. Calculate the currency ratio and the money multiplier for the following numbers:

r = 0.10 C = \$280 billion

D = \$800 billion ER = \$40 billion

c = ____________________________

m = ____________________________

C. Calculate desired reserves (DR), total reserves (R), and the monetary base (MB).

DR = \$____________________________

R = \$____________________________

MB = \$____________________________

D. Calculate the new money multiplier and money supply assuming that banks lower the desired required reserve ratio on chequable deposits to 0.08. Assume that *c* remains unchanged.

m = ____________________________

M = \$____________________________

E. Calculate the new level of deposits (D) and currency in circulation (C).

D = \$____________________________

C = \$____________________________

F. Calculate the new level of desired reserves (DR) and excess reserves (ER).

DR = \$____________________________

ER = \$____________________________

EXERCISE 2: Adding Bank Behaviour into the Money Supply Model

A. Given the following values, calculate the money multiplier and the money supply:

$r = 0.10$ $c = 0.40$

$ER = 0$ $MB_n = \$400$ billion

m = ______________________________

M = $______________________________

B. Calculate the level of currency (C), the level of deposits (D), the level of desired reserves (DR), and the level of total reserves (R) in the banking system.

C = $______________ DR = $______________

D = $______________ R = $______________

C. Suppose that bankers suddenly increase the desired reserve ratio to 0.16. Calculate the new money multiplier, the new money supply, the level of deposits, currency in circulation, and the amount of desired reserves that banks will now hold.

m = ______________________________

M = $______________________________

D = $______________________________

C = $______________________________

DR = $______________________________

EXERCISE 3: Factors that Affect the Money Supply

Indicate how the money supply responds to the following changes by filling in the third column of the table below with either a (↑) to indicate a rise in the money supply or a (↓) to indicate a fall in the money supply.

Player	**Change in Variable**	**Money Supply Response**
Bank of Canada	MB_n decreases	
Depositors	c decreases	
Depositors and banks	Expected deposit outflows decrease	
Borrowers and other players	i decreases	

EXERCISE 4: Depositor and Bank Behaviour and "Y2K"

The Bank of Canada and central banks around the world spent a considerable amount of resources in the late 1990s in anticipation of January 1, 2000. One concern was that banks' computers would fail to operate and thus financial transactions and record keeping would be disrupted.

A. Briefly explain how these concerns might affect depositor behaviour and the currency ratio. What is the effect on the money multiplier and the money supply?

____

____

B. Briefly explain how these concerns might affect bank behaviour and the desired reserve ratio. What is the effect on the money multiplier and the money supply?

____

____

C. How can a central bank reduce the impact of "Y2K" concerns on the money supply?

____

____

Exercise 5: Money Multiplier

The Bank of Canada has a desired reserve ratio of 0.07. The currency in circulation is $70 billion and chequable deposits are $180 billion.

A. Determine the money supply.

____

____

B. What is the value of the currency ratio?

____

____

C. What is the value of the money multiplier?

____

____

SELF-TEST

PART A: True-False Questions

Circle whether the following statements are true (T) or false (F).

T F 1. The ratio that relates the change in the money supply to a given change in the monetary base is called the money multiplier.

T F 2. Another name for the nonborrowed base is high-powered money.

T F 3. The banking system's desired reserve ratio is negatively related to the market interest rate.

T F 4. The desired reserve ratio is negatively related to expected deposit outflows.

T F 5. When individuals reduce their holdings of currency by depositing these funds in their bank accounts, the money multiplier increases.

T F 6. If the Bank of Canada purchases $10,000 in government securities from a bank and simultaneously extends $10,000 in advances to the same bank, then the Bank has kept the monetary base from changing.

T F 7. The Bank of Canada has better control over the nonborrowed base than the borrowed base.

T F 8. As the currency ratio falls, fewer reserves are available to support chequable deposits causing a decrease in the money supply.

T F 9. For a given level of the monetary base, if the Bank of Canada began to pay interest on deposits that banks maintain at the Bank, banks would have greater incentive to hold desired reserves, which would lead to a decline in the money supply, all else constant.

T F 10. The money multiplier from the money supply model that includes depositor and bank behaviour is larger than the simple deposit multiplier.

T F 11. The expected deposit outflow is negatively related to the money supply.

T F 12. The money multiplier and the money supply are positively related to the currency ratio.

T F 13. The money multiplier and the money supply are negatively related to the desired reserve ratio.

T F 14. An increase in the monetary base that goes into currency is not multiplied, whereas an increase that goes into supporting deposits is multiplied.

PART B: Multiple-Choice Questions

Circle the appropriate answer.

1. When comparing the simple model of multiple deposit creation with the money supply model that accounts for depositor and bank behaviour, the more complicated model indicates that
   a. an increase in the monetary base that goes into currency is not multiplied.
   b. the money multiplier is negatively related to the currency ratio.
   c. the money multiplier is positively related to the desired reserve ratio.
   d. all of the above occur.
   e. only (a) and (b) of the above occur

2. The money multiplier increases in value as the
   a. currency ratio increases.
   b. desired reserve ratio increases.
   c. desired reserve ratio decreases.
   d. monetary base increases.

3. Depositors often withdraw more currency from their bank accounts during Christmastime. Therefore, one would predict that
   a. the money multiplier will tend to fall during Christmastime.
   b. the money multiplier will tend to rise during Christmastime.
   c. Bank of Canada lending will tend to fall during Christmastime.
   d. none of the above will occur.

4. The Bank of Canada lacks complete control over the monetary base because
   a. it cannot set the desired reserve ratio on chequable deposits.
   b. it cannot perfectly predict the amount of borrowing by banks.
   c. it cannot perfectly predict shifts from deposits to currency.

d. of each of the above.

e. of only (a) and (b) of the above.

5. The money multiplier is smaller than the simple deposit multiplier when
   a. the currency ratio is greater than zero.
   b. the excess reserves ratio is greater than zero.
   c. the desired reserve ratio on chequable deposits is greater than zero.
   d. all of the above occur.
   e. both (a) and (b) of the above occur.

6. The money multiplier is negatively related to
   a. the desired reserve ratio on chequable deposits.
   b. the currency ratio.
   c. the currency ratio and the desired reserve ratio.
   d. all of the above.
   e. only (a) and (b) of the above.

7. For a given level of the monetary base, a drop in the desired reserve ratio means
   a. an increase in the money supply.
   b. an increase in the monetary base.
   c. an increase in the nonborrowed base.
   d. all of the above.
   e. only (b) and (c) of the above.

8. For a given level of the monetary base, a drop in the currency ratio means
   a. an increase in the nonborrowed base, but a decrease in the borrowed base of equal magnitude.
   b. an increase in the borrowed base, but a decrease in the nonborrowed base of equal magnitude.
   c. an increase in the money supply.
   d. a decrease in the money supply.
   e. none of the above.

9. If banks reduce their holdings of reserves,
   a. the monetary base will increase.
   b. the money supply will increase.
   c. both (a) and (b) of the above will occur.
   d. neither (a) nor (b) of the above will occur.

10. The banking system's desired reserve ratio is
    a. negatively related to both the market interest rate and expected deposit outflows.
    b. positively related to both the market interest rate and expected deposit outflows.
    c. positively related to the market interest rate and negatively related to expected deposit outflows.
    d. negatively related to the market interest rate and positively related to expected deposit outflows.

11. The monetary base less advances to banks is called:
    a. reserves.
    b. high-powered money.
    c. the nonborrowed monetary base.
    d. the borrowed monetary base.

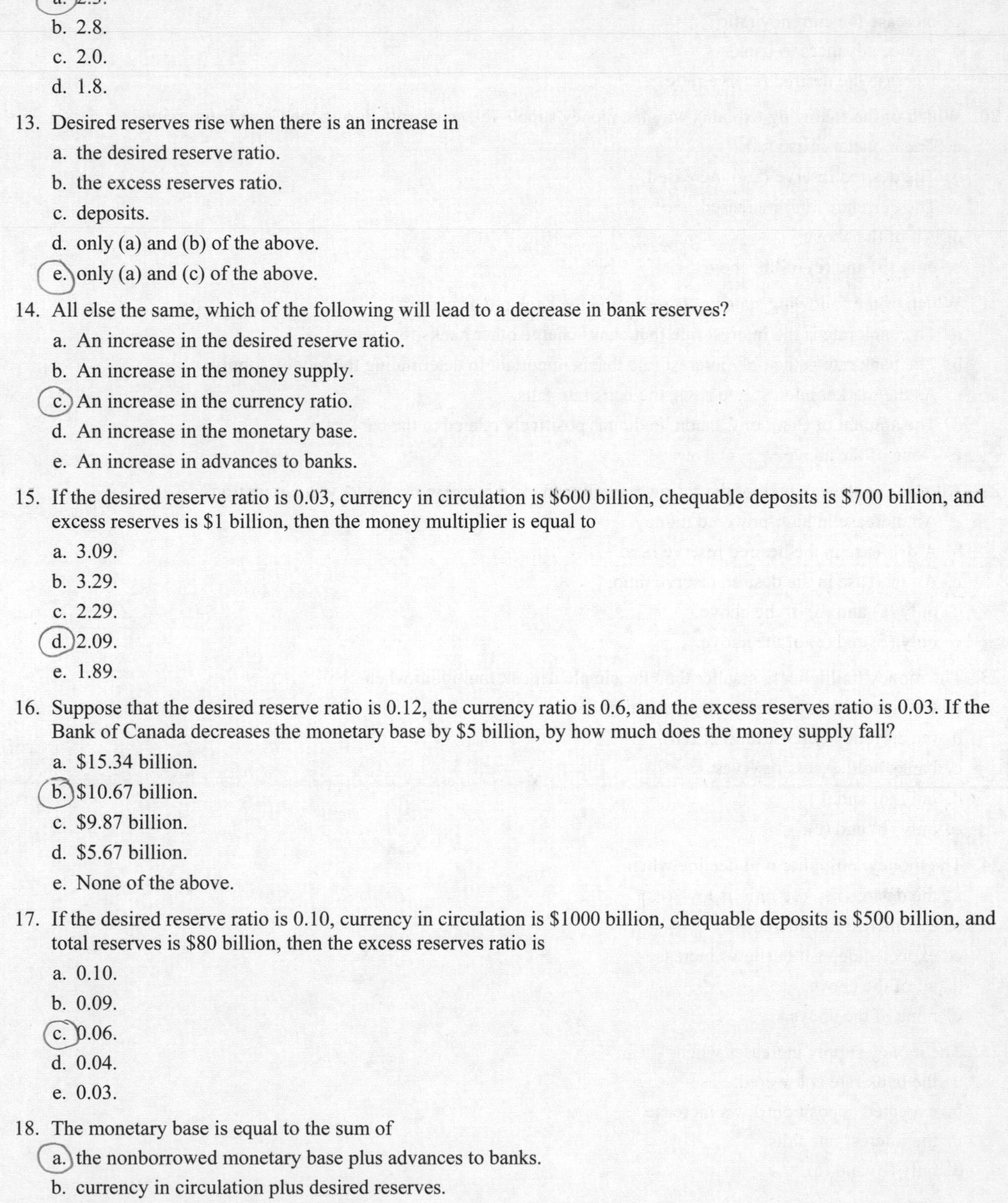

12. If the desired reserve ratio is one-fourth, currency in circulation is $400 billion, excess reserves are not held, and chequable deposits are $1200 billion, then the money multiplier is approximately
    a. 2.3.
    b. 2.8.
    c. 2.0.
    d. 1.8.
13. Desired reserves rise when there is an increase in
    a. the desired reserve ratio.
    b. the excess reserves ratio.
    c. deposits.
    d. only (a) and (b) of the above.
    e. only (a) and (c) of the above.
14. All else the same, which of the following will lead to a decrease in bank reserves?
    a. An increase in the desired reserve ratio.
    b. An increase in the money supply.
    c. An increase in the currency ratio.
    d. An increase in the monetary base.
    e. An increase in advances to banks.
15. If the desired reserve ratio is 0.03, currency in circulation is $600 billion, chequable deposits is $700 billion, and excess reserves is $1 billion, then the money multiplier is equal to
    a. 3.09.
    b. 3.29.
    c. 2.29.
    d. 2.09.
    e. 1.89.
16. Suppose that the desired reserve ratio is 0.12, the currency ratio is 0.6, and the excess reserves ratio is 0.03. If the Bank of Canada decreases the monetary base by $5 billion, by how much does the money supply fall?
    a. $15.34 billion.
    b. $10.67 billion.
    c. $9.87 billion.
    d. $5.67 billion.
    e. None of the above.
17. If the desired reserve ratio is 0.10, currency in circulation is $1000 billion, chequable deposits is $500 billion, and total reserves is $80 billion, then the excess reserves ratio is
    a. 0.10.
    b. 0.09.
    c. 0.06.
    d. 0.04.
    e. 0.03.
18. The monetary base is equal to the sum of
    a. the nonborrowed monetary base plus advances to banks.
    b. currency in circulation plus desired reserves.
    c. total reserves plus chequable deposits.
    d. currency in circulation plus advances to banks.

19. If the Bank of Canada wanted to reduce the monetary base, it could
    a. raise the excess reserves ratio.
    b. buy Canada securities.
    c. increase the currency ratio.
    d. reduce advances to banks.
    e. increase the desired reserve ratio.
20. Which of the following explains why the money supply fell so sharply during the Great Depression?
    a. The monetary base fell.
    b. The desired reserve ratio increased.
    c. The currency ratio increased.
    d. All of the above.
    e. only (b) and (c) of the above.
21. Which of the following statements regarding the bank rate is correct?
    a. The bank rate is the interest rate that banks charge other banks for loans.
    b. The bank rate is the only interest rate that is important in determining the money supply.
    c. As the market interest rate rises, the bank rate falls.
    d. The amount of Bank of Canada lending is positively related to the bank rate.
    e. None of the above.
22. All else the same, which of the following will lead to an increase in currency in circulation?
    a. An increase in high-powered money.
    b. A decrease in the desired reserve ratio.
    c. An increase in the desired reserve ratio.
    d. only (a) and (b) of the above.
    e. only (a) and (c) of the above.
23. The money multiplier is smaller than the simple deposit multiplier when
    a. the currency-deposit ratio is greater than zero.
    b. the currency-deposit ratio is zero.
    c. banks hold excess reserves.
    d. only (a) and (c).
    e. only (b) and (c).
24. The money multiplier will decline when
    a. the desired reserve ratio is lowered.
    b. the interest rate increases.
    c. expected deposit outflows increase.
    d. all of the above.
    e. none of the above.
25. The money supply increases when
    a. the bank rate is lowered.
    b. expected deposit outflows increase.
    c. the interest rate falls.
    d. only (b) and (c).

26. If the market interest rate ________, the opportunity cost of reserves ________ and the desired ratio of reserves rises.
    a. decreases, falls
    b. increases, falls
    c. decreases, rises
    d. increases, rises

27. ________ in the nonborrowed monetary base and ________ in the monetary base will decrease the money supply.
    a. A decrease, an increase
    b. A decrease, a decrease
    c. An increase, an increase
    d. An increase, a decrease

28. The M2+ money multiplier is _______ the M1+ money multiplier.
    a. equal to
    b. smaller than
    c. larger than
    d. larger than or equal to

29. Which of the following will raise the M2+ money supply?
    a. An increase in borrowed reserves.
    b. A decrease in the time deposit ratio.
    c. An increase in the time deposit ratio.
    d. both (a) and (c) of the above.

30. The banking system's desired reserve ratio is
    a. negatively related to the market interest rate.
    b. positively related to the market interest rate.
    c. negatively related to the currency in circulation.
    d. negatively related to the chequable deposits.

31. The M2+ money multiplier and M2+ money supply are
    a. negatively related to the desired reserve ratio and the currency ratio.
    b. positively related to the desired reserve ratio and the currency ratio.
    c. positively related to the desired reserve ratio and negatively related to the currency ratio.
    d. negatively related to the desired reserve ratio and positively related to the currency ratio.

32. When the costs of holding reserves rise, we would expect that
    a. both the desired reserves and the desired reserve ratio will increase.
    b. both the desired reserves and the desired reserve ratio will decrease.
    c. the desired reserves will increase but the desired reserve ratio will decline.
    d. the value of both the desired reserves and the desired reserve ratio will remain the same.

CHAPTER 17

Tools of Monetary Policy

CHAPTER SYNOPSIS/COMPLETIONS

Chapter 17 examines how the Bank of Canada uses its three policy tools (open market operations, government (1)________________________________, and (2)__________________to banks) to manipulate the money supply and interest rates. The chapter begins with a supply and demand analysis of the market for settlement balances to explain how the Bank's settings for these three tools determine the overnight funds interest rate. The (3) _____ _____ _____ is the interest rate that banks charge each other for overnight loans.

Currently, the Bank of Canada implements monetary policy by changing the overnight interest rate. In fact, the Bank's operational objective is to keep the overnight rate within a band of 50 basis points. The upper limit of the operating band for the overnight interest rate defines the bank rate and the lower limit is the rate that the Bank pays LVTS participants with positive settlement balances at the end of the day.

Since December 2000, the Bank operates under a system of eight "fixed" dates throughout the year for announcing any changes to the operating band for the overnight rate, keeping the option of acting between the fixed dates in "extraordinary circumstances."

By far the most important monetary policy tool at the Bank of Canada's disposal is its ability to buy and sell government (4)________________________. Open market operations is the Bank's most important monetary policy tool, because it is the primary determinant of changes in reserves. There are two types of open market operations. Open market operations designed to change the level of settlement balances in an effort to influence economic activity are called (5)__________________ open market operations. Defensive open market operations are intended to offset movements in other factors that affect the monetary base, such as changes in government deposits and float.

Most of the time, the Bank of Canada engages in repurchase agreements (repos) or reverse repurchase agreements (reverse repos). A repo is actually a temporary open market (6)__________________ that will be reversed within a few days, and it is often argued to be an especially effective way of conducting defensive open market operations. Matched sale-purchase transactions or (7)____________________________________ are used when the Bank of Canada wants to temporarily drain reserves from the banking system.

Open market operations have several advantages over the other tools of the Bank of Canada that make them particularly desirable:

1. Open market operations occur at the initiative of the Bank. The Bank has complete control over the volume of open market operations, giving it control over the overnight funds interest rate.
2. Open market operations can be varied in any degree. Thus open market operations are said to be (8)_____________________.
3. Open market operations are easily reversed.
4. Open market operations can be implemented quickly.

EXERCISES

EXERCISE 1: Definitions and Terminology

Match the following terms on the right with the definition or description on the left. Place the letter of the term in the blank provided next to the appropriate definition.

_____ 1. Upper limit of the operating band for the overnight interest rate.

_____ 2. Lower limit of the operating band for the overnight rate of interest.

_____ 3. Intended to offset temporary changes in factors affecting the monetary base.

_____ 4. LVTS participants' borrowing and lending

_____ 5. Intended to affect economic activity by changing the monetary base.

_____ 6. Employed when the Bank of Canada shifts government funds.

_____ 7. Employed when the Bank of Canada wishes to temporarily absorb reserves.

_____ 8. They cause the money multiplier to change.

_____ 9. This monetary policy tool complements the Bank's role as lender of last resort.

_____ 10. Employed when the Bank of Canada wishes to temporarily inject reserves into the system.

a. bank rate-50 basis points

b. daily auctions of government term deposits

c. dynamic open market operations

d. defensive open market operations

e. sale and repurchase agreement (reverse repo)

f. repurchase agreement (repo)

g. bank rate

h. standing facilities

i. currency ratio and reserve ratio

j. advances to banks

EXERCISE 2: Open Market Operations

A. Why is open market operations the most important monetary policy tool?

____

____

B. What are the two types of open market operations?

1. ____

2. ____

C. List the advantages of open market operations.

1. ____

2. ____

3. ____

4. ____

EXERCISE 3: Bank of Canada Lending

A. List the two types of Bank of Canada loans.

1. ______________________________

2. ______________________________

B. Why might it be important to have a lender of last resort even with the existence of deposit insurance?

____

____

EXERCISE 4: Reserve Requirements

One noticeable change in monetary policy is that many central banks have recently reduced or eliminated reserve requirements. This reduces the "tax" that banks implicitly pay because reserves do not pay interest. The reduction of reserve requirements makes banks more competitive with other financial institutions when trying to attract funds.

List two reasons why changes in reserve requirements are rarely used as a policy tool to conduct monetary policy in those countries that still require banks to hold reserves against their deposit liabilities.

1. ______________________________

____

2. ______________________________

____

EXERCISE 5: ACSS Accounting Practices

Until the end of October 2003, the Bank of Canada maintained an ACSS interest rate band, which was 250 basis points wider than that for LVTS balances. In particular, the Bank charged the bank rate plus 150 basis points on ACSS collateralized advances and paid the bank rate less 150 basis points on ACSS positive balances. Effective Nov. 3, 2003, however, the Bank of Canada changed its ACSS accounting practices, in response to a request from the Canadian Payments Association, and abandoned "retroactive settlement" adopting "next-day settlement" in the ACSS.

A. Describe the new ACSS accounting practices.

____

____

____

____

B. What is the effect of next-day settlement on costs for the direct clearers?

____

____

____

____

Exercise 6: Repurchase Transactions

A. What are the Bank of Canada's two buyback operations?

1. ____________________
2. ____________________

B. What are the advantages of buyback operations over other tools of monetary policy?

1. ____________________
2. ____________________
3. ____________________
4. ____________________

SELF-TEST

PART A: True-False Questions

Circle whether the following statements are true (T) or false (F).

T F 1. Open market operations are the most important monetary policy tool because they are the most important determinant of changes in the money multiplier, the main source of fluctuations in the money supply.

T F 2. Open market buyback operations by the Bank of Canada are intended to change the level of reserves and the monetary base in an effort to influence economic activity.

T F 3. When the Bank of Canada purchases or sells a security in the open market, it is most likely trading in Canada bonds.

T F 4. The Bank of Canada has less than complete control over the volume of open market operations because banks can refuse to buy Canada securities.

T F 5. Because banks in agricultural areas experience greater demands for funds in the spring, the Bank of Canada issues adjustment credit to these banks when they have deficient reserves.

T F 6. Central banks in many countries have recently reduced or eliminated reserve requirements.

T F 7. The Bank of Canada's role of lender of last resort may still be useful even though deposit insurance has reduced the probability of bank panics.

T F 8. Banks view Bank of Canada lending as a substitute for borrowing overnight funds.

T F 9. Open market operations are usually carried out once a month.

T F 10. When the overnight interest rate rises, the quantity of excess reserves demanded falls.

T F 11. If the quantity of reserves demanded is larger than the quantity supplied by the Bank of Canada, the equilibrium overnight interest rate will be higher than the bank rate.

T F 12. SPRAs and SRAs are introduced to reduce the undesired downward and upward pressures, respectively, on the overnight rate.

T F 13. The open market purchases expand both the bank reserves and the monetary base, thereby lowering short-term interest rates and raising the money supply.

T F 14. If the overnight rate increases towards the upper limit of the operating band, then the Bank will lend at the bank rate to put a ceiling on the overnight rate.

PART B: Multiple-Choice Questions

Circle the appropriate answer.

1. Open market operations are of two types:
   a. defensive and offensive.
   b. dynamic and reactionary.
   c. actionary and passive.
   d. dynamic and defensive.
2. If the Bank of Canada wants to inject reserves into the banking system, it will usually
   a. purchase government securities.
   b. raise the bank rate.
   c. sell government securities.
   d. lower reserve requirements.
   e. do either (a) or (b) of the above.
3. To temporarily raise reserves in the banking system, the Bank of Canada engages in
   a. a repurchase agreement.
   b. a reverse repo.
   c. a matched sale-purchase transaction.
   d. none of the above.
4. When float increases, causing a temporary increase in reserves in the banking system, the Bank of Canada can offset the effects of float by engaging in
   a. a repurchase agreement.
   b. an interest rate swap.
   c. a matched sale-purchase transaction.
   d. none of the above.
5. The bank rate is the rate at which
   a. the Bank of Canada lends funds to financial institutions.
   b. banks lend funds to their best customers.
   c. banks borrow overnight funds in the interbank market.
   d. none of the above.
6. The interest rate at which the Bank of Canada lends to participating financial institutions is called
   a. prime rate.
   b. overnight rate.
   c. bank rate.
   d. deposit rate.
   e. mortgage rate.
7. A reduction in desired reserves causes the money supply to rise, since the change causes
   a. the money multiplier to fall.
   b. the money multiplier to rise.
   c. reserves to fall.
   d. reserves to rise.
8. The lower limit of the operating band for the overnight interest rate defines
   a. the bank rate.
   b. the prime rate.

c. the rate the Bank of Canada pays LVTS participants with positive settlement balances at the end of the banking day.

d. the rate the Bank of Canada charges LVTS participants with negative settlement balances at the end of the banking day.

9. When the bank of Canada engages in a sale and repurchase agreement, it _____ securities that the other party agrees to _____ back within a few days.
   a. buys; buy
   b. buys; sell
   c. sells; buy
   d. sells; sell

10. When the Bank of Canada wants to conduct a _____ open market _____, it engages in a _____.
    a. permanent; purchase; reverse repo
    b. permanent; purchase; repurchase agreement
    c. temporary; sale; reverse repo
    d. temporary; sale; repurchase agreement
    e. temporary; purchase; reverse repo

11. If the operating band for the overnight interest rate is from 3.5 to 4.0 percent, then
    a. the bank rate is 4.0 percent.
    b. the bank rate is the upper limit of the operating band.
    c. the bank rate is the rate the Bank of Canada charges LVTS participants with negative settlement balances at the end of the banking day.
    d. all of the above.

12. If either government deposits or foreign deposits at the Bank of Canada are predicted to _____, a _____ open market _____ would be needed to offset the expected decrease in the monetary base.
    a. rise; dynamic; purchase
    b. fall; dynamic; sale
    c. rise; defensive; purchase
    d. fall; defensive; purchase

13. The operating band for the overnight interest rate is
    a. 50 basis points wide.
    b. defines the rate of interest the Bank of Canada charges LVTS participants with negative settlement balances at the end of the banking day.
    c. defines the rate of interest the Bank of Canada pays LVTS participants with positive settlement balances at the end of the banking day.
    d. all of the above.
    e. only (a) and (b) of the above.

14. When the Bank of Canada lowers the operating band for the overnight interest rate, it
    a. lowers the bank rate by the same amount.
    b. encourages LVTS participants to borrow reserves either from each other or from the Bank of Canada.
    c. reduces the monetary base and ultimately the money supply.
    d. all of the above.
    e. only (a) and (b) of the above.

15. The overnight interest rate
    a. is the shortest-term rate available.
    b. forms the base of any term structure of interest rates relation.

c. is the rate of interest the Bank of Canada charges LVTS participants with negative settlement balances at the end of the banking day.

d. only (a) and (b) of the above.

16. The overnight market in Canada is
    a. the key market for finance and monetary policy.
    b. the market where the bank rate is determined.
    c. the market where banks borrow overnight funds from each other.
    d. only (a) and (c) of the above.

17. If the Bank of Canada wanted to lower the overnight funds rate, then it would
    a. lower the required reserve ratio.
    b. increase the bank rate.
    c. conduct an open market sale of securities.
    d. lower the operating band.

18. The trading desk at the Federal Reserve Bank of New York contacts primary dealers
    a. in order to learn how dealers view the securities markets.
    b. when the Fed wants to sell government securities.
    c. to ask whether the Fed should buy or sell securities.
    d. all of the above.
    e. only (a) and (b) of the above.

19. A rise in the operating band for the overnight rate of interest is a signal that
    a. the Bank of Canada would like higher short-term interest rates.
    b. the Bank of Canada would like lower short-term interest rates.
    c. the Bank of Canada would like an increase in the monetary base.
    d. none of the above.

20. A fall in the operating band for the overnight rate of interest is a signal that
    a. the Bank of Canada would like higher short-term interest rates.
    b. the Bank of Canada would like lower short-term interest rates.
    c. the Bank of Canada would like a decrease in the monetary base and the money supply.
    d. none of the above.

21. The Channel/Corridor system for setting interest rates
    a. has been adopted by Canada, Australia, and New Zealand.
    b. allows central banks to target interest rates even if there are zero reserve requirements.
    c. strictly limits the amount that banks may borrow from the central bank.
    d. all of the above.
    e. only (a) and (b) of the above.

22. What is the main reason why reserve requirements have been declining around the world?
    a. Central banks are taxing banks in order to raise revenue.
    b. Central banks are trying to make banks more competitive with other financial intermediaries.
    c. The spread between the bank and the market interest rate is growing.
    d. Reserve requirements are a blunt tool for monetary policy.

23. To lower interest rates, the Bank of Canada could
    a. buy government securities.
    b. sell government securities.
    c. raise the operating band.
    d. raise the bank rate.

24. If the Bank of Canada wants to ____ reserves ____ in the banking system, it will execute a repurchase agreement.
    a. increase; temporarily
    b. increase; permanently
    c. decrease; temporarily
    d. decrease; permanently

25. The goal of the Bank of Canada is to keep the inflation rate within a target range of _______ to ________.
    a. 2%, 4%
    b. 1%, 3%
    c. 1%, 4%
    d. 0%, 2%

26. "Core CPI" excludes ________ from "headline CPI".
    a. volatile components
    b. health care costs
    c. housing costs
    d. both (b) and (c) of the above

27. When the Bank of Canada increases the overnight lending rate, the value of the Canadian dollar ________, and the inflation rate ________.
    a. goes up, falls
    b. goes up, rises
    c. remains unchanged, rises
    d. remains unchanged, falls

28. Which of the following is true?
    a. The Bank of Canada has complete control over volumes of SPRAs and SRAs.
    b. Changes in interest rate due to SPRAs and SRAs are not accurate.
    c. SPRA and SRA transactions can be implemented quickly.
    d. both (a) and (c) of the above.

29. The European Central Bank imposes a _______ reserve requirement on all deposit-taking institutions.
    a. 0%
    b. 2%
    c. 3%
    d. 5%

30. The federal funds rate ________ when the Fed makes an open market ________ or lowers reserve requirements.
    a. falls, sale
    b. falls, purchase
    c. rises, sale
    d. rises, purchase

31. A rise in the required reserve ratio will
    a. shift the demand for reserves to the left.
    b. shift the demand for reserves to the right.
    c. shift the supply of reserves to the right.
    d. shift the supply of reserves to the left.

32. If the overnight rate increases towards the upper limit of the operating band, then
    a. the bank will increase the bank rate to put a ceiling on the overnight rate.
    b. the bank will decrease the bank rate to put a ceiling on the overnight rate.
    c. the bank will be lending at the bank rate and reduces the ceiling on the overnight rate.
    d. the bank will be lending at the bank rate to put a ceiling on the overnight rate.

CHAPTER **18**

What Should Central Banks Do? Monetary Policy Goals, Strategy, and Tactics

CHAPTER SYNOPSIS/COMPLETIONS

In this chapter, students discover that central banks in different countries have had remarkable success in conducting monetary policy, bringing inflation down to low levels and promoting stable financial environments that promote general economic health. A central feature of monetary policy strategies in these countries is also the use of a (1) ______________________, a nominal variable such as the inflation rate or the money supply that policymakers use to tie down the price level. The role of the nominal anchor is to guide a nation's monetary authority to conduct monetary policy to keep the nominal anchor variable— the inflation rate or the money supply—within a narrow range.

Adherence to the nominal anchor can limit the (2)__________-______________________ for monetary policymakers. The time-inconsistency problem arises because the effect that monetary policy has on the economy depends on people's expectations. If workers and firms expect the central bank to pursue a tight monetary policy to keep inflation low—because that is the announced policy of the central bank—then the central bank has an incentive to renege on this promise and adopt an (3)______________________ policy to boost output and lower unemployment. Knowing that policymakers may on occasion renege on policy announcements—that is, be inconsistent over time—workers and firms will (4)______________________ central bank announcements. Thus, to make its announcements credible, the central bank will want to commit to a nominal anchor that limits its discretion.

Monetary targeting was adopted by a number of industrialized countries in the 1970s to bring down inflation. Of these countries, both Germany and Switzerland were the most persistent in sticking to this strategy. It is because of their success in keeping inflation under control that monetary targeting still has strong advocates. Germany and Switzerland have shown that monetary targeting can restrain inflation in the long run even when monetary targets are missed by wide margins. Despite frequent misses of announced targets, both countries have openly communicated to the public their intention of keeping inflation under control.

The chapter presents six basic goals most often mentioned by personnel at the Bank of Canada and other central banks as objectives of monetary policy:

(5)____

(6)____

(7)____

(8)____

(9)____

(10)____

By high employment, economists mean a level of unemployment consistent with labour market equilibrium. This level of unemployment is the (11)__________________ ___________ of unemployment.

Because exchange rate fluctuations have a greater relative impact on the domestic economy now that international financial and goods markets have become more integrated, the Bank of Canada no longer treats Canada as a closed economy. Now, when deciding the course of monetary policy, the Bank of Canada pays careful attention to the expected change in the value of the dollar.

Hierarchical mandates put the goal of price stability first, and state that other goals can only be pursued if this goal is achieved. The Bank of Canada and the Bank of England are among the central banks that are following this type of mandate. (12)___________ ___________ has two objectives; these two goals must be achieved at the same time.

The main advantage of monetary targeting is the flexibility it provides to the central bank for dealing with (13)_______________ considerations. The principal problem with monetary targeting occurs when the relationship between the monetary target and the goal variable proves to be too weak to guarantee that the goal can be achieved.

It is because of this breakdown between monetary aggregates and goal variables that many countries have recently adopted (14)______________ ______________ as their monetary policy regime. New Zealand, Canada, and the United Kingdom were the first to adopt explicit inflation-targeting regimes in the early 1990s. Inflation targeting requires a commitment to: emphasizing stability as the primary, long-run goal of monetary policy; public announcement of numerical inflation targets, including the plans and objectives of monetary policymakers; and increased accountability of the central bank to attain its inflation objectives. Consider this last requirement. The governor of the Reserve Bank in (15)__________ ______________ can be dismissed if the publicly announced goals are not satisfied. All three countries have succeeded in bringing inflation down, albeit at the initial cost of higher unemployment.

Inflation targeting is readily understood by the public and is thus highly (16)_________________; it permits monetary policymakers to respond to shocks to the domestic economy, and does not depend on a stable relationship between money and inflation. Because an explicit numerical inflation target increases the (17)_______________________ of the central bank, inflation targeting reduces the likelihood that the monetary authority will fall into the time-consistency trap. Indeed, the success of the Bank of England's inflation-targeting regime proved to be instrumental in the government's decision to grant the Bank its operational independence. An inflation-targeting regime makes it more palatable to have an independent central bank that focuses on long-run objectives but is consistent with a democratic society, because it is accountable.

Critics of inflation targeting contend that long lags in the effects of monetary policy make it too difficult for markets to determine the stance of monetary policy. Also, they claim that inflation targeting limits the discretion of central bankers to respond to domestic shocks, creates the potential for increased fluctuation in aggregate (18)____________, and lowers the economic growth of output and employment. Although the available empirical evidence does not lend much support to these criticisms, some economists claim that targeting nominal GDP would guard against a slow-down in economic activity. A variant of inflation targeting, a nominal GDP targeting regime would suffer the problem of announcing a long-term target for GDP growth, which would be difficult to forecast and politically risky. Moreover, since GDP is not a statistic that is reported monthly, it would make targeting GDP difficult in practice. Inflation targeting has almost all the benefits of nominal GDP targeting, but without its problems.

In recent years the U.S. Fed has pursued a policy of targeting an (19)_____________ nominal anchor in the form of an overriding concern to control inflation in the long run. The Fed's "just do it" approach has many of the advantages of an explicit inflation-targeting regime, but has a disadvantage in that the Fed's policy is much less transparent. In addition, some question whether the Fed's approach is consistent with democratic principles, given the lack of transparency to the Fed's implicit anchor. Perhaps the most serious problem with the "just do it" approach is the strong dependence on the preferences, skills, and trustworthiness of the individuals in charge of the central bank. For these reasons, the "just do it" approach may give way to an explicit inflation-targeting regime.

A controversial theory suggesting how the Bank of Canada should set the overnight funds interest rate has been proposed by Stanford economist John Taylor. The Taylor-rule setting for the overnight funds rate is equal to the inflation rate plus the weighted average of two gaps: (1) an inflation gap, current inflation minus a target rate, and (2) an output gap, the percentage deviation of real GDP from an estimate of its full employment potential.

EXERCISES

EXERCISE 1: Definitions and Terminology

Match the following terms on the right with the definition or description on the left. Place the letter of the term in the blank provided next to the appropriate definition.

_____ 1. Nominal variable that central banks use to tie down the price level such as the inflation rate or the money supply.

_____ 2. Policymakers follow different policies than what had been previously announced.

_____ 3. The revenue that the government receives by issuing money.

_____ 4. Monetary policy that uses a monetary aggregate as an intermediate target.

_____ 5. Central bank publicly announces medium-term numerical targets for inflation.

a. Nominal anchor

b. Time-consistency problem

c. Inflation targeting

d. Seignorage

e. Monetary targeting

EXERCISE 2: Advantages and Disadvantages of Monetary Targeting

A. List the advantages of monetary targeting.

1. ______________________________
2. ______________________________

B. List the one disadvantage of monetary targeting.

1. ______________________________

EXERCISE 3: Advantages and Disadvantages of Inflation Targeting

A. List the advantages of inflation targeting.

1. ______________________________
2. ______________________________
3. ______________________________
4. ______________________________
5. ______________________________

B. List the disadvantages of inflation targeting.

1. ______________________________
2. ______________________________
3. ______________________________

EXERCISE 4: Advantages and Disadvantages of U.S. Fed's Implicit-Targeting Regime

A. List the advantages of the U.S. Fed's "just do it" monetary policy strategy.

1. ______________________________
2. ______________________________
3. ______________________________

B. List the disadvantages of the U.S. Fed's "just do it" monetary policy strategy.

1. ______
2. ______
3. ______

EXERCISE 5: Central Bank's Targeting

A. Show graphically the effect of a central bank's targeting on :

1. Reserve aggregates.

2. The interest rate.

B. What does your graphical analysis imply about the simultaneous usage of the two policy instruments?

______

______

C. What criteria should be used to determine the desirability of using either of the two policy instruments?

______

______

D. Is one preferable to another?

______

______

EXERCISE 6: Taylor Rule

A. Briefly explain the Taylor rule.

______

______

B. What is the equation for the Taylor rule?

______

____

C. Suppose the equilibrium real overnight interest rate is 3%, the target for inflation is also 3%, the inflation rate is 5%, and the real GDP is 2% above its potential. What should the overnight interest rate be?

____

____

SELF-TEST

PART A: True-False Questions

Circle whether the following statements are true (T) or false (F).

T F 1. A key fact about monetary targeting regimes in Germany and Switzerland is that the targeting regimes were not like a Friedman-type monetary targeting rule, in which a monetary aggregate is kept on a constant-growth-rate path and is the primary focus of monetary policy.

T F 2. The European Central Bank has adopted a hybrid monetary policy strategy that has much in common with the monetary targeting strategy previously used by the Bundesbank but also has some elements of inflation targeting.

T F 3. A key reason why monetary targeting has been reasonably successful in both Germany and Switzerland, despite frequent target misses, is that the objectives of monetary policy are clearly stated and both central banks actively engaged in communicating the strategy of monetary policy to the public, thereby enhancing the transparency of monetary policy and the accountability of the central banks.

T F 4. The Bank of Canada desires interest rate stability because it reduces the uncertainty of future planning.

T F 5. The Bank of Canada attempts to get the unemployment rate to zero, since any unemployment is wasteful and inefficient.

T F 6. According to hierarchical mandates, price stability and maximum employment are the most important goals of central banks.

T F 7. A disadvantage of inflation targeting is that it relies on a stable relationship between money and the price level.

T F 8. Two problems with the U.S. Fed's "just do it" approach to monetary policy are the lack of transparency and the low degree of accountability, since the Fed does not announce its long-run goals for policy.

T F 9. Governments of countries that have their own currencies have an incentive to over-expand the money supply to gain the revenue called seignorage. This explains why dollarization may be an effective monetary strategy to convince the public that the monetary authority is serious about reducing inflation.

T F 10. Achieving price stability in the long run and the natural rate of unemployment are not consistent with each other as goals of the central bank.

T F 11. Price stability is desirable because a rising price level creates uncertainty in the economy, and that uncertainty might hamper economic growth.

T F 12. A central bank will have better inflation performance in the long run if it does not conduct unexpected expansionary policies.

T F 13. In the long run, there is inconsistency between the price stability goal and other goals of monetary policy.

T F 14. It is better for an economy to operate under a hierarchical mandate than a dual mandate.

T F 15. When the economy is at full employment, the supply of labour equals the demand for labour, implying that the unemployment rate is zero.

T F 16. The time-inconsistency problem can occur under dual mandate regimes that lead to the Central Bank conducting daily discretionary monetary policy that is less expansionary than what firms and consumers expect.

T F 17. One disadvantage of inflation targeting is that it commits the Central Bank to pursue price stability as its only primary objective.

PART B: Multiple-Choice Questions

Circle the appropriate answer.

1. Using Taylor's rule, the Bank of Canada should raise the overnight funds interest rate when inflation _____ the Bank's inflation target or when real GDP _____ the Bank's output target.
   a. rises above; drops below
   b. drops below; drops below
   c. rises above; rises above
   d. drops below; rises above
2. Bank of Canada watchers are hired by financial institutions in order to
   a. collect data that the Bank of Canada does not share with the public.
   b. explain past Bank of Canada policy.
   c. sell or purchase securities from the Bank of Canada.
   d. predict future monetary policy.
   e. all of the above.
3. The Bank of Canada should not set zero unemployment as a policy goal since
   a. frictional unemployment may be helpful to the economy.
   b. monetary policy cannot eliminate structural unemployment.
   c. it cannot affect the unemployment rate.
   d. all of the above.
   e. only (a) and (b) of the above.
4. A breakdown in the relationship between money growth and inflation is
   a. a disadvantage for countries that use a monetary-targeting regime.
   b. not a disadvantage for countries that use a monetary-targeting regime.
   c. a disadvantage for countries that use an inflation-targeting regime.
   d. both (b) and (c) of the above.
5. Critics of inflation targeting complain that
   a. the signal between monetary policy actions and evidence of success is too long delayed.
   b. it imposes a rule on monetary policymakers that is too rigid, taking away their ability to respond to shocks to the economy.
   c. it has the potential for making output fluctuations more pronounced.
   d. it does all of the above.
   e. it does only (a) and (b) of the above.

6. Some economists question the desirability of the U.S. Fed's implicit targeting strategy by pointing out that
   a. the lack of transparency in the Fed's policy creates uncertainty that leads to unnecessary volatility in financial markets.
   b. the opacity of its policymaking makes it hard to hold the Fed accountable to Congress and the public.
   c. the policy has not been very successful, as inflation and unemployment were too high in the 1990s.
   d. all of the above.
   e. only (a) and (b) of the above.

7. The 1985 Plaza Agreement between central banks from the largest economies
   a. is an example of international policy coordination.
   b. sought to lower the value of the U.S. dollar versus other currencies.
   c. sought to lower inflation in the United States.
   d. only (a) and (b) of the above.
   e. only (a) and (c) of the above.

8. (I) If the relationship between the monetary aggregate and the goal variable is weak, monetary aggregate targeting will not work. (II) Canada was the first country to formally adopt inflation targeting in 1990.
   a. Both are true.
   b. Both are false.
   c. I is true, II is false.
   d. I is false, II is true.

9. Disadvantages of nominal GDP targeting include:
   a. the lack of timely information on nominal GDP since it is reported quarterly, not monthly.
   b. the potential confusion that might arise with the public between nominal and real GDP.
   c. the difficulty that policymakers would encounter in trying to calculate long-run potential GDP growth.
   d. all of the above.
   e. only (a) and (b) of the above.

10. A _____ is used by every central bank to control the price level.
    a. seignorage
    b. nominal anchor
    c. currency board
    d. real GDP target
    e. none of the above

11. The time-inconsistency problem in monetary policy exists because people's behaviour depends on
    a. what the central bank did in the past.
    b. current central bank behaviour.
    c. what the central bank will do in the future.
    d. what people believe the central bank will do in the future.

12. One solution to the time-inconsistency problem is for the central bank to
    a. have discretion over monetary policy.
    b. try to surprise people with unexpected policy.
    c. announce and commit to a policy strategy rule.
    d. only (a) and (c) of the above.
    e. only (b) and (c) of the above.

13. Which of the following statements regarding speculative attacks on currencies is *false*?
    a. Speculative attacks do not strike industrialized countries.
    b. Speculative attacks can be more damaging to emerging market economies than to industrialized economies.
    c. Speculators attack a currency when they believe that the central bank is not willing to increase interest rates high enough to defend the currency.
    d. A speculative attack on one currency may happen if that currency is pegged to another currency.
    e. All of the above.
14. The example of the German and Swiss monetary targeting policy strategies teaches us that
    a. inflation can be restrained even if the monetary target is often missed.
    b. transparency and accountability can be increased by effective communication from the central bank.
    c. a strict policy rule is important to keeping inflation low.
    d. only (a) and (b) of the above.
    e. only (b) and (c) of the above.
15. One advantage of an inflation targeting policy strategy is that
    a. an inflation target policy is very transparent.
    b. the likelihood of the time-inconsistency problem in monetary policy is reduced.
    c. the inflation rate is easily controlled by the central bank.
    d. all of the above.
    e. only (a) and (b) of the above.
16. Which of the following is a feature of Federal Reserve monetary policy?
    a. The Federal Reserve uses "pre-emptive strikes" against the threat of inflation.
    b. The Federal Reserve sets an explicit inflation target.
    c. The Federal Reserve uses policy rules rather than exercising discretion.
    d. Federal Reserve policy is highly transparent.
17. A nominal anchor is
    a. necessary for a successful monetary policy.
    b. used to keep a central bank from letting the price level grow too quickly or fall too fast.
    c. a nominal variable that policymakers use as an intermediate target to achieve their goals.
    d. all of the above.
    e. only (a) and (c).
18. An inflation rate target _____ zero makes periods of deflation _____ likely.
    a. above; more
    b. above; less
    c. below; more
    d. below; less
19. ________ and ________ are two types of policy instruments at the disposal of the Bank of Canada.
    a. Nonborrowed reserves, the monetary base
    b. The monetary base, interest rates
    c. Reserve aggregates, interest rates
    d. Total reserves, the monetary base
20. Which of the following is false?
    a. Inflation targeting is easily understood by the public.
    b. Inflation targeting gives an immediate signal about the achievement of a target.

c. Inflation targeting relies on a stable money-inflation relationship.
d. both (b) and (c) of the above.

21. Which of the following is a criterion in choosing a policy instrument?
    a. The instrument must be easily observable.
    b. The instrument must be controllable.
    c. The instrument must be measurable.
    d. All of the above.

22. Assume that the equilibrium overnight rate is 4%, the target for inflation is 3%, the inflation rate is 5%, and real GDP is 2% below its potential. What will be the overnight rate, according to Taylor's rule?
    a. 10%
    b. 9%
    c. 11%
    d. 12%

23. Inflation targeting involves
    a. public announcement of medium-term numerical targets for inflation.
    b. an institutional commitment to price stability as the primary long-run goal of the monetary policy.
    c. increased transparency of the monetary policy strategy.
    d. all of the above.

24. The rate of inflation tends to remain constant when
    a. the unemployment rate falls faster than the NAIRU falls.
    b. the unemployment rate increases faster than the NAIRU increases.
    c. the unemployment rate equals the NAIRU.
    d. the unemployment rate is above the NAIRU.

25. Interest rates are difficult to measure because
    a. they fluctuate too often.
    b. they cannot be controlled by the Bank of Canada.
    c. real interest rates depend on the expected inflation rate and the expected inflation rate is hard to determine.
    d. all of the above.

26. Full employment indicates that
    a. the unemployment rate is zero.
    b. the unemployment rate is not zero because of frictional unemployment.
    c. the unemployment rate is not zero because of structural unemployment.
    d. both (b) and (c) of the above.

27. Which of the following is false?
    a. Low and stable inflation rates promote economic growth.
    b. Price stability should be the primary short-run goal of monetary policy.
    c. Attempts to keep inflation at the same level in the long run would likely lead to excessive output fluctuations.
    d. Both (b) and (c) of the above.

28. The rate of unemployment at which there is no tendency for inflation to change is called
    a. full unemployment rate.
    b. frictional unemployment rate.
    c. structural unemployment rate.
    d. nonaccelerating inflation rate of unemployment.

29. The type of monetary policy that is used in New Zealand, Canada, and the United Kingdom is
    a. inflation targeting.
    b. monetary targeting.
    c. interest-rate targeting.
    d. both (a) and (c) of the above.
30. Using Taylor's rule, when the positive output gap is 4 percent, the equilibrium overnight rate is 3 percent, the target inflation rate is 2 percent, and the actual inflation rate is 4 percent, the overnight rate should be
    a. 5%.
    b. 10%.
    c. 8%.
    d. 6%.
31. Price stability is desirable because
    a. an unstable price level creates uncertainty in the economy.
    b. uncertainty in the price level might hamper economic growth.
    c. a rising price level creates uncertainty in the economy, and that uncertainty might hamper economic growth.
    d. all of the above.
32. Inflation targeting involves all but one of the following elements:
    a. a public announcement of medium-term numerical targets for inflation.
    b. a public announcement of medium-term numerical targets for government spending.
    c. an institutional commitment to price stability as the primary long-term target.
    d. increased accountability of the central bank to attaining its inflation objectives.
33. The "inflation nutter" problem occurs
    a. when the Central Bank follows a dual mandate of achieving maximum employment and price stability.
    b. when the Central Bank undertakes policies that lead to short-run price and output fluctuations.
    c. when the Central Bank follows a hierarchical mandate that leads to an expected inflation rate of zero and a constant level of output.
    d. when the Central Bank is solely concerned about controlling inflation, but not about output fluctuations.
34. A key similarity between inflation targeting and the Fed's "just do it" approach to monetary policy is:
    a. both involve the use of an implicit nominal anchor, and lower levels of transparency and accountability.
    b. both involve the use of an explicit nominal anchor, and higher levels of transparency and accountability.
    c. both are forward-looking pre-emptive strategies that make the Central Bank more susceptible to the time-inconsistency problem.
    d. none of the above.

CHAPTER 19

The Foreign Exchange Market

CHAPTER SYNOPSIS/COMPLETIONS

Exchange rate movements are extremely important to our economy. Chapter 19 develops a modern analysis of exchange rate determination that explains both recent behaviour in the foreign exchange market, and why exchange rates are so volatile from day to day.

The exchange rate is the price of one country's (1)_________________ in terms of another's. Trades in the foreign exchange market typically involve the exchange of bank (2)_________________ denominated in different currencies. Spot exchange rates involve the immediate exchange of bank deposits, while (3)_________________ exchange rates involve the exchange of deposits at some specified future date. When a currency increases in value, it has (4)_________________; when a currency falls in value and is worth fewer Canadian dollars, it has depreciated. Exchange rates are important because when a country's currency appreciates, its exports become (5)_________________ expensive and foreign imports become less expensive. Conversely, when a country's currency depreciates, its goods become less expensive for foreigners, but foreign goods become more expensive (implying that net exports decline, all else constant).

The starting point for undertaking an investigation of how exchange rates are determined in the long-run is the law of one price, which states the following: If two countries produce an identical good, the price of the good should be the same throughout the world no matter which country produces it. Applying the law of one price to countries' price levels produces the theory of (6)_________________ _________________ _________________, which suggests that if one country's price level rises relative to another's, its currency should (7)_________________.

The theory of purchasing power parity cannot fully explain exchange rate changes because goods produced in different countries are not identical and because many goods and services (whose prices are included in a measure of a country's price level) are not (8)_________________ across borders. Other factors also affect the exchange rate in the long run, including trade barriers such as (9)_________________ and quotas, the demand for imports and exports, and relative productivity.

The key to understanding the short-run behaviour of exchange rates is to recognize that an exchange rate is the price of domestic bank deposits in terms of foreign bank deposits. Because the exchange rate is the price of one asset in terms of another, the natural way to investigate the short-run determination of exchange rates is through an asset-market approach using the theory of asset demand.

The theory of asset demand indicates that the most important factor affecting the demand for both domestic (dollar) and foreign deposits is the (10)_________________ _________________ on these assets relative to one another. According to the interest parity condition, however, the expected return on both domestic and foreign deposits is identical in a world in which there is (11)_________________ _________________. Because the interest parity condition is an equilibrium condition, it provides a framework for understanding short-run movements in exchange rates as a result of factors that cause the expected return on either domestic or foreign deposits to change.

Therefore, changes in foreign interest rates, the domestic (12)________________ ________________, or a change in the expected future exchange rate will cause the exchange rate to change in the short run. Because long-run determinants of the exchange rate influence the expected future exchange rate, the determinants of long-run exchange rates affect short-run exchange rates. For example, any factor that raises the expected return on domestic deposits relative to foreign deposits causes the domestic currency to appreciate. These factors include a (13)________________ in the domestic interest rate, a decline in the foreign interest rate, or any long-run factor that causes the expected future exchange rate to (14)________________.

A rise in domestic interest rates relative to foreign interest rates can result in either an appreciation or a depreciation of the domestic currency. If the rise in the domestic interest rate is due to a rise in expected inflation, then the domestic currency depreciates. If the rise in the domestic interest rate, however, is due to a rise in the real interest rate, then the domestic currency (15)________________. Higher domestic money growth leads the domestic currency to (16)________________.

Exchange rates have been very volatile in recent years. The theory of asset demand explains this volatility as a consequence of changing expectations that are also volatile, and play an important role in determining the demand for domestic assets and, thereby, affects the value of the exchange rate.

EXERCISES

EXERCISE 1: Foreign Exchange Rates and Goods Prices

A. Suppose the exchange rate between the Swiss franc and the Canadian dollar is $0.50 per franc. What would be the exchange rate if it is quoted as francs per dollar? ________

B. If you are contemplating buying a fancy Swiss watch that costs 1000 francs, how much will it cost you in dollars? ________

C. If a Swiss is contemplating buying a Canadian pocket calculator that costs $100, how much will it cost him in francs? ________

D. If the exchange rate changes to $.25 per Swiss franc, has there been an appreciation or depreciation of the Swiss franc? ________ Of the Canadian dollar? ________

E. Now if you buy the Swiss watch that costs 1000 francs, how much will it cost you in Canadian dollars? ________ Does the Swiss watch cost you more or less than before? ________

F. Now how much will it cost the Swiss in francs for the $100 pocket calculator? ________ Does it cost more or less than before? ________

G. What does the example here indicate about the effect on prices of foreign goods in a country and domestic goods sold abroad when the exchange rate appreciates? ________

EXERCISE 2: Definitions and Terminology

Match the following terms on the right with the definition or description on the left. Place the letter of the term in the blank provided next to the appropriate definition. Terms may be used once, more than once, or not at all.

	Definition		Term
_____	1. The price of one country's currency in terms of another's.	a.	law of one price
_____	2. Condition in which exchange rate falls more in short run than long run when money supply increases.	b.	interest parity condition
_____	3. States that the domestic interest rate equals the foreign interest rate plus the expected depreciation of the domestic currency.	c.	capital mobility
		d.	devaluation
		e.	exchange rate
_____	4. Value of the domestic currency increases relative to one or more foreign currencies.	f.	quota

_____	5. Value of foreign currency increases relative to the domestic currency.	g.	tariff
_____	6. When two countries produce an identical good, the price of the good should be the same throughout the world no matter which country produces it.	h.	exchange rate overshooting
_____	7. Theory that exchange rates between any two countries will adjust to reflect changes in price levels of the two countries.	i.	spot exchange transaction
_____	8. Barrier to trade restricting the quantity of foreign goods that can be imported.	j.	forward exchange transaction
_____	9. The predominant type of exchange rate transaction that involves the immediate exchange of bank deposits denominated in different currencies.	k.	purchasing power parity
_____	10. Canadians can easily purchase foreign assets; foreigners can easily purchase Canadian assets.	l.	appreciation
_____	11. An exchange rate transaction that involves the exchange of bank deposits denominated in different currencies at a specified future date.	m.	depreciation

EXERCISE 3: Law of One Price and Purchasing Power Parity

PART A

Suppose that Polish wheat costs 3000 zloties per bushel and that Canadian wheat costs $6 per bushel. In addition, assume that Canadian wheat and Polish wheat are identical goods.

1. If the exchange rate is 300 Polish zloties per Canadian dollar, what is the price of Polish wheat in dollars?
   ____
2. What is the price of Canadian wheat in zloties? ____________________
3. What will be the demand for Polish wheat? __________ Why? ____________________
   ____
4. If the exchange rate is 600 Polish zloties per Canadian dollar, what is the price of Polish wheat in dollars?
   ____
5. What is the price of Canadian wheat in zloties? ____________________
6. What will be the demand for Canadian wheat? __________ Why? ____________________
   ____
7. What does the law of one price indicate will be the exchange rate between the Polish zloty and the Canadian dollar? ____________________

   Why? ____________________
8. If the price of Canadian wheat rises to $10 per bushel, what does the law of one price suggest will be the new exchange rate? ____________________

   Is this an appreciation or depreciation of the Canadian dollar? __________

PART B

1. If the Canadian price level doubles while that in Poland remains unchanged, what does the theory of purchasing power parity suggest will happen to the exchange rate which initially is at 500 zloties to the dollar?

____

2. If the Canadian inflation rate is 5% and the Polish inflation rate is 7%, then what does the theory of purchasing power parity predict will happen to the value of the dollar in terms of zloties in one year's time?

____

EXERCISE 4: Factors that Affect Exchange Rates

In the second column of the following table indicate with an arrow whether the exchange rate will rise (↑) or fall (↓) as a result of the change in the factor. (Recall that a rise in the exchange rate is viewed as an appreciation of the domestic currency.)

Change in Factor	Response of the Exchange Rate
Domestic interest rate decreases	↓
Foreign interest rate decreases	↓
Expected domestic price level decreases	↓
Expected tariffs and quotas decreases	↓
Expected import demand decreases	↓
Expected export demand decreases	↓
Expected productivity decreases	↓

EXERCISE 5: Asset Demand and the Interest Parity Condition

Suppose that you are considering placing $100 in either a British or a Canadian bank account for one period, and that you would like to earn the greatest return possible. Further suppose that today's spot exchange rate is 0.56 pounds per Canadian dollar, the British interest rate is 3% (=.03), the Canadian interest rate is 7% (=.07), and that the expected exchange rate one period from today is 0.48 pounds per dollar.

A. If you place $100 in a Canadian bank account, how much do you expect to have after one period?

____

B. If you instead buy pounds in today's spot market, place them in a British bank account for one period, and then convert them to dollars, how many dollars do you expect to have?

____

C. Do you prefer the Canadian or British bank account? What do you predict will happen to the spot exchange rate?

____

____

D. Given today's interest rates and the expected exchange rate in one period, and using the interest parity condition, what must today's spot exchange rate be such that the expected return is the same for holding either pounds or dollars for one period?

____

____

EXERCISE 6: INVESTMENT DECISION

Imagine yourself as an investor who is considering investing in domestic assets. Suppose further that $i^D = 0.05$; $i^F = 0.045$; $E_{t+1} = 1.15$ euro per dollar, $E_t = 1.20$.

A. Would you make the decision to hold domestic assets? Why or why not?

B. If the domestic interest rate increases to $i^D = 0.06$, would you change your decision? Why or why not?

C. Suppose that the current exchange rate falls below its long-run value of 1.20 to $E_t = 1.10$.
   i) Would you invest in domestic assets?
   ii) What are the factors that would initiate a decline in E_t?
   iii) Demonstrate the effect of these factors graphically.
   iv) Explain, in words, why your demand curve takes the shape it does.

EXERCISE 7: EXCHANGE RATE

A. The Economist Big Mac Index deals with the purchasing power parity of the currency of a number of currencies around the world. The Big Mac Index measures the price of Big Macs around the world, measured in converted US dollars. The purchasing power parity theory states that, in theory, in the long run, the price of Big Macs in adjusted US dollars should:

B. If the Bank of Canada increases Canadian interest rates, one should expect the Canadian dollar to do what and why?

C. The interest parity condition states that, when the expected rate of return on assets in Canada is higher than the expected rate of return on assets in the US, both Canadians and Americans will want to invest in Canadian assets.

In order for there to be a demand for dollar supplies of both countries, the difference between their expected returns must be zero. If the Canadian interest rate is 10%, and the US interest rate is 5%, according to the interest parity condition, if the difference between Canadian and US returns is zero, what accounts for the other 5% of the difference?

____

____

SELF-TEST

PART A: True-False Questions

Circle whether the following statements are true (T) or false (F).

T F 1. Most trades in the foreign exchange market involve the buying and selling of bank deposits.

T F 2. If the interest rate on euro-denominated assets is 5% and is 8% on dollar-denominated assets, then the expected return on dollar-denominated assets is higher than that on euro-denominated assets if the dollar is expected to depreciate at a 5% rate.

T F 3. When a country's currency appreciates, its goods abroad become more expensive, and foreign goods in that country become cheaper, all else constant.

T F 4. The interest parity condition does not hold if there is perfect capital mobility in international finance.

T F 5. The model of foreign exchange rate behaviour indicates that whenever the domestic interest rate rises relative to the foreign interest rate, the exchange rate appreciates.

T F 6. If a central bank lowers the growth rate of the money supply, then its currency will appreciate.

T F 7. If expected inflation in Canada rises from 5 to 8% and the interest rate rises from 7 to 9%, the dollar will appreciate.

T F 8. Forward transactions involve the immediate exchange of bank deposits.

T F 9. The phenomenon in which the exchange rate falls by more in the short run than it does in the long run when the money supply increases is called exchange rate overshooting.

T F 10. The high volatility of exchange rate movements indicates that participants in the foreign exchange market do not behave in a rational manner.

T F 11. The theory of PPP suggests that if one country's price level declines relative to another's, its currency should appreciate.

T F 12. The PPP theory provides perfect guidance to the long run and short run movements of exchange rates.

T F 13. In the long run, as a country becomes more productive relative to other countries, its currency depreciates.

T F 14. An increase in the foreign interest rate shifts the demand curve for domestic assets to the left and causes the domestic currency to depreciate.

T F 15. When domestic real interest rates rise, the domestic currency appreciates.

T F 16. A higher domestic money supply causes the domestic currency to depreciate.

T F 17. The presence of a weighted average of the inflation gap and the output gap in Taylor's rule for calculating the overnight rate may indicate that central banks should not behave as "inflation nutters".

T F 18. For the law of one price to hold, a decline in the price of the US-produced Dell computer relative to the Japanese-produced Toshiba computer means that the Yen must depreciate by the amount of the relative price increase of Dell computers over Toshiba computers.

T F 19. As the relative expected return on foreign assets increases relative to the return on domestic assets, only domestic residents will want to hold more foreign assets and fewer domestic assets.

PART B: Multiple-Choice Questions

Circle the appropriate answer.

1. When the Swiss franc appreciates (holding everything else constant), then
   a. Swiss watches sold in Canada become more expensive.
   b. Canadian computers sold in Switzerland become more expensive.
   c. Swiss army knives sold in Canada become cheaper.
   d. Canadian toothpaste sold in Switzerland becomes cheaper.
   e. both (a) and (d) of the above are true.
2. The theory of purchasing power parity indicates that if the price level in Canada rises by 5% while the price level in Mexico rises by 6%, then
   a. the dollar appreciates by 1% relative to the peso.
   b. the dollar depreciates by 1% relative to the peso.
   c. the exchange rate between the dollar and the peso remains unchanged.
   d. the dollar appreciates by 5% relative to the peso.
   e. the dollar depreciates by 5% relative to the peso.
3. If, in retaliation for "unfair" trade practices, the government imposes a quota on Japanese cars, but at the same time Japanese demand for Canadian goods increases, then in the long run
   a. the Japanese yen should appreciate relative to the dollar.
   b. the Japanese yen should depreciate relative to the dollar.
   c. the dollar should depreciate relative to the yen.
   d. it is not clear whether the dollar should appreciate or depreciate relative to the yen.
4. If the interest rate on dollar-denominated assets is 10% and it is 8% on euro-denominated assets, then if the euro is expected to appreciate at a 5% rate,
   a. dollar-denominated assets have a lower expected return than euro-denominated assets.
   b. the expected return on dollar-denominated assets in euros is 2%.
   c. the expected return on euro-denominated assets in dollars is 3%.
   d. none of the above will occur.
5. Of the following factors, which will not cause the expected return schedule for foreign deposits to shift?
   a. A change in the expected future exchange rate.
   b. A change in the foreign interest rate.
   c. A change in the current exchange rate.
   d. A change in the productivity of Canadian workers.
6. A rise in the expected future exchange rate shifts the expected return schedule on foreign deposits to the _____ and causes the exchange rate to _____.
   a. right; appreciate
   b. right; depreciate
   c. left; appreciate
   d. left; depreciate

7. A rise in the domestic interest rate is associated with
   a. a shift in the expected return schedule for domestic deposits to the right.
   b. a shift in the expected return schedule for domestic deposits to the left.
   c. a shift in the expected return schedule for foreign deposits to the right.
   d. a shift in the expected return schedule for foreign deposits to the left.
8. If the foreign interest rate rises and people expect domestic productivity to rise relative to foreign productivity, then (holding everything else constant)
   a. the expected return schedule for domestic deposits shifts left and the domestic currency appreciates.
   b. the expected return schedule for domestic deposits shifts right and the domestic currency appreciates.
   c. the expected return schedule for foreign deposits shifts left and the domestic currency depreciates.
   d. the expected return schedule for foreign deposits shifts right and the domestic currency depreciates.
   e. the effect on the exchange rate is uncertain.
9. When domestic real interest rates rise, the
   a. the expected return schedule for dollar deposits shifts to the right, and the dollar appreciates.
   b. the expected return schedule for dollar deposits shifts to the left, and the dollar appreciates.
   c. the expected return schedule for dollar deposits shifts to the right, and the dollar depreciates.
   d. the expected return schedule for dollar deposits shifts to the left, and the dollar depreciates.
10. If the interest rate on dollar deposits is 10 percent, and the dollar is expected to appreciate by seven percent over the coming year, then the expected return on the dollar deposit in terms of foreign currency is
    a. 3%.
    b. 17%.
    c. −3%.
    d. 10%.
11. If the interest rate on dollar deposits is 10 percent, and the dollar is expected to appreciate by seven percent over the coming year, then the expected return on the dollar deposit in terms of dollars is
    a. 3%.
    b. 17%.
    c. −3%.
    d. 10%.
12. Reasons why the theory of purchasing power parity might not fully explain exchange rate movements include
    a. differing monetary policies in different countries.
    b. changes in the prices of goods and services not traded internationally.
    c. changes in the domestic price level that exceed changes in the foreign price level.
    d. changes in the foreign price level that exceed changes in the domestic price level.
13. An expected _____ in _____ productivity relative to _____ productivity (holding everything else constant) causes the domestic currency to _____.
    a. rise; foreign; domestic; depreciate
    b. rise; domestic; foreign; depreciate
    c. decline; foreign; domestic; depreciate
    d. rise; foreign; domestic; appreciate
14. When the domestic nominal interest rate falls because of a decrease in expected inflation, the expected appreciation of the dollar rises, R^F shifts _____ than R^D, and the exchange rate _____.
    a. less; falls
    b. less; rises

c. more; falls
d. more; rises

15. Lowering the domestic money supply causes the domestic currency to
   a. depreciate more in the short run than in the long run.
   b. depreciate more in the long run than in the short run.
   c. appreciate more in the short run than in the long run.
   d. appreciate more in the long run than in the short run.

16. According to the theory of purchasing power parity, the rupee will depreciate by 10% against the dollar if the Canadian price level increases by _____ and the Indian price level increases by _____.
   a. 10%; 10%
   b. 10%; 0%
   c. 10%; 20%
   d. 0%; 20%
   e. 10%; 15%

17. Suppose that the current exchange rate is 1200 won per dollar. If inflation in South Korea is 8% while inflation in Canada is 5%, then PPP predicts that the exchange rate will become
   a. 1200 won per dollar.
   b. 1236 won per dollar.
   c. 1260 won per dollar.
   d. 1296 won per dollar.
   e. 1310 won per dollar.

18. Suppose that sunglasses cost 30 real in Brazil and 12 dollars in Canada. According to the law of one price, the exchange rate should be
   a. 24 dollars per real.
   b. 24 real per dollar.
   c. 0.4 real per dollar.
   d. 2.5 real per dollar.
   e. 2.5 dollars per real.

19. Currencies are traded in markets
   a. that are organized into large centralized exchanges.
   b. with over $1 trillion in exchange volume per day.
   c. where banks trade deposits denominated in various currencies.
   d. all of the above.
   e. only (b) and (c) of the above.

20. If the Mexican peso depreciates against the Canadian dollar, then which of the following is true?
   a. It takes more dollars to buy a peso.
   b. It takes fewer pesos to buy a dollar.
   c. Mexico has lost foreign exchange.
   d. The dollar has appreciated against the peso.
   e. Canadian goods are less expensive in Mexico.

21. If Canada produces a new electric automobile that is very popular and Canada exports many to Europe, then over time
    a. the euro per dollar exchange rate will fall.
    b. European cars will become less expensive in Canada.
    c. Canadian wine will become less expensive in Europe.
    d. all of the above.
    e. none of the above.

22. The interest parity condition
    a. assumes that capital is immobile.
    b. assumes that deposits in different currencies are not substitutes.
    c. explains exchange rate movements in the long run.
    d. explains interest rate movements in the short run.
    e. none of the above.

23. If the domestic real interest rate rises, then
    a. the nominal interest rate will rise if there is no change to expected inflation.
    b. the return on domestic deposits falls.
    c. the expected return on foreign deposits rises.
    d. the expected return on foreign deposits falls.

24. Exchange rates are extremely volatile because
    a. expectations about many variables change frequently.
    b. the volume of exports and imports changes every day.
    c. money neutrality may lead to exchange rate overshooting.
    d. only (a) and (b) of the above.
    e. only (a) and (c) of the above.

25. If people expect the inflation rate to rise in Europe, then
    a. the expected return on Canadian deposits falls and the Euro appreciates.
    b. the expected return on European deposits falls and the Euro depreciates.
    c. the expected return on Canadian deposits rises and the Euro depreciates.
    d. the expected return on European deposits rises and the Euro appreciates.
    e. the effect on the exchange rate is uncertain.

26. If the interest rate on euro-denominated assets is 13 percent, the interest rate on peso-denominated assets is 15 percent, and the euro is expected to appreciate by 4 percent, then the expected euro rate of return on peso-denominated assets is
    a. 19 percent.
    b. 17 percent.
    c. 15 percent.
    d. 11 percent.
    e. 9 percent.

27. The interest parity condition tells us that if the domestic interest rate is 12 percent and the foreign interest rate is 10 percent, then the expected _____ of the foreign currency is _____ percent.
    a. appreciation; 4
    b. depreciation; 4
    c. appreciation; 2
    d. depreciation; 2

28. An appreciation of the US dollar __________ the cost of American goods in Canada but __________ the cost of Canadian goods in the U.S.
    a. raises, lowers
    b. raises, keeps constant
    c. lowers, raises
    d. lowers, keeps constant
29. Which of the following affect the exchange rate?
    a. Relative price level.
    b. Trade barriers.
    c. Transportation costs.
    d. both (a) and (b).
30. Assume that $i^D=0.15$, $i^F=0.2$, $E_t=0.65$, and $E_{t+1}=0.8$. What is the rate on a one-year investment in the home and foreign country.
    a. -5%, 20%
    b. 15%, -2.5%
    c. 15%, 22%
    d. More information is needed.
31. The PPP theory holds true *only if* the following assumption is satisfied:
    a. relative goods prices are not affected by changes in the exchange rates.
    b. the exchange rate is determined by the law of one price.
    c. countries produce identical goods, and transportation costs and trade barriers are low.
    d. both countries become relatively more productive over time.
32. If Seychelles experiences increased demand for its exports and, at the same time, becomes more productive relative to other countries, then
    a. its currency will appreciate.
    b. its currency will depreciate.
    c. the effect on the value of the currency is uncertain.
    d. none of the above.
33. Defining the exchange rate as the value of domestic currency in terms of foreign currency means
    a. an appreciation of the domestic currency leads to an increase in the exchange rate.
    b. an appreciation of the domestic currency leads to a decline in the exchange rate.
    c. a depreciation of the domestic currency leads to a decline in the exchange rate.
    d. both (a) and (c) only.

CHAPTER 20

The International Financial System

CHAPTER SYNOPSIS/COMPLETIONS

The growing interdependence of Canada with other economies of the world means that our monetary policy is influenced by international financial transactions. Chapter 20 examines the international financial system and explores how it affects the way our monetary policy is conducted.

The current international environment in which exchange rates fluctuate from day to day is called a managed-float or a (1)________________ float regime. In a managed-float regime, central banks allow rates to fluctuate but intervene in the foreign exchange market in order to influence exchange rates. Interventions are of two types. An unsterilized central bank intervention in which the domestic currency is sold to purchase foreign assets leads to a gain in international reserves, an (2)________________ in the money supply, and a depreciation of the domestic currency. Sterilized central bank interventions, which involve offsetting any increase in international reserves with equal open market sales of domestic securities, have little effect on the exchange rate.

The balance of payments is a bookkeeping system for recording all payments that have a direct bearing on the movement of funds between countries. The (3)_______ _____ shows international transactions that involve currently produced goods and services. The difference between merchandise exports and imports is called the (4)________________ ________________. The capital account shows the net receipts from capital transactions, such as sales of stocks and bonds to foreigners. The official reserves transaction balance is the sum of the current account balance plus the items in the capital account. It indicates the net amount of international reserves that must move between countries to finance international transactions.

Before World War I, the world economy operated under a gold standard, under which the currencies of most countries were convertible directly into gold, thereby fixing exchange rates between countries. After World War II, the Bretton Woods system was established in order to promote a (5)________________ exchange rate system in which the U.S. dollar was convertible into gold. The Bretton Woods agreement created the International Monetary Fund (IMF), which was given the task of promoting the growth of world trade by setting rules for the maintenance of fixed exchange rates and by making loans to countries that were experiencing balance of payments difficulties. The Bretton Woods agreement also set up the World Bank in order to provide long-term loans to assist developing countries to build dams, roads, and other physical capital.

A change in a country's holdings of international reserves leads to an equal change in its monetary base, which, in turn, affects the money supply. A currency like the U.S. dollar and the euro, which is used by other countries to denominate the assets they hold as international reserves, is called a (6)________________ ________________. A reserve currency country (such as the United States) has the advantage over other countries that balance of payments deficits or surpluses do not lead to changes in holdings of international reserves and the monetary base.

The Bretton Woods system—because it did not allow for smooth and gradual adjustments in exchange rates when they became necessary—was often characterized by destabilizing balance-of-payments crises. Because countries resisted revaluing their currencies, they were often characterized by a "fundamental disequilibrium." The Bretton Woods system finally collapsed in 1971. The European Monetary System, because it is a (7)________________ exchange rate system like the Bretton Woods system, suffers the potential weakness of exchange rate crises characterized by "speculative attacks"—that is, a massive sale of a weak currency (or purchases of a strong currency) that would hasten the change in exchange rates.

Because capital flows were an important element in the currency crises in Mexico (1994), East Asia (1997), Brazil (1999), and Argentina (2001), politicians and some economists have advocated restricting capital mobility in emerging market countries. Controls on capital outflows could potentially prevent an emerging market country from being forced to (8)________________ its currency, which would otherwise exacerbate a financial crisis. Empirical evidence, however, indicates that controls are seldom effective during a crisis. Indeed, controls on capital outflows may be counterproductive because confidence in the government is weakened.

The case for controls on capital (9)________________ is stronger, as capital inflows can lead to a lending boom and excessive risk taking on the part of banks, which then helps trigger a financial crisis. Although the case for controls on capital inflows seems plausible, this regulation can lead to corruption and a serious misallocation of resources in the emerging market country.

Three international considerations affect the conduct of monetary policy: direct effects of the foreign exchange market on the money supply, balance of payments considerations, and (10)________________ considerations. If a central bank intervenes in the foreign exchange market to keep its strong currency from appreciating, as did the German central bank in the early 1970s, it (11)________________ international reserves, and the monetary base and the money supply (12)________________. In order to prevent balance of payments deficits, a country's central bank might pursue (13)________________ monetary policy.

Monetary policy is also affected by exchange rate considerations. Because an appreciation of the currency causes domestic businesses to suffer from increased foreign competition, a central bank might (14)________________ the rate of money growth in order to lower the exchange rate. Similarly, because a (15)________________ of the currency hurts consumers and stimulates inflation, a central bank might slow the rate of money growth in order to prop up the exchange rate. Because the United States has been a reserve-currency country in the post-World War II period, U.S. monetary policy has been less affected by developments in the foreign exchange market than is true for other countries.

EXERCISES

EXERCISE 1: Definitions and Terminology

Match the following terms on the right with the definition or description on the left. Place the letter of the term in the blank provided next to the appropriate definition. Terms may be used once, more than once, or not at all.

____	1. A bookkeeping system for recording all payments that have a direct bearing on the movement of funds between a country and foreign countries.	a. Speculative attack
____	2. Account that shows international transactions that involve currently produced goods and services.	b. Balance of payments
____	3. Merchandise exports less imports	c. Gold standard
____	4. Account that describes the flow of capital between Canada and other countries.	d. Trade balance
____	5. Massive sales of a weak currency or purchases of a strong currency that hasten a change in the exchange rate.	e. Current account

_____	6. The current account balance plus items in the capital account.	f.	Reserve currency
_____	7. A situation in which the par value of a currency is reset at a lower level.	g.	Capital account
_____	8. A currency (like the U.S. dollar) that is used by other countries to denominate the assets they hold as international reserves.	h.	Bretton Woods
_____	9. A regime under which the currency of most countries is directly convertible into gold.	i.	Devalue
_____	10. The international monetary system in use from 1945 to 1971 in which exchange rates were fixed and the U.S. dollar was freely convertible into gold (by foreign governments and central banks only).	j.	Official Reserve Transactions Balance

EXERCISE 2: International Reserves, the Balance of Payments, and the Monetary Base

Suppose that Canadians are buying $1 billion more goods and assets from Mexicans than the Mexicans are buying from Canadians. If Canadians pay for the Mexican goods and assets with dollars, and if Mexicans carry out their daily purchases with pesos, Mexicans will sell their dollars in the foreign exchange market to buy pesos. If the Mexican central bank does not want the pesos to appreciate, they must buy the dollars the Mexican public is holding.

A. After the Mexican central bank intervenes in the foreign exchange market, what is the effect on the balance sheet of the Mexican central bank? Answer this question by filling in the amounts in the balance sheet below.

Mexican Central Bank

Assets	Liabilities
Canadian dollars	Mexican pesos

What is the effect on the Mexican monetary base from the Mexican central bank's purchase of the $1 billion of dollars?

____

What is the effect on the Mexican central bank's holdings of international reserves?

____

Is a surplus or deficit created in the official reserve transactions balance in the Mexican balance of payments?

____

B. If the Canadian dollar is a reserve currency so that the Mexican central bank uses its $1 billion of dollars to buy Canadian securities from the Canadian public, then what is the final outcome for the balance sheet of the Mexican central bank? Answer this question by filling in the amounts in the balance sheet below.

Mexican Central Bank

Assets	Liabilities
Canadian dollars	Mexican pesos
Canadian securities	

What is the net effect on the Canadian monetary base from the Mexican central bank's intervention in the foreign exchange market?

____

Is a surplus or deficit created in the official reserve transactions balance in the Canadian balance of payments?

____

EXERCISE 3: An Unsterilized Intervention

Suppose that South Korea wants to raise the value of its currency, the won, in order to continue attracting foreign investment. The South Korean central bank, The Bank of Korea, purchases won by selling Japanese bonds denominated in yen.

A. What effect will this have on the expected return on won-denominated deposits, the future exchange rate (yen per won), and the expected return (in terms of won) on Japanese deposits?

____

____

B. Show the effect of the sale of Japanese bonds by The Bank of Korea in the foreign exchange market in the short run and the long run in Figure 20A.

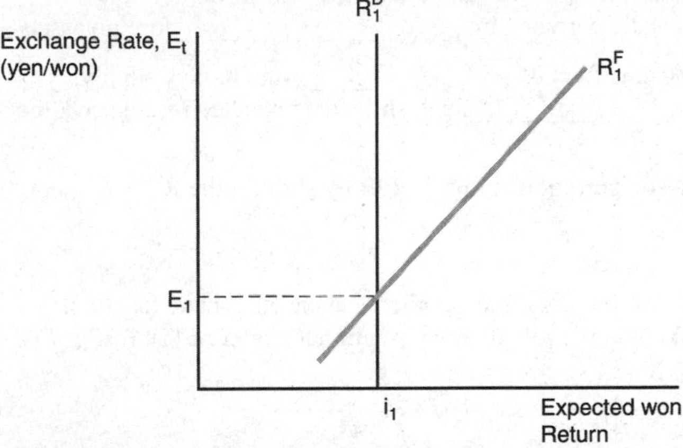

Figure 20A

EXERCISE 4: How a Fixed Exchange Rate Regime Works

The most important feature of the Bretton Woods system was that it established a fixed exchange rate regime. Figure 20B illustrates a situation in which the domestic currency is initially overvalued: the expected return on the foreign deposits schedule (R_1^F) intersects the expected return on domestic deposits schedule (R_1^D) at an exchange rate that is below the fixed par rate, E_{par}.

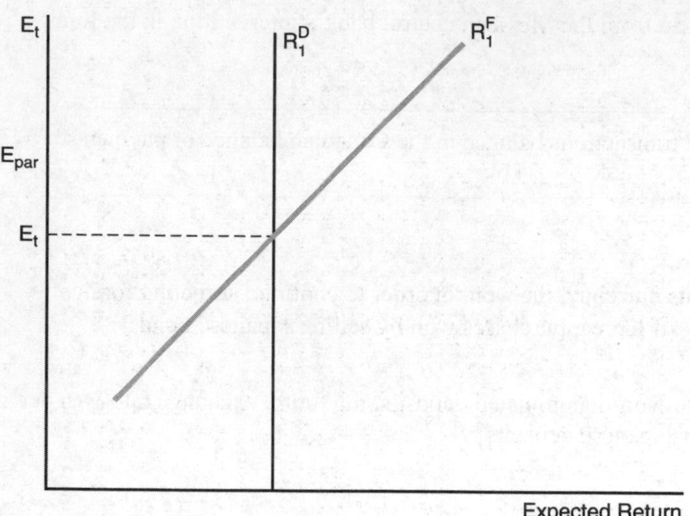

Figure 20B

A. Complete the following statements:

1. In order to return the exchange rate to equilibrium at E_{par}, the central bank must intervene in the foreign exchange market to ____________________ the domestic currency by ____________________ foreign assets.
2. The central bank's purchase of domestic currency has the effect of ________________ the money supply, causes the interest rate on domestic deposits to ____________________, and shifts the expected return schedule on domestic deposits to the ____________________.

B. Illustrate the effect of a central bank's purchase of domestic currency in Figure 20B by shifting the R^D.

EXERCISE 5: The IMF as a Lender of Last Resort

The IMF no longer attempts to encourage fixed exchange rates, but as is true of other agencies that have lost their missions, the IMF has discovered a new mission—it has taken on the role of an international lender of last resort. List the advantages and disadvantages of this new role for the IMF.

A. Advantages of the IMF as an international lender of last resort.

1. ____

____

2. ____

____

B. Disadvantages of the IMF as an international lender of last resort.

1. ____

____

2. ____

____

3. ____

____

4. ____

____

EXERCISE 6: CURRENCY BOARD AND MONETARY POLICY STRATEGY

There are two exchange-rate strategies that make it less likely that the exchange rate regime will break down in emerging-market economies – the currency board arrangement and dollarization.

A. What is a currency board regime and how does it operate?

____

____

B. Is there a difference between a currency board regime and the typical fixed exchange rate regime?

____

____

C. List two advantages of the currency board regime over a monetary policy strategy that only uses an exchange-rate target.

____

____

D. What is dollarization? List at least two ways in which dollarization differs from a currency board regime.

____

____

E. List at least three disadvantages common to both dollarization and the currency board regime. Is there an additional disadvantage to dollarization that is not common to a currency board?

____

____

____

SELF-TEST

PART A: True-False Questions

Circle whether the following statements are true (T) or false (F).

T F 1. The capital account balance indicates whether the country is increasing or decreasing its claims on foreign wealth.

T F 2. The current account balance equals the difference between exports and imports.

T F 3. When the domestic currency is undervalued in a fixed exchange rate regime, the country's central bank must intervene in the foreign exchange market to purchase the domestic currency by selling foreign assets.

T F 4. The gold standard of the late nineteenth century always prevented inflation from developing.

T F 5. A particular problem with a fixed exchange rate system (or regime) is that it is periodically subject to speculative attacks on currencies.

T F 6. Special drawing rights (SDRs) are IMF loans to member countries.

T F 7. The World Bank makes loans to countries suffering balance of payments difficulties.

T F 8. The current international financial system is perhaps best described as a hybrid of fixed and flexible exchange rate systems.

T F 9. The IMF has, since the 1980s, been acting as an international lender of last resort.

T F 10. Monetary policy in a reserve currency country is less influenced by balance of payments deficits because they will be financed by other countries' interventions in the foreign exchange market.

T F 11. When the domestic currency is overvalued, the central bank must purchase domestic currency to keep the exchange rate fixed, but as a result it loses international reserves.

T F 12. A central bank's sale of domestic currency to purchase foreign assets in the foreign exchange market results in an equal rise in its international reserves and the monetary base.

T F 13. Under the Bretton Woods system, the U.S. dollar was overvalued if the equilibrium exchange rate was below the par value.

T F 14. A sterilized intervention in the foreign exchange market by a central bank will have no effect on the exchange rate because the central bank does not purchase or sell international reserves.

PART B: Multiple-Choice Questions

Circle the appropriate answer.

1. Which of the following appear as payments in the Canadian balance of payments?
   a. French purchases of Canadian jeans
   b. Purchases by Japanese tourists in Canada
   c. Interest payments to Germans who hold Canadian bonds
   d. Income earned by Nortel from its business abroad

2. Which of the following appears in the current account part of the balance of payments?
   a. An Italian's purchase of Nortel stock
   b. Income earned by Barclay's Bank of London, England, from subsidiaries in Canada
   c. A loan by a Swiss bank to a Canadian corporation
   d. A purchase by the Bank of Canada of an English Treasury bond
   e. None of the above

3. If Canadians are buying $1 billion more English goods and assets than the English are willing to buy from Canada, and so the Bank of England therefore sells $1 billion worth of pounds in the foreign exchange market, then
   a. England gains $1 billion of international reserves and its monetary base rises by $1 billion.
   b. England loses $1 billion of international reserves and its monetary base falls by $1 billion.
   c. England gains $1 billion of international reserves and its monetary base falls by $1 billion.
   d. England loses $1 billion of international reserves and its monetary base rises by $1 billion.
   e. England's level of international reserves and monetary base remains unchanged.

4. An important advantage for a reserve currency country is that
   a. its balance of payments deficits are financed by other countries' interventions in the foreign exchange market.
   b. it has more control over its monetary policy than non-reserve currency countries.
   c. it has more control over its exchange rate than non-reserve currency countries.
   d. both (a) and (b) of the above are true.

5. Under a gold standard in which one dollar could be turned into the U.S. Treasury and exchanged for 1/20th of an ounce of gold and one Swiss franc could be exchanged for 1/60th of an ounce of gold,
   a. at an exchange rate of 4 francs per dollar, gold would flow from the United States to Switzerland and the Swiss monetary base would fall.
   b. at an exchange rate of 4 francs per dollar, gold would flow from Switzerland to the United States and the Swiss

monetary base would rise.

c. at an exchange rate of 2 francs per dollar, gold would flow from the United States to Switzerland and the U.S. monetary base would fall.

d. at an exchange rate of 2 francs per dollar, gold would flow from Switzerland to the United States and the U.S. monetary base would rise.

6. In a speculative attack against a weak currency under a fixed exchange rate system, the central bank for this country must shift the expected return schedule for domestic deposits further to the _____ through the _____ of international reserves.
   a. left; purchase
   b. right; sale
   c. left; sale
   d. right; purchase

7. Countries with deficits in their balance of payments often do not want to see their currencies depreciate because
   a. this would hurt consumers in their country by making foreign goods more expensive.
   b. this would stimulate inflation.
   c. this would hurt domestic businesses by making foreign goods cheaper in their country.
   d. this would hurt domestic businesses by making their goods more expensive abroad.
   e. of both (a) and (b) of the above.

8. The International Monetary Fund is an international organization that
   a. promotes the growth of trade by setting rules for how tariffs and quotas are set by countries.
   b. makes loans to countries to finance projects such as dams and roads.
   c. since the 1980s, has been acting as an international lender of last resort.
   d. does each of the above.

9. When a central bank buys its currency in the foreign exchange market,
   a. they acquire international reserves.
   b. they lose international reserves.
   c. the money supply will increase.
   d. both (a) and (b) of the above occur.

10. A central bank's international reserves rise when
    a. it sells domestic currency to purchase foreign assets in the foreign exchange market.
    b. it sells foreign currency to purchase domestic assets in the foreign exchange market.
    c. it buys domestic currency with the sale of foreign assets in the foreign exchange market.
    d. it buys gold with the sale of foreign assets in the foreign exchange market.

11. Under the Bretton Woods system, the U.S. dollar was _____ if the _____ exchange rate (expressed as units of foreign currency per dollar) was _____ the _____ value of the exchange rate.
    a. overvalued; equilibrium; below; par
    b. overvalued; equilibrium; above; par
    c. undervalued; par; above; equilibrium
    d. undervalued; equilibrium; below; par

12. A central bank that wants to _____ its currency is likely to adopt a _____ monetary policy.
    a. strengthen; less contractionary
    b. strengthen; more contractionary
    c. weaken; less expansionary
    d. weaken; more contractionary

13. A central bank _____ of domestic currency and corresponding _____ of foreign assets in the foreign exchange market leads to an equal decline in its international _____ and the monetary base.
    a. sale; purchase; reserves
    b. sale; sale; liabilities
    c. purchase; sale; reserves
    d. purchase; purchase; liabilities
14. A higher domestic money supply leads to a higher domestic price level in the long run, resulting in an expected _____ of the domestic currency that shifts the _____ schedule to the _____.
    a. depreciation; R^F; right
    b. appreciation; R^F; right
    c. depreciation; R^D; left
    d. appreciation; R^D; left
15. If the central bank decreases the money supply, domestic interest rates rise causing R^D to shift _____, while causing R^F to shift _____ because of the expected appreciation of the dollar.
    a. right; left
    b. right; right
    c. left; left
    d. left; right
16. A case can be made for controls on capital inflows because capital inflows
    a. can lead to a lending boom and encourage excessive risk taking.
    b. never go to financing productive investments.
    c. never finance productive investments and can lead to a lending boom and encourage excessive risk taking.
    d. are more effective in preventing financial crises than are policies that regulate banking activities.
17. A sterilized intervention in the foreign exchange market by a central bank will have no effect on the exchange rate because
    a. the central bank does not purchase or sell international reserves.
    b. the amount of international reserves held by the central bank is unchanged.
    c. the monetary base of the central bank is unchanged.
    d. the central bank simultaneously sells and buys foreign exchange.
18. When a central bank performs an unsterilized intervention in the foreign exchange market, the money supply _____ changes.
    a. always
    b. usually
    c. sometimes
    d. never
19. Which of the following will make the exchange rate rise from 3.5 Brazilian real per Canadian dollar to 3.7 real per dollar?
    a. The Brazilian central bank sells Brazilian government bonds.
    b. The Brazilian central bank sells Canadian dollars.
    c. The Bank of Canada sells Canadian dollars.
    d. The Bank of Canada sells Canada bonds.
    e. None of the above.

20. The current account balance may indicate future changes in the exchange rate because
    a. the current account shows what is happening to the demand for imports and exports.
    b. the current account indicates what will happen to claims on foreign wealth in the future.
    c. any change to the current account must be paid for by a change in net government international reserves.
    d. only (a) and (b) of the above.
    e. only (a) and (c) of the above.
21. If Singapore's current account is $300 billion, and its capital account is –$250 billion, then the central bank of Singapore _____ net holdings of international reserves by _____ .
    a. increased; $550 billion
    b. decreased; $550 billion
    c. increased; $50 billion
    d. decreased; $50 billion
22. If a newspaper reports that Nigeria's balance of payments has a deficit of $50 billion, then which of the following is true?
    a. The capital account is –$50 billion.
    b. The current account minus the capital account is $50 billion.
    c. The official reserve transactions balance is –$50 billion.
    d. The Nigerian central bank acquired $50 billion worth of international reserves.
23. One benefit of the gold standard is that
    a. a country has greater control of its money supply.
    b. inflation and deflation are less severe.
    c. exchange rates tend to return to their par value.
    d. gold is not traded between countries.
24. Countries experiencing a foreign exchange crisis, such as Mexico and Brazil did in the 1990s,
    a. are also experiencing a balance-of-payments crisis.
    b. may turn to the World Bank for help.
    c. are gaining international reserves.
    d. can revalue their currencies to end the crisis.
    e. only (a) and (c) of the above.
25. If the exchange rate between the Thai baht and the U.S. dollar is fixed, and if the Thai baht is overvalued, then Thailand will need to _____ international reserves or _____ the baht.
    a. sell; devalue
    b. purchase; revalue
    c. sell; revalue
    d. purchase; devalue
26. A disadvantage of capital controls in emerging market economies is that
    a. there are ways for capital to avoid the controls.
    b. they divert attention away from other important causes of financial instability.
    c. they may lead to corruption and bribery of governmental officials.
    d. all of the above.
    e. only (b) and (c) of the above.
27. If a central bank engages in a sterilized intervention, then there is no
    a. impact on the monetary base.

b. effect on the exchange rate.
c. impact on the money supply.
d. all of the above.
e. only (a) and (b) of the above.

28. The "rules of the game" under a gold standard means that a country
a. experiences deflation when world gold production increases.
b. experiences inflation when world gold production slows.
c. loses control over monetary policy.
d. all of the above.
e. only (a) and (c).

29. In the case of an unsterilized intervention, if the Bank of Canada decides to sell foreign assets, the Canadian price level will _______ in the long run and the expected future exchange rate will _______.
a. fall, fall
b. rise, rise
c. rise, fall
d. fall, rise

30. Exchange-rate targeting _______ the probability of speculative attacks, and provides ________ control on inflation.
a. increases, more
b. decreases, more
c. increases, less
d. decreases, less

31. An unsterilized intervention in which the domestic currency is sold to purchase foreign assets leads to
a. a gain in international reserves, an increase in the money supply, and a depreciation of the domestic currency.
b. a gain in international reserves, an increase in the money supply, and an appreciation of the domestic currency.
c. a gain in international reserves, a decrease in the money supply, and a depreciation of the domestic currency.
d. a gain in international reserves, a decrease in the money supply, and an appreciation of the domestic currency.

32. When the domestic currency is undervalued, in order to keep the exchange rate fixed, the central bank must
a. sell domestic currency .
b. buy domestic currency.
c. sell foreign currency.
d. buy foreign currency.

33. The higher the money supply, the ____ price level in the long run; and so, the future exchange rate is _____.
a. lower; lower
b. lower; higher
c. higher; lower
d. higher; higher

34. If Canada's current account is $900 billion, and its capital account is -$800 billion, then the central bank of Canada has a(n) _____ net holdings of international reserves of ______.
a. increased; $1700 billion
b. decreased; $1700 billion
c. increased; $100 billion
d. decreased; $100 billion

CHAPTER 21

The Demand for Money

CHAPTER SYNOPSIS/COMPLETIONS

Chapter 21 discusses in chronological order the major developments in the theory of the demand for money. These developments have attempted to explain the reasons people hold money and to what extent the quantity of money demanded is affected by changes in interest rates.

The earliest treatment of the demand for money was offered by the classical economists. The classical economists—most notably Irving Fisher—argued that the demand for money was a function of nominal aggregate income. This followed from their assumptions regarding (1)__________________ (the average number of times per year that a dollar is spent on final goods and services produced in the economy) and the equation of exchange.

The classical economists argued that the speed with which money is spent is a function of the institutional features of the economy. Although these features certainly change over time (due to improvements in technology, for example), velocity could be regarded as (2)__________ in the short run.

Nothing more than an identity, the equation of (3)______________________ states that the quantity of money times velocity must equal nominal income. But when combined with Irving Fisher's assumption of a constant velocity, the equation of exchange is transformed into the quantity theory of (4)__________________. Given the assumption of constant velocity, the quantity theory of money implies that changes in nominal income are determined solely by changes in the quantity of money. The classical economists also assumed that prices and wages were completely (5)______________________, meaning that the economy would always remain at full employment. This last assumption meant that changes in the money supply had no effect on aggregate output and could therefore affect only the (6)__________________ __________________.

Dividing both sides of the equation of exchange by the constant velocity makes clear that the quantity of money people hold is a constant fraction of nominal income. Thus, the classical economists regarded the demand for money as a demand for a medium of exchange.

John Maynard Keynes believed that a decline in velocity helped to explain the Great Depression, and his efforts to explain this decline in velocity led to his theory of money demand, which he called the (7)______________________ ______________________ theory. Keynes contended that there were three separate and distinct motives for holding money: the transactions motive, the precautionary motive, and the (8)______________________ motive.

It was the speculative motive that distinguished Keynes's theory from the other theories. Keynes argued that interest rates played an important role in determining the amount of wealth people desire to hold in the form of money. Though bonds pay interest, a rise in interest rates causes bond values to (9)__________________, subjecting their holders to capital losses and even negative returns if bond values fall significantly. Thus at low rates of interest, people reduce their holdings of bonds and hold more money as they expect interest rates to rise, returning to their normal levels. Therefore, Keynes concluded that the demand for money was (10)________________________ related to the level of interest rates.

Since Keynes's early attempt, economists have improved on his analysis providing a better rationale for the (11)__________________ relationship between interest rates and velocity. The works of Baumol and Tobin indicate that the transaction component (and, by extension, the precautionary component) of the demand for money is negatively related to the level of interest rates.

Friedman—noting that the interest rate paid on chequing deposits tends to move with market rates so that the differential between market interest rates and the interest rate paid on money remains relatively constant—believes that changes in interest rates will have little effect on the demand for money. This result does not require the absence of deposit rate ceilings, as banks pay implicit interest on deposits by providing "free" services such as branch offices, more tellers, or "free" chequing. Additionally, Friedman differs from Keynes in believing that the money demand function is stable and therefore velocity is predictable. To Friedman, the money supply is the main determinant of nominal income.

Milton Friedman has offered an alternative explanation for the (12)__________________ behaviour of velocity. Rather than rely on the procyclical behaviour of interest rates, Friedman argues that since changes in actual income exceed changes in permanent income, velocity will tend to move procyclically.

Research on the demand for money indicates that while the demand for money is sensitive to interest rates, there is little evidence that the liquidity trap has ever existed. Also, because of the rapid pace of financial innovation, since 1973, the demand for money has been quite unstable. It is because of this instability that setting rigid money supply targets in order to control aggregate spending in the economy may not be an effective way to conduct monetary policy.

EXERCISES

EXERCISE 1: The Keynesian Approach to Money Demand

A. What are the three motives behind the demand for money postulated by Keynes?

1. ______________________________
2. ______________________________
3. ______________________________

B. What motive did Keynes believe was a function of the interest rate?

1. ______________________________

C. Tobin's model of the speculative demand for money shows that people hold money as a store of wealth as a way of reducing

____

EXERCISE 2: Velocity and the Quantity Theory of Money

Complete the following table.

	M	V	P	Y
	200	5	1	1000
1.	200	6	2	____
2.	300	5	1.5	____
3.	400	6	____	1200
4.	400	____	1	1600
5.	____	5	2	2000

EXERCISE 3: The Demand for Money

Indicate whether the following statements are associated with Fisher's quantity theory of money (Q), Keynes's liquidity preference theory (K), or with Friedman's modern quantity theory of money (F). Place the appropriate letter in the blank to the left of the statement.

_____ 1. Interest rates have no effect on the demand for money.

_____ 2. There are three distinct motives for holding money: (a) a transactions motive, where money balances are held if there is imperfect synchronization between receipts and expenditures; (b) a precautionary motive, where money is held because of uncertainty of future expenditures; and (c) a speculative motive, where money is held if bonds are expected to fall in value.

_____ 3. Permanent income is the primary determinant of money demand, and changes in interest rates should have little effect on the demand for money.

_____ 4. The demand for money is insensitive to interest rates, not because the demand for money is insensitive to changes in the opportunity cost of holding money, but because changes in interest rates actually have little effect on the opportunity cost of holding money.

_____ 5. More recent developments in this approach suggest that interest rates are important to the transactions and precautionary components of money demand, as well as to the speculative component.

_____ 6. The transactions and precautionary components of the demand for money are proportional to income, while the speculative component is negatively related to the level of interest rates.

_____ 7. Movements in the price level result solely from changes in the quantity of money.

_____ 8. The demand for money is purely a function of income; interest rates have no effect on the demand for money.

_____ 9. Theory that offered an explanation for the decline in velocity during the Great Depression.

_____ 10. The demand for money is a function of both permanent income and the opportunity cost of holding money.

EXERCISE 4: The Interest Rate in the Keynesian Money Demand Function

Keynes believed that the demand for real money balances, $\frac{M^d}{P}$, is a function of the interest rate, i, and real income, Y.

Suppose that the Keynesian money demand function is

$$\frac{M^d}{P} = f(i, Y) = \frac{Y}{100i}$$

and that real income is 1000.

A. If the interest rate is 4% (=0.04) then what is the demand for real money balances?

____

____

B. What is the velocity of money?

____

____

C. If the interest rate rises to 5% (=0.05) then what is the demand for real money balances? How does this compare to your answer in part (A)?

D. What is the velocity of money at the higher interest rate? How does this compare to your answer in part (B)?

EXERCISE 5: Quantity Theory of Money

A. If a country's price level is $12 and a country's aggregate output is 5, and the quantity of money is 4, what is the number of times per year that a dollar is spent?

B. What did Keynes' liquidity preference theory state were the three motives for holding money?

C. What did Keynes' liquidity preference theory state with respect to money demand and interest rates?

SELF-TEST

PART A: True-False Questions

Circle whether the following statements are true (T) or false (F).

T F 1. The equation of exchange states that the product of the quantity of money and the average number of times that a dollar is spent on final goods and services in a given period must equal nominal income.

T F 2. Irving Fisher argued that velocity would be relatively constant in the short run, since institutional features of the economy, such as the speed at which cheques were cleared, were likely to change only slowly over time.

T F 3. The classical economists' contention that velocity could be regarded as a constant transformed the equation of exchange (an identity) into the quantity theory of money.

T F 4. Friedman believes that the demand for money is affected by changes in current income.

T F 5. At relatively low interest rates, people might be reluctant to hold money due to a concern about capital losses should interest rates rise.

T F 6. Keynes's liquidity preference theory offered an explanation for why velocity had fallen during the Great Depression.

T F 7. The demand for money approach developed by Keynes is consistent with the procyclical movements in velocity observed in Canada.

T F 8. Studies by economists show that the liquidity trap was common before 1973.

T F 9. James Tobin suggested that people might prefer to hold money to bonds as a store of wealth in an effort to reduce risk.

T F 10. The permanent income argument in Friedman's demand for money formulation suggests that velocity will fluctuate with business cycle movements.

T F 11. The main difference between Keynes's formulation and the classical demand for money is that the former relates it to the interest rate.

T F 12. The liquidity preference theory of Keynes states that the demand for precautionary money is determined by the interest rate.

T F 13. The transaction component of the demand for money is negatively related to the level of the interest rate.

T F 14. Unlike Keynes's theory, Friedman's theory suggests that changes in interest rates should have little effect on the demand for money.

T F 15. With Keynes's liquidity preference theory, permanent income is the primary determinant of money demand, and changes in interest rates should have little effect on the demand for money.

PART B: Multiple-Choice Questions

Circle the appropriate answer.

1. The quantity theory of money suggests that cutting the money supply by one-third will lead to
   a. a sharp decline in output by one-third in the short run and a decline in the price level by one-third in the long run.
   b. a decline in output by one-third.
   c. a decline in output by one-sixth and a decline in the price level by one-sixth.
   d. a decline in the price level by one-third.
   e. none of the above.
2. The classical economists believed that velocity could be regarded as constant in the short run, since
   a. institutional factors, such as the speed with which cheques were cleared through the banking system, changed slowly over time.
   b. the opportunity cost of holding money was close to zero.
   c. financial innovation tended to offset changes in interest rates.
   d. none of the above are true.
3. Empirical evidence supports the contention that
   a. velocity tends to be procyclical; that is, velocity declines (increases) when economic activity contracts (expands).
   b. velocity tends to be countercyclical; that is, velocity declines (increases) when economic activity contracts (expands).
   c. velocity tends to be countercyclical; that is, velocity increases (declines) when economic activity contracts (expands).
   d. velocity is essentially a constant.

4. Keynes's liquidity preference theory explains why velocity can be expected to rise when
   a. income increases.
   b. wealth increases.
   c. brokerage commissions increase.
   d. interest rates increase.
5. Keynes argued that people were more likely to increase their money holdings if they believed that
   a. interest rates were about to fall.
   b. bond prices were about to rise.
   c. bond prices were about to fall.
   d. none of the above are true.
6. The Baumol-Tobin analysis suggests that
   a. velocity is relatively constant.
   b. the transactions component of money demand is negatively related to the level of interest rates.
   c. the speculative motive for money is nonexistent.
   d. both (a) and (c) of the above are true.
   e. both (b) and (c) of the above are true.
7. One possible implication of the elimination of deposit rate ceilings is that the implicit interest rate on money will more closely approach bond rates. This suggests that changes in interest rates will
   a. have a greater impact on money demand.
   b. have less effect on the demand for money.
   c. no longer affect the speculative demand for money.
   d. cause velocity to become more volatile.
8. Milton Friedman argues that the demand for money is relatively insensitive to interest rates because
   a. the demand for money is insensitive to changes in the opportunity cost of holding money.
   b. competition among banks keeps the opportunity cost of holding money relatively constant.
   c. people base their investment decisions on expected profits, not interest rates.
   d. transactions are not subject to scale economics as wealth increases.
9. Friedman's belief regarding the interest insensitivity of the demand for money implies that
   a. the quantity of money is the primary determinant of aggregate spending.
   b. velocity is countercyclical.
   c. both (a) and (b) of the above are correct.
   d. neither (a) nor (b) of the above are correct.
10. In Friedman's view, because income tends to decline relative to permanent income during business cycle contractions, the demand for money with respect to actual income will increase, causing velocity to
    a. rise.
    b. decline.
    c. remain unchanged, since velocity is only sensitive to changes in interest rates.
    d. decline, provided that interest rates increase when the economy contracts.
11. The velocity of money is best defined as
    a. the average real money balances that are held in one month.
    b. the average number of times per year that a dollar is spent in buying aggregate output.
    c. the average amount of money that a person spends over one year.
    d. the average number of months that a currency bill circulates.

12. The equation of exchange, MV = PY,
    a. is an equation that is always true.
    b. is an equation that is never true.
    c. is an equation that holds only if velocity is constant.
    d. was disproved by Keynes.
    e. was proved correct by Friedman.
13. Which of the following may lead to a change in velocity?
    a. A reduction in the interest rate.
    b. A change in monetary institutions.
    c. A change in the money demand function.
    d. All of the above.
    e. None of the above.
14. The quantity theory of money predicts that movements in the price level result solely from changes in the quantity of money because
    a. velocity and aggregate real output are assumed to be constant in the short run.
    b. velocity is assumed to be constant in the short run.
    c. the price level changes slowly.
    d. the money supply is constant in the long run.
    e. None of the above.
15. Keynes' _____ motive states that people hold real money balances as a cushion against unexpected need.
    a. quantity
    b. speculative
    c. transactions
    d. savings
    e. precautionary
16. Keynes' speculative demand for money predicts that people will hold either money or bonds, but not both money and bonds at the same time. This shortcoming was overcome by Tobin who reasoned that _____ , in addition to expected return, was important to the demand for money.
    a. capital gain
    b. longevity
    c. risk
    d. the interest rate
17. According to Keynes, the demand for real money balances _____ and velocity falls when the interest rate _____.
    a. falls; falls
    b. rises; falls
    c. falls; rises
    d. rises; rises
18. Friedman applied the theory of _____ to the demand for money.
    a. liquidity preference
    b. permanent wealth
    c. asset demand
    d. speculation

19. Friedman's concept of permanent income is best defined as
    a. transitory income.
    b. the opportunity cost of holding money.
    c. expected average holdings of stocks and bonds.
    d. expected average long-run income.
    e. none of the above.

20. According to Friedman, velocity is predictable because
    a. the relationship between income and permanent income is predictable.
    b. interest rates do not change very much.
    c. the money demand function is stable.
    d. only (a) and (b) of the above.
    e. only (a) and (c) of the above.

21. According to Keynes, when the interest rate was below a "normal" value, people would expect the price of bonds to _____ and the quantity demanded of money would _____.
    a. increase; increase
    b. increase; decrease
    c. decrease; increase
    d. decrease; decrease

22. If money demand is _____ sensitive to interest rates, then velocity will be _____ predictable.
    a. more; more
    b. less; more
    c. more; less
    d. less; less

23. The demand for real money will increase if
    a. interest rates increase.
    b. interest rates decrease.
    c. income increases.
    d. income decreases.
    e. both (b) and (c) of the above.

24. The liquidity preference theory indicates that a rise in the interest rate ______ velocity.
    a. decreases
    b. increases
    c. has no effect on
    d. might change

25. According to the demand for money model of Baumol and Tobin, in which case does the demand for transactions money increase?
    a. A rise in brokerage fee.
    b. An increase in interest rate.
    c. An increase in income.
    d. All of the above.

26. Which one of the following money demand functions includes inflation?
    a. Money demand function of Keynes.
    b. Money demand function of Fisher.
    c. Money demand function of Baumol and Tobin.
    d. Money demand function of Friedman.

27. According to Friedman's modern quantity theory of money, if the expected inflation rate is 5% and the expected return of money is 2.5%, then the demand for money will
    a. increase.
    b. decrease.
    c. remain unchanged.
    d. double.

28. Speculative component of money demand is sensitive to
    a. interest rate.
    b. expectations about interest rate.
    c. income and interest rate.
    d. both (a) and (b) of above.

29. It is believed that the main source of unstable money demand after 1973 is the
    a. increase in velocity.
    b. rapid pace of financial innovation.
    c. business cycles.
    d. fluctuations in interest rate.

30. Fisher emphasized ________ and ruled out any possible effect of interest rates on the demand for money in the ________.
    a. technological factors, long run.
    b. technological factors, short run.
    c. individual choice, long run.
    d. individual choice, short run.

CHAPTER 22

The ISLM Model

CHAPTER SYNOPSIS/COMPLETIONS

This chapter presents the simple Keynesian model and introduces the ISLM model of simultaneous money and goods markets equilibrium. These models allow us to better understand the functioning of the economy and to better assess the effects of fiscal and monetary policy actions. In addition, the ISLM model is used to derive the aggregate demand curve that is used in aggregate demand and supply analysis.

The Keynesian model arose from John Maynard Keynes's concern with explaining the cause of the Great Depression. Keynes came to the conclusion that the dramatic decline in economic activity was the result of insufficient (1)____________________ ____________________. Aggregate demand in an open economy is the sum of four components of spending: consumer expenditure, (2)____________________, government expenditure, and net exports. A decline in any one of these components causes output to decline, potentially leading to recession and rising unemployment.

The Keynesian model, though highly simplified, provides a framework that is very useful for understanding fluctuations in aggregate output. This is more easily accomplished by examining the individual spending components separately.

Keynes argued that consumer expenditure is primarily determined by the level of disposable (3)____________________. As income increases, consumers will increase their expenditures. The change in consumer expenditures that results from an additional dollar of disposable income is referred to as the (4)____________________ ____________________ to consume, or simply *mpc*. At low levels of income it is likely that individuals consume more than their disposable income. Thus some amount of consumer expenditure is (5)____________________, that is, independent of disposable income. This description of consumption behaviour is summarized by the consumption function, where autonomous consumption is represented by a constant term, *a*, and the positive slope of the function is given by the *mpc*.

Investment spending includes fixed investment (spending by business on equipment and structures, and by households on residential houses) and planned inventory investment. (6)____________________ ____________________ is the spending by business on additional holdings of raw materials, parts, and finished goods.

Keynes believed that managers' expectations of future conditions, as well as interest rates, explained the level of planned investment. If actual investment (the sum of fixed investment and unplanned inventory investment) differs from desired investment (fixed investment plus (7)____________________ inventory investment), then the actions of business firms will move the economy toward a new equilibrium. Consider a situation where business firms' inventories have risen above desired levels. Because firms find inventories costly to hold, they will cut production in an attempt to reduce their excess inventories. Aggregate output will fall and the desired level of inventories will eventually be restored.

After this equilibrium is achieved, business firms may become more optimistic about the future health of the economy. As business firms spend more, inventory levels will fall below desired levels, inducing a further expansion in aggregate output. Hence, the initial increase in investment spending is likely to cause a multifold increase in aggregate output. The ratio of the change in aggregate output to the change in investment spending is called the expenditure (8)____________________.

An increase in investment spending causes aggregate output to expand by an amount greater than the initial change because consumer expenditure also increases. As firms expand output, they hire more factor inputs such as labour, raising households' disposable incomes. Consumers respond by spending more, leading to a further expansion in output and creating a multifold increase. Since this multifold increase is dependent on additional consumer expenditure, it is not surprising that the value of the *mpc* is used to determine the value of the multiplier.

Once government spending and taxes are added to the simple Keynesian model, policy decisions can be evaluated. Although the tax multiplier is smaller than the government expenditure multiplier, changes in either taxes or government spending can be effective in returning the economy to a full (9)______________ equilibrium.

The ISLM model allows one to determine the influence monetary policy has on the economy in the Keynesian framework. The (10)________ curve illustrates that at lower interest rates, the level of investment spending and aggregate output is greater. Because the IS curve represents goods market equilibrium, the economy must be on the IS curve to be in general equilibrium. Goods market equilibrium is not, however, sufficient to guarantee general equilibrium; the economy must also be on the LM curve.

The LM curve slopes up, indicating that as income rises, a (11)________________ interest rate is required to maintain money market equilibrium. The increase in money demand due to an increase in (12)______________ must be exactly offset by the decrease in money demand due to the increase in the interest rate.

The ISLM model determines both the level of aggregate output and interest rates when the price level is fixed. Therefore, the ISLM model can be used to illustrate the effect on aggregate output and interest rates of monetary or fiscal policy actions, a topic extensively discussed in the next chapter.

EXERCISES

EXERCISE 1: Definitions and Terminology

Match the following terms on the right with the definition or description on the left. Place the letter of the term in the blank provided next to the appropriate definition.

	Definition		Term
_____	1. Spending by business firms on equipment and structures, and planned spending on residential houses.	a.	Planned investment
_____	2. Spending by business firms on additional holdings of raw materials, parts, and finished goods, calculated as the change in holdings in a given time period.	b.	Consumer expenditure
_____	3. Used by economic forecasters, this model explains how interest rates and aggregate output are determined for a fixed price level.	c.	"Animal spirits"
_____	4. Total demand for consumer goods and services.	d.	IS Curve
_____	5. Planned spending by business firms on equipment, structures, raw materials, parts and finished goods, and planned spending on residential houses.	e.	Expenditure multiplier
_____	6. Total quantity demanded of output produced in the economy.	f.	LM Curve
_____	7. Aggregate income less taxes, or the total income available for spending.	g.	Fixed investment
_____	8. Consumer expenditure that is independent of disposable income.	h.	Inventory investment

_____ 9. The change in consumer expenditure that results from an additional dollar of disposable income.

_____ 10. Government purchases of goods and services.

_____ 11. The relationship that describes the combinations of aggregate output and interest rates for which the goods market is in equilibrium.

_____ 12. The relationship that describes the combination of interest rates and aggregate output for which the money market is in equilibrium.

_____ 13. Emotional waves of business optimism and pessimism that Keynes believed dominated fluctuations in planned investment spending.

_____ 14. The ratio of the change in aggregate output to the change in planned investment spending.

_____ 15. The relationship between aggregate output and aggregate demand that shows the expenditure quantity of aggregate output demanded for each level of aggregate output.

i. ISLM model

j. Disposable income

k. Marginal propensity to consume

l. Aggregate demand

m. Government spending

n. Aggregate demand function

o. Autonomous consumer expenditure

EXERCISE 2: The Consumption Function

This exercise examines the relationship between the level of disposable income and consumer expenditures known as the consumption function.

A. Assume that the consumption function is given by $C = 50 + 0.75Y_D$. Complete the following table:

Point	Disposable Income (Y_D)	Change in Y_D	Change in C	Autonomous Consumption	Total Consumption
A	0	_____	_____	50	_____
B	100	_____	_____	_____	_____
C	200	_____	_____	_____	_____
D	300	_____	_____	_____	_____
E	400	_____	_____	_____	_____
F	500	_____	_____	_____	_____

B. In Figure 22A, plot the points on the consumption function you derived in the table.

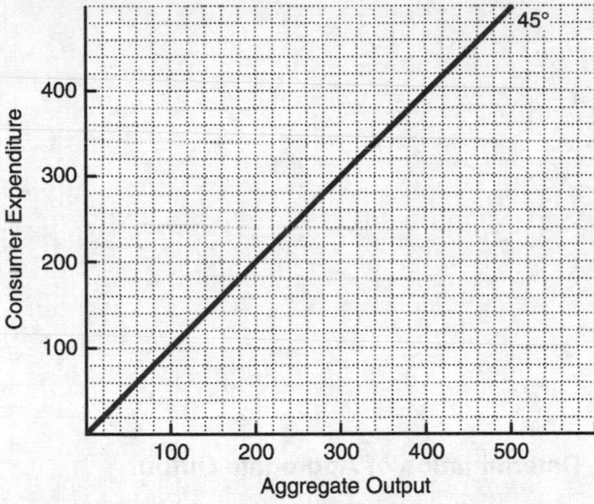

Figure 22A

EXERCISE 3: Determination of Equilibrium Aggregate Output

Suppose that for a particular economy, planned investment spending is 10, government spending is 10, taxes are zero, net exports are zero, and consumer expenditure is given by the consumption function:

$$C = 20 + 0.8\ Y_D$$

which is plotted in Figure 22B.

A. Plot the aggregate demand function and mark it as Y_1^{ad} in Figure 22B.

B. What is the equilibrium level of aggregate output? $Y_1 =$ ______________

C. If planned investment spending rises to 30, draw in the new aggregate demand function, Y_2^{ad}. What is the new equilibrium level of aggregate output?

$Y_2 =$ ______________

D. What is the value of the expenditure multiplier? ______________

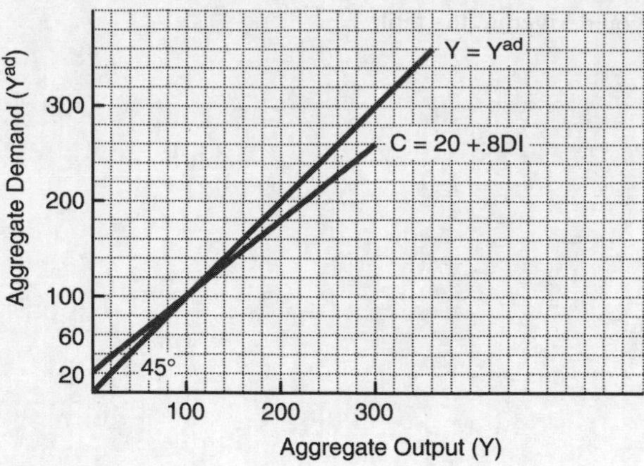

Figure 22B

EXERCISE 4: Unplanned Inventory Investment and the Determination of Aggregate Output

Assume that planned investment spending is equal to 100, government spending is equal to 200, taxes are zero, net exports are zero, and consumer expenditure is given by:

$$C = 100 + 0.9Y_d$$

A. Write down the equation describing the aggregate demand function.

____

B. If current aggregate output is 3000, what is the level of unplanned inventory investment?

____

C. What will happen to the level of aggregate output in the next time period?

____

D. At what level of aggregate output will unplanned inventory disinvestment be zero?

____

E. At what level will aggregate output eventually settle?

____

EXERCISE 5: The Response of Aggregate Output

In the following matrix there is noted at the top of each column Autonomous Consumer Expenditure, Induced Consumer Expenditure, Planned Investment Spending, Government Spending, and Equilibrium Aggregate Income. At the beginning of each row there is a hypothetical change in some variable in the model. In each cell of the matrix indicate by a, +, –, or 0 whether the assumed change will increase, decrease, or cause no change in the variables in each column for the model in the text.

	Consumer Autonomous	Expenditure Induced	Planned Investment Spending	Government Spending	Equilibrium Aggregate Income
Decrease in interest rate					
Decrease in mpc					
Increase in planned investment spending					
Increase in autonomous consumer expenditure					
Decrease in government spending					

EXERCISE 6: The Expenditure Multiplier

Assume that the equilibrium level of income is 4000 and the mpc = 0.8.

A. Calculate the value of the government expenditure multiplier. ______________________

B. Suppose that the government knows that the full-employment level of income is 4200. Calculate the increase in government spending necessary to raise equilibrium income to the full employment level.

Change in government spending = ______________________

EXERCISE 7: Deriving the LM Curve

The LM curve is the relationship that describes the combinations of interest rates and aggregate output for which the quantity of money demanded equals the quantity of money supplied. Panel (a) of Figure 22C shows the equilibrium values of interest rates in the money market for aggregate income levels of $400 billion, $600 billion, and $800 billion. Complete panel (b) by plotting the level of equilibrium output corresponding to each of the three interest rates. Connect the three points with straight-line segments.

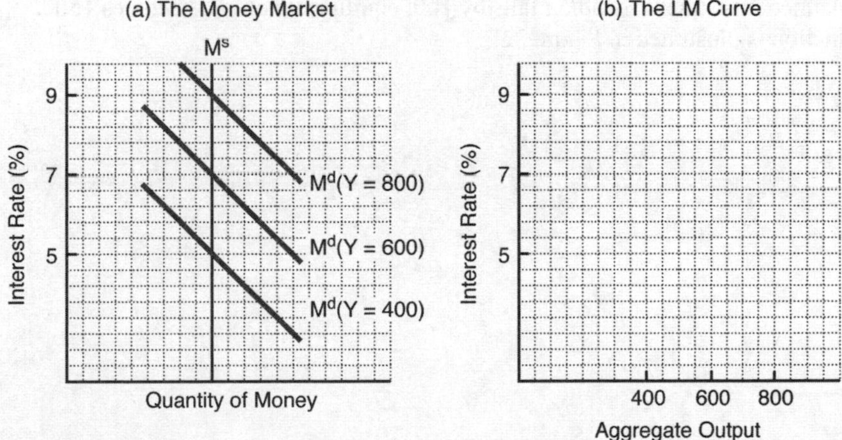

Figure 22C

EXERCISE 8: Deriving the IS Curve

The IS curve is the relationship that describes the combinations of aggregate output and interest rates for which the total quantity of goods produced equals the total quantity demanded. The investment schedule in panel (a) of Figure 22D shows that as the interest rate rises from 5 to 7 to 9 percent, planned investment spending falls from $150 billion to $100 billion to $50 billion. Panel (b) of Figure 22D indicates the levels of equilibrium output $400 billion, $600 billion, and $800 billion that correspond to those three levels of planned investment. Complete panel (c) by plotting the level of equilibrium output corresponding to each of the three interest rates. Then connect the points with straight-line segments.

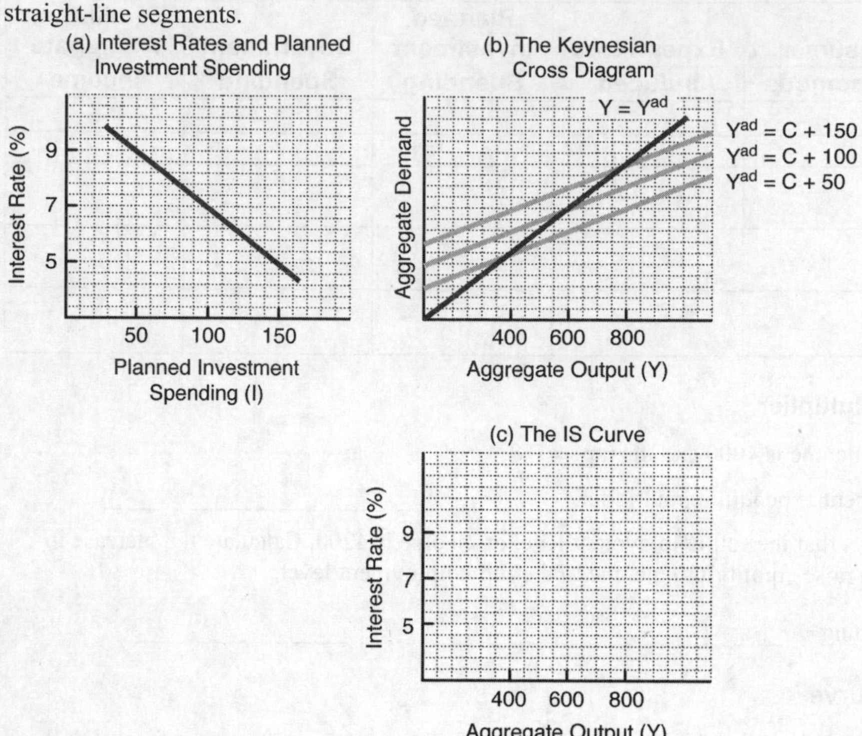

Figure 22D

EXERCISE 9: The MPC and the Expenditure Multiplier

Consider an economy with no foreign trade and no government. Suppose that autonomous spending is originally 600 and equilibrium output is 1800. When planned investment spending falls by 100, equilibrium output becomes 1500. This change to the aggregate demand function is illustrated in Figure 22E.

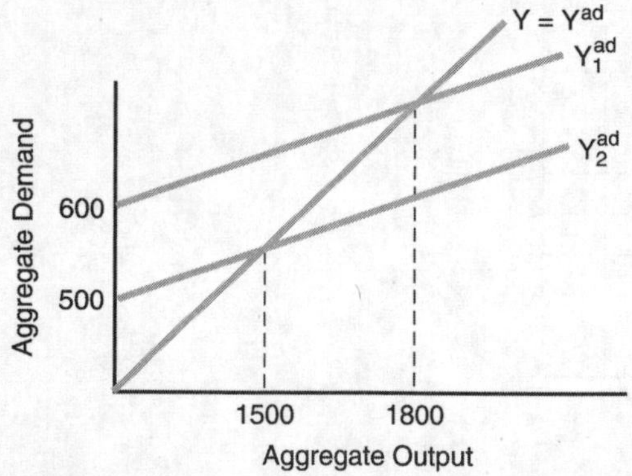

Figure 22E

A. What is the value of the expenditure multiplier in this economy?

____

B. What is the marginal propensity to consume?

____

C. Suppose that the marginal propensity to consume in an economy is less than what is calculated in Part B. If planned investment falls by 100, then would equilibrium output be higher or lower than 1500?

____

SELF-TEST

PART A: True-False Questions

Circle whether following statements are true (T) or false (F).

T F 1. The investment spending component of aggregate demand does not include unplanned inventory investment.

T F 2. Jean purchases 1000 shares of Exxon common stock through her broker. This transaction is included in the investment component of aggregate demand.

T F 3. The 45-degree line in the Keynesian cross diagram represents all possible or potential equilibrium points.

T F 4. If the level of aggregate output exceeds aggregate demand, income will rise, causing the level of output to expand.

T F 5. Unplanned inventory investment occurs when the level of aggregate demand exceeds aggregate output.

T F 6. Business firms are likely to cut production in the face of rising unplanned inventory levels.

T F 7. The simple Keynesian model suggests that an increase in planned investment will actually lead to an expansion in aggregate output that exceeds the initial change in investment spending. This is known as the multiplier effect.

T F 8. Keynes believed that business cycle fluctuations were dominated by changes in autonomous consumer expenditure.

T F 9. The slope of the IS curve reflects the fact that investment is negatively related to the interest rate.

T F 10. At any point along an IS curve the level of unplanned inventory investment is zero.

T F 11. The money demand curve is downward sloping, because a lower interest rate means that the opportunity cost of holding money is lower and therefore the quantity demanded of money is higher.

T F 12. Aggregate demand function y^{ad} is the horizontal sum of the consumption and planned investment spending.

T F 13. As long as output is below the equilibrium level, unplanned inventory investment will remain negative and firms will continue to raise production and output will continue to rise.

T F 14. The larger the marginal propensity to consume, the higher the expenditure multiplier.

T F 15. If the economy is located in the area to the right of the LM curve, there is an excess demand for money.

T F 16. When the equilibrium condition is satisfied, producers are able to sell all of their output and have no reason to change their production.

T F 17. The dollar amount for all variables in the figures corresponds to real quantities because we assume that the price level is fixed.

T F 18. When there is no government sector to collect taxes, disposable income equals aggregate output.

PART B: Multiple-Choice Questions

Circle the appropriate answer.

1. Which of the following describes the equilibrium condition in the simple Keynesian model?
   a. Aggregate output equals aggregate demand.
   b. Unplanned inventory investment is zero.
   c. Actual investment equals planned investment.
   d. All of the above.
   e. Only (a) and (b) of the above.
2. Keynes believed that the economy could achieve an equilibrium level of output
   a. only at the full-employment level of output.
   b. below the full-employment level of output.
   c. only if the government took a "hands off" approach.
   d. by doing none of the above.
3. Inventory investment is distinguished from fixed investment in that
   a. fixed investment is never unplanned.
   b. inventory investment is never planned.
   c. unplanned inventory investment is always zero.
   d. there is no distinction.
4. If one knows the value of the multiplier and the change in the level of autonomous investment, one can determine
   a. the change in the interest rate.
   b. the change in the money supply.
   c. the change in the aggregate output.
   d. all of the above.
5. Keynes believed that fluctuations in aggregate output were largely the result of fluctuations in
   a. the money supply.
   b. autonomous investment spending.
   c. autonomous consumer expenditure.
   d. government spending.
6. If the MPC is 0.75, the multiplier is
   a. 3.00.
   b. 3.75.
   c. 0.25.
   d. 4.00.
7. Assume that an economy characterized by the simple Keynesian model is in equilibrium at full employment but the government budget is in deficit. If the government raises taxes to balance the budget, then
   a. the rate of unemployment will increase.
   b. the level of aggregate output will increase.
   c. the price level will increase.
   d. all of the above will occur.
8. An increase in the interest rate will cause
   a. investment spending to fall.
   b. investment spending to rise.
   c. tax rates to rise.

d. no change in aggregate spending.

9. Points to the left of the IS curve represent interest rate and output combinations characterized by reductions in
   a. unplanned inventory accumulations.
   b. unplanned inventory reductions.
   c. an excess demand for money.
   d. an excess supply of money.

10. The money market is in equilibrium
    a. at any point on the LM curve.
    b. at only one point on the IS curve.
    c. at any point on the IS curve.
    d. at only one point on the LM curve.
    e. when only (a) and (b) of the above occur.

11. At points to the _____ of the LM curve there is an excess _____ of money which causes interest rates to fall.
    a. left; supply
    b. left; demand
    c. right; supply
    d. right; demand

12. If the economy is on the *IS* curve, but is to the _____ of the *LM* curve, then the _____ market is in equilibrium, but the interest rate is _____ the equilibrium level.
    a. left; goods; below
    b. left; goods; above
    c. right; money; below
    d. right; goods; above
    e. left; money; above

13. The multiplier effect means that a given change in _____ expenditures will change equilibrium _____ by an amount _____ than the initial change in autonomous expenditures.
    a. autonomous; income; greater
    b. autonomous; income; less
    c. induced; income; greater
    d. induced; employment; greater
    e. autonomous; employment; less

14. If I^u is positive, firms will _____ production and output will _____.
    a. cut; rise
    b. cut; fall
    c. increase; rise
    d. increase; fall

15. In the Keynesian framework, as long as output is _____ the equilibrium level, unplanned inventory investment will remain negative and firms will continue to _____ production.
    a. below; lower
    b. above; lower
    c. below; raise
    d. above; raise

16. The price level in the Keynesian framework
    a. signals to firms whether they should increase or decrease production.
    b. is assumed to be constant.
    c. is the difference between real and nominal interest rates.
    d. changes in order for equilibrium to be reached.
    e. None of the above.

17. If Lisa finds $50 and purchases a sweater for $40 and saves the remaining $10, then her MPC is
    a. 0.10.
    b. 0.40.
    c. 0.80.
    d. $10.
    e. $40.

18. Aggregate demand includes _____ but it does not include _____.
    a. consumer expenditures; net exports
    b. planned investment spending; unplanned investment spending
    c. government spending; investment spending
    d. unplanned investment spending; planned investment spending
    e. unplanned investment spending; inventory investment

19. Which of the following is considered fixed investment?
    a. Government bonds
    b. Raw materials
    c. Inventory investment
    d. A warehouse
    e. All of the above.

20. If the MPC is 0.60, and if government spending rises by $500, then equilibrium output rises by
    a. $1,250.
    b. $1,000.
    c. $600.
    d. $500.
    e. $60.

21. Which of the following is a reason why the *IS* curve slopes downward?
    a. Investment rises as the interest rate rises.
    b. Net exports fall as the interest rate rises.
    c. Money demand rises as the interest rate rises.
    d. Only (a) and (b) of the above.
    e. Only (b) and (c) of the above.

22. If the consumption function is $C = 100 + 0.50Y_D$, then which of the following statements is true?
    a. Consumption is zero when disposable income is zero.
    b. Consumption is 100 when disposable income is zero.
    c. Consumption is 50 when disposable income is 100.
    d. Consumption is 100 when disposable income is 100.
    e. Consumption is 100 when disposable income is 50.

23. If the government raises taxes by $40 and simultaneously raises government spending by _____, then equilibrium

output will _____.

a. $40; fall

b. $50; fall

c. $0; rise

d. $80; rise

24. The *ISLM* model differs from the Keynesian framework in that

a. the price level is assumed to be constant.

b. the interest rate is determined within the model.

c. monetary policy can be studied within the model.

d. only (a) and (b) of the above.

e. only (b) and (c) of the above.

25. The LM curve slopes upward because as income rises, the _____ must _____ in order for the money market to remain in equilibrium.

a. money supply; rise

b. interest rate; fall

c. money supply; fall

d. interest rate; rise

e. MPC; rise

26. If government purchases increase by $100 million and if autonomous taxes increase by $100 million, then in the simple Keynesian model

a. aggregate output will increase by more than $100 million.

b. aggregate output will increase by less than $100 million.

c. aggregate output will increase by exactly $100 million.

d. the effect on aggregate output cannot be determined.

27. In Keynes' model, if output is below equilibrium, then unplanned inventory investment will be negative, firms will ______ production, and output will ______.

a. raise; rise

b. raise; fall

c. lower; rise

d. lower; fall

28. Suppose that the consumption function is C=100+0.8Y and that planned investment spending increases from $50 to $150. The equilibrium output will then rise by ______ dollars.

a. 100

b. zero

c. 500

d. 200

29. If autonomous spending decreases by $100 and planned investment spending increases by $100 at the same time, the equilibrium output

a. increases by $100.

b. decreases by $100.

c. decreases by $200.

d. remains unchanged.

30. When the interest rate is ________, few investments in physical capital will earn more than the cost of borrowed funds, so planned investment spending is ________.
    a. high, high
    b. high, low
    c. low, low
    d. low, high

31. Aggregate output is
    a. positively related to consumer expenditure, investment spending, government spending, and negatively related to net exports and the level of taxes.
    b. positively related to consumer expenditure, investment spending, government spending, net exports and negatively related to the level of taxes.
    c. positively related to consumer expenditure, investment spending, net exports and negatively related to government spending and the level of taxes.
    d. positively related to investment spending, the level of taxes and net exports, and negatively related to consumer expenditure and government spending.

CHAPTER 23

Monetary and Fiscal Policy in the ISLM Model

CHAPTER SYNOPSIS/COMPLETIONS

In this chapter we explore the mechanics of the *ISLM* model, discovering how monetary policy—the control of the money supply and interest rates—and (1)_______________ policy—the control of government spending and taxes—affect the level of aggregate output and interest rates. Since policymakers have these two tools at their disposal they will be interested in knowing the effects each policy can be expected to have on the economy. The ISLM model provides a convenient but powerful framework for comparing the relative effects of proposed monetary and fiscal actions. By comparing these predicted effects, policymakers can better decide which policy is most appropriate.

The ISLM model also provides a framework that allows one to compare the desirability of interest rate targeting against money supply targeting. In addition, the aggregate demand curve is derived using the ISLM model. It is for these three important reasons that we study the ISLM model in the money and banking course.

As is true of any economic model, we can better comprehend the workings of the ISLM model by first examining the behaviour of the individual curves. Once this has been done, the effects that changes in fiscal and monetary variables will have on interest rates and aggregate output can be determined.

The (2)_______ curve shows the combinations of interest rates and aggregate output that ensure equilibrium in the goods market. Therefore, changes in autonomous consumer expenditures, autonomous (3)_______________ spending, and government spending or taxes are all factors that shift the IS curve. For example, if the government enacts legislation to spend $100 billion over the next ten years to repair the decaying infrastructure (roads, bridges, canals) of the economy, the added government spending shifts the IS curve to the (4)_______. An example of a leftward shift in the IS curve is provided by the precipitous drop in autonomous investment spending during the Great Depression. It is important to distinguish between autonomous changes in investment and changes in investment due to changes in interest rates. A change in investment that results from a change in interest rates is shown as a movement along a given IS curve, not as a shift in the IS curve.

Interest rate and aggregate output combinations that represent equilibrium in the money market define an (5)_______ curve. Therefore, changes in either money supply or money demand can cause the LM curve to shift.

Consider the effect an increase in money supply has on the LM curve. At the initial interest rate, an increase in the money supply creates an (6)_______________ supply of money. Holding output constant, equilibrium is regained in the money market by a fall in the interest rates. Alternatively, the interest rate held constant, equilibrium is regained in the money market when the increase in aggregate (7)_______________ is sufficient to raise money demand to a level that eliminates the excess supply of money.

Changes in money demand also shift the LM curve. If more people come to expect a surge in the stock market, they will try to conserve their holdings of money, filling their portfolios with more stocks (recall the analysis of Chapter 5 on asset demand). The drop in money demand creates an excess supply of money at the initial interest rate. Therefore, interest rates will (8)__________________, holding output constant, and the LM curve shifts to the (9)__________________. Conversely, an increase in the demand for money shifts the LM curve left.

Putting the IS and LM curves together allows us to consider the effects of autonomous spending and policy changes on the equilibrium levels of the interest rate and aggregate output. For example, a tax cut aimed at reducing the budget surplus shifts the IS curve (10)__________________ due to the increase in spending by consumers. The increase in output causes the demand for money to rise, which in turn creates an excess demand for money, putting upward pressure on interest rates. Although the rise in interest rates causes interest sensitive investment to decrease, the decrease is not enough to offset the expansionary effects of the tax cut. No wonder tax cuts are so popular among incumbent politicians: a tax cut may cause rising employment and a net gain of votes on election day.

Some economists contend that there is a tendency for the money supply to expand prior to elections. Since the ISLM model indicates that an increase in the money supply causes aggregate output to (11)__________________ and interest rates to fall, and since both are likely to help the incumbent politician, such a contention has credibility.

The ISLM framework also has been used to analyze the appropriateness of Bank of Canada operating procedures. While interest rate targets can be shown to be more consistent with stable economic activity when the LM curve is unstable, a money supply target helps ensure greater stability when the (12)________ curve is unstable. Since neither targeting procedure outperforms the other in every situation, it becomes an empirical question as to which curve is more stable and under which conditions. Thus it is not surprising that economists still debate over the appropriate targeting procedure the Bank should employ.

Another debate has centered around the slope of the LM curve. If the LM curve is very steep, approaching a vertical line, then an expansionary fiscal policy is likely to be an (13)__________________ tool for expanding aggregate output since investment spending will be crowded out by the rising interest rates.

Finally, the ISLM model is useful in deriving the aggregate demand curve used in aggregate demand and supply analysis. Since aggregate demand and supply analysis is so powerful, this function of the ISLM model is especially important. A decline in the price level raises the real money supply, causing interest rates to fall and investment spending to rise. Simultaneous goods and money market equilibrium will correspond to higher levels of aggregate output as the price level falls, indicating that the aggregate demand curve slopes (14)__________________ to the right.

The aggregate demand curve shifts in the same direction as a shift in the IS or LM curves. Increases in the money supply and government spending or decreases in taxes all cause the aggregate demand curve to shift to the (15)__________________. We see in the next chapter that the aggregate demand and supply model provides a powerful framework for understanding recent economic events.

EXERCISES

EXERCISE 1: Factors that Cause the IS and LM Curves to Shift

This exercise provides a summary of the factors that cause the IS and LM curves to shift.

A. List the factors that cause the IS curve to shift to the right.

1. ____________________________________
2. ____________________________________
3. ____________________________________
4. ____________________________________

B. List the factors that cause the IS curve to shift to the left.

1. ____________________________________
2. ____________________________________
3. ____________________________________
4. ____________________________________

C. List the factors that cause the LM curve to shift to the right.

1. ______________________________

2. ______________________________

D. List the factors that cause the LM curve to shift to the left.

1. ______________________________

2. ______________________________

EXERCISE 2: Response to a Change in Both Monetary and Fiscal Policy

The United States experienced its deepest post-World War II recession in the years 1981 and 1982 despite the fiscal stimulus provided by the Reagan tax cut. The recession was somewhat unusual in that interest rates rose throughout 1981 and the first half of 1982. In Figure 23A the stimulus provided by the tax cut is shown as the rightward shift of the IS curve from IS_1 to IS_2, moving the economy from point 1 to point 2. Draw in the new LM curve in Figure 23A consistent with the decline in aggregate output and rise in interest rates.

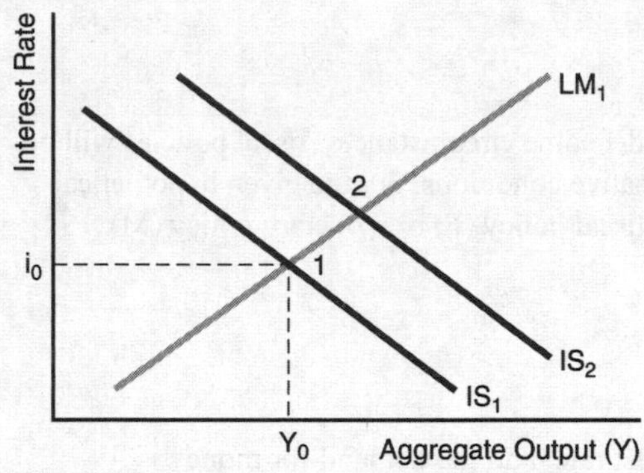

Figure 23A

Explain why the LM curve might have shifted in the direction it did.

____

____

EXERCISE 3: Contractionary Monetary and Fiscal Policies

Use the ISLM model and explain what happens to output and the interest rate when both fiscal and monetary policies are contractionary, but fiscal policy turns out to be less contractionary than monetary policy.

EXERCISE 4: Monetary and Fiscal Policy

Indicate whether the following statements are a description of monetary policy (M), fiscal policy (F), or both (B). Place the appropriate letter in the blank next to the statement.

_____ 1. Changes in money supply and interest rates.

_____ 2. Shown as a shift in the IS curve.

_____ 3. Changes in government spending and taxing.

_____ 4. Shown as a shift in the LM curve.

_____ 5. Policy made by the Bank of Canada.

_____ 6. Policy made by the government.

_____ 7. Shown as a shift in the aggregate demand curve.

EXERCISE 5: Effectiveness of Monetary Versus Fiscal Policy

Policymakers often must choose between monetary and fiscal policies. Under some circumstances, fiscal policies will be preferred to monetary policies, while the converse may be true under alternative conditions. For the given hypothetical conditions, indicate whether the policymaker would have a preference for fiscal policy (F) or monetary policy (M).

_____ 1. Investment is relatively responsive to changes in interest rates.

_____ 2. The demand for money is unaffected by the interest rate.

_____ 3. Investment is relatively responsive to changes in the interest rate, and the demand for money is unaffected by the interest rate.

_____ 4. The demand for money is relatively responsive to changes in the interest rate, and investment is relatively unresponsive to changes in the interest rate.

_____ 5. Investment is completely crowded out when taxes are cut or government spending is increased.

EXERCISE 6: Short run and Long run Response to a Drop in Investment Spending

Suppose that the economy is initially at the natural rate level of output, Y_n, as shown by point 1 in Figure 23B.

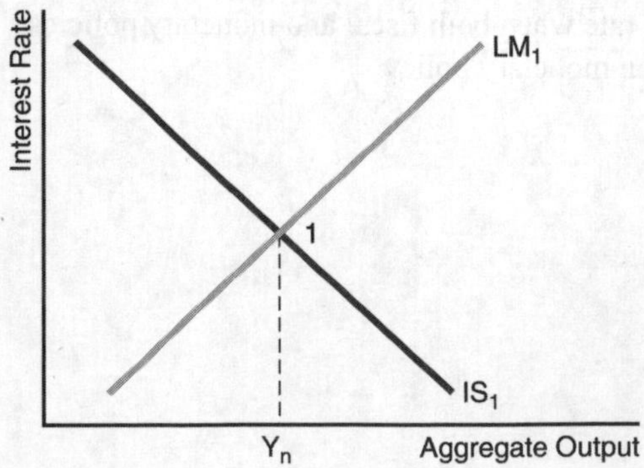

Figure 23B

A. If many businesses predict that a recession is coming, and if planned investment falls, what is the effect in the short run on aggregate output and the interest rate? Graphically draw the effect in Figure 23B and label the new equilibrium point 2.

____

____

B. In the short run, what could the Bank of Canada do to avoid this effect on aggregate output? Draw the effect in Figure 23B and label the new equilibrium point 3.

____

____

C. Suppose instead that the Bank of Canada chooses not to engage in any active policy after the initial drop in investment spending. Starting from point 2, describe what will happen to the economy in the long run.

____

____

EXERCISE 7: Factors that Cause the Aggregate Demand Curve to Shift

In the following table, factors that cause the aggregate demand curve to shift are listed. For a decrease in the variable, indicate whether the aggregate demand shifts to the right (→) or to the left (←).

Factors that Cause the Aggregate Demand Curve to Shift

Change in Variable		Direction of Aggregate Demand Curve Shift
A. Taxes	↓	____
B. Money supply	↓	____
C. Government spending	↓	____
D. Autonomous consumption	↓	____
E. Money demand	↓	____
F. Business confidence	↓	____

SELF-TEST

PART A: True-False Questions

Circle whether the following statements are true (T) or false (F).

T F 1. An increase in the interest rate causes the IS curve to shift to the left, since investment spending will fall.

T F 2. If businesses should suddenly become "bearish" (pessimistic) about the future profitability of investment, aggregate output will fall, all else constant. This is shown as a leftward shift of the IS curve.

T F 3. Financial innovation—by increasing the liquidity of financial assets—has enabled some people to reduce their demand for money. The decline in the demand for money has the effect of shifting the LM curve to the left.

T F 4. An expansion of the money supply will lead to lower interest rates and an increase in investment spending as people attempt to rid themselves of excess money balances.

T F 5. The condition known as complete crowding out occurs when the demand for money is insensitive to the interest rate.

T F 6. The effect of an open market purchase is to shift the LM curve to the left.

T F 7. Assume that money demand is very unstable and the IS curve is stable. Such knowledge makes the case for monetary targeting stronger, since the IS curve will be stable relative to the LM curve.

T F 8. A decline in taxes causes the aggregate demand curve to shift to the left.

T F 9. Monetary policy changes have no effect on the aggregate demand curve, since it is only factors that shift the IS curve which affect aggregate demand.

T F 10. High unemployment leads the Bank of Canada to expand the money supply. Such a policy will shift both the LM and aggregate demand curves to the right.

T F 11. Aggregate output and interest rates are negatively related to government spending and positively related to taxes.

T F 12. The less interest-sensitive money demand is, the more effective monetary policy is, relative to fiscal policy.

T F 13. If the IS curve is more unstable than the LM curve, a money supply target is preferred.

T F 14. Any factor that shifts the IS curve shifts the aggregate demand curve in the same direction.

T F 15. If the LM curve is more unstable than the IS curve, an interest rate target is preferred.

T F 16. If the IS curve is more unstable than the LM curve, a money supply target is not preferred.

T F 17. Ceteris paribus, all factors that shift the IS curve to the right shift the aggregate demand curve to the left.

T F 18. The less interest-sensitive the money demand, the more effective the monetary policy, relative to increases in government spending.

T F 19. When output is above the equilibrium level in the long run, the booming economy will cause prices to fall.

T F 20. An increase in money supply will increase the money demand, thus, an excess demand for money is created. However, rising interest rates will reduce the quantity of money demanded.

T F 21. Aggregate output is positively related to the money supply.

T F 22. When demand for money is unaffected by changes in the interest rate, increases in the money supply will increase output, but changes in government spending will not affect aggregate output.

T F 23. In the long run, because of the natural rate level of output, monetary and fiscal policy does not affect output.

PART B: Multiple-Choice Questions

Circle the appropriate answer.

1. Which of the following causes the IS curve to shift to the left?
   a. Increase in taxes.
   b. Increase in government spending.
   c. Increase in the money supply.
   d. All of the above.
   e. Only (b) and (c) of the above.

2. An increase in government spending causes both interest rates and aggregate output to increase. In the ISLM framework, this is represented by a _____ shift of the _____ curve.
   a. leftward; LM
   b. rightward; LM
   c. leftward; IS
   d. rightward; IS

3. In the early 1930s there was a significant contraction in the money supply. In the ISLM framework, such a contraction is illustrated as a _____ shift of the _____ curve.
   a. rightward; IS
   b. rightward; LM
   c. leftward; IS
   d. leftward; LM
4. In 1981, President Reagan in the United States was able to get through Congress a fiscal package containing a tax cut and increased federal expenditures. Such a policy shifts the _____ curve to the _____.
   a. LM; left
   b. IS; right
   c. LM; right
   d. IS; left
5. Assume that an economy suffers a recession in spite of an expansionary monetary policy. The ISLM framework suggests that even if the LM curve shifts to the right, the level of aggregate output might fall if the
   a. IS curve shifts to the right.
   b. investment function shifts to the right.
   c. IS curve shifts to the left.
   d. taxes are cut.
6. Suppose that the economy is suffering from both high interest rates and high unemployment. Viewed from an ISLM framework, we can conclude that _____ policy has been too _____.
   a. fiscal; expansionary
   b. monetary; expansionary
   c. monetary; contractionary
   d. fiscal; contractionary
7. Assume that econometric studies indicate that the demand for money is highly sensitive to interest rate changes. Such evidence would tend to support the belief that
   a. fiscal policy has no aggregate output effects.
   b. fiscal policy is effective in increasing output.
   c. monetary policy is effective in increasing output.
   d. none of the above is true.
8. Investment spending in the country Curtonia is highly unstable, making the IS curve very unstable relative to the LM curve. Given the nature of the economy, the Central Bank of Curtonia will want to target the
   a. money supply.
   b. interest rate.
   c. exchange rate.
   d. bank rate.
   e. monetary base.
9. The aggregate demand curve slopes downward to the right, since
   a. a decline in the price level raises the real money supply, lowering interest rates.
   b. a decline in the price level raises the real money supply, causing output to fall.
   c. an increase in the price level raises the real money supply, causing output to rise.
   d. none of the above occurs.
10. A Bank of Canada purchase of government securities will shift the aggregate demand curve in which direction?
    a. Right.
    b. Left.

c. A Bank of Canada purchase of securities does not shift the aggregate demand curve.

d. All of the above are a possible result of an expansion in the money supply.

11. Assume that the Bank of Canada pursues a policy of pegging the interest rate. If government policymakers _____ government spending, the Bank will be forced to _____ the money supply to keep interest rates from _____.
    a. decrease; decrease; rising
    b. decrease; increase; falling
    c. increase; increase; rising
    d. increase; decrease; rising

12. Within the ISLM framework an expansionary fiscal policy causes a(n) _____ in aggregate output and causes interest rates to _____.
    a. increase; fall
    b. increase; rise
    c. decrease; fall
    d. decrease; rise

13. Interest rates in Canada rose over the period 1965 through 1966. Since this coincided with the Vietnam War buildup, we can assume that the _____ curve shifted to the _____.
    a. LM; left
    b. LM; right
    c. IS; left
    d. IS; right

14. The _____ responsive is money demand to the interest rate, the _____ effective is _____ policy.
    a. more; more; fiscal
    b. more; less; fiscal
    c. less; more; fiscal
    d. less; less; monetary

15. A _____ in the price level, ceteris paribus, will mean _____ interest rates and thus a _____ level of investment.
    a. rise; higher; higher
    b. rise; lower; higher
    c. decline; higher; lower
    d. decline; lower; higher

16. Fiscal policy that moves the budget toward a larger surplus will _____ aggregate output and _____ interest rates.
    a. lower; raise
    b. raise; raise
    c. lower; lower
    d. raise; lower

17. After being elected in 2000, President Bush in the United States reduced taxes, which helped to move the federal government budget from a surplus to a deficit. The ISLM framework predicts that the effect was to
    a. shift the LM curve to the left.
    b. shift the IS curve to the left.
    c. raise aggregate output and lower interest rates.
    d. only (a) and (b) of the above.
    e. none of the above occur.

18. Which of the following has the same effect on the LM curve, all else the same, as does a decrease in the money supply?

a. An increase in the interest rate.
b. An increase in autonomous consumption expenditures.
c. An increase in money demand.
d. An increase in taxes.
e. None of the above.

19. If investment spending is relatively insensitive to the interest rate, then the _____ curve is relatively _____ and monetary policy is relatively less effective than fiscal policy.
a. IS; flat
b. IS; steep
c. LM; flat
d. LM; steep

20. When the central bank reduces the money supply
a. the interest rate rises in order to induce people to hold less money.
b. the interest rate rises and investment spending declines.
c. aggregate output rises as investment spending declines.
d. only (a) and (b) of the above.
e. only (a) and (c) of the above.

21. If the LM curve is relatively flat because money demand is relatively interest-sensitive, then a given reduction in taxes will lead to a _____ increase in aggregate output and a _____ increase in the interest rate.
a. larger; smaller
b. smaller; larger
c. smaller; smaller
d. larger; larger

22. If complete crowding out occurs, then
a. an increase in the money supply will not decrease the interest rate.
b. an increase in government spending will not increase the interest rate.
c. a decrease in the money supply will not decrease aggregate output.
d. an increase in government spending will not increase aggregate output.

23. If money demand is unstable, then the LM curve will not be stable. In this case, the best monetary policy for minimizing output fluctuations is
a. a money supply target.
b. an increase in the money supply.
c. a reduction in government spending.
d. an interest rate target.

24. The fact that changes in the money supply will not affect output and the interest rate in the long run, known as long-run monetary neutrality, results because
a. the inflation rate is permanently changed when the money supply changes.
b. the price level changes and leaves real money balances constant in the long run.
c. complete crowding out prevents any effect on aggregate output.
d. none of the above occur.

25. Which of the following will shift the aggregate demand curve to the left?
a. An increase in the money supply.
b. A reduction in investment spending.
c. An increase in government spending.

d. A reduction in taxes.

e. None of the above.

26. Other things being equal, if the price level increases, then the _____ curve shifts to the _____.

a. LM; right

b. LM; left

c. IS; right

d. IS; left

27. In the long-run ISLM model, when the level of output _____ the natural rate level, the price level _____, which shifts the LM curve to the _____ until output returns to the natural rate level.

a. exceeds; rises; right

b. exceeds; rises; left

c. remains below; falls; left

d. remains below; rises; right

28. An increase in net exports will shift the ________ curve to the ______.

a. LM, right

b. LM, left

c. IS, right

d. IS, left

29. An increase in the volatility of bond returns would _______ the quantity of demanded money and this will shift the ________ curve to the ________.

a. increase, LM, left

b. decrease, LM, right

c. increase, IS, left

d. decrease, IS, left

30. A contractionary fiscal policy shifts the ________ curve to the _______, and the aggregate demand (AD) curve shifts to the _______.

a. LM, left, right

b. LM, left, left

c. IS, left, right

d. IS, left, left

31. Holding price level constant, any factor that shifts the LM curve shifts the

a. aggregate supply curve in the same direction.

b. aggregate supply curve in the opposite direction.

c. aggregate demand curve in the opposite direction.

d. aggregate demand curve in the same direction.

32. When the demand for money is unaffected by the interest rate, an expansionary fiscal policy will

a. increase both interest rate and aggregate output.

b. increase output and leave the interest rate unchanged.

c. increase the interest rate and leave aggregate output unchanged.

d. reduce both interest rate and aggregate output.

CHAPTER 24

Aggregate Demand and Supply Analysis

CHAPTER SYNOPSIS/COMPLETIONS

This chapter develops the basic tool of aggregate demand and supply analysis in order to study the effects of money on aggregate output and the price level. The model is very powerful in gaining insight into the workings of the economy, yet it is relatively simple and, with a little work, relatively easy to master.

We construct the aggregate demand and aggregate supply model by first examining the individual curves. The aggregate demand curve describes the relationship between the (1)________________ level and the quantity of aggregate output demanded. The monetarists derive the aggregate demand curve from the quantity theory of money. Holding the money supply and velocity constant, an increase in the price level reduces the quantity of aggregate output demanded. A falling price level implies an increase in the quantity of aggregate output demanded. Keynesians argue that a falling price level—because it causes the real (2)________________________________ to increase which in turn lowers interest rates—causes both investment spending and the quantity of aggregate output demanded to (3)__________________. Both explanations are consistent with a downward sloping aggregate demand curve.

Though both monetarists and Keynesians agree that the aggregate demand curve is downward sloping, they hold different views about the factors that cause the aggregate demand curve to shift. Monetarists contend that changes in the (4)__________________ supply are the primary source of changes in aggregate demand. An increase in the money supply shifts the aggregate demand curve to the (5)__________________, while a decrease in the money supply shifts it to the left.

Keynesians do not dispute that a change in the money supply shifts aggregate demand, but they regard changes in fiscal policy and autonomous expenditure as additional factors that shift the aggregate demand curve. For example, Keynesians believe that increased government expenditures or a cut in taxes will shift the aggregate demand curve to the (6)__________________, while a decrease in government expenditures or a tax increase shifts the aggregate demand curve to the left.

The aggregate supply curve is upward sloping, illustrating that an increase in the price level will lead to an increase in the quantity of output supplied, all else constant. Explaining why the aggregate supply curve slopes upward is fairly straightforward. Since the costs of many inputs (factors of production) tend to be (7)__________________ in the short run, an increase in the price of the output will mean greater profits, encouraging firms to (8)__________________ production, increasing the quantity of aggregate output supplied.

Note, however, that this increase in output cannot last. Eventually workers will demand higher wages, and resource suppliers will demand higher prices. As factor prices (9)__________________, the aggregate supply curve shifts in, causing aggregate output supplied to fall back to its original level.

Combining the aggregate supply and the aggregate demand curves allows one to consider the effects on the price level and aggregate output when one of the factors affecting either aggregate demand or aggregate supply changes. For example, an increase in the money supply shifts the aggregate demand curve to the right. This implies that an increase in the money supply will cause both (10)________________ and the price level to increase in the short run. In the long run, the (11)________________ curve will shift in as workers demand higher nominal wages to compensate for the increase in prices. Since the aggregate supply curve will shift when unemployment and aggregate output differ from their natural rate levels, the long-run equilibrium will coincide with the natural rate level of output.

Therefore, changes in either monetary or fiscal policies can have only temporary effects on unemployment and aggregate output. In the long run, monetary and fiscal expansions can do nothing more than raise the (12)________________. This concept is illustrated by the long run aggregate supply curve, a vertical line passing through the natural rate of aggregate output.

The aggregate supply curve will shift inward not only as workers come to expect higher inflation, but when negative supply (13)________________ hit the economy (as in the 1970s when OPEC dramatically increased the price of oil) or when workers push for higher real wages. Unfortunately, the economy experiences both rising prices and falling aggregate output in the short run, an outcome referred to as (14)________________. Eventually, the aggregate supply curve will shift outward returning the economy to the natural rate of output.

The aggregate demand and supply analysis indicates that aggregate output and unemployment can deviate from their natural-rate levels for two reasons: shifts in aggregate demand and shifts in aggregate supply. Whether these shifts cause aggregate output to rise or fall, the change will be temporary. Factor prices eventually adjust, moving the economy back to the vertical long-run aggregate supply curve. In the long run, shifts in aggregate demand merely change the price level, and shifts in short-run aggregate supply have no permanent effects.

EXERCISES

EXERCISE 1: Factors that Shift the Aggregate Demand Curve

A. List the factors that cause the aggregate demand curve to shift to the right.

1. ________________
2. ________________
3. ________________
4. ________________
5. ________________
6. ________________

B. List the factors that cause the aggregate demand curve to shift to the left.

1. ________________
2. ________________
3. ________________
4. ________________
5. ________________
6. ________________

EXERCISE 2: The Monetarist View of Aggregate Demand

A. The equation of exchange tells us that aggregate spending will equal the product of the money supply and income velocity. Assume that the money supply is $600 billion and velocity is 6. Graph the aggregate demand function in Figure 24A.

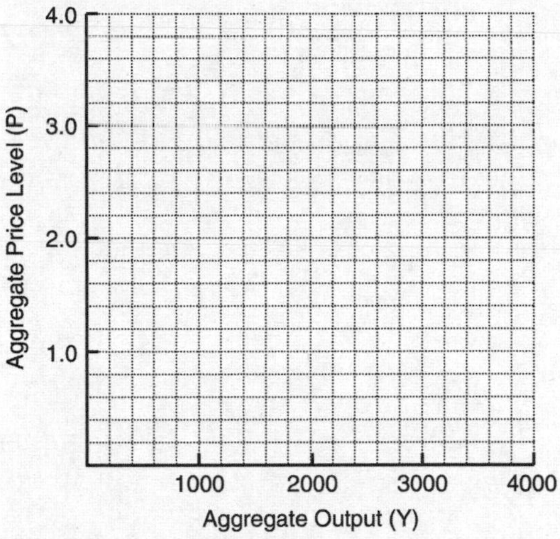

Figure 24A

B. If the Bank of Canada lowers the money supply to $500 billion, what will happen to aggregate spending if velocity remains unchanged?

____

C. Graph the new aggregate demand curve in Figure 24A representing the aggregate output price level combinations for the level of aggregate spending in part B.

EXERCISE 3: Factors that Shift the Aggregate Supply Curve

In the following table, factors that cause the aggregate supply curve to shift are listed. For each factor indicate whether the aggregate supply curve shifts in (←) or shifts out (→).

Factors that Shift the Aggregate Supply Curve

Factor	Shift in Aggregate Supply
1. OPEC increases the price of oil	
2. "Tightening" up of the labour market	
3. A decline in the expected price level	
4. Drought conditions in most of the country	
5. Fruit crops in British Columbia freeze	
6. Improved productivity	

EXERCISE 4: Shifts in Aggregate Supply

A. Using information provided in the following table and assuming that the aggregate demand curve remained at AD_1 in both periods, graph in Figure 24B the short-run aggregate supply curves for the two years.

Year ($1972)	Real GNP (1972 = 100)	GNP Deflator	Unemployment Rate	Natural Unemployment Rate
1974	1248.0	114.9	5.6	5.4
1975	1233.9	125.5	8.5	5.4

Source: R. Gordon, *Macroeconomics*, 3d Ed. (Boston: Little, Brown, 1984), Appendix B.

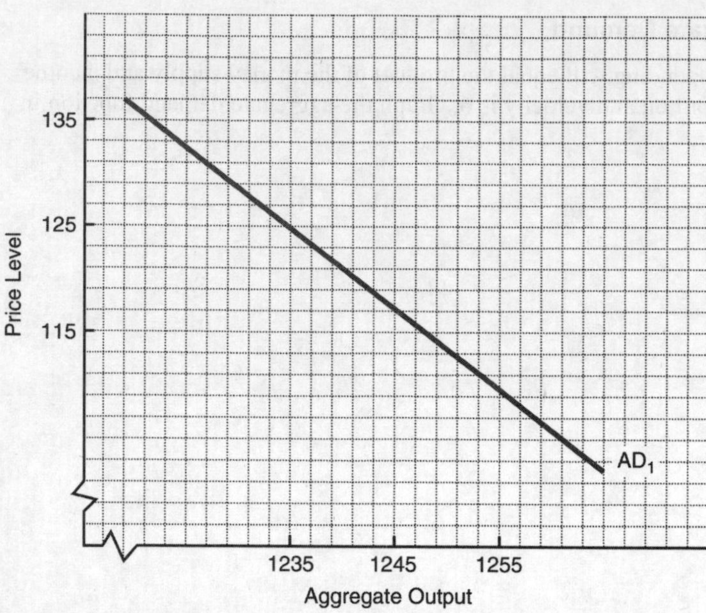

Figure 24B

B. Is it likely that workers' expectations of higher wages were the force that shifted the aggregate supply curve in?

____

____

EXERCISE 5: Differences Between Monetarist and Keynesian Analyses

Indicate whether the following statements are consistent with monetarist aggregate demand and supply analysis (M), Keynesian aggregate demand and supply analysis (K), both (B), or neither (N).

_____ 1. The aggregate demand curve is downward sloping and shifts in response to changes in the money supply.

_____ 2. The short-run aggregate supply curve is vertical at the natural rate of output.

_____ 3. Movements in the price level and aggregate output are driven by changes in government spending and taxes in addition to changes in the money supply.

_____ 4. The economy will return to full employment in the face of shocks but active use of government intervention to stabilize the economy is to no avail.

_____ 5. An increase in government spending will not cause aggregate output to increase, since private spending will be "crowded out" by government spending.

_____ 6. Changes in consumer and business confidence, imports and exports, and government spending and taxes shift the aggregate demand curve.

_____ 7. Adjustments in wages and prices may be quite prolonged delaying the self-correction of the economy back to the natural-rate level.

_____ 8. Changes in aggregate spending are primarily determined by changes in the money supply.

_____ 9. The aggregate supply curve does not remain fixed over time. Rather, it shifts whenever aggregate output is either above or below the natural-rate level.

_____ 10. A rise in the expected price level causes the aggregate supply curve to shift inward.

EXERCISE 6: The Labour Market and the Self-correcting Mechanism

Suppose that in the short run the economy is initially at point 1 in Figure 24C, where Y_n is the natural level of output.

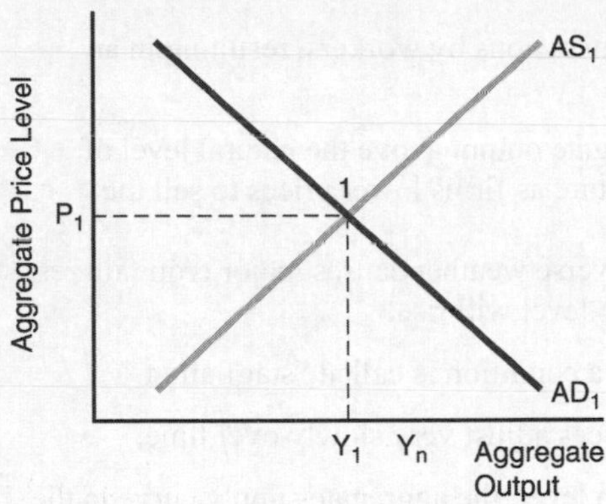

Figure 24C

A. Is the unemployment rate above or below the natural rate of unemployment? How do you know?

____

____

B. Explain what will happen in the labour market in the long run.

____

____

C. Show and explain the effect of this labour market change in Figure 24C. Indicate what the price level and aggregate output level are in the long run.

____

____

EXERCISE 7: AGGREGATE DEMAND AND AGGREGATE SUPPLY MODEL

A. Using short-run aggregate supply and aggregate demand analysis depict graphically the scenario for an economy experiencing stagflation. Be sure to interpret your graphical analysis clearly in words.

B. Using the same graph, show graphically and explain in words what happens to the aggregate demand and aggregate supply in the long-run.

C. What assumption underlies your graphical aggregate demand and supply analysis with respect to the natural rate level of output? Would the real business cycle theorists agree with your assumption? Why or why not?

SELF-TEST

PART A: True-False Questions

Circle whether the following statements are true (T) or false (F).

T F 1. Monetarists argue that a change in the money supply is the primary factor causing aggregate demand to shift.

T F 2. Income velocity is defined as the value of nominal gross national product divided by the money supply.

T F 3. Milton Friedman argues that changes in the money supply affect output almost immediately as if it were injected directly into the bloodstream of the economy.

T F 4. Along a given aggregate supply curve, input prices are assumed fixed.

T F 5. If workers come to expect higher inflation, the aggregate supply curve will shift out to reflect the expectation of lower real wages.

T F 6. Persistently high unemployment is likely to force wage concessions by workers, resulting in an eventual outward shift in the aggregate supply curve.

T F 7. Suppose that the economy is currently producing an aggregate output above the natural level of aggregate output. We can expect price reductions in the future as firms lower prices to sell the excess output.

T F 8. Aggregate demand and supply analysis indicates that if adverse weather causes major crop failures throughout Canada, aggregate output will fall and the price level will rise.

T F 9. In 1970 both inflation and unemployment increased. Such a condition is called "stagflation."

T F 10. Monetarists, unlike Keynesians, believe that wages and prices adjust very slowly over time.

T F 11. Since prices and wages take time to adjust to their long-run level, the aggregate supply curve in the short run differs from the aggregate supply curve in the long run.

T F 12. According to the quantity theory of money, changes in aggregate spending are determined primarily by changes in government spending.

T F 13. The amount of aggregate output supplied at any given price level goes to the natural rate level of output in the long run, so that the long-run aggregate supply curve is a vertical line at the natural rate of output.

T F 14. A rise in the expected price level causes the aggregate supply curve to shift to the right.

PART B: Multiple-Choice Questions

Circle the appropriate answer.

1. Keynesians and monetarists have different views regarding the factors that cause the aggregate demand curve to shift. This difference is best explained by which of the following statements?
   a. Monetarists place greater emphasis on the importance of money yet believe that fiscal actions can shift the aggregate demand curve, while Keynesians contend that money has no effect on aggregate demand.
   b. Keynesians believe that only fiscal policy can affect aggregate demand, while monetarists believe that fiscal policy is ineffective in altering the level of aggregate demand.
   c. Keynesians contend that both fiscal and monetary policy actions influence the level of aggregate demand, while monetarists claim that monetary policy is far more important than fiscal policy in affecting the level of aggregate demand.
   d. Keynesians place more significance on monetary actions than on fiscal actions, while monetarists believe that neither monetary nor fiscal actions influence the level of aggregate demand.
2. In Keynesian analysis, if investment is unresponsive to changes in the interest rate, the aggregate demand curve will be
   a. downward sloping.
   b. horizontal.
   c. downward sloping if consumer expenditures are sensitive to the interest rate.
   d. none of the above.
3. The upward slope of the short-run aggregate supply curve reflects the belief that
   a. factor prices are more flexible than output prices.
   b. output prices are more flexible than factor prices.
   c. factor prices are fixed in the long run.
   d. factor prices are completely flexible even in the short run.

4. Which of the following factors cause the aggregate supply curve to shift?
   a. Changes in the tightness of the labour market
   b. Changes in expectations of inflation
   c. Supply shocks such as commodity price changes
   d. Attempts by workers to push up their real wages
   e. All of the above

5. The aggregate demand and supply analysis suggests that the economy has a self-correcting mechanism which ensures that aggregate output and unemployment will move toward their natural-rate levels. However, Keynesians contend that this mechanism
   a. is unacceptably slow due to the stickiness of wages.
   b. cannot be improved on, even though the adjustment process is slow.
   c. while slow, can be improved through activist policy.
   d. does both (a) and (b) of the above.
   e. does both (a) and (c) of the above.

6. If the economy experiences a period of both a rising price level and rising unemployment, one can reasonably infer
   a. that the aggregate demand curve has shifted to the right.
   b. that the aggregate demand curve has shifted to the left.
   c. that the aggregate supply curve has shifted out.
   d. that the aggregate supply curve has shifted in.

7. Which of the following statements accurately describes the difference between monetarists and Keynesians?
   a. Monetarists believe that crowding out can be a major problem reducing the effectiveness of fiscal policy, while Keynesians contend that crowding out will not be complete.
   b. Keynesians regard wage stickiness as a factor that prevents quick adjustment back to the natural rate of unemployment, while monetarists believe that wages are sufficiently flexible to ensure relatively quick adjustment.
   c. Monetarists do not see a need for activist policies, while Keynesians argue that activist policies can prove highly beneficial.
   d. All of the above.
   e. Only (a) and (c) accurately represent differences between monetarists and Keynesians.

8. The long-run aggregate supply curve is a vertical line running through
   a. the natural rate of output.
   b. the natural-rate price level.
   c. the natural rate of unemployment.
   d. none of the above.

9. Which of the following statements is not one commonly associated with Keynesian analysis?
   a. "The economy is inherently unstable, and failure to take corrective action now could mean prolonged unemployment."
   b. "It would be foolish to tie the hands of government policymakers and prevent them from responding to a negative supply shock."
   c. "Wages and prices, while not perfectly flexible, do respond quickly, and in the correct direction, to economic disturbances."
   d. "Crowding out is unlikely to be a problem in the current economic recovery."

10. If policymakers accommodate supply shocks by increasing the money supply, unemployment will return to its natural level sooner, but
    a. even Keynesians, in general, will oppose such a policy.
    b. the price level will increase in the long run.
    c. prices will take much longer in returning to their original level.
    d. none of the above will occur.

11. Keynesians contend that at a _____ price level the real quantity of money _____, _____ higher spending.
    a. lower; expands; encouraging
    b. lower; expands; discouraging
    c. lower; contracts; discouraging
    d. higher; expands; encouraging
    e. higher; expands; discouraging

12. OPEC oil price increases or fruit crop freezes are referred to as _____ price shocks and cause the aggregate _____ curve to shift _____.
    a. negative; demand; inward
    b. negative; demand; outward
    c. negative; supply; inward
    d. positive; supply; inward
    e. positive; supply; outward

13. The aggregate demand and supply framework indicates that in the long run the ultimate effect of a _____ in the money supply is an increase in _____.
    a. fall; aggregate output
    b. fall; the price level
    c. rise; aggregate output
    d. rise; the price level

14. _____ tend to question the effectiveness of _____ policy in shifting aggregate _____, since they believe that crowding out of investment will be nearly complete.
    a. Keynesians; fiscal; demand
    b. Keynesians; monetary; demand
    c. Monetarists; monetary; demand
    d. Monetarists; fiscal; demand
    e. Keynesians; monetary; supply

15. The _____ supply shock from declining oil prices in 1986 did not produce the business cycle boom that some had predicted, in part, because a _____ in net exports that year caused a weakening in aggregate _____.
    a. negative; decline; demand
    b. negative; rise; supply
    c. negative; decline; supply
    d. positive; rise; supply
    e. positive; decline; demand

16. Which of the following explains why Monetarists believe that the demand curve is downward sloping?
    a. The quantity theory of money shows that as the money supply rises, aggregate output rises.
    b. The quantity theory of money shows that for a fixed money supply and velocity, as the price level rises, aggregate real output falls.
    c. Since the velocity of money is fixed, changes in the money supply lead to changes in aggregate spending.
    d. All of the above.
17. If Italian goods became more popular around the world, and if Italian net exports grow, then
    a. Italy's aggregate demand curve will shift inward to the left.
    b. Italy's aggregate demand curve will shift outward to the right.
    c. Italy's aggregate supply curve will shift outward to the right.
    d. Italy's aggregate supply curve will shift inward to the left.
18. To Keynes, an important influence on business cycle fluctuations is _____, which is described as waves of optimism and pessimism.
    a. crowding out
    b. stagflation
    c. the velocity of money
    d. animal spirits
    e. hysteresis
19. If complete crowding out occurs, then as government spending increases
    a. private spending falls by the same amount.
    b. the aggregate demand curve is unaffected.
    c. the aggregate supply curve shifts outward to the right.
    d. All of the above.
    e. only (a) and (b) of the above.
20. If _____ is above the short run equilibrium, then there is excess _____ and the price level will fall until it reaches its equilibrium level.
    a. aggregate output; demand
    b. aggregate output; equilibrium
    c. the price level; supply
    d. the price level; crowding out
21. The natural rate of unemployment
    a. is the rate of unemployment to which the economy tends toward in the long run.
    b. occurs when there is zero unemployment.
    c. is estimated to be around 10% by most economists.
    d. rises when output is above the natural level of output.
22. The self-correcting mechanism predicts that if aggregate output is initially above the natural level of output, then in the long run _____ will rise and the _____ curve will shift inward to the left.
    a. the price level; aggregate demand
    b. the natural rate of unemployment; aggregate supply
    c. the real wage; aggregate supply
    d. aggregate output; aggregate demand

23. According to _____ the self-correcting mechanism works very quickly and there is no need for government policy to restore output to the natural rate level of output.
    a. activists
    b. passivists
    c. nonactivists
    d. Keynesians
24. If the price level rises and aggregate output rises, then which of the following is the most likely cause?
    a. An increase in investment spending.
    b. A rise in household income taxes.
    c. A rise in the expected inflation rate.
    d. A positive supply shock.
    e. A negative supply shock.
25. If the natural rate of unemployment experiences hysteresis, then recent _____ unemployment will _____ the natural rate of unemployment and lower the natural rate level of output.
    a. high; lower
    b. high; raise
    c. low; lower
    d. low; raise
26. A decrease in the availability of raw materials is called a
    a. negative demand shock.
    b. positive demand shock.
    c. negative supply shock.
    d. positive supply shock.
27. The initial effect of a _____ shift in the aggregate _____ curve is a rise in the price level and a rise in aggregate output, while the ultimate effect is only a rise in the price level.
    a. leftward; supply
    b. leftward; demand
    c. rightward; supply
    d. rightward; demand
28. An increase in price level, holding the nominal quantity of money constant, leads to ________ interest rates and in turn to a _______ level of the quantity of aggregate output demanded.
    a. higher, lower
    b. lower, lower
    c. higher, higher
    d. lower, higher
29. __________, _________, and __________ will shift the aggregate demand curve to the right.
    a. An increase in G, an increase in T, an increase in NX
    b. An increase in G, an increase in T, a decrease in NX
    c. An increase in C, an increase in I, a decrease in T
    d. An increase in price level, an increase in G, a decrease in T

30. According to real business cycle theory, _______ and _______ are the major driving forces behind short-run fluctuations in the business cycle.
    a. technological shocks, sticky wages
    b. sticky wages, sticky prices
    c. supply shocks, technological shocks
    d. shocks to tastes, technological shocks
31. A successful wage push by workers will shift
    a. the aggregate demand curve to the right.
    b. the aggregate supply curve to the right.
    c. the aggregate demand curve to the left.
    d. the aggregate supply curve to the left.
32. When the costs of production increase
    a. the long-run aggregate supply curve shifts to the left.
    b. the long-run aggregate supply curve shifts to the right.
    c. the short-run aggregate supply curve shifts to the left.
    d. the short-run aggregate supply curve shifts to the right.

CHAPTER 25

Transmission Mechanisms of Monetary Policy: The Evidence

CHAPTER SYNOPSIS/COMPLETIONS

This chapter examines the connection between monetary policy and economic activity, focusing on the debate between the (1)__________________ and the Keynesians over the years since the Great Depression, and illustrates how the accumulation of evidence has led to greater consensus regarding the importance of monetary policy on economic activity. Although views have converged, differences still exist, primarily because monetarists and Keynesians prefer different types of (2)____________________.

Monetarists regard monetary policy's effect on economic activity as diverse and constantly changing; thus they prefer to model the impact of money supply changes directly. Evidence indicating a high correlation between changes in money growth and fluctuations in economic activity is referred to as (3)__________________ __________________ evidence. Reduced form evidence merely indicates the existence of a relationship; it does not describe how monetary policy affects economic activity.

Keynesians tend to be skeptical of reduced form evidence, preferring to model the channels by which monetary policy affects the economy. Keynesian models are constructed using a system of equations, each equation describing part of the monetary transmission mechanism. These models are called (4)__________________ models because they attempt to describe the relationships among the various segments of the economy; that is, they attempt to describe how the pieces of the structure fit together.

The structural model approach has three major advantages over the reduced form approach:

1. Structural models allow us to evaluate each segment separately for its plausibility. This investigation improves our understanding of monetary policy's effect on economic activity.
2. Our improved understanding of the economy's workings may mean more accurate economic (5)__________________.
3. Our ability to predict the consequences of institutional change may be improved from the knowledge of economic relationships provided by structural model evidence.

One disadvantage of the structural model approach is that it must be correctly (6)________________ or it will tend to give poor predictions. For example, suppose that a change in money growth causes stock prices to change, which in turn causes consumer expenditures to change. If this transmission mechanism is not part of the model, then the model will provide inaccurate results. In weighing the advantages and disadvantages monetarists conclude that reduced form models give more reliable results.

Although less sensitive to the correct specification, reduced form models can prove to be misleading. Since reduced form models focus on correlations, they may imply that movements in one variable cause the movements in another when causality actually runs in the other direction or is nonexistent. (7)________________ ________________ refers to the condition where influence runs in the direction opposite that hypothesized. If two variables are highly correlated, it is possible that an independent (8)________________ factor influences the behaviour of both variables in a way that gives the appearance that one influences the other.

Early Keynesian models were poorly specified, leading to results indicating that monetary policy had little effect on economic activity. Had the early Keynesians specified relationships in terms of (9)________________ interest rates, rather than nominal interest rates, they would have been less likely to conclude that monetary policy does not matter.

In the early 1960s, the monetarists presented evidence indicating that monetary policy had never been more contractionary than during the Great Depression. The implication was that monetary policy mattered a great deal in determining aggregate economic activity. Milton Friedman and other monetarists emphasized three types of evidence when making their case about the importance of monetary growth: timing evidence, (10)________________ evidence, and historical evidence. Of the three types of evidence, most economists find (11)________________ evidence to be the most supportive of monetarist theory.

The impact of the monetarist attack on early Keynesian models led to improvements in these models to account for more channels of monetary influence on aggregate economic activity. Initial efforts extended the traditional interest-rate channel to account for changes in *consumer durable expenditure*. An important feature of the interest-rate mechanism is its emphasis on *real* rather than the nominal interest rate as the rate that influences business and consumer decisions. Because it is the real interest rate that affects spending, monetary policy can stimulate spending even when the nominal interest rate drops to zero. An expansionary monetary policy will raise the expected (12)________________ ________________ and hence expected inflation, thereby lowering the real interest rate.

In addition to the interest-rate transmission mechanism, monetary policy can affect spending through asset prices (primarily foreign exchange and equities) other than interest rates and through asymmetric information effects on credit markets (the so-called *credit view*). For example, an expansionary monetary policy, because it lowers the real interest rate, causes the domestic currency to depreciate, which stimulates net exports and gross domestic product. Tobin's q theory indicates that (13)________________ (or equity) prices can have an important effect on investment spending. Under this monetary channel, increasing stock prices stimulate investment as firms discover that the cost of replacement capital declines relative to the market value of business firms.

According to the credit view, an expansionary monetary policy increases bank reserves and deposits, increasing the volume of bank loans available to borrowers who do not have access to credit markets to finance their spending. In addition to this bank lending channel, monetary policy may influence spending through the balance sheet channel. An expansionary monetary policy raises the net (14)________________ of firms (improves their balance sheets), reducing adverse selection and moral hazard problems, increasing the willingness of banks to extend loans to these firms.

Other credit channels include: the cash flow channel, the unanticipated price level channel, and household liquidity effects. Expansionary monetary policy lowers nominal interest rates, reducing interest payments and thereby increasing (15)________________ ________________. Because banks know that borrowers' improved liquidity reduces adverse selection and moral hazard problems, lending increases. Similarly, expansionary monetary policy raises the price level, lowering the real value of firms' liabilities. This improvement in firms' balance sheets reduces adverse selection and moral hazard problems, thereby increasing banks' willingness to lend. The view that unanticipated movements in the price level have important effects on aggregate demand is a key feature of the *debt-deflation* view of the Great Depression. Because households' interest payments, cash flow, liquidity, and real value of assets and liabilities are affected by changes in interest rates and the price level, monetary policy influences consumer spending too.

These three monetary transmission mechanisms indicate that changes in monetary policy can have a significant effect on aggregate demand. Research findings from the Great Depression support the economic significance of these monetary channels. Declining stock prices, the decline in consumers' wealth, and the increase in real consumer debt (due to falling prices) depressed consumption, consumer durable expenditure, and expenditure on housing .

Although not all issues about monetary policy have been fully resolved, four lessons for monetary policy can be drawn from this chapter. First, changes in short-term nominal interest rates do not provide clear signals about monetary policy. Second, changes in prices of assets other than short-term debt instruments contain information about monetary policy. Third, fears about a liquidity trap are likely unfounded, as monetary policy can be effective in reviving a weak economy even when short-term interest rates are quite low. Fourth, price level stability is an important goal for monetary policy.

EXERCISES

EXERCISE 1: Two Types of Empirical Evidence

For each of the following statements, indicate whether reduced form evidence or structural model evidence is being presented by writing in the space provided an R for reduced form evidence and an S for structural model evidence.

_____ 1. Dutch researchers report that eating fish is associated with a lower risk of heart attack.

_____ 2. Eating fish appears to be effective in reducing heart attack risk. Fish oil reduces fat and cholesterol in the blood thereby preventing heart disease, the underlying cause of heart attacks.

_____ 3. Medical research has found that men who take one aspirin per day following a coronary attack significantly reduced the probability of a second coronary.

_____ 4. Drinking one ounce of alcohol per day seems to reduce cholesterol levels in the bloodstream, reducing the likelihood of coronary heart disease and heart attack.

_____ 5. Canadian researchers report that beer drinkers are less likely to report illness than nondrinkers, although they could not directly link the beverage itself to better health.

_____ 6. A reduction in the money supply causes the volume of loans to fall, which causes investment to fall as banks ration credit. This in turn causes aggregate output to fall.

_____ 7. An increase in the money supply causes interest rates to fall. Consumer durable expenditures rise in response, leading to an increase in aggregate output.

_____ 8. An increase in the money supply increases the demand for stocks. Rising stock prices cause Tobin's q to increase, which induces firms to undertake more investment spending.

_____ 9. An increase in the money supply is followed by an increase in aggregate output.

EXERCISE 2: Monetarists Versus the Keynesians

Listed below are a number of statements. Indicate which of the following statements are associated with monetarists (M) and which are associated with Keynesians (K).

_____ 1. Structural model evidence is superior to reduced form evidence because it allows us to better understand how the economy works.

_____ 2. Reduced form evidence allows for the luxury of not having to know all the many ways in which money might affect economic activity.

_____ 3. The channels through which changes in the money supply affect output and employment are numerous and ever changing.

_____ 4. The problem with looking at simple correlations is that it may be extremely difficult to determine the direction of causation. How can one be sure that aggregate output does not affect money growth rather than the reverse?

_____ 5. Changes in the money supply are the most important determinants of economic fluctuations in output, employment, and prices.

_____ 6. The main advantage of employing a monetary rule is that it would greatly diminish the use of discretionary stabilization policies.

_____ 7. The economy tends to be very unstable, making the use of discretionary monetary and fiscal policy essential to the maintenance of full employment.

_____ 8. We agree with the belief that money matters, but the weight of empirical evidence suggests that money is not all that matters.

_____ 9. Money is extremely important, but fiscal policy as well as net exports and "animal spirits" also contribute to fluctuations in aggregate demand.

EXERCISE 3: Interpreting Reduced Form Evidence

Some economists contend that inflation is the result of cost-push pressures exerted on the economy by powerful labour unions and big businesses. To support their position, they produce empirical results which clearly indicate that rising costs tend to precede rising prices in many instances. Despite the existence of such evidence, many economists in Canada are highly skeptical of cost-push theories.

1. Could there be a problem of reverse causation in the data that makes it appear as though cost increases precede price increases?

____

____

2. How might the prevalence of three-year labour contracts help account for the perception that costs lead prices?

____

____

3. Many economists dismiss the cost-push theory of inflation by pointing to a third factor that is believed to drive both costs and prices. What do you suppose this third factor is?

____

____

EXERCISE 4: Transmission Mechanisms of Monetary Policy

The traditional Keynesian view of the monetary transmission mechanism can be characterized as follows:

$$M\uparrow \rightarrow i_r\downarrow \rightarrow I\uparrow \rightarrow Y\uparrow$$

In response to monetarist challenges in the 1960s, many Keynesian economists began searching for new channels of monetary influence on economic activity. Match the names of transmission mechanisms on the right with their schematic depictions on the left.

_____ 1. $M\uparrow \rightarrow$ stock prices $\uparrow \rightarrow$ value of financial assets $\uparrow \rightarrow$ likelihood of financial distress $\downarrow \rightarrow$ consumer durable expenditures $\uparrow$ and residential housing $\uparrow \rightarrow Y\uparrow$ a. Balance sheet channel

_____ 2. $M\uparrow \rightarrow$ unanticipated $P\uparrow \rightarrow$ adverse selection $\downarrow$ moral hazard $\downarrow \rightarrow$ lending $\uparrow \rightarrow I\uparrow \rightarrow Y\uparrow$ b. Cash flow channel

_____ 3.	$M\uparrow \rightarrow$ bank deposits $\uparrow \rightarrow$ bank loans $\uparrow$ $I\uparrow \rightarrow Y\uparrow$	c. Exchange-rate effect
_____ 4.	$M\uparrow \rightarrow P_e\uparrow \rightarrow$ adverse selection $\downarrow$, moral hazard $\downarrow \rightarrow$ lending $\uparrow \rightarrow I\uparrow \rightarrow Y\uparrow$	d. Household liquidity effect
_____ 5.	$M\uparrow \rightarrow$ stock prices $\uparrow \rightarrow q\uparrow$investment $\uparrow \rightarrow Y\uparrow$	e. Unanticipated price level channel
_____ 6.	$M\uparrow \rightarrow i\downarrow \rightarrow$ cash flow $\uparrow \rightarrow$ adverse selection $\downarrow$, moral hazard $\downarrow \rightarrow$ lending $\uparrow \rightarrow I\uparrow \rightarrow Y\uparrow$	f. Bank lending channel
_____ 7.	$M\uparrow \rightarrow i_r\downarrow \rightarrow$ exchange rate $\downarrow \rightarrow$ exports $\uparrow \rightarrow Y\uparrow$	g. Tobin's *q* theory

EXERCISE 5: Japan's Recent Slump and Monetary Transmission Channels

Since the early 1990s the Japanese economy has experienced low growth and deflation. To fight the stagnation, the Bank of Japan lowered interest rates to near zero by the late 1990s and early 2000s. This was accomplished through open market operations, which increased bank reserves. Given this large drop in interest rates, why didn't the Japanese economy respond to monetary policy? One explanation is that there was a "credit crunch." Despite the fact that the Bank of Japan was increasing reserves, the evidence shows that bank lending to businesses was stagnant in the 1990s. For some reason, banks were not issuing loans.

For both of the following causes explain which monetary transmission channel it may interfere with and disrupt.

A. Banks had just experienced large losses on real estate loans in the 1980s.

____

____

B. The balance sheets of many businesses were worsened by the large debt burdens acquired in the 1980s.

____

____

EXERCISE 6: MONETARY POLICY

A. How does the structural model describe the transmission mechanism of monetary policy?

____

____

B. How does reduced-form evidence describe the transmission mechanism of monetary policy?

____

____

C. Briefly explain three advantages of structural model evidence.

____

____

D. Briefly explain two disadvantages of structural model evidence.

____

E. What is the main advantage of reduced-form evidence?

F. What is the reverse causation problem and what does it imply about reduced-form evidence?

G. Is the structural model approach better than the reduced-form approach, or vice versa?

SELF-TEST

PART A: True-False Questions

Circle whether the following statements are true (T) or false (F).

T F 1. Reduced-form evidence examines whether one variable has an effect on another by looking at a sequence of steps and describing the process at each step so that the channels of influence can be better understood.

T F 2. One advantage of the structural-model approach is that it can give us a better understanding of how money influences economic activity.

T F 3. Correlation does not necessarily imply causation.

T F 4. Though nominal interest rates fell during the Great Depression to extremely low levels, real interest rates rose.

T F 5. Historical evidence that has focused on the effects of exogenous changes in the money supply indicates that changes in aggregate output are related to changes in money growth.

T F 6. Keynesians argue that while banks may tend to ration credit in response to "tight" monetary policy, such credit rationing has no effect on economic activity.

T F 7. Friedman and Schwartz argue that money growth affects output with "long and variable lags."

T F 8. Though Tobin's *q* theory provides a good explanation for the economic recovery that started in late 1982, it is inconsistent with the events of the Great Depression.

T F 9. Assume that the stock market index falls by over 500 points in one week and remains at this level long enough that people adjust their expectations downward regarding the average level of the stock market index. One should expect this event to affect the level of consumption.

T F 10. Economic theory suggests that the stock market crash of 1929 depressed consumer expenditures due to the loss of wealth and the increase in financial distress.

T F 11. By using structural model evidence, monetarists believe that monetary policy is very important to economic fluctuations.

T F 12. A weak link between nominal interest rates and investment indicates that there is no strong link between real interest rates and investment.

T F 13. Monetary policy can be highly effective in reviving a weak economy even if the short-term interest rate is already near zero.

T F 14. Early empirical studies found a strong linkage between movements in nominal interest rates and investment spending.

PART B: Multiple-Choice Questions

Circle the appropriate answer.

1. Monetarists prefer reduced-form models because they believe that
   a. reverse causation is never a problem.
   b. structural models may understate money's effect on economic activity.
   c. money supply changes are always exogenous.
   d. each of the above is true.
2. Scientists tend to be skeptical of reduced-form evidence because
   a. the finding of a high correlation between two variables does not always imply that changes in one cause changes in the other.
   b. reduced-form evidence may not account for all the channels of influence.
   c. it fails to add insight to the process that leads movements in one variable to cause movements in another.
   d. if the model is poorly specified it can lead to poor predictions about the future behaviour of the variable of interest.
   e. of both (a) and (c) of the above.
3. Monetarist evidence in which declines in money growth are followed by recessions provides the strongest support for their position that monetary policy matters.
   a. statistical
   b. historical
   c. timing
   d. structural
4. Early Keynesians tended to dismiss the importance of monetary policy due to their findings that
   a. indicated the absence of a link between movements in nominal interest rates and investment spending.
   b. interest rates had fallen during the Great Depression.
   c. surveys of businessmen revealed that market interest rates had no effect on their decisions of how much to invest in new physical capital.
   d. all of the above are true.

5. Monetarists contend that reduced-form evidence provides valid proof that monetary policy affects economic activity when it can be shown that the change in the money supply
   a. is an endogenous event.
   b. is an exogenous event.
   c. preceded the change in economic activity.
   d. was expected.
6. What were the monetarists' main conclusions from the early reduced-form evidence?
   a. One had to be careful to distinguish between real and nominal magnitudes.
   b. The early Keynesian models were incorrectly specified because they accounted for too few channels of monetary influence.
   c. Monetarists models showed that fiscal policies had little or no effect on economic activity.
   d. Both (a) and (b) are correct.
   e. Both (b) and (c) are correct.
7. The availability hypothesis suggests that in periods characterized by "tight" money, banks may
   a. stop making any loans.
   b. continue to make loans, but only at much higher interest rates.
   c. ration credit rather than significantly raise interest rates.
   d. make available more loans to businesses with which they have had no previous dealings.
8. Because of asymmetric information problems in credit markets, monetary policy may affect economic activity through the balance sheet channel, which holds that an increase in money supply
   a. raises equity prices, which lowers the cost of new capital relative to the market value of firms, thereby increasing investment spending.
   b. raises the net worth of firms, decreasing adverse selection and moral hazard problems, thereby increasing banks' willingness to lend to finance investment spending.
   c. raises the level of bank reserves, deposits, and the quantity of bank loans available, which raises the spending by those individuals who do not have access to credit markets.
   d. does none of the above.
9. Assume that a contractionary monetary policy lowers the price level by more than anticipated, raising the real value of consumer debt. New Keynesian structural models suggest that a contractionary monetary policy is channeled into lower consumer expenditure through which of the following effects?
   a. Bank lending channel
   b. Tobin's q
   c. Traditional interest-rate effect
   d. Household liquidity effect
10. The household liquidity effect suggests that higher stock prices lead to increased consumer expenditures because consumers
   a. feel more secure about their financial position.
   b. will want to sell their stocks and spend the proceeds before stock prices go back down.
   c. believe that they will receive higher wages in the near future because companies are now more profitable.
   d. believe none of the above.
11. _____ prefer to emphasize _____ model evidence because they believe that _____ models do not add insight into how monetary policy affects the economy.
   a. Keynesians; structural; reduced form
   b. Keynesians; reduced form; structural
   c. Monetarists; structural; reduced form

d. Monetarists; reduced form; structural

12. Monetarists claim that simple _____ models, because they may ignore important transmission mechanisms, tend to _____ the importance of monetary policy's effect on the economy.
    a. structural; overstate
    b. reduced form; overstate
    c. structural; understate
    d. reduced form; understate

13. Because they believed that _____ policy was _____, early Keynesians stressed the importance of _____ policy.
    a. fiscal; ineffective; monetary
    b. monetary; ineffective; fiscal
    c. monetary; potent; monetary
    d. fiscal; too potent; monetary

14. Economic theory suggests that _____ interest rates are a _____ important determinant than _____ interest rates in explaining the behaviour of investment spending.
    a. nominal; more; real
    b. real; less; nominal
    c. real; more; nominal
    d. market; more; real
    e. real; less; market

15. Which of the following accurately describe the current state of the monetarist-Keynesian debate on monetary policy and economic activity?
    a. Keynesians still insist that monetary policy is not an important source of business cycle fluctuations.
    b. Although Keynesians now agree that monetary policy matters, they do not believe that it is all that matters.
    c. There is now general agreement among Keynesians that fiscal policy is indeed an extremely important source of business cycle fluctuations.
    d. Only (a) and (c) of the above.

16. Suppose that a structural model specifies that X influences Z and that Y influences Z. In which of the following is the structural model appropriate for determining the influence of X on Z?
    a. X influences Y.
    b. X does not influence Y.
    c. X influences W and W influences Z.
    d. In none of the above is the structural model appropriate.

17. The statement "correlation does not imply causation" means that if two variables are correlated, then
    a. they cannot cause a third variable.
    b. they always cause a third variable.
    c. one variable causes the other, but it is not known which direction causality runs.
    d. one variable may or may not cause the other.

18. If one event happens before a second event, then this supports the assertion that the first event caused the second event
    a. as long as the first event was an endogenous event.
    b. as long as the first event was an exogenous event.
    c. as long as reverse causality exists.
    d. as long as the first event occurred after the second event.
    e. none of the above.

19. Even if the _____ interest rate is zero, the _____ interest rate can still be lowered by expansionary monetary policy as long as _____ is increased.
    a. real; nominal; government spending
    b. real; nominal; expected inflation
    c. nominal; real, expected inflation
    d. real; nominal; the money supply
    e. nominal; real; moral hazard
20. Tobin's *q* theory predicts that as the money supply increases
    a. the price of stocks will rise.
    b. the ratio of firm market value to capital replacement cost will fall.
    c. investment goods are relatively expensive and firms will reduce investment spending.
    d. only (a) and (b) of the above.
    e. only (b) and (c) of the above.
21. According to the lifecycle hypothesis of consumption, consumption will _____ when the money supply falls, since the value of stocks and housing is _____ and consumer lifetime resources are _____.
    a. increase; higher; higher
    b. increase; lower; lower
    c. decrease; lower; higher
    d. decrease; higher; higher
    e. decrease; lower; lower
22. The bank lending channel suggests that monetary policy will have a larger influence on spending by _____ firms, since _____ firms have _____ access to credit through stocks and bonds.
    a. small; large; greater
    b. small; large; less
    c. large; small; greater
    d. large; small; less
23. The cash flow monetary transmission channel suggests that as the _____ interest rate falls, firms' cash flow and _____ increase, which _____ adverse selection and moral hazard problems.
    a. real; liquidity; increases
    b. real; stock price; decreases
    c. real; liquidity; decreases
    d. nominal; liquidity; decreases
    e. nominal; stock price; increases
24. When the price level rises unexpectedly, firms' debt burdens _____ and net worth increases. The effect is to _____ adverse selection and moral hazard problems, which results in increased lending.
    a. increase; increase
    b. increase; decrease
    c. decrease; increase
    d. decrease; decrease
25. Credit channels are likely to be important monetary transmission mechanisms because
    a. asymmetric information, which forms the core of credit channel theory, does a good job of explaining financial market institutions.
    b. small firms, which are more likely to be credit-constrained, appear to be most affected by monetary policy.
    c. credit market imperfections appear to influence firms' expenditure decisions.

d. all of the above.

e. only (b) and (c) of the above.

26. If a high correlation of variable A and variable B misleadingly suggests that controlling variable A would help to control the level of variable B, then it is likely that

a. changes in variable B affect changes in variable A on account of reverse causation.

b. variable A and variable B are both affected by some other factor.

c. either (a) or (b) of the above are possible.

d. none of the above.

27. An increase in stock prices _____ the net worth of firms and _____ investment spending because of the reduction in moral hazard.

a. lowers; lowers

b. raises; lowers

c. lowers; raises

d. raises; raises

28. Which of the following is the key element in monetarists' discussions of why actual economies were not stuck in a liquidity trap during the Great Depression?

a. The rational expectations.

b. The fact that the real interest rate rather than nominal rate affects spending.

c. Sticky prices.

d. The fact that money does not matter at all.

29. Which of the following is true?

a. Monetary policy is not effective if short-run interest rates are close to zero.

b. Monetary policy is effective even if short-run interest rates are close to zero.

c. Monetary policy is effective only if this policy is anticipated.

d. none of the above.

30. In which of the following cases do stock prices transmit the effect of monetary policy to GDP?

a. Traditional interest rate effects, Household liquidity effects

b. Tobin's q theory, Wealth effects

c. Exchange rate effects, Bank lending channel

d. both (a) and (b) of the above.

31. When Tobin's q is low, firms will not purchase new investment goods

a. because the market value of the firm is high relative to the cost of capital.

b. because the cost of capital is lower than the market value of the firm.

c. because the market value of the firm is low relative to market interest rate.

d. because the market value of the firm is low relative to the cost of capital.

32. According to the traditional components view of the monetary transmission mechanism, an expansionary monetary policy leads to

a. a fall in real interest rate, which in turn lowers the cost of capital, causing a rise in investment spending , thereby leading to an increase in aggregate demand and output.

b. a rise in real interest rate, which in turn increases the cost of capital, causing a fall in investment spending , thereby leading to a decrease in aggregate demand and output.

c. a fall in real interest rate, which in turn increases the cost of capital, causing a fall in investment spending , thereby leading to a decrease in the aggregate demand and output.

d. a fall in real interest rate, which in turn lowers government spending, thereby leading to an increase in aggregate demand and output.

CHAPTER 26

Money and Inflation

CHAPTER SYNOPSIS/COMPLETIONS

In this chapter the aggregate demand and supply analysis introduced in Chapter 24 is used to examine the role of monetary policy in creating inflation. It will be shown that sustained inflation is always the result of sustained growth in the money supply.

The German experience from 1921 to 1923 illustrates a classical scenario of (1)__________________. The unwillingness of German government officials to raise taxes and their inability to borrow an amount sufficient to finance huge budget deficits left money creation as the only available means of financing government expenditures. This scenario has been repeated many times, for example, in Argentina and Brazil in the 1980s. In both instances, massive government budget deficits initiated rapid expansions in the money supply, which in turn led to rapidly accelerating rates of inflation.

While these episodes, along with others, confirm that sustained inflation can only occur if there is a continually increasing money supply, a variety of sources are actually responsible for the inflationary monetary policies of many countries. Budget deficits, concerns over unemployment, negative supply shocks, union wage pushes, and concerns over interest rates often lead to inflationary monetary expansions.

Economists are in general agreement that inflation is always and everywhere a (2) "__________________ phenomenon." Evidence from both historical and recent inflationary episodes confirms the proposition that sustained inflation results from excessive monetary expansion.

The consensus must appear at first to be highly unusual, given that much of the two previous chapters has been devoted to the disagreements between monetarists and Keynesians. The apparent paradox is solved by the precise way in which economists define inflation. A one-shot (or one-time) increase in the price level is simply not defined as inflation by economists. Only when the price level is continually rising do economists consider such episodes to be inflationary.

Keynesians, unlike monetarists, believe that one-shot tax cuts or government-spending boosts are likely to raise aggregate demand, and thus the price level, but they contend that any effect on inflation will be merely (3)__________________. In their view, fiscal actions are incapable of generating sustained price increases. Thus monetarists and Keynesians agree that rapid money growth is both a sufficient and necessary condition explaining inflation.

Regarding negative supply shocks, economists are again in general agreement that it is only through monetary (4)__________________ that such shocks prove inflationary. In the absence of an increase in money growth, the price level would rise, but it would not continue to do so.

One must naturally wonder why, if it is well understood, inflation continues to plague so many countries to this day. Examination of the Canadian experience suggests that governments pursue many goals, some of which are not (5)__________________ with price stability. Specifically, federal government efforts designed to reduce unemployment in the 1960s proved incompatible with the goal of general price stability. In the 1970s, a series of negative (6)__________________ __________________ compounded the problem by pressuring government policymakers toward accommodation in order to prevent high rates of unemployment.

Higher wage demands by workers can lead to inflation if policymakers fear that such demands will cause rising unemployment. Additionally, the government may set its (7)__________________ target too low, causing overexpansion and inflation.

Large government budget deficits are another possible source of excessive money growth. Politicians are extremely reluctant to cut government expenditures and raise taxes because such actions are often politically unpopular. Thus the political process is likely to generate a bias toward large budget deficits and inflation.

Economists often find it difficult to distinguish between demand-pull and (8)__________________ inflation. Both types of inflation result when money growth becomes excessive. At first glance, one distinguishes between the two by looking at the behaviour of employment. Demand-pull inflation is associated with high employment, and cost-push inflation is associated with (9)____________ employment. Once inflation is underway, however, demand-pull inflations may exhibit cost-push tendencies as workers demand higher wages in expectation of higher inflation.

The government budget (10)__________________ indicates that an increase in the government budget deficit must lead to an increase in the sum of the monetary base and outstanding government bonds held by the public. If the government pays for additional spending with higher taxes, the deficit does not increase and the monetary base does not change. Should the government run a deficit, it must issue bonds to pay for the additional spending. If individuals buy these newly issued bonds, there will be no change in the monetary base. When the public purchases the bonds, the government spends the proceeds returning the funds to the public. Hence the government sale of bonds to the public has no effect on the monetary base.

Deficit financing through central bank security purchases, however, leads to an increase in the monetary base. This method of deficit financing is often referred to as "printing money" because high-powered money is created in the process. The action is probably better referred to as *monetizing the debt* because the money supply increases as a result of the increase in government debt.

An examination of inflation in Canada from 1960 through 1980 dismisses the importance of budget deficits in explaining rapid money growth. It appears that the concern over unemployment led to over-expansionary policies which kept unemployment low over the period 1965 to 1973. In the latter half of the 1970s, inflation resembles the (11)__________________ variety as unemployment rose to a level that exceeded the natural rate level.

The debate over the appropriateness of activist stabilization policy has important implications for anti-inflationary policies. Monetarists argue against the use of activist policy to reduce unemployment. They believe the effort is fruitless because any reduction in unemployment will be merely temporary, and it may hinder anti-inflationary efforts. Monetarists hold that the economy is inherently (12)______________, as wages are sufficiently flexible so that deviations from the natural rate of output are quickly reversed. Further, monetarists contend that even in those instances where adjustment tends to be relatively slow, activist policies are not likely to improve circumstances. In their view, policy responses are ineffectual, or even harmful, due to the long (13)______________ ______________ that plague government decision making. For this reason, monetarists tend to support monetary rules that limit the discretion of policymakers.

Keynesians are optimistic about the effectiveness of (14)__________________ policies. They believe that available evidence indicates that wages and prices are sticky, implying prolonged deviations from the natural rate of output and unemployment. Therefore, they contend that government fiscal or monetary actions are required to restore the economy to full employment. Unlike the monetarists, Keynesians contend that fiscal policy actions will be effective and dismiss the possibility of complete crowding out.

The phenomenon of "stagflation" in the latter half of the 1970s focused greater attention on the importance of expectations. People had come to expect that macroeconomic policies would always be accommodating; thus, when policymakers announced intentions of fighting inflation, few people believed them. Following this experience, economists in greater numbers began to question the desirability of activist policy. Some economists argued that nonaccommodating policy would yield better inflation performance with no more unemployment. Importantly, policy must be (15)________, which means that the public must expect that policymakers will carry out their promises. Although this conclusion is not universally accepted, the recognition of the importance expectations play in economics has led to a new field of macroeconomics which is presented in Chapter 27.

EXERCISES

EXERCISE 1: Forces of Inflationary Monetary Policy

Monetarists and Keynesians agree that inflation is a monetary phenomenon. In other words, inflation would not persist in the absence of excessive money growth. Of interest to many economists, therefore, is the source of inflationary monetary policy. Why at times does the Bank of Canada expand the money supply at a rapid rate? Two explanations have been offered, both of which give us an insight into the forces that affect Bank decision making. List below the two explanations presented in the text that help explain expansionary monetary policy. Provide a brief explanation for each factor listed.

1. ____

____

2. ____

____

EXERCISE 2: High Employment Targets and Inflation

Suppose that the government's target unemployment rate is 3% (corresponding to an output level of $Y_{3\%}$ in Figure 26A). Assume that the economy is initially at the natural-rate level of output, where the aggregate demand curve, AD_1, and aggregate supply curve, AS_1, intersect at point 1 in Figure 26A. If the government is targeting a 3% unemployment rate, show where the government would shift the aggregate demand curve in Figure 26A and mark it as AD_2.

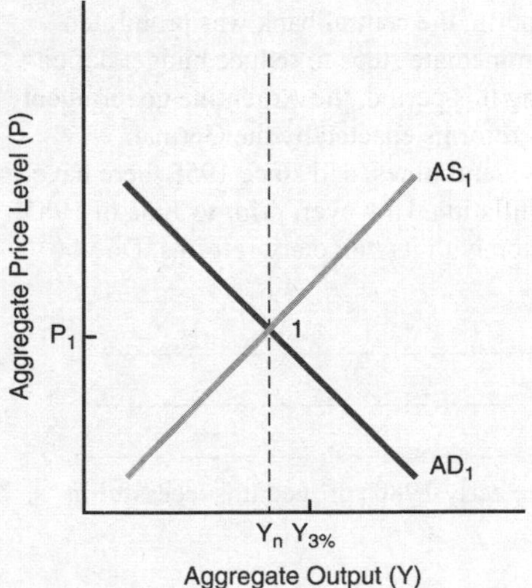

Figure 26A

What would now happen to the aggregate supply curve?

Why?

Draw in the new aggregate supply curve as AS_2. Now what would the government do to aggregate demand?

Draw in the new aggregate demand curve as AD_3. Where will the aggregate supply curve shift to now?

Draw it in as AS_3. What is the outcome as the scenario discussed above repeats itself?

EXERCISE 3: Budget Deficits and Money Creation

When the Canadian government is running a budget deficit, does this necessarily cause the rate of money growth to increase?

What two facts must be true in order for budget deficits to lead to higher money growth?

1.

2.

Do you think that both facts were true during the 1960–1980 period?

Why or why not?

EXERCISE 4: Eliminating Inflation: The Importance of Credibility

The German hyperinflation provides a classic example of how mistaken policies can generate dire consequences. More importantly, the successful cure of the hyperinflation at a relatively low cost illustrates the importance of adopting an anti-inflationary policy that the citizenry views as credible.

The German government adopted several reforms at the time it announced its intention of controlling inflation. First, the government transferred the responsibility for monetary control to a new authority. Second, new currency was issued. Third, an upper limit was placed on the issue of this new currency. Fourth, the central bank was prohibited from issuing paper money to the government. Finally, the government took immediate steps to reduce budget deficits.

In the first half of the 1980s, Argentina was beset by hyperinflation. During this period, the Argentine government and central bank adopted numerous reforms, including some of the monetary reforms enacted by the German government of the 1920s. For example, Argentina has issued new currency, several times, and since 1955 there have been more than 30 different finance ministers, each of whom vowed to stop inflation. However, prior to June of 1985, Argentina made no effort to appreciably reduce its budget deficit in conjunction with its monetary reforms. Do you think that Argentina's monetary reforms were credible? Why or why not?

Can the lack of credibility explain why the Argentine monetary reforms of the early 1980s proved unsuccessful in fighting inflation while the Germans were successful in the 1920s?

In June of 1985, Argentina instituted a set of policies to reduce its 1000% inflation rate. Argentina declared a one-week bank holiday, created a new currency in the interim, imposed wage and price controls, and implemented budget reforms that reduced the budget deficit from 8% to 4% of GDP. The strict anti-inflation plan proved successful in lowering the annual inflation rate to 50% by August of 1986. Disappointingly, however, the austerity plan only produced short-run benefits. By March of 1988, inflation was running at an annual rate of 207%—four times higher than predicted one year earlier by the economic team of President Raul Alfonsin. Recurrent price and wage freezes during 1987 and 1988 could not counteract the inflationary effects of budget deficits that had once again reached 8% of GDP by late 1987. Does the temporary success of the Argentine reforms suggest a key element to reducing inflation? Explain.

____

____

____

EXERCISE 5: The Budget Deficit and the Monetary Base

A. List the three methods that can be used to finance government spending.

1. ____
2. ____
3. ____

B. Which of the three methods has an affect on the monetary base?

____

C. When the government borrows from the Bank of Canada, the monetary base increases. This method of finance is referred to as

____

D. Does a large government deficit necessarily lead to a rapid growth in the monetary base? Why or why not?

____

____

EXERCISE 6: Expectations and Policy Choice

A. Assume that the economy is originally at the natural rate level of output, Y_n, and price level P_1. This is shown by point 1 in Figure 26B. Suppose that workers are able to insist upon large wage increases. Show the effect of higher wages in Figure 26B and label the new aggregate supply curve AS_2, the new price level P_2, and the new output level Y_2.

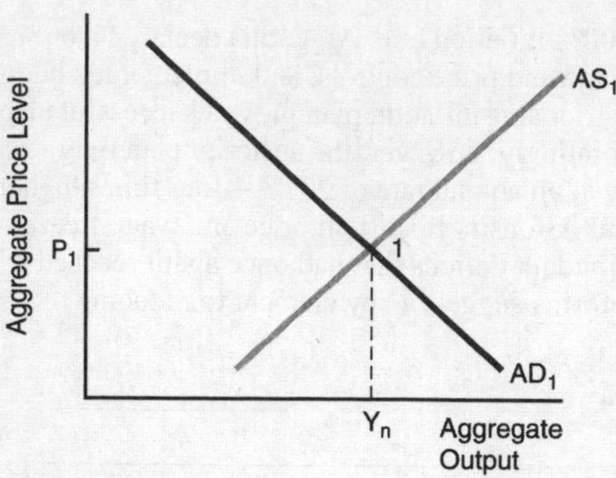

Figure 26B

B. The government has two possible responses to combat the increase in unemployment that results. First, it could pursue a nonactivist policy by doing nothing. Eventually, the economy's self-correcting mechanism will return output back to the natural rate level of output. Show the effect of nonactivist policy and the self-correcting mechanism in Figure 26B.

____

____

C. Alternatively, the government could combat high unemployment at Y_2 by pursuing an activist policy and increasing the money supply. Show the effect of such a policy in Figure 26B. Label the new aggregate demand curve AD_2 and the new price level P_3.

____

____

D. Will the nonactivist or activist response to the initial wage increase be more likely to encourage further wage pushes by workers? Explain.

____

____

EXERCISE 7: INFLATION, MONETARY AND FISCAL POLICIES

A. What does Friedman's statement that "inflation is always and everywhere a monetary phenomenon" mean?

B. Depict graphically the monetarist view of the source of high inflation. Give a clear explanation of your graphical analysis.

C. Depict graphically and explain, in words, why fiscal policy by itself cannot produce high inflation.

D. Depict graphically and explain, in words, why supply-side phenomena by themselves cannot produce high inflation.

SELF-TEST

PART A: True-False Questions

Circle whether the following statements are true (T) or false (F).

T F 1. If inflation is defined as a continuous rise in the price level, then it is true that inflation can be eliminated by reducing the growth rate of the money supply to a low level.

T F 2. Keynesians disagree with the monetarists' proposition that inflation is a monetary phenomenon. That is, Keynesians believe that inflation can occur even when money growth has not been excessive.

T F 3. Any shift to the right in AD, regardless of its cause, will generate a higher inflation.

T F 4. The price level may rise in any one month due to factors unrelated to changes in the money supply. Thus one can conclude that continual price-level increases need not be related to changes in the money supply.

T F 5. Keynesians argue that factors other than a continually increasing money supply may lead to sustained inflation.

T F 6. Sustained inflation occurs when unions successfully push up wages, even if the monetary authorities refuse to accommodate the higher wages by expanding the money supply.

T F 7. Inflation, according to one view, is the side effect of government efforts to cure high unemployment.

T F 8. At first glance, one would expect falling unemployment to be associated with demand-pull inflation.

T F 9. Huge government budget deficits have been the initiating source of inflationary monetary policies in every instance of hyperinflation.

T F 10. An examination of the period from 1960 through 1980 suggests that large government deficits are to blame for the inflationary monetary policies of this period.

T F 11. Accommodating policy refers to an activist policy with a low inflation target.

T F 12. Studies have shown that the welfare cost of inflation in Canada is much higher than in the U.S.

T F 13. Cost–push inflation is a monetary phenomenon because it cannot occur without the monetary authorities pursuing an accommodating policy of a higher rate of money growth.

T F 14. Supply-side phenomena cannot be the source of high inflation.

PART B: Multiple-Choice Questions

Circle the appropriate answer.

1. A continual increase in the money supply, according to Keynesian analysis, will cause
   a. the price level to increase, but have no lasting effect on the inflation rate.
   b. the price level to fall.
   c. inflation.
   d. output to increase and will have no effect on either the price level or inflation.
   e. none of the above.

2. Monetarists believe that a continually rising price level ______ due to factors other than growth in the money supply.
   a. may be
   b. is never

c. is sometimes
d. is always

3. In general, most economists believe that inflation can only occur if
   a. government spending increases.
   b. strong labour unions demand higher wages.
   c. negative supply shocks continuously hit the economy.
   d. the money supply is continually expanded.
4. Monetarists emphasize the importance of a constant money growth rate rule more than the balanced-budget amendment or restrictions on union power because
   a. they tend to regard excessive money growth as the cause of inflation.
   b. while they do not believe that excessive money growth is the cause of inflation, they do believe that it is related to excessive government expenditures.
   c. while they regard unions as the source of inflation, they know that they are too powerful politically to deal with.
   d. of each of the above.
5. Analysis of hyperinflationary episodes indicates that the rapid money growth leading to the inflation results when
   a. governments finance massive budget deficits by printing money.
   b. central banks attempt to peg interest rates.
   c. government taxes become too excessive.
   d. central banks lower reserve requirements too much.
6. A one-shot increase in government spending will have what effect on the inflation rate, according to the Keynesian analysis?
   a. Permanent increase
   b. Temporary increase
   c. Temporary decrease
   d. No effect
7. Assume workers know that government policymakers, because unemployment is politically unpopular, always accommodate wage increases by expanding the money supply. What type of inflation is likely to result if workers demand higher wages not fearing a rise in unemployment?
   a. Demand-pull inflation
   b. Hyperinflation
   c. Cost-push inflation
   d. Demand-shock inflation
8. If an economist were interested in testing whether federal budget deficits had been the source of excessive money growth for a particular country during the time period 1900–1930, she would be interested in the behaviour of
   a. inflation.
   b. the money supply-to-monetary-base ratio.
   c. interest rates.
   d. the government debt-to-GDP ratio.
9. When the government sets an unemployment target that is unrealistically low without realizing it, what is the likely result?
   a. Inflation
   b. An unemployment rate that may actually drop below the natural rate for a period of time
   c. Excessive money growth
   d. All of the above

10. Governments are likely to lose credibility in fighting inflation when
    a. government budget deficits remain high.
    b. government policymakers continue to accommodate wage demands and negative supply shocks.
    c. the commitment to high employment is viewed as government's number-one goal for political reasons.
    d. all of the above are true.
11. The German hyperinflation of the 1920s supports the proposition that excessive money growth leads to higher prices, and not the other way around, since the increase in money growth appears to have been
    a. unintentional.
    b. intentional.
    c. exogenous.
    d. endogenous.
12. A common element of hyperinflationary episodes discussed in the text is government unwillingness to
    a. finance expenditures by raising taxes.
    b. increase expenditures.
    c. finance expenditures by printing money.
    d. finance transfer payments by printing money.
13. Which of the following statements is true?
    a. The price level may rise in any one month due to factors unrelated to changes in the money supply. Thus one can conclude that continual price-level increases need not be related to changes in the money supply.
    b. Within the aggregate demand and supply framework, a continually increasing money supply has the effect of continually shifting the aggregate demand curve to the right.
    c. Keynesians argue that factors other than a continually increasing money supply may lead to sustained inflation.
    d. Sustained inflation occurs when unions successfully push up wages, even if the monetary authorities refuse to accommodate the higher wages by expanding the money supply.
14. Workers will have greater incentives to push for higher wages when government policymakers place greater concern on _____ than _____ and are thus _____ likely to adopt accommodative policies.
    a. inflation; unemployment; less
    b. inflation; unemployment; more
    c. unemployment; inflation; less
    d. unemployment; inflation; more
15. Which of the following statements is true?
    a. Cost-push inflation is not a monetary phenomenon.
    b. At first glance, one would expect rising unemployment to be associated with demand-pull inflation.
    c. Huge government budget deficits have been the initiating source of inflationary monetary policies in every instance of hyperinflation.
    d. Large government deficits are to blame for the inflationary monetary policies of the 1970s in Canada.
16. Economists such as Robert Barro hold the view that deficits
    a. cause the monetary base to decrease.
    b. cause the monetary base to increase.
    c. have no effect on the monetary base.
    d. are inflationary even when financed by tax hikes.

17. The reason that Keynesians do not believe that fiscal policy alone can lead to a continually rising price level is that
    a. fiscal and monetary policies will cancel each other out in the long run.
    b. the self-correcting mechanism will lower the inflation rate in the long run.
    c. there is a limit to how much taxes can be reduced or how much the government can spend.
    d. all of the above.
    e. only (b) and (c) of the above.
18. If energy prices rise tremendously, then which of the following is true?
    a. The aggregate supply curve will shift inward to the left in the short run.
    b. The aggregate supply curve will shift inward to the left in the long run after the self-correcting mechanism begins.
    c. The aggregate demand curve will shift inward to the left in the short run.
    d. The aggregate demand curve will shift outward to the right in the long run after the self-correcting mechanism begins.
    e. None of the above.
19. Demand-pull inflation
    a. may be the result of a high money growth rate.
    b. results from the aggregate demand curve shifting outward to the right.
    c. can eventually trigger cost-push inflation if inflation expectations rise.
    d. will usually be accompanied by unemployment rates below the natural rate of unemployment.
    e. All of the above.
20. How can a government pay for a budget deficit?
    a. Lower taxes
    b. Borrow by issuing government bonds
    c. Decrease the monetary base
    d. Increase government expenditures
    e. None of the above
21. When government spending is paid for by monetizing the debt
    a. the Bank of Canada pays for items with new currency.
    b. the central bank sells bonds to pay for items.
    c. the monetary base is reduced and the amount of government bonds held by the public is increased.
    d. the monetary base is increased and the amount of government bonds held by the public is reduced.
    e. none of the above.
22. Proponents of the theory of Ricardian equivalence believe that when the government runs a deficit
    a. the demand for bonds increases.
    b. household saving decreases.
    c. the interest rate rises.
    d. only (a) and (b) of the above.
    e. only (a) and (c) of the above.
23. The length of time that passes before policymakers can correctly interpret economic data is known as the _____ lag.
    a. data
    b. recognition
    c. legislative

d. implementation
e. effectiveness

24. The case for an activist policy is made stronger if
    a. the political process takes longer to pass economic policy.
    b. it takes less time for the impact of policy to be felt.
    c. worker expectations regarding policy are unimportant when wages are negotiated.
    d. only (a) and (b) of the above.
    e. only (b) and (c) of the above.

25. Policy __________ tend to recommend the use of policy _________.
    a. activists; rules
    b. activists; lags
    c. nonactivists; rules
    d. nonactivists; discretion
    e. nonactivisits; expectations

26. A one-time increase in wages due to a successful wage push by labour unions causes
    a. continual inflation.
    b. a one-time increase in the price level.
    c. a one-time increase in real output.
    d. both (b) and (c) of the above.

27. Chronic government budget deficits will lead to inflation if
    a. they are financed by government sales of bonds to the public.
    b. they are financed by government sales of bonds to the central bank.
    c. they are financed by government sales of bonds to commercial banks.
    d. any of the above occurs.

28. A deficit can be the source of a sustained inflation only if it is ________ and if the government finances it by _________.
    a. temporary, issuing bonds to the public
    b. temporary, creating money
    c. persistent, creating money
    d. persistent, issuing bonds to the public

29. Inflation is defined as
    a. a rise in prices.
    b. a rapid rise in prices.
    c. a continuing and rapid rise in the price of necessary goods.
    d. a sustained increase in the general level of prices.

30. _________ happens when the amount of goods and services people are willing and able to buy goes up, leading to an increase in prices.
    a. Demand-pull inflation
    b. Demand-push inflation
    c. Cost-pull inflation
    d. Cost-push inflation

31. Whenever a country's inflation rate is extremely high for a sustained period of time,
    a. its rate of money supply growth is extremely low.
    b. its rate of money supply growth is constant.
    c. its rate of money supply growth is also extremely high.
    d. its rate of money supply growth is lower than the aggregate output growth.

CHAPTER 27

Rational Expectations: Implications for Policy

CHAPTER SYNOPSIS/COMPLETIONS

Chapter 27 discusses the implications of rational expectations theory for macroeconomic stabilization policies. Rational expectations theory arose in the 1970s as an attempt to explain "stagflation" and the failure of government policies to prevent this unhappy state. How can the apparent ineffectiveness of government stabilization policies be explained? This chapter introduces models that attempt to answer this question.

In his famous paper, "Econometric Policy Evaluation: A Critique," Robert Lucas argues that stabilization policies formulated on the basis of conventional econometric models will fail to stabilize the economy since (1)__________________ about policy will alter the intended effects. Lucas argues that while conventional econometric models may be useful for forecasting economic activity, they cannot be used to evaluate the potential impact of particular policies on the economy. The short-run forecasting ability of these models provides no evidence of the accuracy to be expected from simulations of hypothetical policy alternatives.

To understand Lucas's argument, one needs to recognize that conventional econometric models contain equations that describe the relationships between hundreds of variables. These relationships (parameters), estimated using past data, are assumed to remain (2)______________________. Lucas contends that such models will likely provide misleading results about the effects of a policy change (say, a monetary expansion); the actual effects are likely to be different than predicted because the change in policy will mean that the way expectations are formed will change, causing the real-world relationships (parameters) to change. Thus the effects of a particular policy depend heavily on the public's expectations about the policy.

Two schools of rational expectations economists have formed: the new classical and the new Keynesian schools. (3)________________ ____________________ rational expectationists contend that anticipated macroeconomic policies have no effect on aggregate output and employment. This conclusion rests on the assumption that all wages and prices are completely (4)____________________ with respect to expected changes in the price level. For example, if policymakers are known to act in certain systematic ways, the public will come to anticipate policy changes, causing the aggregate (5)___________________________ curve to shift. People will respond to expected expansionary macropolicies by raising wages and factor prices. The aggregate demand curve shifts out, but the aggregate supply curve shifts in, neutralizing the impact on aggregate output. The (6)______________________ _______________________ rises, but output remains unchanged at the natural-rate level.

Policymakers can affect the level of aggregate output and employment in the new classical rational expectations model only through policy surprises. Unanticipated policies will cause the aggregate demand curve to shift while leaving the aggregate supply curve unchanged, resulting in a change in the price level and aggregate output. Only unanticipated macropolicies can affect the level of output in the new classical model; anticipated policies cannot affect the level of output. This conclusion is referred to as the policy (7)____. The proposition depends critically on two assumptions: rational expectations and perfect wage and price flexibility.

Many economists find the assumption of wage and price flexibility unacceptable. They note that the prevalence of long-term labour and supply contracts create (8)___________________________ which prevent wages and prices from fully responding to expected changes in the price level.

New Keynesians argue that the existence of long-term labour contracts—both explicit and implicit—leads to wage and price stickiness. In contrast to the new classical school, the assumption of rational expectations does not imply that (9)______________________________ policies are ineffectual in altering the level of aggregate output. The public may understand the consequences of a newly announced macropolicy yet be unable to fully respond in the face of contracted fixities.

(10)____ agree that unanticipated policies are more effective than anticipated policies in changing the level of aggregate output. Anticipated policies are effective in altering the level of aggregate output, but unanticipated policies have a larger impact. The new Keynesians suggest that activist stabilization policies can be used to affect the level of output in the economy, but policymakers must be cognizant of the Lucas (11)____. In other words, since expectations affect the outcome of policies, making predictions about a proposed policy's effects is more difficult than is implied by the traditional model.

New classical economists are less optimistic. They contend that (12)________________________ macropolicies can only be counterproductive. Activist policies are likely to be destabilizing and inflationary.

A significant implication of rational expectations is that anti-inflationary policies can achieve their goal at a lower cost if these policies are viewed as (13)__________________________ by the public. The traditional model suggests that fighting inflation will be quite costly in terms of lost output and higher unemployment. Arthur Okun's rule of thumb indicates that a reduction of one point in the inflation rate requires a four percent loss in a year's GNP, a staggering cost for such a small gain. Recall that Okun's rule of thumb holds in a world where anti-inflation policies are not viewed as credible. To the extent that such policies foster credibility, fighting inflation will be less costly.

Evidence indicates that credible policies do reduce the adverse consequences of anti-inflationary policies. Actions designed to reduce government (14)____ appear to be particularly important in this regard. It appears that anti-inflationary policies that do not address budget-deficit problems may be viewed with little credibility and prove to be relatively costly. Some economists contend that recessions in Great Britain and the United States in the early 1980s were more severe because deficit issues went unresolved. Although this conclusion is controversial, it indicates the importance expectations play in economic theory.

EXERCISES

EXERCISE 1: The Effects of Anticipated Policy

Suppose the economy is initially at point 1 in Figure 27A, at the intersection of the AD_1 and AS_1 curves. If the government decides to cut military spending in an attempt to ease world tensions, draw in Figure 27A the new aggregate demand curve AD_2. If this spending cut were widely anticipated, draw in the new aggregate supply curve AS_{NC} if the new classical model is the best description of the economy.

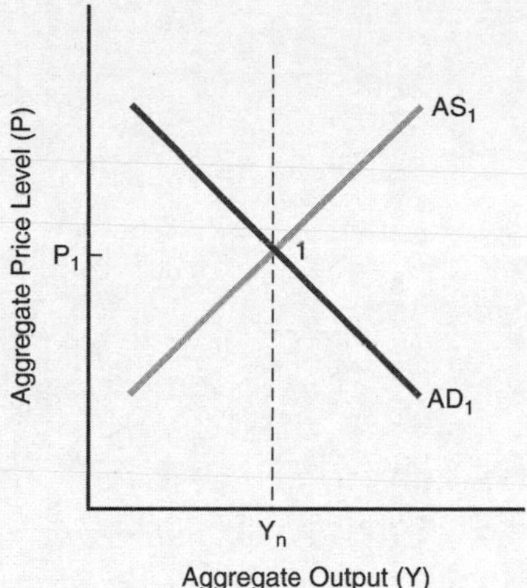

Figure 27A

What is the effect on output and price level?

____

____

If, instead, the new Keynesian model is the best description of the economy, draw in the new aggregate supply curve AS_{NK} when the policy is anticipated.

What is the effect on output and price level?

____

____

Would output rise by more or by less than your answers above if the traditional model best describes the economy?

____

____

____

EXERCISE 2: The Effects of Unanticipated Policy

Suppose the economy is initially at point 1 in Figure 27B, at the intersection of the AD_1 and AS_1 curves. If the government reduces military spending in an attempt to ease world tensions, but reduces it by less than expected (where the aggregate demand curve for the expected policy is AD_e), draw in the new aggregate demand curve AD_2 and the new aggregate supply curve AS_{NC} if the new classical model is the best description of the economy.

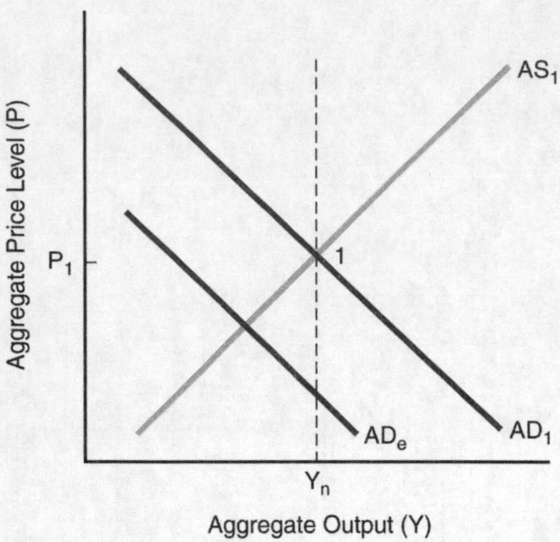

Figure 27B

Does aggregate output fall as a result of the decline in government spending?

If, instead, the new Keynesian model is the best description of the economy, draw in the new aggregate supply curve AS_{NK} when the spending reduction is less than anticipated. Will aggregate output fall in this case?

If the traditional model best describes the economy, will aggregate output fall in response to the spending reduction?

EXERCISE 3: The Lucas Critique and Monetary Policy

Suppose that the Bank of Canada follows a monetary rule designed to stabilize nominal interest rates. If interest rates suddenly rise, what will most likely be the Bank's response? If people come to expect this response, will the Bank's efforts be helped or hindered? Explain.

EXERCISE 4: A Comparison of the Schools of Thought

In the space provided next to each statement, indicate whether the statement reflects a view held by Keynesians (K), monetarists (M), new classical rational expectationists (NC), or new Keynesians (NK). Use more than one letter if appropriate.

_____ 1. Any policy move that is widely expected will have no impact at the time it is taken, since it will have already been discounted by the public.

_____ 2. No systematic economic policy can be devised that is capable of affecting anything other than the inflation rate.

_____ 3. The private economy is inherently unstable; thus monetary and fiscal policy can be important in stabilizing the economy whether or not the policy is anticipated.

_____ 4. There is no serious need to stabilize the economy, and even if there were a need, it could not be done, for stabilization policies would be more likely to increase than to decrease instability.

_____ 5. Only policy moves that people do not expect will cause changes in aggregate output and employment.

_____ 6. Traditional econometric models cannot be relied on to evaluate the potential impact of particular policies on the economy. In other words, the short-run forecasting ability of these models provides no evidence of the accuracy to be expected from simulations of hypothetical policy rules.

_____ 7. The existence of long-term labour contracts are one source of rigidity that prevents instantaneous price and wage adjustment. Thus, even with rational expectations, anticipated monetary and fiscal policies may affect output in the short run.

_____ 8. The policy ineffectiveness proposition does not hold in a world such as ours where both explicit and implicit long-term labour contracts impart a degree of wage and price rigidity in the economy.

EXERCISE 5: A Comparison of Rational Expectations Models with the Traditional Model

Listed below are statements that reflect the beliefs of economists regarding stabilization policy. If the statement most closely reflects views held by the new classical economists, write NC in the space provided. If the statement most closely reflects views held by new Keynesians, place an NK in the space provided. If the statement does not reflect views held by either school of rational expectationists, place a T in the space. You may use more than one letter if the statement reflects views held by more than one of the groups.

_____ 1. An unanticipated expansion in the money supply will boost employment in the short run, but after a period of from 12 to 24 months, prices will begin to rise.

_____ 2. Stabilization policy—what some might call an activist policy—can and should be employed in an effort to eliminate the high level of unemployment.

_____ 3. An increase in government spending or a tax cut would be appropriate at this time because unemployment is too high and inflation is almost nonexistent. In addition, the announcement of such a plan would bode well for stock prices—this is the policy the market has been expecting to hear from Ottawa.

_____ 4. Mr. Minister of Finance, since you have decided that an anti-inflation policy of slower money growth and higher taxes is appropriate at this time, I think it will be wise that you make the announcement at your televised press conference tonight. Remember, it is important for you to convince the public that you plan to stick with the contractionary strategy even if unemployment begins to rise.

_____ 5. Fighting inflation is extremely costly—probably more costly than it's worth—and announcing an anti-inflationary policy in advance does nothing to lower that cost.

_____ 6. An activist stabilization policy will have no predictable effect on output, and it cannot be relied on to stabilize economic activity.

EXERCISE 6: The Effects of Announced Policy and Credibility

Assume for a moment that you are the prime minister of Canada and currently running for reelection. The unemployment rate is 5.8% and the inflation rate is 2.0%. In a private meeting with the governor of the Bank of Canada you are given assurances that monetary policy will be expansionary in the next few months in an attempt to lower the unemployment rate. If the traditional model best describes the economy, does it matter if you publicly announce the governor's assurances?

____

____

If the new classical model best describes the economy?

If the new Keynesian model best describes the economy?

If no one believes you when you make your announcement, how does it affect the answers above?

EXERCISE 7: Transparency and Policy

The Bank of Canada has become much more open in informing the public of its actions and intentions. If the public has rational expectations, and if the Bank is credible, then the public will anticipate Bank policy.

A. Consider policy that is designed to raise aggregate output. We learned that if people have rational expectations then unanticipated policy has a greater effect on output than anticipated policy. This implies that the Bank should try to surprise the public with its policy. What is the advantage of making the policy anticipated through increased transparency?

B. Consider an anti-inflationary policy that is designed to lower the price level. What is the advantage of making the policy anticipated through increased transparency?

EXERCISE 8: ANTI-INFLATION POLICIES

Suppose that you have been asked by the Governor of the Bank of Zimbabwe to make a presentation on the consequences of adopting both an anticipated and an unanticipated anti-inflation policy on the level of aggregate output.

A. Depict graphically and explain, in words, what would be the outcome of this policy in the traditional model.

B. Depict graphically and explain, in words, what would be the outcome of this policy in the new classical model.

C. Depict graphically and explain, in words, what would be the outcome of this policy in the new Keynesian model.

D. According to the new classical and the new Keynesian model, what must happen for inflation to be reduced successfully at the lowest possible output cost?

SELF-TEST

PART A: True-False Questions

Circle whether the following statements are true (T) or false (F).

T F 1. Robert Lucas in his famous critique argued that econometric model simulations provide no useful information with which to evaluate the effects of alternative economic policies.

T F 2. A monetary acceleration may have different effects in 2004 than in 2005 if the public's expectations about the policy are different in those two years.

T F 3. The new classical economists argue that neither anticipated nor unanticipated policies affect the level of unemployment.

T F 4. The new classical economists argue that only unanticipated increases in the money supply can affect the general level of prices.

T F 5. While an expansionary monetary policy can never lead to a decline in output in the traditional model, such a result is possible in the new classical model.

T F 6. Anticipated policies have no effect on aggregate output or the rate of unemployment in the New Keynesian model.

T F 7. The expansion of aggregate output will be smaller for an anticipated policy than for an unanticipated policy in the nonclassical rational expectations model.

T F 8. It is the existence of rigidities such as sticky wages and prices, not adaptive expectations, that explains why anticipated policies can affect output in the New Keynesian model.

T F 9. If expectations about policy are formed adaptively, then anticipated policies will actually have greater output effects than unanticipated policies.

T F 10. If expectations are formed rationally, and prices and wages are completely flexible, then the best anti-inflation policy is likely to consist of a gradual reduction in the money supply over a period of several years.

T F 11. Anticipated and unanticipated policies have an identical effect in the traditional models.

T F 12. Expectation formation will change when the behaviour of forecasted variables changes.

T F 13. The new classical model suggests that an expansionary monetary policy can lead to an increase in aggregate output if the public expects an even more expansionary policy than the one actually implemented.

T F 14. Unlike the new classical model, in the new Keynesian model, the anticipated policy does have an effect on aggregate output.

T F 15. The new classical macroeconomic model demonstrates that aggregate output does not increase as a result of unanticipated expansionary policy.

PART B: Multiple-Choice Questions

Circle the appropriate answer.

1. Robert Lucas argues that using an econometric model that has been constructed on the basis of past data
   a. may be appropriate for short-run forecasting, but is inappropriate for evaluating alternative policies.
   b. may be appropriate for alternative policies, but is not appropriate for evaluating short-run forecasting.
   c. is appropriate for both short-run forecasting and policy evaluation.
   d. is not appropriate for either short-run forecasting or policy evaluation.

2. An anticipated expansion in the money supply will have no effect on aggregate output in which model?
   a. New Keynesian model
   b. Traditional model
   c. New classical rational expectations model
   d. All of the above models

3. In which of the following models does an anticipated increase in money growth affect the price level?
   a. Traditional model
   b. New classical model
   c. New Keynesian model
   d. All of the above models
4. The new Keynesian model indicates that anticipated policies affect aggregate output because of rigidities resulting from
   a. long-term contracts.
   b. adaptive expectations.
   c. the reluctance of some firms to alter prices and wages frequently, creating what can be considered implicit contracts.
   d. All of the above.
   e. Only (a) and (c) of the above.
5. The traditional model is distinguished from both the new classical and the new Keynesian model by the following:
   a. The traditional model assumes that expectations are formed adaptively, that is, on past behaviour of the relevant variable.
   b. The traditional model does not distinguish between anticipated and unanticipated policies.
   c. The traditional model assumes that the price level remains fixed.
   d. Both (b) and (c) of the above.
   e. Both (a) and (b) of the above.
6. Assume that the economy is characterized by sticky wages and prices, and rational expectations. If the Bank of Canada wishes to reduce unemployment by expanding the money supply, how will the preannouncement of such a policy influence the policy's effectiveness?
   a. The preannouncement eliminates the policy's effectiveness.
   b. The preannouncement diminishes the policy's effectiveness.
   c. The preannouncement has no effect on the policy's effectiveness.
   d. The preannouncement enhances the magnitude of the policy's effectiveness.
7. Kristin argues at a meeting of the Governing Council that the Bank of Canada should vote to quickly lower the overnight rate in an attempt to return the economy to full employment. One can infer from her argument that Kristin is
   a. either a new classical or a traditional economist.
   b. either a new classical or a new Keynesian economist.
   c. definitely not a new classical economist.
   d. definitely not a new Keynesian economist.
8. If people form rational expectations, an anti-inflation policy will be more successful if it
   a. is credible.
   b. comes as a surprise.
   c. is unanticipated.
   d. does all of the above.
9. At a meeting of the central bank's policy-making committee, Meghan argues that any decision regarding a contractionary monetary policy should be postponed until the legislative body votes on a deficit-reduction package currently before it. Meghan seems to be implying that
   a. an anti-inflationary policy would make more sense if people saw evidence of lower deficits.
   b. an anti-inflationary policy might be too costly in terms of lost output if such a policy was not believed to be credible.

c. both (a) and (b) of the above are possible.
d. neither (a) nor (b) of the above are a concern.

10. Assume that irrefutable evidence proves that while anticipated monetary expansions cause aggregate output to expand, unanticipated monetary expansions proved more potent than anticipated policies. What economic model would the evidence support?
    a. New classical model
    b. New Keynesian model
    c. Traditional model
    d. Uninformed median-voter model

11. _____ policies have no effect on aggregate output or the rate of unemployment in the _____ model.
    a. anticipated; new Keynesian
    b. unanticipated; new Keynesian
    c. anticipated; new classical
    d. unanticipated; new classical

12. The expansion of aggregate output will be _____ for an _____ policy than for an _____ policy in the _____ model.
    a. smaller; unanticipated; anticipated; new classical
    b. smaller; anticipated; unanticipated; new classical
    c. smaller; unanticipated; anticipated; new Keynesian
    d. smaller; anticipated; unanticipated; new Keynesian
    e. larger; anticipated; unanticipated; new Keynesian

13. It is the existence of rigidities such as sticky wages and prices, not adaptive expectations, that explains why _____ policies can affect output in the _____ model.
    a. unanticipated; new classical
    b. anticipated; new classical
    c. unanticipated; new Keynesian
    d. anticipated; new Keynesian

14. According to _____ economists, policymakers' attempts to stabilize the economy will be ineffective and may even make conditions worse.
    a. new classical
    b. new Keynesian
    c. Keynesian
    d. activist

15. If the government _____ budget deficits, an anti-inflationary policy is _____ likely to be regarded as credible.
    a. reduces; less
    b. reduces; more
    c. increases; more
    d. eliminates; less

16. Econometric models
    a. are ones in which the public is assumed to have rational expectations.
    b. are estimated using data and statistics.
    c. can be used to forecast future economic conditions.
    d. are no longer used by economists.
    e. only (b) and (c) of the above.

17. Suppose that a new professor is teaching a course for the first time and that students try to guess which questions will be on the midterm examination. Students display rational expectations most clearly if they base their guess on
    a. midterm examinations from previous semesters.
    b. suggestions from friends at other universities.
    c. the midterm review session taught by the professor.
    d. advice from students who took the class last semester.
    e. all of the above.
18. In the new classical model, policy that is designed to increase output will be successful if
    a. the price level rises less than anticipated.
    b. the price level rises more than anticipated.
    c. the price level rises exactly as anticipated.
    d. the price level does not rise.
    e. either (a) or (c) of the above.
19. The policy ineffectiveness proposition states that policy will have no effect on _____ as long as policy is anticipated, people have rational expectations, and _____.
    a. prices; prices and wages are sticky.
    b. prices; prices and wages are fully flexible.
    c. output; prices and wages are sticky.
    d. output; prices and wages are fully flexible.
20. Suppose that the central bank decides to lower the rate of inflation by lowering the growth rate of the money supply. If the inflation rate actually increases, then which of the following is a possible explanation?
    a. The central bank lowered the growth rate of the money supply more than was expected by the public.
    b. The public did not believe that the central bank would lower the price level, and the central bank did not lower the growth rate of the money supply.
    c. The public believed that the central bank would lower the price level, but the central bank did not lower the growth rate of the money supply.
    d. only (a) and (b) of the above.
    e. only (b) and (c) of the above.
21. In the new Keynesian model, if the central bank credibly announces that it will fight inflation, and if the public has rational expectations, then
    a. output will fall and the price level will fall.
    b. output will rise and the price level will fall.
    c. output will fall but it is impossible to determine what will happen to the price level.
    d. it is impossible to determine what will happen to output, but the price level will fall.
    e. output will remain constant and the price level will fall.
22. In the new Keynesian model, if the public has rational expectations then anticipated policy will generally lead to _____ changes in output and _____ changes in the price level as compared to unanticipated policy.
    a. larger; larger
    b. smaller; larger
    c. larger; smaller
    d. smaller; smaller

23. Despite the fact that only unanticipated policy affects output in the new classical model, why is it not recommended that policymakers attempt to continually "fool" the public with unanticipated policy?
    a. Policymakers will have a difficult time knowing what public expectations are, and as a result the effect of policy on output will be unknown.
    b. It is impossible to continually fool the public by changing policy frequently.
    c. Unanticipated policy will not change the price level and therefore is inconsistent with reducing inflation.
    d. All of the above.
    e. None of the above.
24. In which model of the economy can inflation be reduced with the least cost in terms of lost output by using a "cold turkey" approach?
    a. The traditional model.
    b. The new Keynesian model.
    c. The new classical model.
    d. The Keynesian model.
    e. The monetarist model.
25. A _____ anti-inflation policy may be more costly than a _____ approach since it may be more difficult to be credibly implemented.
    a. "cold turkey"; rational
    b. traditional; rational
    c. gradual; "cold turkey"
    d. gradual; flexible
    e. "cold turkey"; sticky
26. Eric the economist tells his students that all anticipated policy has no effect on aggregate output. You can probably infer that he is a
    a. Keynesian economist
    b. Monetarist
    c. Proponent of activist policies
    d. New classical economist
27. If long-term contracts create wage and price rigidities, then an anticipated monetary policy expansion will cause
    a. aggregate output to increase in the short run.
    b. the price level to rise.
    c. a permanent increase in aggregate output.
    d. both (a) and (b) of the above to occur.
    e. both (b) and (c) of the above to occur.
28. When an expansionary policy by the Bank of Canada is ________ and the expectations are rational, the output and price will increase. However, when this policy is ________, the output level remains unchanged and the price level ________.
    a. anticipated, unanticipated, goes up
    b. anticipated, unanticipated, goes down
    c. unanticipated, anticipated, goes up
    d. unanticipated, anticipated, goes down

29. According to the new classical model, an expansionary policy can lead to a decline in aggregate output if __________.
    a. the expectations are adaptive
    b. prices are sticky
    c. the public expects an even more expansionary policy than the one actually implemented
    d. both (a) and (b) of above
30. According to traditional models, in response to an unanticipated anti-inflation policy, the output level ________ and credibility __________ important.
    a. increases, is
    b. increases, is not
    c. decreases, is not
    d. decreases, is

ANSWERS

CHAPTER 1

Chapter Synopsis/Completions

1. financial
2. exchange rates
3. stock market
4. stronger
5. expensive
6. financial institutions
7. bank
8. spend
9. financial intermediation
10. business cycle
11. inflation
12. spending
13. saving
14. high
15. money

Exercise 1

1. B
2. S
3. S
4. F
5. S
6. F

Exercise 2

Yes, pawnbrokers are financial intermediaries since they bring savers (the pawnbroker) and spenders (the borrower) together. Just like banks, the borrower leaves collateral for the loan, the conditions of the loan are written, and interest is charged. However, interest rates and collateral requirements are often higher than what is available through banks.

Exercise 3

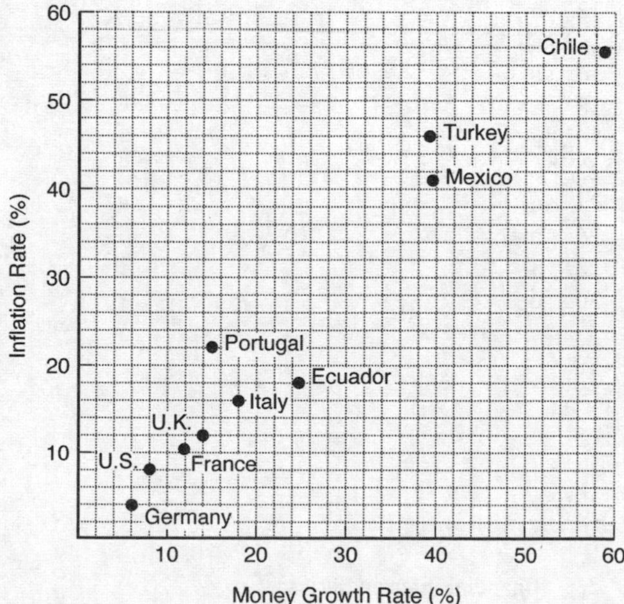

Exercise 4

One would predict a fall in prices and economic output. This is in fact what happened. In 1929, real GDP was $52 billion (in 1986 dollars) and the GDP deflator was 11.9. By 1933, real GDP declined by 30% to $36 billion and the deflator by 18% to 9.7.

Exercise 5

1. A
2. A
3. D
4. D
5. A
6. D

Exercise 6

A. 19.8

B. 1620

Self-Test

Part A

1. T
2. F
3. F
4. T
5. F
6. T
7. T
8. T
9. F
10. T
11. F
12. F
13. F

Part B

1. d
2. d
3. a
4. d
5. c
6. e
7. b
8. b
9. a
10. a
11. c
12. b
13. e
14. b
15. d
16. d
17. c
18. a
19. e
20. a
21. c
22. c
23. c
24. e
25. d
26. b
27. a
28. a
29. a
30. d
31 e

CHAPTER 2

Chapter Synopsis/Completions

1. direct
2. financial intermediaries
3. equity
4. over-the-counter
5. capital
6. short

7. equity
8. exchanges
9. money
10. bonds
11. Eurodollar
12. liabilities
13. risk sharing
14. diversification
15. adverse selection
16. depository

Exercise 1

1. I
2. D
3. D
4. I
5. D
6. I
7. I
8. D
9. I
10. D

Exercise 2

Part A

1. a, b, d, f, h
2. a
3. a
4. b
5. a, e
6. e, g
7. e, f, g, h
8. e, g
9. c
10. b

Part B

1. a, c
2. a, c
3. a, c
4. a, c
5. b
6. d
7. b
8. f
9. f
10. e, g, h

Exercise 3

Julie will face many transaction costs, including both lost time and lost profit. First, she will need to locate someone who wants to borrow exactly $15,000 for a car loan. She will need to determine the creditworthiness of the borrower. She will also need to write a loan contract and collect loan payments. She faces legal and towing fees if the borrower defaults and the car needs to be repossessed. Lastly, she may be liable for damages caused by the car, since she is the legal owner until the car loan is repaid.

Exercise 4

1. a, c, d, e, g
2. c, d
3. e
4. a, c, d
5. a, c, d
6. g
7. b, f

Exercise 5

1. Government of Canada treasury bills
2. Certificates of deposit
3. Commercial paper
4. Banker's acceptances
5. Repurchase agreements
6. Overnight funds

Self-Test

Part A

1. T
2. T
3. T
4. F

5. T
6. F
7. T
8. T
9. F
10. T
11. F
12. T
13. F
14. T
15. F

Part B

1. c
2. c
3. a
4. b
5. d
6. e
7. c
8. e
9. b
10. c
11. e
12. d
13. c
14. b
15. b
16. d
17. b
18. d
19. c
20. d
21. c
22. a
23. c
24. b
25. b
26. d
27. d
28. a
29. b
30. c
31. a

CHAPTER 3

Chapter Synopsis/Completions

1. money
2. money supply
3. flow
4. specialization
5. store of value
6. barter
7. time
8. liquid
9. paper currency
10. e-money
11. monetary aggregates
12. initial

Exercise 1

In this example the R.E.M. CD has actually served the function of money. It has served as a medium of exchange, since Barbi took an inferior position (trading for the R.E.M. CD) in hopes of getting something she valued more than she gave up. This is exactly what you do when you accept money in exchange for your labour efforts. It really is not money that you want, but the things that money can be exchanged for.

Individual	Initial CD	Intermediate CD	Final CD
A	R	S	S
B	S	R	T
C	T	T	R

Exercise 2

1. M
2. S
3. U
4. U
5. S
6. U

7. M
8. M
9. U
10. S

Exercise 3

Number of Goods	Number of Prices in a Barter Economy	Number of Prices in a Money Economy
5	10	5
25	300	25
50	1225	50
500	124,750	500
5000	12,497,500	5000

Exercise 4

When dollars cease to function as money, they will become near worthless pieces of paper, and you don't want to be stuck holding dollars when they become worthless. Therefore, you spend your dollars today, rather than tomorrow, because no one will accept dollars tomorrow. If you expect dollars to become worthless next week, you still want to spend them today, because others will do the same. Since no one wants to be stuck holding the dollars on the day that they become worthless, everyone tries to spend the dollars as soon as they believe that dollars will become worthless.

Exercise 5

Part A

435

Part B

1. d
2. a
3. b
4. c
5. b

Self-Test

Part A

1. T
2. F
3. F
4. T
5. F
6. T
7. T
8. T
9. T
10. F
11. F
12. F
13. T
14. F
15. F

Part B

1. e
2. a
3. b
4. c
5. b
6. c
7. b
8. b
9. b
10. a
11. c
12. c

13. d
14. d
15. d
16. b
17. b
18. b
19. d
20. a
21. c
22. a
23. c
24. d
25. d
26. a
27. d
28. b
29. c
30. c
31. b
32. c
33. c
34. b

CHAPTER 4

Chapter Synopsis/Completions

1. present value
2. negatively
3. fixed payment
4. coupon rate
5. discount
6. coupon
7. discount
8. rise
9. return
10. maturity
11. interest rates
12. credit market

Exercise 1

a. $\$50/(1 + i)$
b. $\$50/(1 + i)^2$
c. $\$50 * (1 + i)^2$
d. $\$50 * (1 + i)$

Exercise 2

1. $\$453.51 = \$500/(1 + .05)^2$
2. $\$413.22 = \$500/(1 + .10)^2$
3. $\$341.51 = \$500/(1 + .10)^4$
4. The present value falls.
5. The present value falls.

Exercise 3

Part A

1. $\$1{,}000 = \$600/(1 + i) + \$600/(1 + i)^2$
2. $1,041
3. Above
4. $975
5. Below

Part B

1. Below, because the price of the bond is above the par value.
2. $\$1{,}079 = \$100/(1 + i) + \$100/(1 + i)^2 + \$1{,}100/(1 + i)^3$
3. $1,052
4. Below
5. $1,136
6. Above

Exercise 4

Price of the Discount Bond	Maturity	Yield on a Discount Basis	Yield to Maturity
$900	1 year (365 days)	11.1%	11.1%
$950	6 months (182 days)	10.56%	10.84%
$975	3 months (91 days)	10.28%	10.68%

Exercise 5

Coupon Rate	Maturity Date	Price	Yield to Maturity	Current Yield
10.75	May 2003	110 11/32	6.87%	9.74%
12.375	May 2004	118 31/32	6.86%	10.40%
6.75	May 2005	100 5/32	6.71%	6.74%
6.50	Nov 2026	101 12/32	6.39%	6.41%
6.25	May 2030	101 26/32	6.12%	6.14%

The 6 1/4 of May 2030, the 6 1/2 of November 2026, and the 6 3/4 of May 2005 are the bonds for which the current yield is a good measure of the interest rate. The reason for this is that all three are selling at a price close to par, while the 6 1/2 of November 2026 and the 6 1/4 of May 2030 both have long terms to maturity.

Exercise 6

1. 110 percent, which is calculated as follows: The initial price of the consol is $1000 = $100/0.10 while next year the price is $2000 = $100/0.05. The return is therefore 110 percent = 1.10 = ($2000 – $1000 + $100)/$1000.

2. 14.8 percent, which is calculated as follows: The initial price of the coupon bond is $1000, since the interest rate equals the coupon rate when the bond is at par. Next year, when the bond has 1 year to maturity, the price is $1048 = $100/(1 + 0.05) + $1000/(1 + 0.05). The return is therefore 14.8 percent = 0.148 = ($1048 – $1000 + $100)/$1000.

The consol is a better investment because when the interest rate on two bonds has the same decline, the bond with the longer maturity—the consol—has a larger increase in its price.

Exercise 7

1. 6%
2. –10%
3. 3%
4. 0%

You would rather be a lender in situation 1 because the real interest rate is the highest, while you would rather be a borrower in situation 2 because the real interest rate is lowest.

Exercise 8

1. $963.42
2. $1232.91
3. $1174.60
4. $1295.05

Self-Test

Part A

1.	T	2.	F
3.	F	4.	F
5.	F	6.	T
7.	F	8.	F
9.	T	10.	F
11.	F	12.	F
13.	T	14.	F

Part B

1.	d	2.	a
3.	b	4.	c
5.	c	6.	b
7.	c	8.	b
9.	e	10.	c
11.	d	12.	e
13.	d	14.	c
15.	d	16.	c
17.	a	18.	a
19.	a	20.	b
21.	d	22.	d
23.	b	24.	c
25.	d	26.	d
27.	a	28.	b
29.	d	30.	c
31.	c	32.	a
33.	b	34.	a

CHAPTER 5

Chapter Synopsis/Completions

1.	demand	2.	inversely
3.	higher	4.	up
5.	lower	6.	equilibrium
7.	increases	8.	increases
9.	decreases	10.	increases
11.	increases	12.	Fisher
13.	increase	14.	increases
15.	declines	16.	decline
17.	opposite	18.	higher

Exercise 1

Variable	Change in Variable	Change in Quantity Demanded
Wealth	↓	↓
Liquidity of asset	↓	↓
Riskiness of asset	↓	↑
Expected return of asset	↓	↓

Riskiness of other assets	↓	↓
Liquidity of other assets	↓	↑
Expected return of other assets	↓	↑

Exercise 2

1. D →
2. ← D, S →
3. D →
4. S →
5. S →
6. ← D
7. D →, S →
8. D →
9. D →
10. ← D

Exercise 3

The new supply and demand curves are B_2^s and B_2^d, and the market equilibrium moves from point 1 to point 2. As can be seen in Figure 5A, the interest rate rises to i_2.

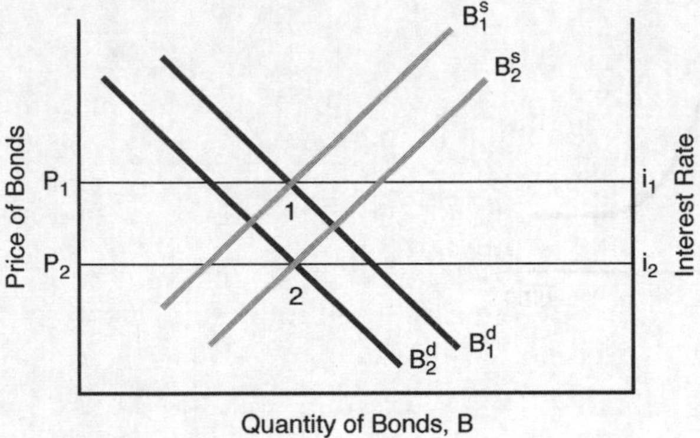

Figure 5A

Exercise 4

The Orange County default raises the awareness that local governments could default on bonds. This made holding municipal bonds more risky relative to other assets, such as U.S. Treasury bills or corporate bonds. Thus, the demand for municipal bonds fell, which lowered the market equilibrium price, and raised the interest rate. Since local governments had to pay higher interest rates on the bonds they issued, the costs of many projects grew too high, and some were cancelled.

Exercise 5

The new supply and demand curves are M_2^s and M_2^d, and the market equilibrium moves from point 1 to point 2. As the figure is drawn, the interest rate rises, but if the shift of the demand curve is greater, then the interest rate could fall, instead of rise. What we are seeing here is a combination of the liquidity effect and the income effect of a money supply decrease. Since they have opposite effects the overall impact on the interest rate is ambiguous.

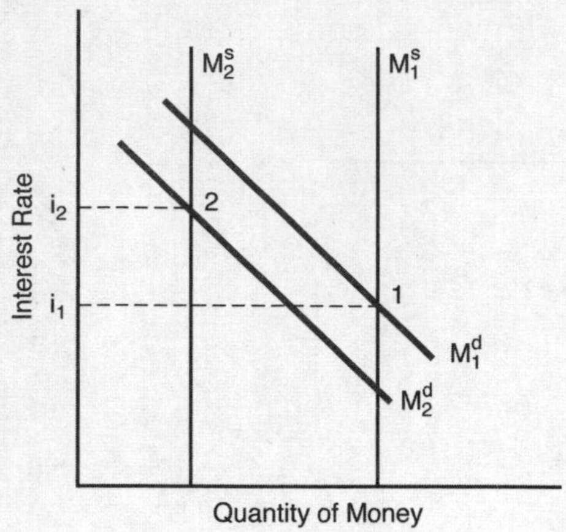

Exercise 6

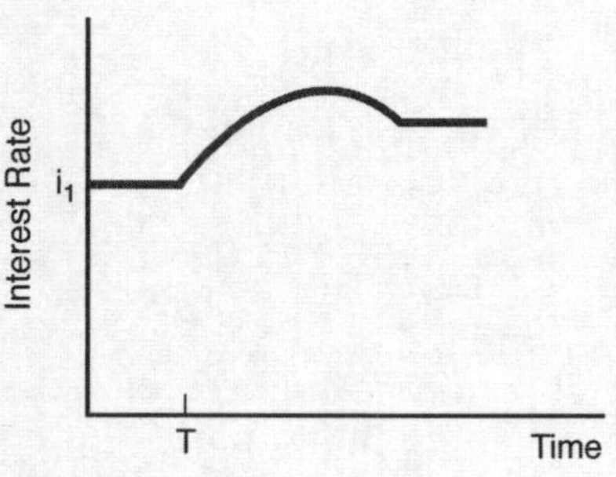

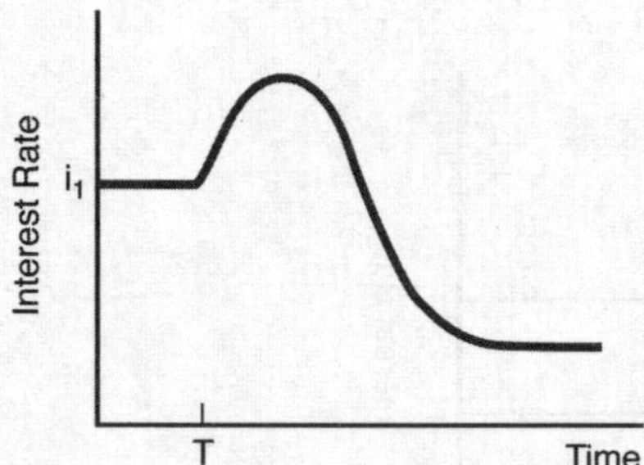

Exercise 7

A. 70

B. 100

Exercise 8

A. The 4 determinants of asset demand are Wealth (the total resources owned by the individual, including all assets), which has a positive relationship with quantity demanded, Expected Return (the return expected over the next period on one asset relative to alternative assets) , which has a positive relationship with quantity demanded, Risk (the degree of uncertainty associated with the return on one asset relative to alternative assets), which has a negative relationship with quantity demanded, and Liquidity (the ease and speed with which an asset can be turned into cash relative to alternative assets), which has a positive relationship with quantity demanded.

B. An increase in wealth will shift the demand curve to the right, while a decrease in wealth and income as seen in a recession will shift the demand curve left. Higher expected interest rates in the future lower the expected return for long-term bonds, decrease the demand, and shift the demand curve left, whereas lower expected interest rates in the future increase the demand for long-term bonds and shift the demand curve to the right. An increase in the riskiness of bonds causes the demand for bonds to fall and the demand curve shifts left. An increase in the riskiness of alternative assets causes the demand for bonds to rise and the demand curve to shift to the right. Increased liquidity of bonds results in higher demand for bonds, and the demand curve shifts to the right. Similarly, increased liquidity of alternative assets lowers the demand for bonds and shifts the demand curve to the left.

C. An increase in expected profitability of investment opportunities will shift the supply curve to the right, and a decrease in expected profitability of investment opportunities will shift the supply curve to the left. Therefore it is positively correlated. The other factors are expected inflation, and the government deficit and they are positively correlated as well.

i) Demand = Supply

$-x+1=2x+1$

X=0
Supply=Demand =1
ii) 2x+3=-x+1
3x=-2
X=-2/3
Supply = Demand = 1 2/3

Although we cannot have a negative value as a quantity or price of a bond, the Bank of Canada should reexamine their policy. This would shift the supply curve left and the expected inflation would decrease in this case.

Self-Test

Part A

1. T
2. F
3. F
4. F
5. T
6. F
7. T
8. F
9. T
10. F
11. F
12. F
13. T

Part B

1. b
2. b
3. a
4. b
5. b
6. b
7. c
8. c
9. a
10. c
11. e
12. a
13. b
14. d
15. a
16. d
17. a
18. d
19. d
20. a
21. d
22. d
23. d
24. a
25. d
26. a
27. c
28. c
29. b
30. b
31. a
32. d
33. c

CHAPTER 6

Chapter Synopsis/Completions

1. risk
2. risk of default
3. risk
4. liquidity
5. increases
6. lowers
7. term
8. yield curve
9. upward
10. segmented markets
11. liquidity
12. substitutes
13. higher
14. positive
15. rise

Exercise 1

1. The interest rate on corporate bonds would probably fall. Both the demand and supply curves shift to the right. If the demand curve shifts out more than the supply curve, the interest rate falls.
2. The interest rate on Canada bonds rises.
3. The risk premium falls.

Exercise 2

1. 8%
2. 7.5% = 10% × (1 – 0.25)
3. You would prefer to hold the tax-exempt bond because it has a higher after-tax return.
4. Since you would prefer the tax-exempt bond with a lower interest rate, this example indicates that tax-exempt bonds will have lower market interest rates than they otherwise would because of their tax advantages.

Exercise 3

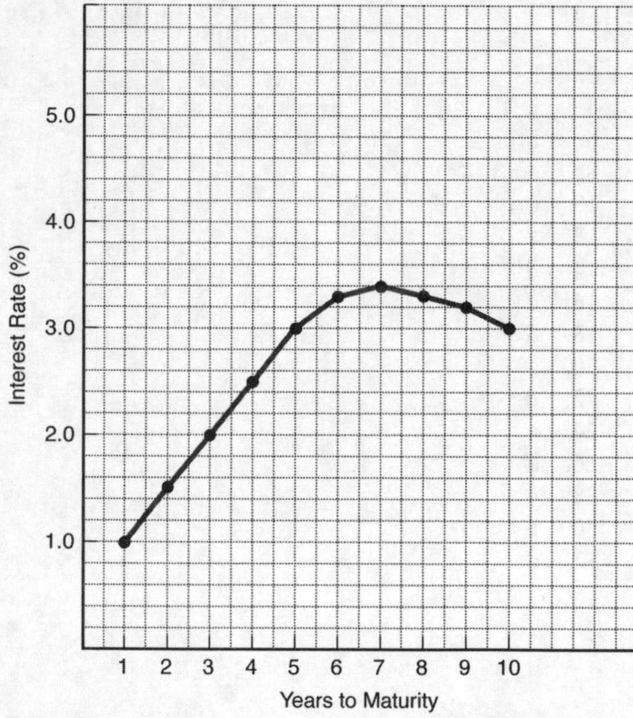

Figure 6A

Exercise 4

1. 6% = 0.06 = [0.06 + 0.06 + 0.06]/3
2. 6% = 0.06 = [0.07 + 0.06 + 0.05]/3
3. The expected returns are identical.
4. Our analysis of the expectations hypothesis indicates that when the 3 year interest rate equals the average of the expected future 1 year rates over the life of the 3 year bond, the expected returns on strategies 1 and 2 are equal. In our example here, the 3 year interest rate of 6% is the average of the 1 year rates over the life of the 3 year

bond (6% = [7% + 6% + 5%]/3), so the expected return from the two strategies must be the same.

Exercise 5

A. The market is predicting that there will be a mild decline in short-term interest rates in the near future and an even steeper decline further out in the future.

B. The market is predicting that there will be a steep decline in short-term interest rates in the near future and a sharp increase further out in the future.

Exercise 6

1. Yes, the market expected short-term interest rates to fall in the near future.
2. No, the market expects short-term interest rates to rise in the near future, and expectations for short-term interest rates in the distant future are the same as expectations were one year ago.

Exercise 7

1. 3.67%
2. 4.25%
3. 5.92%

Exercise 8

A. Junk bonds are bonds with ratings below BB and have higher default risk. Fallen angels are investment grade securities whose rating has fallen to junk levels.

B. Canadian bonds are the most liquid of all long-term bonds because they are so widely traded that they are the easiest to sell quickly and the cost of selling them is low. Corporate bonds are not as liquid because fewer bonds for any one corporation are traded; thus it can be costly to sell these bonds in an emergency because it may be harder to find buyers quickly.

C. Interest rates on bonds of different maturities move together over time. When short-term interest rates are low, yield curves are more likely to have an upward slope; when short term interest rates are high, yield curves are more likely to slope downward and be inverted.

D. The expectations theory, the segmented markets theory, the liquidity premium theory, and the preferred habitat theory.

E.

$$i_{3t} = \frac{i_t + i_{t+1} + i_{t+2}}{n} + l_{3t}$$

$$i_{3t} = \frac{4\% + 4.5\% + 4.75\%}{3} + (\frac{2.0\% + 2.1\%}{2})$$

$$i_{3t} = 4.412\% + 2.05\%$$

$$i_{3t} = 6.462\%$$

Self-Test

Part A

1. F
2. T
3. T
4. F
5. F
6. T
7. T
8. F
9. T
10. F
11. T
12. F
13. T
14. T
15. F

Part B

1. c
2. c
3. d
4. a
5. a
6. d
7. a
8. a
9. c
10. c
11. b
12. e
13. b
14. d
15. a
16. b
17. a
18. c
19. d
20. c
21. c
22. e
23. b
24. a
25. a
26. b
27. a
28. c
29. a
30. d
31. d
32. b

CHAPTER 7

Chapter Synopsis/Completions

1. cash flows
2. generalized dividend
3. constant
4. information
5. adaptively
6. past
7. rational expectations
8. predictions
9. optimal forecasts
10. efficient market hypothesis
11. prices
12. equilibrium
13. random walk
14. financial analysts
15. expected
16. brokerage

Exercise 1

1. c
2. f
3. d
4. b
5. e
6. g
7. h
8. a
9. a
10. c

Exercise 2

A. Long-term interest rates are likely to be unaffected. Since asset prices, and hence financial market yields, reflect currently available information, efficient markets theory suggests that the anticipated Bank of Canada action will not change long-term interest rates.

B. Long-term interest rates might fall as people revise their expectations of inflation downward.

C. Long-term interest rates are likely to rise as the excess demand for money leads to falling bond prices (see Chapter 6).

D. Thus, when the Bank of Canada slows the growth of the money supply, predicting the interest-rate outcome requires some knowledge of people's expectations. While there is dispute as to whether or not unexpected money growth influences long-term interest rates, this example illustrates that expectations can play an important role in determining the effectiveness of monetary policy.

Exercise 3

A. $P(0) = 1/(1.09) + 1/(1.09)^2 + 1/(1.09)^3 + 20/(1.09)^3 = \$17.97$

B. $P(0) = 0.73/(1.09) + 0.73/(1.09)^2 + 0.73/(1.09)^3 + 20/(1.09)^3 = \$17.29$

The stock value falls.

Exercise 4

1. $69.67
2. 17.5%

Exercise 5

A. The price would decline to $85.47 ($100/1.17) after the opening.

B. Microsoft's returns would be abnormally high, leading to an unexploited profit opportunity.

C. This situation could not be maintained because in an efficient market, all unexploited profit opportunities will be eliminated.

Self-Test

Part A

1. F
2. F
3. T
4. T
5. T
6. T
7. F
8. F
9. F
10. F
11. F
12. T
13. F
14. T
15. F

Part B

1. c
2. e
3. d
4. c
5. c
6. b

7. c
8. b
9. a
10. c
11. c
12. b
13. d
14. c
15. d
16. a
17. b
18. b
19. c
20. b
21. a
22. b
23. d
24. d
25. e
26. d
27. d
28. a
29. c
30. c
31. A

CHAPTER 8

Chapter Synopsis/Completions

1. intermediaries
2. adverse selection
3. moral hazard
4. bonds
5. one-third
6. financial
7. external
8. complicated
9. information
10. adverse selection
11. agency theory
12. worthiness
13. equity
14. restrictive covenants
15. financial crises

Exercise 1

1. B
2. B
3. B
4. B
5. B
6. B
7. B
8. M

Exercise 2

1. j
2. i
3. h
4. g
5. f
6. e
7. d
8. c
9. b
10. a
11. k

Exercise 3

Part A

1. Sharp decline in the stock market
2. Unanticipated decline in the aggregate price level
3. Unanticipated depreciation of the domestic currency
4. A rise in interest rates that reduces cash flow

Part B

1. Sharp increases in interest rates
2. Asset market effects on balance sheets (steep stock market decline)
3. An increase in financial market uncertainty

4. Problems in the banking sector

Exercise 4

When Bowie issues the bond, he receives funds today and promises to pay back the funds in ten years. The two asymmetric information problems are adverse selection and moral hazard. Adverse selection problems occur before Bowie issues the bonds, while moral hazard problems occur after the bonds are issued. Royalty sales from future albums are collateral and the value of collateral depends on the number and quality of future albums that Bowie records. However, once he raises the funds by issuing the bonds, the bond contract does not provide incentive for Bowie to sell records. Therefore, a moral hazard problem exists if future album royalties are the collateral. This likely explains why the bondholders want past rather than future album royalty sales to serve as collateral.

Exercise 5

Part A
1. Underwriting and research in investment banking.
2. Auditing and consulting in accounting firms.

Part B
1. The Sarbanes-Oxley Act in the U.S.
2. The Global Legal Settlement in the U.S.
3. Bill 198 in Ontario.

Self-Test

Part A

1. F
2. T
3. F
4. T
5. T
6. T
7. F
8. T
9. T
10. T
11. F
12. T
13. T

Part B

1. c
2. a
3. a
4. d
5. e
6. e
7. a
8. d
9. d
10. b
11. b
12. a
13. b
14. c
15. d
16. b
17. e
18. d
19. a
20. d
21. a
22. b
23. e
24. e
25. d
26. a
27. b
28. c
29. d
30. b
31. c
32. b

CHAPTER 9

Chapter Synopsis/Completions

1. capital
2. sources
3. vault cash
4. desired reserves
5. reserves
6. outflows
7. liquidity
8. default
9. diversifying
10. overnight funds
11. dividends

Exercise 1

1. i
2. c
3. e
4. a
5. f
6. b
7. h
8. g
9. d

Exercise 2

Part A

First Bank

Assets		Liabilities	
Reserves	+ $2,000	Chequable deposits	+$2,000

Part B

First Bank

Assets		Liabilities	
Reserves	–$1,000	Chequable deposits	–$1,000

Second Bank

Assets		Liabilities	
Reserves	+$1,000	Chequable deposits	+$1,000

Part C
Both banks end up with an increase of $1,000 in reserves.

Exercise 3

Part A

Assets		Liabilities	
Reserves	$19 million	Deposits	$94 million
Loans	$75 million	Bank capital	$10 million
Securities	$10 million		

No. The bank does not need to make any adjustment to its balance sheet because it initially is holding $25 million of reserves when desired reserves are only $20 million (20% of $100 million). Because of its initial holding of $5 million of excess reserves, when it suffers the deposit outflow of $6 million it can still satisfy its reserve requirements: Desired reserves are $18.8 million (20% of $94 million) while it has $19 million of reserves.

Part B

Assets		Liabilities	
Reserves	$15 million	Deposits	$90 million
Loans	$75 million	Bank capital	$10 million
Securities	$10 million		

Yes. The bank must make an adjustment to its balance sheet because its desired reserves are $18 million (20% of $90 million), but it is only holding $15 million of reserves. It has a reserve deficiency of $3 million.

Part C
$3 million. As we see above the bank has a reserve shortfall of $3 million, which it can acquire by selling the $3 million of securities.

Part D

Assets		Liabilities	
Reserves	$18 million	Deposits	$90 million
Loans	$75 million	Bank capital	$10 million
Securities	$7 million		

Part E

Assets		Liabilities	
Reserves	$15 million	Deposits	$80 million
Loans	$75 million	Bank capital	$10 million
Securities	$0 million		

The bank could fail. The desired reserves for the bank are $16 million (20% of $80 million), but it has $15 million of reserves. The proceeds from a distress sale of loans could result in a loss that exceeds bank capital, causing the bank to become insolvent.

Exercise 4

1. Finding borrowers who will pay high interest rates, yet are unlikely to default on their loans.
2. Purchasing securities with high returns and low risk.
3. Attempt to minimize risk by diversifying both holdings of loans and securities.
4. Manage the liquidity of its assets so that it can satisfy its reserve requirements without bearing huge costs.

Exercise 5

1. Banks now aggressively set target goals for asset growth and then acquire funds by issuing liabilities as they are needed.
2. Chequable deposits became a less important source of bank funds, while negotiable CDs and bank borrowings have increased in importance.
3. Banks have increased the proportion of their assets in loans.

Exercise 6

Part A
ROA = (net profit after taxes)/(assets) = 0.9/45 = 2%

ROE = (net profit after taxes)/(equity capital) = 0.9/10 = 9%

Part B
Reserves = (50 ∗ 0.10) = $5 million (no change in reserves)

Loans = (40 + 15) = $55 million (increase of 15)

Part C
net profit after taxes= (ROA) ∗ (assets) = 2% ∗ 60 = $1.2 million

Part D
ROE = (net profit after taxes)/(equity capital) = 1.2/10 = 12%

Exercise 7

Part A
ROA=0.72%, ROE=16.36%

Part B
NIM=0.6%, EM=22.73

Part C
ROA × EM=0.72 × 22.73 =16.36

Exercise 8

A. The equity multiplier for the Bretton Woods Bank is 75, and the equity multiplier for the Doha Development Bank is 50.
B. The return on equity for the Bretton Woods Bank is 75%. It is 112.5% for the Doha Development Bank.
C. Equity holders from the Bretton Woods Bank will be more satisfied with their returns.

Exercise 9

A.

Assets		Liabilities	
Reserves	$0	Deposits	$130
Loans	$130	Bank capital	$20
Securities	$20		

B. With a reserve ratio of 25%, the deposit outflow of $50 caused a total depletion of reserves. Therefore, the Bank of Cambridge did not have ample reserves to deal with the withdrawal.

C. Borrow reserves from other banks; sell securities; acquire reserves from the central bank; reduce loans.

D. Excess reserves are insurance against the costs associated with deposit outflows. The higher the costs associated with deposit outflows, the more excess reserves the bank will want to hold. Yet banks suffer losses from holding too much excess reserves because the opportunity cost of holding reserves is the interest income that could be accumulated from issuing loans.

Self-Test

Part A

1. F
2. T
3. F
4. T
5. F
6. F
7. F
8. T

9. T
10. F
11. T
12. F
13. F
14. F

Part B

1. d
2. c
3. d
4. d
5. e
6. a
7. d
8. b
9. c
10. b
11. a
12. b
13. a
14. b
15. e
16. e
17. d
18. e
19. a
20. b
21. b
22. d
23. c
24. d
25. c
26. d
27. d
28. a
29. b
30. c
31. b
32. c

CHAPTER 10

Chapter Synopsis/Completions

1. Constitution
2. banknotes
3. Dominion notes
4. Bank of Canada
5. mortgages
6. loophole mining
7. disintermediation
8. cost
9. commercial
10. junk
11. small
12. branches
13. Schedule III
14. international
15. Eurodollars

Exercise 1

1. e
2. d
3. a
4. g
5. c
6. b
7. f

Exercise 2

Part A

Foregone interest = 1000 * (i * r) = 1000 * 8% * 10% = $8

Part B

Less incentive, since the foregone interest from keeping reserves is lower.

Exercise 3

A.

1. Money market mutual funds (decline in cost advantages in acquiring funds).
2. Commercial paper market
3. Junk bonds
4. Securitization

B. The junk bond market has allowed traditional borrowers to by-pass banks, thereby reducing the income advantages banks once had on uses of funds.

Exercise 4

1. Bank holding companies
2. Automated teller machines (ATMs)

Exercise 5

A. It would be more profitable for households to borrow using fixed-rate mortgages. They will avoid higher mortgage payments when the volatile market interest rate increases.

B. It would be more profitable for banks to issue adjustable-rate mortgages as they would collect higher mortgage payments when the market interest rate increases.

Self-Test

Part A

1. T
2. T
3. F
4. T
5. T
6. T
7. T
8. T
9. T
10. T
11. T
12. F
13. F
14. T
15. T

Part B

1. d
2. d
3. d
4. a
5. b
6. c
7. d
8. d
9. e
10. a
11. d
12. d
13. e
14. e
15. a
16. a
17. a
18. b
19. d
20. c
21. d
22. c
23. a
24. a
25. c
26. d
27. d
28. c
29. d
30. c
31. d
32. d
33. d

CHAPTER 11

Chapter Synopsis/Completions

1. withdraw
2. moral hazard
3. adverse selection
4. moral hazard
5. examinations
6. financial
7. Differential Premiums By-law
8. four
9. Opting-Out By-law
10. regulatory forbearance
11. moral hazard

Exercise 1

1. Banks with deposit insurance are likely to take on greater risks than they otherwise would. This is the moral hazard problem.
2. Deposit insurance attracts risk-prone entrepreneurs to the banking industry. This is the adverse selection problem.
3. Deposit insurance reduces the incentives of depositors to monitor the riskiness of their banks' asset portfolios. This is the free-rider problem (see chapter 8).

Exercise 2

Part A

1. Adverse selection problems can be reduced through a chartering process that prevents crooks or risk-prone entrepreneurs from getting control of banks.
2. Moral hazard problems can be reduced through regulatory restrictions that prevent banks from acquiring certain risky assets such as common stocks or junk bonds.
3. High bank capital requirements raise the cost of a bank failure to the owners, thereby reducing the incentives of bank owners to take on too much risk, and reducing the moral hazard to depositors.
4. Regular bank examinations reduce moral hazard problems by reducing opportunities for bank owners to skirt regulations concerning asset holdings and minimum capital requirements.

Part B

Regular bank examinations, restrictions on asset holdings, and minimum capital requirements help to reduce the adverse selection problem because, given fewer opportunities to take on risk, risk-prone entrepreneurs will be discouraged from entering the banking industry.

Exercise 3

The failure of a large bank could lead to greater uncertainty in financial markets, potentially causing a major financial crisis that could result in adverse macroeconomic consequences. The too-big-to-fail policy is intended to prevent greater financial market instability and adverse economic conditions.

Exercise 4

Part A

1. A burst of financial innovation in the 1970s and early 1980s that produced new financial instruments and markets widened the scope for greater risk taking.
2. Financial deregulation opened up more avenues to banks and near banks to take on more risk.
3. In the early stages of the 1980s' banking crisis, financial institutions were harmed by the sharp increases in interest rates from late 1979 until 1981 and the severe recession in 1981–82.

Part B

Regulators adopted a policy of regulatory forbearance toward insolvent financial institutions in the 1980s.

Part C

1. The CDIC lacked sufficient funds to cover insured deposits in the insolvent banks.
2. The regulators were reluctant to close the firms that justified their regulatory existence.

Exercise 5

1. Set new ownership rules.
2. Established a process for reviewing mergers for large banks.
3. Allowed bank financial groups to organize under a holding company structure.
4. Allowed greater flexibility for bank involvement in the information technology area.
5. Allowed non-banks access to the payments and clearance systems.

Exercise 6

Regulators' desire to escape blame for poor performance, led them to adopt a perverse strategy of "regulatory gambling," whereby capital requirements were lowered and insolvent institutions were allowed to continue operating in the hope that conditions in the banking industry would improve. Rather than mandate stricter controls, politicians encouraged lax monitoring and regulatory forbearance, even hampering regulatory efforts to close insolvent banks by cutting regulatory appropriations.

Exercise 7

1. The Differential Premiums By-law that came into force on March 31, 1999.
2. The Opting-Out By-law that came into effect on October 15, 1999.
3. The Modernized Standards By-law adopted in early 2001.

Exercise 8

A. $80,000 will be insured (USD deposits and term deposits longer than 5 years are not insured).

B. The CDIC will use the purchase and assumption method, whereby all of the failed bank's deposits will be taken over by a merger partner, effectively insuring all of the deposits.

C. Because the failure of a very large bank makes it more likely that a major financial disruption will occur, bank regulators are naturally reluctant to allow a big bank to fail and cause losses to depositors.

Self-Test

Part A

1. T
2. T
3. F
4. T
5. T
6. T
7. F
8. F
9. F
10. F
11. T
12. F
13. T
14. F

Part B

1. e
2. e
3. c
4. c

5. e
6. d
7. e
8. a
9. d
10. e
11. b
12. a
13. d
14. d
15. b
16. b
17. c
18. d
19. c
20. c
21. d
22. e
23. d
24. a
25. a
26. b
27. d
28. d
29. d
30. b

CHAPTER 12

Chapter Synopsis/Completions

1. more
2. gap
3. duration

Exercise 1

1. Screening good credit risks from bad and monitoring
2. Long-term customer relationships
3. Loan commitments
4. Collateral
5. Compensating balances
6. Credit rationing

Exercise 2

A. \$30 million – \$50 million = –\$20 million.

B. Profits will decline.

C. –\$20 million × 0.02 = –\$400,000.

D. Profits will increase by \$600,000 (= \$20 million × 0.03).

Exercise 3

A. $DUR_{gap} = DUR_a - (L/A * DUR_l)$
$= 2.50 - (180/200 * 1.10)$
$= 2.50 - (0.99)$
$= 1.51$

B. $\Delta NW/A = -DUR_{gap} * \Delta i/(i+1)$
$= -1.51 * (-0.01)/(1+0.06)$
$= 0.014$
$= 1.4\%$

C. Initial asset value was $200 million, with an increase of net worth as a percentage of assets of 1.4%. Therefore the market value of net worth increases by $2.8 million.

Self-Test

Part A

1. F
2. T
3. T
4. T
5. F
6. F
7. F
8. F
9. F
10. T

Part B

1. b
2. d
3. d
4. b
5. d
6. a
7. a
8. d
9. b
10. c
11. b
12. b
13. a
14. c
15. a

CHAPTER 13

Chapter Synopsis/Completions

1. hedge
2. short
3. risk
4. opposite
5. standardized
6. reduces
7. lowering
8. right
9. strike
10. European
11. sell
12. long

Exercise 1

1. Futures are standardized contracts
2. Futures can be bought and sold up until maturity
3. Futures can be satisfied with any similar security
4. Futures are marked to market daily

Exercise 2

1. d
2. h
3. f
4. c
5. g
6. i
7. j
8. a
9. e
10. b

Exercise 3

1. j
2. d

3. f
4. b
5. h
6. i
7. c
8. e
9. a
10. g

Exercise 4

1. selling
2. short
3. default
4. arbitrage
5. standardized
6. reduce

Exercise 5

1. option
2. call
3. put
4. strike
5. European
6. American
7. swap

Exercise 6

Table 13.A Gain or Loss

	Price of Asset				
	$85,000	**$90,000**	**$95,000**	**$100,000**	**$105,000**
Part A. Selling Canada bonds	–$10	–$5	$0	$5	$10
Part B. Selling Futures contract	$10	$5	$0	–$5	–$10
Part C. Purchasing Put option	$8	$3	–$2	–$2	–$2

Exercise 7

A. Plain vanilla swap

1. the interest rate on the payments that are being exchanged
2. the type of interest payments (variable or fixed-rate)
3. the amount of notional principal
4. the time period over which the exchanges continue to be made

B. 1. Allow financial institutions to convert fixed-rate assets into rate-sensitive assets without affecting the balance sheet.
2. Can be written for very long horizons.

C. 1. Swap markets can suffer from a lack of liquidity.
2. Swap contracts are subject to default risk.
3. Swap markets require information about the counterparties.

Self-Test

Part A

1. F
2. T
3. T
4. F
5. T
6. T
7. F
8. T
9. T
10. T
11. F
12. F

13. F
14. F
15. T
16. T

Part B

1. d
2. a
3. c
4. a
5. c
6. a
7. d
8. e
9. a
10. b
11. a
12. b
13. c
14. c
15. a
16. c
17. c
18. a
19. c
20. e
21. b
22. a
23. e
24. a
25. e
26. a
27. b
28. a
29. c
30. a
31. c
32. b

CHAPTER 14

Chapter Synopsis/Completions

1. Board of Directors
2. Governing Council
3. Board of Governors
4. New York
5. interest
6. bureaucratic
7. independence
8. inflationary
9. undemocratic

Exercise 1

1. c
2. a
3. c
4. b
5. b
6. b
7. a
8. c
9. c

Exercise 2

Part A

1. Greater focus on long-run objectives.
2. Less pressure to finance deficits and less pressure to pursue inflationary policies.
3. More likely to pursue policies in the public interest even if politically unpopular.

Part B

1. Greater accountability. If Bank of Canada policymakers make mistakes there is no way of voting them out, thus system is undemocratic.
2. Coordination of fiscal and monetary policy would be easier.
3. Lack of evidence indicating that an independent Bank of Canada performs well.

Exercise 3

Part A
1. Bank note issue
2. Government debt and asset management services
3. Central banking services
4. Monetary policy

Part B
1. Board of Governors
2. Federal Reserve Banks
3. Federal Open Market Committee
4. Federal Advisory Council
5. Member commercial banks

Exercise 4

A. Partisan business cycles.

B. Overnight interest rate; an explicit inflation-control target.

C. The purchase and sale of government securities that affect both interest rates and the amount of reserves in the banking system.

D. Clears and settles payments and transactions; 15 times our GDP per year.

E. Preserve the integrity and safety of Canadian currency in the most economical and efficient manner possible.

F. Debt-management services for the federal government; advising on borrowings, managing new debt offerings, and servicing outstanding debt.

G. Instrument independence; goal independence.

H. Follow the incoming data from government agencies and private sector organizations on the economy; provide guidance to the policymakers on where the economy may be heading and what the impact of monetary policy actions on the economy might be.

I. Remained relatively unchanged.

J. Principal-agent; politicians; the central bank; politicians have fewer.

Self-Test

Part A

1. T
2. F
3. F
4. T
5. F
6. T
7. T
8. F
9. T
10. T
11. F
12. F
13. T

Part B

1.	d	2.	c
3.	d	4.	c
5.	c	6.	b
7.	b	8.	c
9.	c	10.	d
11.	d	12.	a
13.	d	14.	e
15.	d	16.	c
17.	d	18.	a
19.	a	20.	d
21.	d	22.	d
23.	d	24.	c
25.	a	26.	c
27.	a	28.	c
29.	d	30.	a
31.	d	32.	a
33.	b	34.	d

CHAPTER 15

Chapter Synopsis/Completions

1.	central	2.	banks
3.	Bank of Canada	4.	settlement balances
5.	monetary base	6.	open market
7.	identical	8.	currency
9.	declines	10.	deposits
11.	multiple	12.	simple deposit multiplier
13.	excess	14.	smaller

Exercise 1

Part A

Banking System

Assets		Liabilities	
Securities	+$100		
Reserves	–$100		

The Bank of Canada

Assets		Liabilities	
Government securities	–$100	Reserves	–$100

Change in the monetary base = –$100

Change in reserves = –$100.

Part B

Nonbank Public

Assets		Liabilities	
Securities	+$100		
Chequable deposits	–$100		

Banking System

Assets		Liabilities	
Reserves	–$100	Chequable deposits	–$100

The Bank of Canada

Assets		Liabilities	
Government securities	–$100	Reserves	–$100

Change in the monetary base = –$100

Change in reserves = –$100.

Part C

Nonbank Public

Assets		Liabilities	
Securities	+$100		
Currency	–$100		

The Bank of Canada

Assets		Liabilities	
Government securities	–$100	Currency in circulation	–$100

Change in the monetary base = –$100

Change in Reserves = 0.

In all cases, the open market sale leads to a $100 decline in the monetary base. In part C, however, reserves do not change, while they decline by $100 in parts A and B.

Exercise 2

Part A

First Bank

Assets		Liabilities	
T-bills	+$100,000		
Reserves	–$100,000		

The Bank of Canada

Assets		Liabilities	
T-bills	–$100,000	Reserves	–$100,000

Reserves in the banking system have fallen by $100,000.

Part B

First Bank

Assets		Liabilities	
Reserves	–$100,000	Advances	–$100,000

The Bank of Canada

Assets		Liabilities	
Advances	–$100,000	Reserves	–$100,000

Reserves in the banking system have again fallen by $100,000.

Exercise 3

A. $100
B. $100, the amount of its excess reserves.
C.

Panther Bank

Assets		Liabilities
Reserves	–$100	
Loans	+$100	

Exercise 4

Part A
The deposit liabilities of Bank A increase by $1000 and desired reserves increase by $200 (20 percent of $1,000). Bank A can safely lend $800.

Part B
In the process of lending $800, chequable deposits of Bank A increase by $800. However, once the loan is deposited into Bank B, chequable deposits at Bank A fall by $800. Thus, chequable deposits at Bank A increase by $1,000, which is the amount of the original deposit.

Part C

Bank	Change in Deposits	Change in Loans	Change in Reserves
First Bank of Toronto	+$0.00	+$1000.00	+$0.00
A	+1000.00	+800.00	+200.00
B	+800.00	+640.00	+160.00
C	+640.00	+512.00	+128.00
D	+ 512.00	+409.60	+102.40
.	.	.	.
.	.	.	.
.	.	.	.
Total All Banks	+$5000.00	+$5000.00	+$1000.00

Exercise 5

1. The simple deposit multiplier formula is D = (1/r)R.

2. The $10 billion dollar sale of government bonds causes bank reserves to fall by $10 billion. This is partially offset by the $5 billion in advances that increase bank reserves by $5 billion. Thus on net, bank reserves fall by

$5 billion.

3. The change in chequable deposits is calculated by multiplying the $5 billion decline by 5 (= 1/0.20). Chequable deposits fall by $25 billion in the simple model.

Exercise 6

Part A

Mark's bank

Assets		Liabilities	
Reserves	–$50	Chequable deposits	–$50

Lisa's bank

Assets		Liabilities	
Reserves	+$50	Chequable deposits	+$50

Part B

Mark's bank lost $50 in chequable deposits, so desired reserves fell by $5 (= $50 ∗ 10%). However, since actual reserves fell by $50, Mark's bank is $45 below its desired reserve amount. Lisa's bank gained $50 in chequable deposits, so desired reserves increased by $5 (= $50 ∗ 10%). However, since actual reserves increased by $50, Lisa's bank is $45 above its desired reserve amount.

Part C

When Mark writes a cheque to Lisa, Lisa's bank eventually finds itself with excess reserves and begins to issue loans. This starts multiple deposit creation. However, once Mark's bank loses reserves, it must reduce loans or buy securities, which starts multiple deposit contraction. The net result is that chequable deposits in the banking sector do not change.

Exercise 7

A. The bank will find itself with $5000 more reserves and a reduction in its holdings of securities of $5000.

B. Its liabilities have increased by the additional $5000 of settlement balances. Its assets have now increased by the $5000 of additional securities it now holds.

C. Reserves have increased by $5000, the amount of the open market purchase. With no change in currency circulation, the monetary base rises by $5000.

Self-Test

Part A

1. F
2. F
3. F
4. F
5. T
6. F
7. T
8. F
9. F
10. F
11. F
12. F
13. T
14. T
15. T
16. F
17. T

Part B

1. c
2. c
3. b
4. c
5. d
6. a
7. c
8. d

9. e
10. c
11. e
12. b
13. c
14. a
15. e
16. b
17. a
18. e
19. a
20. d
21. b
22. b
23. e
24. d
25. a
26. d
27. b
28. d
29. b
30. d
31. d
32. c

CHAPTER 16

Chapter Synopsis/Completions

1. reserves
2. currency
3. chequable deposits
4. monetary base
5. overstates
6. increase
7. decline
8. interest rate
9. positively
10. multiplier
11. increases

Exercise 1

A. m = [1 + c]/[r + c]

B. c = \$280b/\$800b = 0.35

m = 1.35/0.45 = 3

C. DR = r(D) = 0.10(800) = \$80 b

R = DR + ER = \$120 b

MB = C + R = \$280 + \$120 = \$400 b

D. m = 1.35/0.43 = 3.139

M = \$400 × 3.139 = \$1255.6 b

E. M = C + D

M = (c × D) + D

M = (c + 1) × D

M = 1.35 × D

D = \$1255.6/1.35 = \$930.07 b

C = c × D

C = 0.35 × \$930.07 = \$325.52 b

F. DR = 0.08(930.07) = \$74.40 b

ER = \$120 − \$74.40 = \$45.6 b

Exercise 2

A. $m = 1.4/0.5 = 2.8$

$M = m \times MB = 2.8 \times \$400 = \$1120$ b

B. $C + D = M$

$(0.04 \times D) + D = \$1120$ b

$1.4 \times D = \$1120$ b

$D = \$1120/1.4 = \$800$ b

$C = \$1120 - \$800 = \$320$ b

$DR = 0.1(800) = \$80$ b

$R = DR + ER = \$80$ b

C. $m = 1.4/0.56 = 2.5$

$M = 2.5 \times \$400 = \$1000$ b

$D = \$1000/1.4 = \$714.29$ b

$C = 0.4 \times \$714.29 = \$285.71$ b

$DR = 0.16(714.29) = \$114.29$ b

Exercise 3

Change in Variable		Money Supply Response
MB_n	↓	↓
c	↓	↑
Expected deposit outflows	↓	↑
i	↓	↓

Exercise 4

A. Depositors may worry that they will not have access to their funds. They may withdraw cash and this will increase the currency ratio. All else the same, this will reduce the money multiplier and reduce the money supply.

B. Banks may expect larger-than-usual deposit outflows and will therefore keep more vault cash available. This will increase the desired reserve ratio and, all else the same, reduce the money multiplier and reduce the money supply.

C. A central bank will stand ready to increase the monetary base through increased lending (advances to banks) or open market purchases of securities. This will maintain the money supply in the face of a falling money multiplier. A central bank can also try to assure depositors that it has inspected banks' computers and they will not fail.

Exercise 5

A. $M = \text{Money Supply (M1+)} = C + D = \$70 + \$180 = \$250$ b

B. $$c = \frac{\text{currency in circulation}}{\text{chequable deposits}} = \frac{70}{180} = 0.39$$

C. $m = \frac{1 + c}{c + r} = \frac{1 + 0.39}{0.39 + 0.07} = \frac{1.39}{0.46} = 3.0\%$

Self-Test

Part A

1. T
2. F
3. T
4. F
5. T
6. F
7. T
8. F
9. T
10. F
11. T
12. F
13. T
14. T

Part B

1. e
2. c
3. a
4. b
5. d
6. d
7. a
8. c
9. b
10. d
11. c
12. a
13. e
14. c
15. d
16. b
17. c
18. a
19. d
20. e
21. e
22. d
23. d
24. c
25. a
26. a
27. b
28. c
29. d
30. a
31. a
32. b

CHAPTER 17

Chapter Synopsis/Completions

1. deposit shifting
2. advances
3. overnight interest rate
4. securities
5. dynamic
6. purchase
7. reverse repos
8. flexible

Exercise 1

1. g
2. a
3. d
4. h
5. c
6. b
7. e
8. i
9. j
10. f

Exercise 2

Part A
The Bank of Canada uses open market operations to target the overnight interest rate.

Part B
1. Dynamic open market operations
2. Defensive open market operations

Part C
1. Open market operations occur at the initiative of the Bank of Canada.
2. Open market operations can be used to any degree.
3. Open market operations are easily reversed.
4. Open market operations can be implemented quickly.

Exercise 3

Part A
1. Standing liquidity facility loans
2. Last-resort lending

Part B
Many deposits exceed the $100,000 limit that the CDIC promises to pay. Thus the lender of last resort prevents bank failures due to large depositor withdrawals. In addition, the CDIC contingency fund is limited and a wave of bank failures could seriously jeopardize the solvency of the system leading to a severe financial panic that only a lender of last resort might prevent.

Exercise 4

1. Small changes in reserve requirements are too costly to administer, so it is too blunt a tool to be used effectively.
2. Raising reserve requirements can cause immediate liquidity problems for banks with small amounts of excess reserves.

Exercise 5

Part A
With the adoption of next-day settlement accounting, direct clearers with positive clearing balances receive an interest payment and those with net debit positions make interest payments. The interest compensation is calculated using the Bank of Canada's target overnight interest rate.

Part B

Next-day settlement accounting eliminates many of the costs for the direct clearers, although it results in a small capital charge being imposed. In fact, given the 300-basis-point band in the previous retroactive settlement, it is estimated that with next-day settlement the direct clearers will save about $15 million per year at the expense of Bank of Canada profits.

Exercise 6

Part A
1. Special Purchase and Resale Agreements (SPRAs)
2. Sale and Repurchase Agreements (SRAs).

Part B
1. The Bank of Canada has complete control over the volume of SPRAs and SRAs.
2. Repurchase transactions are flexible and precise.

3. Repurchase transactions are easily reversed.
4. Repurchase transactions can be implemented quickly.

Self-Test

Part A

1. F
2. F
3. T
4. F
5. F
6. T
7. T
8. T
9. F
10. T
11. F
12. F
13. T
14. T

Part B

1. d
2. a
3. a
4. c
5. a
6. c
7. b
8. c
9. d
10. c
11. d
12. c
13. d
14. e
15. d
16. d
17. d
18. e
19. a
20. b
21. e
22. b
23. a
24. a
25. b
26. a
27. a
28. d
29. b
30. b
31. b
32. d

CHAPTER 18

Chapter Synopsis/Completions

1. nominal anchor
2. time-inconsistency problem
3. expansionary
4. distrust
5. high employment
6. economic growth
7. price stability
8. interest rate stability
9. financial market stability
10. foreign exchange market stability
11. natural rate
12. dual mandate
13. domestic
14. inflation targeting
15. New Zealand
16. transparent
17. accountability
18. output
19. implicit

Exercise 1

1. a
2. b
3. d
4. e
5. c

Exercise 2

Part A

1. It enables the central bank to adjust its monetary policy to cope with domestic considerations.
2. Information on whether the central bank is achieving its target is known almost immediately.

Part B

1. It works well only if there is a reliable relationship between the monetary aggregate and inflation.

Exercise 3

Part A

1. It enables monetary policy to focus on domestic considerations.
2. Stability in the relationship between money and inflation is not crucial to its success.
3. It's readily understood by the public and is highly transparent.
4. It increases the accountability of the central bank.
5. It appears to ameliorate the effects of inflationary shocks.

Part B

1. An inflation target does not send immediate signals to both the public and markets.
2. It might impose a rigid rule on policymakers.
3. Sole focus on the inflation rate could mean larger output fluctuations.
4. It may lead to low growth in output and employment.

Exercise 4

Part A

1. It enables monetary policy to focus on domestic considerations.
2. Stability in the relationship between money and inflation is not crucial to its success.
3. It has had demonstrated success.

Part B

1. It has a lack of transparency.
2. It is strongly dependent on the preferences, skills, and trustworthiness of the individuals at the central bank.
3. It has some inconsistencies with democratic principles because the central bank is not highly accountable.

Exercise 5

A. 1

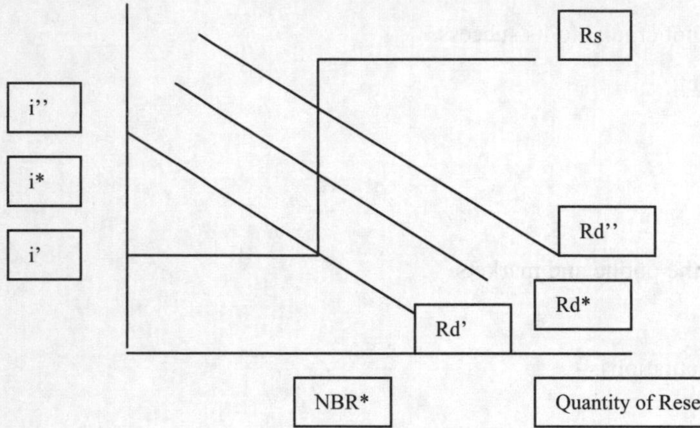

A. 2. Same graph as that on p.456.

B. Simultaneous usage of the two policy instruments is not possible. Graph a) tells us that targeting on reserve aggregates involves losing control of the interest rate. Graph b) tells us that interest-rate targeting leads to fluctuating quantity of reserve aggregates and the money supply. A central bank can therefore hit one or the other, but not both.

C. Three criteria apply when choosing a policy instrument: The instrument must be observable and measurable, it must be controllable by the central bank, and it must have a predictable effect on the goals.

D. Both interest rates and aggregates have observability and measurability problems, so it is not clear whether one should be preferred to the other. On the controllability criterion, a clear cut case cannot be made that short-term interest rates are preferable to reserve aggregates since the central bank cannot set short-term real interest rates because it does not have control over expectation of inflation. On the predictability criterion, interest rates seem to be more preferable than reserve aggregates. In recent years, most central banks have concluded that the link between interest rates and goals such as inflation is tighter than the link between aggregates and inflation. For this reason, central banks throughout the world now generally use short-term interest rates as their policy instruments.

Exercise 6

A. The Taylor rule has come up with an answer to suggest how the target for short term interest rates should be chosen. It indicates that the overnight interest rate should be equal to the inflation rate plus an "equilibrium" overnight rate, an inflation gap and an output gap.

B. $i_{or} = \pi + \bar{i}_{or} + \frac{1}{2}(\pi - \pi^*) + \frac{1}{2}(y - \bar{y})$

C. $i_{or} = 3\% + 5\% + \frac{1}{2}(5\% - 3\%) + \frac{1}{2}(2\%)$

$i_{or} = 10\%$

Self-Test

Part A

1. T
2. T
3. T
4. T
5. F
6. T
7. F
8. T
9. T
10. F
11. T
12. T
13. F
14. T
15. F
16. F
17. F

Part B

1. c
2. d
3. e
4. a
5. d
6. e
7. d
8. c
9. d
10. b
11. d
12. c
13. a
14. d
15. e
16. a
17. d
18. b
19. c
20. d
21. d
22. b
23. d
24. c
25. c
26. d
27. d
28. d
29. a
30. b
31. d
32. b
33. d
34. d

CHAPTER 19

Chapter Synopsis/Completions

1. currency
2. deposits
3. forward
4. appreciated
5. more
6. purchasing power parity
7. depreciate
8. traded
9. tariffs
10. expected return
11. capital mobility
12. interest rate

13. rise
14. appreciate
15. appreciates
16. depreciate

Exercise 1

1. 2 francs per dollar
2. $500
3. 200 francs
4. Depreciation of the franc; appreciation of the dollar
5. $250; less
6. 400 francs; more
7. When a country's currency appreciates, its goods abroad become more expensive and foreign goods in that country become cheaper (holding domestic prices constant in the two countries).

Exercise 2

1. e
2. h
3. b
4. l
5. m
6. a
7. k
8. f
9. i
10. c
11. j

Exercise 3

Part A
1. $10
2. 1800 zloties
3. None, because Polish wheat is more expensive in both countries and the goods are identical.
4. $5
5. 3600 zloties
6. None, because Canadian wheat is more expensive in both countries and the goods are identical.
7. 500 zloties per dollar, because only at this exchange rate will both Canadian and Polish wheat be purchased.
8. 300 zloties per dollar; a depreciation of the dollar

Part B
1. The value of the dollar will fall to 250 zloties per dollar.
2. The dollar will appreciate by 2%.

Exercise 4

Change in Factor		Response of the Exchange Rate
Domestic interest rate	↓	↓
Foreign interest rate	↓	↑
Expected domestic price level	↓	↑
Expected tariffs and quotas	↓	↓
Expected import demand	↓	↑

Expected export demand	↓	↓
Expected productivity	↓	↓

Exercise 5

1. $\$100 * 1.07 = \$107$

2. $\$100 * (.56) = 56$ pounds

   56 pounds $* (1.03) = 57.68$ pounds

   57.68 pounds $* [1/(0.48\text{pounds/dollar})] = \$120.17$

3. The return is higher when British bank accounts are purchased. As people purchase pounds, the exchange rate will fall (the pound will depreciate).

4. $i^{\$} = i^{pounds} - [(E^e_{t+1} - E_t)/E_t]$

   $0.07 = 0.03 - [(0.48 - E_t)/E_t]$

   $E_t = 0.50$ pounds per dollar

Exercise 6

A. No.
B. No. The relative expected return is still negative.
C. i.: Yes.
   ii & iii:
   1. A fall in the domestic interest rate

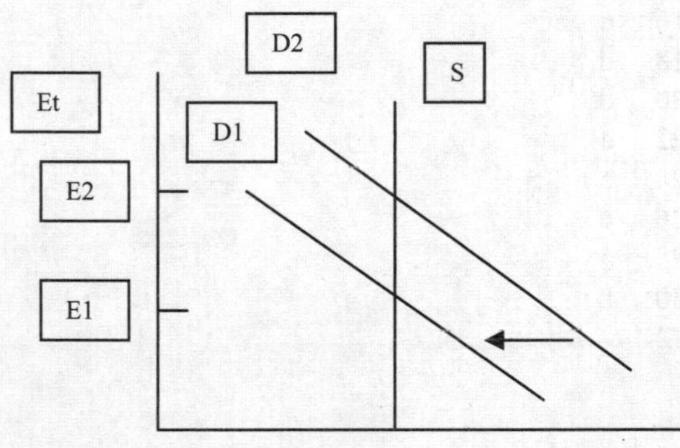

   2. An increase in the foreign interest rate (graph same as above)
   3. An increase in the expected domestic price level (graph same as above)
   4. Decrease in expected trade barriers (graph same as above)
   5. Increase in expected import demand (graph same as above)
   6. Decrease in expected export demand (graph same as above)
   7. Decrease in expected productivity (graph same as above)

   iv. Be able to explain why the demand curve for domestic assets is downward-sloping through the relationship between E_t and E_{t+1}. The lower the current exchange rate, Et, the greater the expected appreciation of the dollar, and thus the higher the expected return on dollar assets relative to foreign assets. The lower the current exchange rate, the higher the quantity demanded of dollar assets (everything else held equal), so that the demand curve slopes down. (Answer, p. 482).

Exercise 7

A. Be the same all over the world.

B. To increase in value against other currencies because of an increase in the demand for domestic assets.
C. A 5% expected appreciation of the US dollar.

Self-Test

Part A

1. T
2. F
3. T
4. F
5. F
6. T
7. F
8. F
9. T
10. F
11. T
12. F
13. F
14. T
15. T
16. T
17. T
18. F
19. F

Part B

1. e
2. a
3. b
4. a
5. c
6. c
7. a
8. e
9. a
10. b
11. d
12. b
13. a
14. d
15. c
16. c
17. b
18. d
19. e
20. d
21. b
22. e
23. a
24. e
25. b
26. d
27. c
28. a
29. d
30. b
31. c
32. c
33. b

CHAPTER 20

Chapter Synopsis/Completions

1. dirty
2. increase
3. current account
4. trade balance
5. fixed
6. reserve currency
7. fixed
8. devalue
9. inflows
10. exchange rate
11. purchases
12. increase
13. contractionary
14. increase
15. depreciation

Exercise 1

1.	b	2.	e
3.	d	4.	g
5.	a	6.	j
7.	i	8.	f
9.	c	10.	h

Exercise 2

Part A

Mexican Central Bank

Assets		Liabilities	
Canadian dollars	+$1 billion	Mexican pesos	+$1 billion

The effect of the Mexican central bank's intervention in the foreign exchange market is a $1 billion increase in the Mexican monetary base and a $1 billion increase in the Mexican central bank's holdings of international reserves (dollar-denominated assets). The Mexican official reserve transactions balance has a surplus of $1 billion.

Part B

Mexican Central Bank

Assets		Liabilities	
Canadian dollars	0	Mexican pesos	+$1 billion
Canadian securities	+$1 billion		

Since there is no change in the Bank of Canada's dollar liabilities, the Canadian monetary base is unaffected. In the Canadian balance of payments, the official reserve transactions balance has a deficit of $1 billion, since reserves have moved to the Mexican central bank.

Exercise 3

Part A

In the short run, the expected return on Korean deposits rises since the Korean monetary base falls. In the long run, however, the interest rate returns to the original level.

The exchange rate is expected to be higher in the future, since the drop in the Korean monetary base will lead to an appreciation of the won.

The expected return (in terms of won) on Japanese deposits is lower, since the yen is expected to depreciate.

Part B

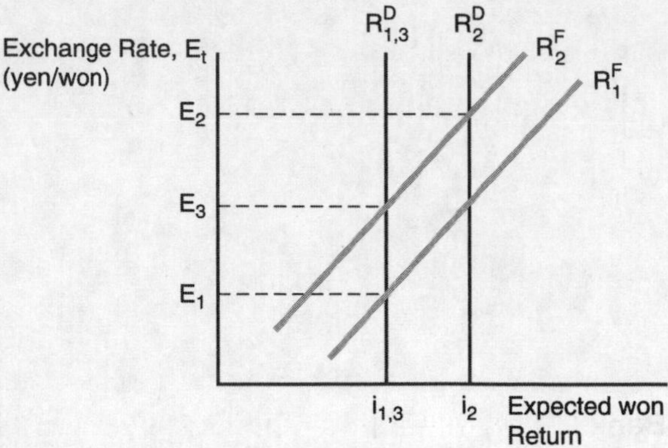

Figure 20A

In the short run, the R^D schedule shifts right as the South Korean interest rate rises. The return on Japanese assets, R^F, shifts left. In the long run, the interest rate in South Korea is unaffected, and the R^D schedule returns to the original position. However, the exchange rate is higher and the won has appreciated.

Exercise 4

Part A

1. purchase; selling
2. reducing; rise; right

Part B

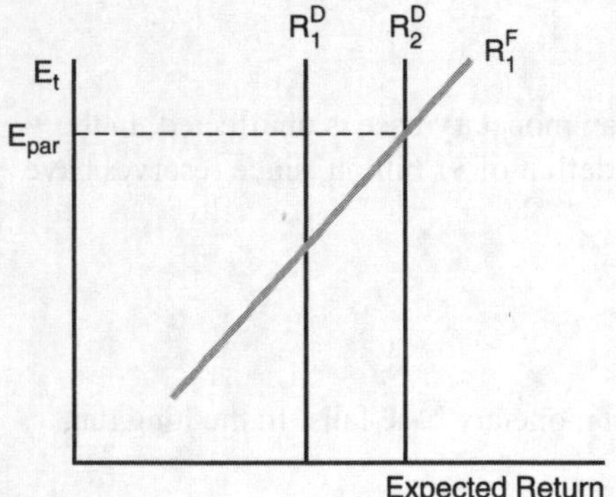

Figure 20B

Exercise 5

Part A

1. An international lender of last resort can provide liquidity without the undesirable side effect of raising inflation expectations.

2. An international lender of last resort may be able to prevent contagion.

Part B

1. The existence of an international lender of last resort creates the moral hazard problem in that irresponsible financial institutions may take excessive risks that make financial crises more likely.

2. The IMF as lender of last resort may feel forced to come to the rescue, even if the emerging market country

resists adopting necessary reforms.

3. The IMF has been criticized for imposing austerity programs on the East Asian countries, rather than microeconomic policies to fix the crisis-causing problems in the financial sector.

4. The IMF may take too much time to provide sufficient funds to keep the crisis from becoming worse

Exercise 6

A. A currency board is a regime in which the domestic currency is backed 100% by a foreign currency, and in which the note-issuing authority, whether the central bank or the government, establishes a fixed exchange rate to this foreign currency and stands ready to exchange domestic currency for the foreign currency at this rate whenever the public requests it.

B. In a currency board regime, the conduct of monetary policy is taken completely out of the hands of the central bank and the government. In contrast, the typical fixed exchange-rate regime does allow the monetary authorities some discretion in their conduct of monetary policy because they can still adjust interest rates or print money.

C. 1. The money supply can expand only when foreign currency is exchanged for domestic currency at the central bank. Since the central bank has no longer the ability to print money, it no longer is able to cause inflation.
2. The currency board involves a stronger commitment by the central bank to the fixed exchange rate and may therefore be effective in bringing down inflation quickly and in decreasing the likelihood of a successful speculative attack against the currency.

D. Dollarization involves the adoption of a sound currency, like the U.S. dollar, as a country's money. 1. The currency board can be abandoned, allowing a change in the value of the currency, but a change of value is impossible with dollarization. 2. Dollarization avoids the possibility of a speculative attack on the domestic currency, whereas such an attack is still a danger even under a currency board arrangement.

E. 1. The loss of an independent monetary policy
2. Increased exposure of the economy to shocks from the anchor country
3. Inability of the central bank to create money and act as a lender of last resort
Dollarization has one additional disadvantage – the country adopting dollarization loses the revenue that a government receives by issuing money, which is called seignorage.

Self-Test

Part A

1. F
2. F
3. F
4. F
5. T
6. F
7. F
8. T
9. T
10. T
11. T
12. T
13. T
14. F

Part B

1. c
2. b
3. a
4. d
5. d
6. c
7. e
8. c
9. b
10. a
11. a
12. b
13. c
14. a
15. a
16. a
17. c
18. a
19. d
20. d
21. c
22. c
23. c
24. a

25. a
26. d
27. d
28. c
29. d
30. a
31. a
32. a
33. c
34. c

CHAPTER 21

Chapter Synopsis/Completions

1. velocity
2. fixed
3. exchange
4. money
5. flexible
6. price level
7. liquidity preference
8. speculative
9. decline
10. negatively
11. positive
12. procyclical

Exercise 1

Part A

1. transactions motive
2. precautionary motive
3. speculative motive

Part B

Speculative motive

Part C

Risk

Exercise 2

1. 600
2. 1000
3. 2
4. 4
5. 800

Exercise 3

1. Q
2. K
3. F
4. F
5. K
6. K
7. Q
8. Q
9. K
10. F

Exercise 4

A. $\frac{M^d}{P} = \frac{1,000}{100 * 0.04} = 250$

B. $V = \frac{PY}{M} = \left(\frac{P}{M}\right)Y = \left(\frac{1}{250}\right)1,000 = 4$

C. $\frac{M^d}{P} = \frac{1,000}{100 * 0.05} = 200$. The demand for real money balances is lower.

D. $V = \frac{PY}{M} = \left(\frac{P}{M}\right)Y = \left(\frac{1}{200}\right)1{,}000 = 5$. Velocity is higher.

Exercise 5

A. 15 times
B. The transactions motive, the precautionary motive, and the speculative motive.
C. Money demand is negatively related to the level of interest rates.

Self-Test

Part A

1. T
2. T
3. T
4. F
5. F
6. T
7. T
8. F
9. T
10. T
11. T
12. F
13. T
14. T
15. F

Part B

1. d
2. a
3. a
4. d
5. c
6. b
7. b
8. b
9. a
10. b
11. b
12. a
13. d
14. a
15. e
16. c
17. b
18. c
19. d
20. e
21. c
22. c
23. e
24. b
25. d
26. d
27. b
28. d
29. b
30. b

CHAPTER 22

Chapter Synopsis/Completions

1. aggregate demand
2. investment spending
3. income
4. marginal propensity
5. autonomous
6. inventory investment
7. planned
8. multiplier
9. employment
10. IS
11. higher
12. income

Exercise 1

1. g
2. h
3. i
4. b
5. a
6. l
7. j
8. o
9. k
10. m
11. d
12. f
13. c
14. e
15. n

Exercise 2

Part A

Point	Disposable Income (Y_D)	Change in Y_D	Change in C	Autonomous Consumption	Total Consumption
A	0			50	50
B	100	100	75	50	125
C	200	100	75	50	200
D	300	100	75	50	275
E	400	100	75	50	350
F	500	100	75	50	425

Part B

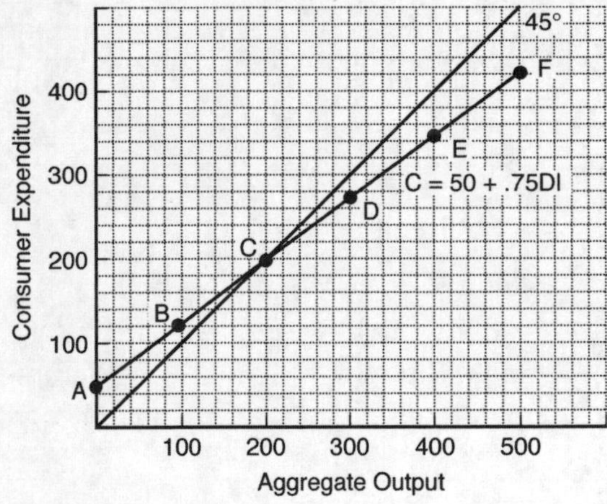

Figure 22A

Exercise 3

Part A

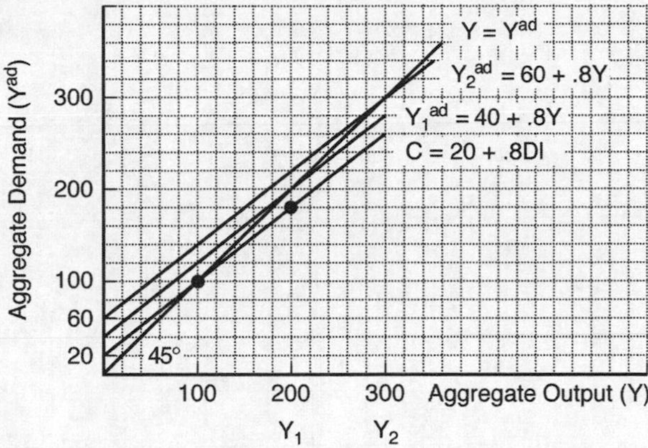

Figure 22B

B. $Y_1 = 200$

C. $Y_2 = 300$

D. 5

Exercise 4

A. $Y^{ad} = 100 + 0.9Y + 100 + 200 = 400 + 0.9Y$

B. Inventory investment $= -100 = (Y - Y^{ad}) = 3000 - 400 - 0.9(3000)$

C. Output will increase since business will expand production in the second time period.

D. 4000: Because $Y - Y^{ad} = 0 = Y - 400 - 0.9Y$; $0.1Y = 400$; $Y = 4000$

E. 4000: The same level where unplanned inventory investment is zero.

Exercise 5

	Consumer Autonomous	Expenditure Induced	Planned Investment Spending	Government Spending	Equilibrium Aggregate Income
Decrease in interest rate	0	+	+	0	+
Decrease in mpc	0	–	0	0	–
Increase in planned investment spending	0	+	+	0	+
Increase in autonomous consumer expenditure	+	+	0	0	+
Decrease in government spending	0	–	0	–	–

Exercise 6

A. $5 = 1/(1 - 0.8)$

B. Change in G = 40

Exercise 7

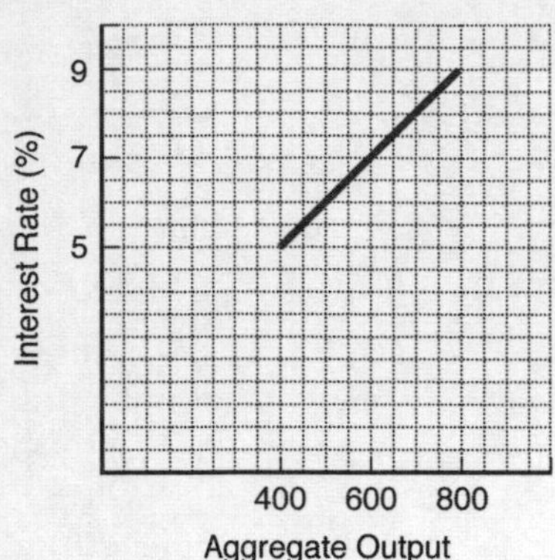

Exercise 8

(c) The IS Curve

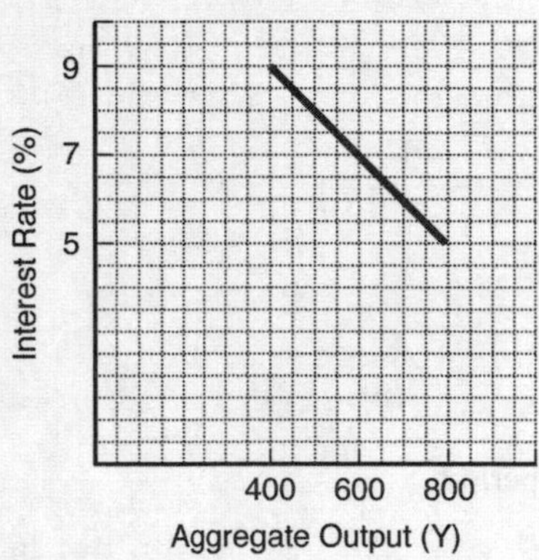

Exercise 9

Part A

$\Delta Y/\Delta I = 300/100 = 3$

Part B

$[1/(1 - mpc)] = 3$

$1 = 3 - 3mpc$

$mpc = 2/3$

Part C

If the mpc is lower, then the expenditure multiplier is lower, and the change in output is less for a given change in planned investment spending. Thus, equilibrium output would be higher than 1500.

Self-Test

Part A

1. T
2. F
3. T
4. F
5. F
6. T
7. T
8. F

9. T
10. T
11. T
12. F
13. T
14. T
15. T
16. T
17. T
18. T

Part B

1. d
2. b
3. a
4. c
5. b
6. d
7. a
8. a
9. b
10. e
11. a
12. b
13. a
14. b
15. c
16. b
17. c
18. b
19. d
20. a
21. b
22. b
23. d
24. e
25. d
26. c
27. a
28. c
29. d
30. b
31. b

CHAPTER 23

Chapter Synopsis/Completions

1. fiscal
2. IS
3. investment
4. right
5. LM
6. excess
7. income
8. fall
9. right
10. rightward
11. rise
12. IS
13. ineffective
14. downward
15. right

Exercise 1

Part A

1. increase in autonomous consumer expenditures
2. increase in autonomous investment
3. increase in government spending
4. decline in taxes

Part B

1. decline in autonomous consumer expenditures
2. decline in autonomous investment
3. decline in government spending
4. increase in taxes

Part C

1. increase in the money supply
2. decline in money demand

Part D

1. decline in the money supply
2. increase in money demand

Exercise 2

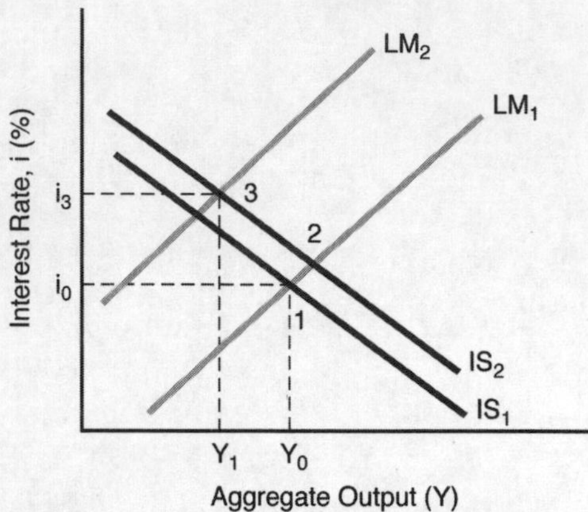

Figure 23A

The LM curve must have shifted to the left (to LM2), moving the economy to point 3. The leftward shift in the LM curve is best explained by the combination of two factors. First, the Fed, in an attempt to slow inflation which had reached double-digit levels in 1979 and 1980, slowed money growth. Second, people's concerns about recession and rising unemployment led to an increase in money demand. Both of these factors cause the LM curve to shift to the left and thus reinforce each other. Some economists have argued that the Fed was slow to realize the increase in money demand. Had the Fed known earlier, it is possible that the Fed would not have slowed money growth so sharply.

Note that the contractionary monetary policy explains the decline in real GDP, while the combination of an expansionary fiscal policy and contractionary monetary policy pushed interest rates up. In 1982, these interest rates adjusted for inflation (real interest rates) proved to be very high, leading to concerns that the fiscal-monetary policy mix of the Reagan administration would prove harmful to investment.

Exercise 3

The LM curve shifts to the left by more than the IS curve. This increases the interest rate and reduces the level of output (thereby increasing the unemployment rate).

Exercise 4

1. M
2. F
3. F
4. M
5. M
6. F
7. B

Exercise 5

1. M
2. M
3. M
4. F
5. M

Exercise 6

A. The IS curve will shift to the left which leads to lower aggregate output and a lower interest rate.

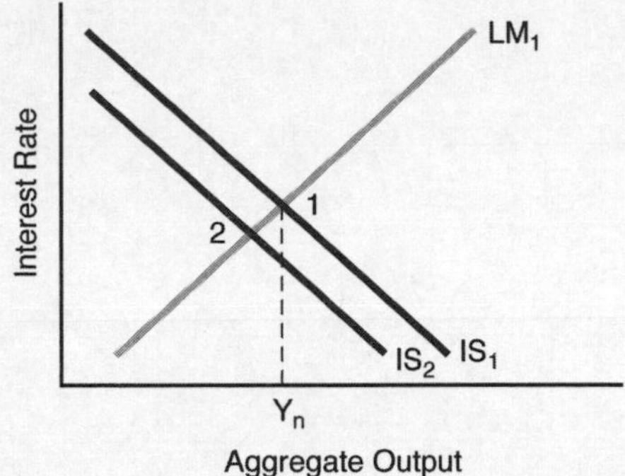

B. The Bank of Canada could increase the money supply, which shifts the LM curve to the right. This returns aggregate output to the natural rate level of output and lowers the interest rate.

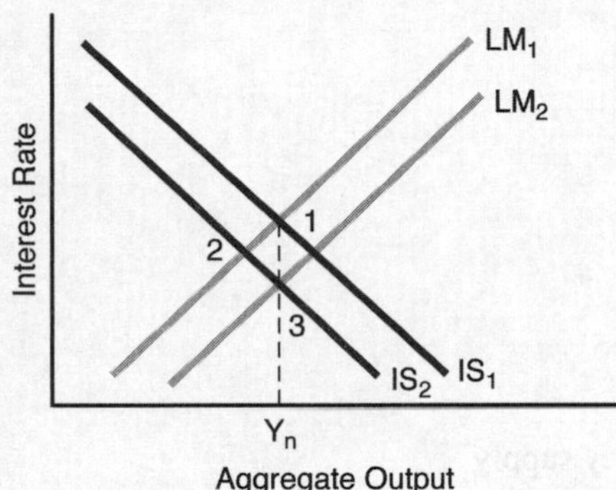

C. Since the economy is below the natural rate level of output at point 2, the price level begins to fall. This raises real money balances, which shifts the LM curve to the right. The price level continues to fall until the economy reaches the natural rate level of output at point 3.

Exercise 7

A. →
B. ←
C. ←
D. ←
E. →
F. ←

Self-Test

Part A

1.	F	2.	T
3.	F	4.	T
5.	T	6.	F
7.	F	8.	F
9.	F	10.	T
11.	F	12.	F
13.	T	14.	T
15.	T	16.	F
17.	F	18.	T
19.	F	20.	F
21.	T	22.	T
23.	T		

Part B

1. a
2. d
3. d
4. b
5. c
6. c
7. b
8. a
9. a
10. a
11. c
12. b
13. d
14. a
15. d
16. c
17. e
18. c
19. b
20. d
21. a
22. d
23. d
24. b
25. b
26. b
27. b
28. c
29. a
30. d
31. d
32. c

CHAPTER 24

Chapter Synopsis/Completions

1. price
2. money supply
3. increase
4. money
5. right
6. right
7. fixed
8. expand
9. rise
10. aggregate output
11. aggregate supply
12. price level
13. shocks
14. stagflation

Exercise 1

Part A

1. increase in the money supply
2. increase in government spending
3. increase in net exports
4. reduction in taxes
5. improved consumer optimism
6. improved business optimism

Part B

1. decline in the money supply
2. decline in government spending
3. decline in net exports
4. increase in taxes
5. increase in consumer pessimism
6. increase in business pessimism

Exercise 2

Parts A and C

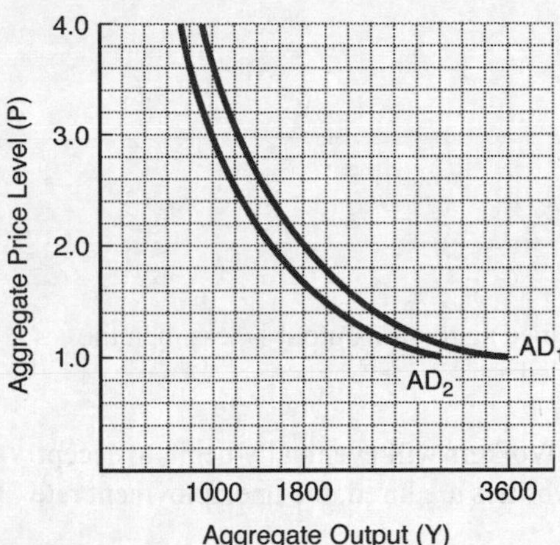

Figure 24A

Part B

Aggregate spending will fall from \$3600 to \$3000

Exercise 3

1. ←
2. ←
3. →
4. ←
5. ←
6. →

Exercise 4

Part A

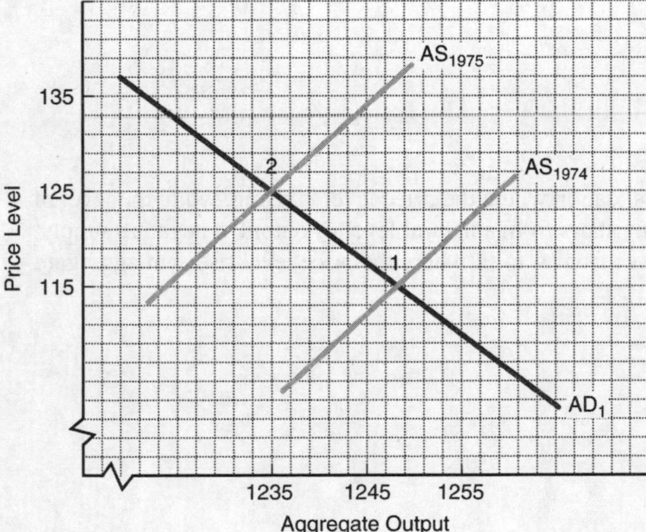

Figure 24B

Part B

Since the actual unemployment rate exceeds the natural unemployment rate in 1974, the labour market was slightly "easy" at this time, suggesting that the aggregate supply curve would have shifted out, all else constant. Most of the blame for the shifting of the aggregate supply curve must go to OPEC, which had significantly raised the price of oil in 1974, crop failures, and the lifting of wage and price controls.

Exercise 5

1. B	2. N
3. K	4. M
5. M	6. K
7. K	8. M
9. B	10. B

Exercise 6

Part A. The unemployment rate is above the natural rate of unemployment since aggregate output is less than the natural rate of output. When less output is produced, fewer workers are needed.

Part B. The relatively high unemployment describes an easy labour market. Workers will eventually begin to accept lower real wages in return for employment. As the wage falls and as more workers are hired, the unemployment rate declines.

Part C. Production costs for firms fall as the real wage falls. This shifts the aggregate supply curve outwards to the right. In the long run (point 2) output is equal to the natural level of output, and the price level falls to P_2.

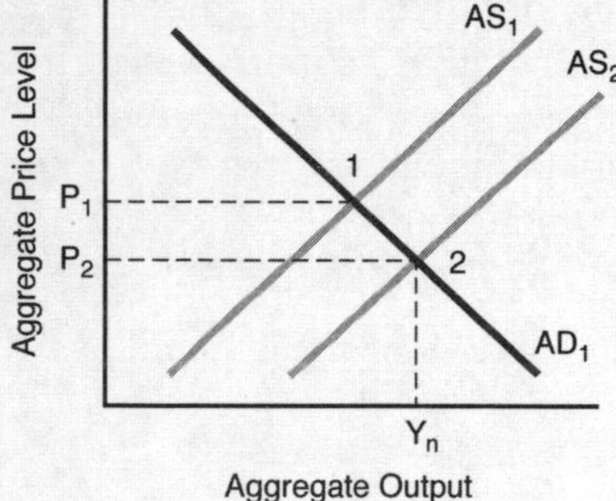

Figure 24C

Exercise 7

A. Students should be able to realize that stagflation is a situation where the price level is rising, while the level of aggregate output is falling. Supposing that the economy starts from a natural level of output, a negative supply shock shifts the AS curve leftward. The economy moves from A to B, where the price level rises but aggregate output falls – i.e., stagflation.

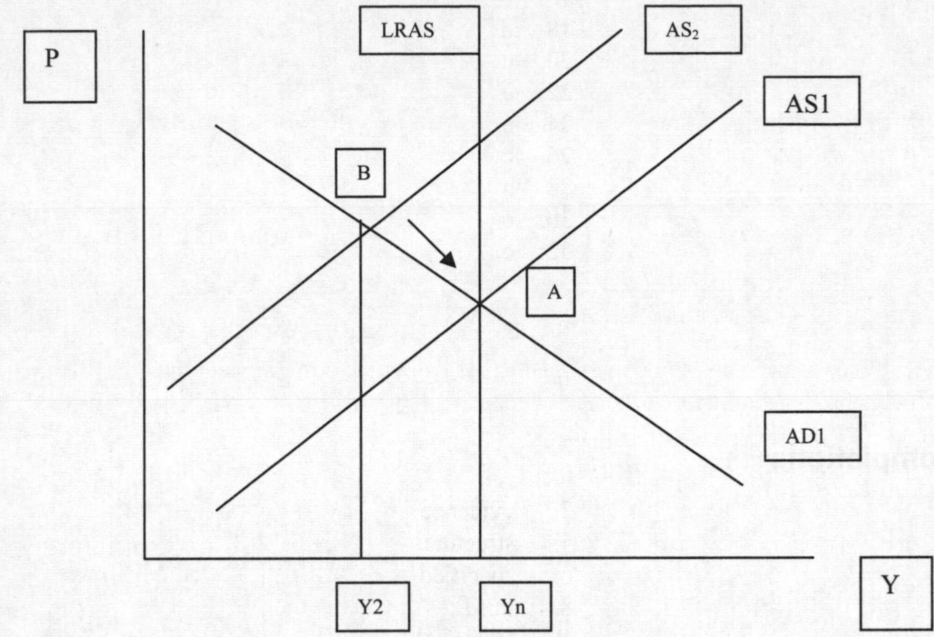

B. In the long run, the aggregate supply curve shifts back to its initial position. This is because Y2 < Yn. Wages fall because labour markets are slack, production costs fall at any given price level and the AS curve shifts rightward to AS1. The AD curve is not affected; the economy only moves down the AD1 curve returning to the long-run equilibrium at A. Hence, although a leftward shift in the short-run AS curve initially raises the price level and lowers output, the ultimate effect is that output and price level are unchanged (holding the AD curve constant).

C. Students should be able to recognize that the above analysis assumes that the natural rate level of output Yn and hence the long-run AS curve are given. This means that the shifts in either the aggregate demand or aggregate supply curve have no effect on the natural rate level of output. Real business cycle theorists take issue with the assumption that Yn is unaffected by AD and supply shocks. This theory views aggregate supply shocks as the major driving forces behind short-run fluctuations in the business cycle because these shocks lead to substantial short-run fluctuations in Yn.

Self-Test

Part A

1. T
2. T
3. F
4. T
5. F
6. T
7. F
8. T
9. T
10. F
11. T
12. T
13. F
14. T

Part B

1. c
2. c
3. b
4. e
5. e
6. d
7. d
8. a
9. c
10. b
11. a
12. c
13. d
14. d

15. e
16. b
17. b
18. d
19. e
20. c
21. a
22. c
23. c
24. a
25. b
26. c
27. d
28. a
29. c
30. d
31. d
32. c

CHAPTER 25

Chapter Synopsis/Completions

1. Monetarists
2. evidence
3. reduced form
4. structural
5. forecasts
6. specified
7. reverse causation
8. third
9. real
10. statistical
11. historical
12. price level
13. stock
14. worth
15. cash flow

Exercise 1

1. R
2. S
3. R
4. S
5. R
6. S
7. S
8. S
9. R

Exercise 2

1. K
2. M
3. M
4. K
5. M
6. M
7. K
8. K
9. K

Exercise 3

1. If workers and other resource suppliers anticipate future price increases, they may attempt to hedge against inflation by increasing their prices now, especially if longer term contracts are prevalent.
2. When parties enter into longer term agreements they will have expectations of what the future will be like. If high rates of inflation are anticipated, wages will tend to reflect these anticipations. Thus, it is possible that wages rise in anticipation of higher prices rather than cause higher prices.
3. Many economists would argue that changes in monetary growth drive both input costs, such as wages, and prices.

Exercise 4

1. d
2. e

3. f
4. a
5. g
6. b
7. c

Exercise 5

Part A. Bank lending channel. With losses on real estate loans and therefore a reduction of bank assets, banks needed to increase their capital relative to assets. They were therefore less likely to lend and acquire new assets.

Part B. Balance sheet channel. With more debt, the net worth of businesses was reduced. This may increase adverse selection and moral hazard problems associated with lending. Thus, banks would be less likely to lend.

Exercise 6

A. The structural model describes the transmission mechanism of monetary policy as follows: the change in the money supply M affects interest rates i, which in turn affect investment spending I, which in turn affects aggregate output or aggregate spending Y. Structural model evidence on the relationship between M and Y looks at empirical evidence on the specific channels of monetary influence, such as the link between interest rates and investment spending.

B. Reduced-form evidence does not describe specific ways in which the money supply affects aggregate spending. Instead, it suggests that the effect of money on economic activity should be examined by looking at whether movements in Y are tightly linked with movements in M. Reduced-form evidence analyzes the effect of changes in M on Y as if the economy were a black box whose workings cannot be seen.

C. Three advantages of structural model evidence:
   1. Provides more confidence in the direction of causation between M and Y.
   2. Helps us to predict the effect of changes in M on Y more accurately.
   3. Allows predictions of the effect of monetary policy when institutions change

D. A disadvantage of structural model evidence: The structural model evidence works only if we know the correct structure of the model. Failing to include one or two relevant transmission mechanisms for monetary policy in the structural model might result in a serious misjudgment about the impact of changes in M on Y.

E. The main advantage of reduced-form evidence over structural model evidence is that no restrictions are imposed on the way monetary policy affects the economy and may be more likely to spot the full effect of changes in M on Y.

F. The reverse causation problem can lead to misleading conclusions when interpreting correlations. This is the most notable objection to reduced-form evidence which may misleadingly suggest that changes in M cause changes in Y when that is not the case. In other words, correlation does not necessarily imply causation.

G. No clear-cut case can be made that reduced-form evidence is preferable to structural model evidence or vice versa.

Self-Test

Part A

1. F
2. T
3. T
4. T
5. T
6. F
7. T
8. F
9. T
10. T
11. F
12. F
13. T
14. F

Part B

1. b
2. e
3. b
4. d
5. b
6. d

7. c
8. b
9. d
10. a
11. a
12. c
13. b
14. c
15. b
16. b
17. d
18. b
19. c
20. a
21. e
22. a
23. d
24. d
25. d
26. c
27. d
28. b
29. b
30. b
31. d
32. a

CHAPTER 26

Chapter Synopsis/Completions

1. hyperinflation
2. monetary
3. temporary
4. accommodation
5. compatible
6. supply shocks
7. unemployment
8. cost-push
9. low
10. constraint
11. cost-push
12. stable
13. time lags
14. activist
15. credible

Exercise 1

1. Concern over unemployment. Expansionary macropolicies reduce unemployment in the short run, but raise the price level in the long run. Such policies may prove inflationary if the unemployment target is set too low. Alternatively, monetary authorities may expand the money supply in response to cost-push pressures that threaten to raise unemployment.

2. Budget deficits. If deficits push interest rates upward, the Bank of Canada may automatically accommodate them if it pursues an interest-rate targeting strategy. Even if the Bank does not attempt to peg interest rates, the Bank may feel pressure to expand the money supply to keep interest rates from rising.

Exercise 2

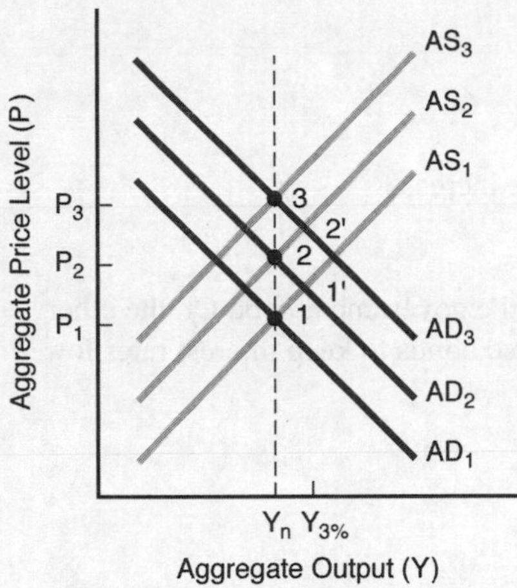

Figure 26A

The target level of unemployment is below the natural rate level so $Y_{3\%}$ is above Y_n, as is drawn in the figure. Hence in trying to reach an output level of $Y_{3\%}$, the government will shift the aggregate demand curve to AD_2. Because the resulting level of output at point 1' is above the natural-rate level, the aggregate supply curve shifts in to AS_2 and output falls to the natural-rate level. To raise aggregate output to $Y_{3\%}$, the government again pursues expansionary policy to shift the aggregate demand curve to AD_3. The aggregate supply curve again shifts up to AS_3 because $Y > Y_n$. The outcome of this process is that the price level continually rises from P_1 to P_2 to P_3 and so on. The result is a demand-pull inflation.

Exercise 3

Canadian govemment budget deficits do not necessarily lead to monetary expansion because the Bank of Canada is not obligated to monetize the debt.

1. The budget deficit must lead to upward pressure on interest rates.
2. The Bank of Canada will try to prevent any rise in interest rates.

Although the Bank of Canada may have tried to prevent interest rate rises in the 1960-1980 period, the budget deficits could not have led to upward pressure on interest rates since the debt-to-GNP ratio did not rise in this period. Thus the budget deficits in this period could not have been the source of higher money growth.

Exercise 4

A comparison of the Argentine experience with that of post-World War I Germany suggests that changing the person in charge and issuing new currency may be insufficient by itself to rid a country of inflation. The German government constrained itself by limiting currency issue and moving toward a balanced budget. The deflation proved costly as the German economy went into recession. However, one can reasonably assume that the recession would have been longer and deeper had their policies not been viewed as credible by the citizenry. Especially important to achieving credibility is the reduction of budget deficits, since many people associate large deficits with inflation. Unfortunately, the failure of past reforms probably means that even serious reforms may, at first, be regarded with skepticism. Thus one might anticipate that deflationary policies will prove relatively more costly in Argentina than they did in 1920s Germany. The initial success of the Argentine anti-inflation program differed from previous attempts by addressing the problem of government budget deficits. Reducing the budget deficit likely changed inflationary expectations, contributing to the dramatic drop in the Argentine inflation rate in 1986. The government's failure to constrain budget deficits explains, in part, the return of triple-digit inflation rates.

Exercise 5

A.

1. The government can increase taxes.
2. The government can borrow from the public.
3. The government can borrow from the Bank of Canada.

B. When the government borrows from the Bank of Canada, the monetary base increases.

C. Monetizing the debt or it is sometimes called printing money.

D. No, because the Bank of Canada does not have to monetize it—that is, buy the government debt. On the other hand, if the Bank wants to prevent a rise in interest rates, then it will purchase bonds to keep interest rates low and the result will be expansion of the monetary base.

Exercise 6

Part A.

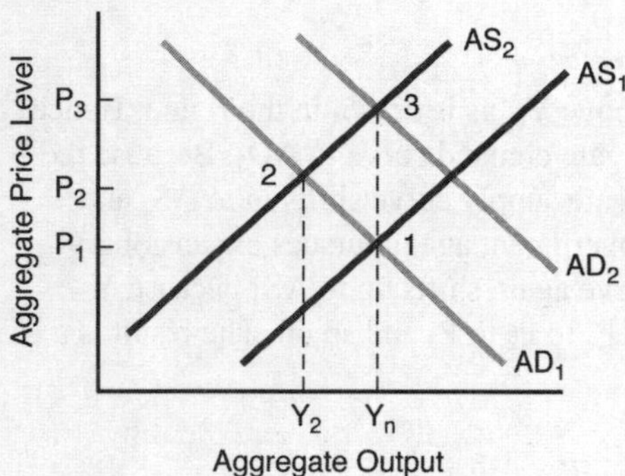

Figure 26B

Part B. The aggregate supply curve will shift back to AS_1, and output and the price level will return to their original levels at point 1.

Part C. The aggregate demand curve will shift outward to the right, the price level will rise to P_3 and output will return to the natural rate level of output.

Part D. The activist policy will be more likely to encourage workers to seek higher wages, because the accommodative monetary policy results in output returning to the natural rate level fairly quickly without an accompanying tight labour market. In other words, employment rises as demand for workers increases. In the nonactivist response, the self-correcting mechanism involves painful wage reductions that eventually encourage firms to hire more workers.

Exercise 7

A. Friedman's statement that "inflation is always and everywhere a monetary phenomenon" means that upward movements in the price level are a monetary phenomenon only if this is a sustained process. Hence, inflation is defined as a situation in which the price level is continually rising at a rapid rate.

B. We can use the aggregate supply and demand analysis to show that large and persistent upward movements in the price level (high inflation) can occur only if there is a continually growing money supply. Using monetarist analysis,

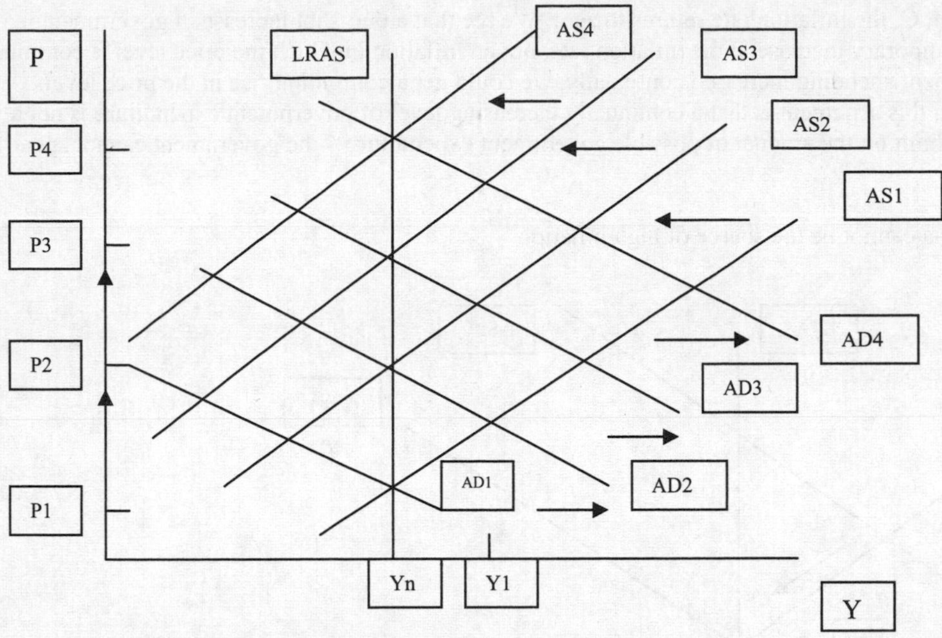

A continually rising money supply shifts the AD curve to the right from AD1 to AD2 to AD3 to AD4, while the supply curve shifts to the left from AS1 to AS2 to AS3 to AS4. The result is that the price level rises continually from P1 to P2 to P3 to P4. The AS curve shifts leftward because only for a brief time can output increase above the natural rate level to Y1. The resulting decline in unemployment below the natural level will cause wages to rise, and the short-run AS curve will quickly begin to shift leftward. It will stop shifting when it returns to the natural rate level of output on the LRAS. The rightward shifts of the AD curve will continue as long as money supply grows and inflation will occur. High money growth produces high inflation.

C. Fiscal policy by itself cannot generate high inflation.

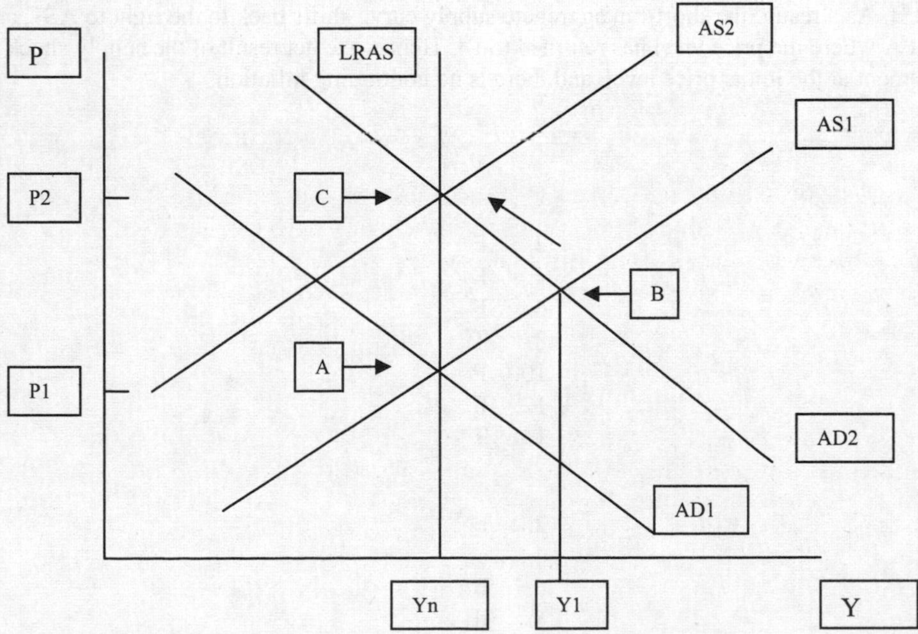

Assume a one-shot permanent increase in government spending. This generates a one-shot permanent increase in the price level. When we move from point A to B to C, the price level rises, and we have a positive inflation rate. But when we finally get to point C, the inflation rate returns to zero. We see that a one-shot increase in government spending leads to only a temporary increase in the inflation rate, not an inflation in which the price level is continually rising. Even if the government spending increased continually, we could get a continuing rise in the price level. However, the problem with this argument is that a continually increasing level of government expenditure is not a feasible policy. There is a limit on the amount of possible government expenditure – the government cannot spend more than 100% of GDP.

D. Supply-side phenomena cannot be the source of high inflation.

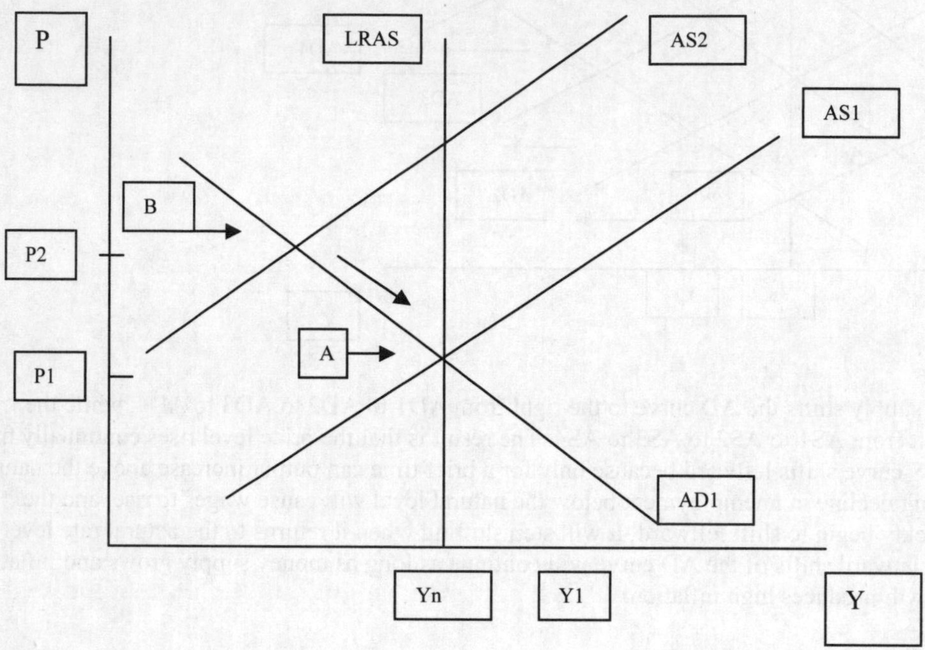

A negative supply shock (or a wage push) shifts the short-run aggregate supply curve leftward to AS2 and results in high unemployment at point B. As a result, the short-run aggregate supply curve shifts back to the right to AS1, and the economy returns to point A where the price level has returned to P1. Hence, the net result of the supply shock is that we return to full employment at the initial price level, and there is no continuing inflation.

Self-Test

Part A

1. T
2. F
3. F
4. F
5. F
6. F
7. T
8. T
9. T
10. F
11. F
12. F
13. T
14. T

Part B

1. c
2. b
3. d
4. a
5. a
6. b
7. c
8. d
9. d
10. d
11. c
12. a
13. b
14. d

15. c
16. c
17. c
18. a
19. e
20. b
21. d
22. a
23. b
24. e
25. c
26. b
27. b
28. c
29. d
30. a
31. c

CHAPTER 27

Chapter Synopsis/Completions

1. expectations
2. constant
3. new classical
4. flexible
5. supply
6. price level
7. ineffectiveness proposition
8. rigidities
9. anticipated
10. New Keynesians
11. policy critique
12. activist
13. credible
14. budget deficits

Exercise 1

In the new classical model, the aggregate supply curve shifts out to AS_{NC} and the economy goes to point NC. Aggregate output does not fall, while the price level falls to P_{NC}.

In the new Keynesian model, the aggregate supply shifts out but only to AS_{NK} and the economy goes to point N. Aggregate output falls below Y_N and the price level falls to P_{NK}, which is higher than that found in the new classical model.

In the traditional model, the aggregate supply curve does not shift out at all and the economy goes to point T. Aggregate output falls to Y_T, which is lower than in the other models, and the price level falls to P_T, which is higher than in the other models.

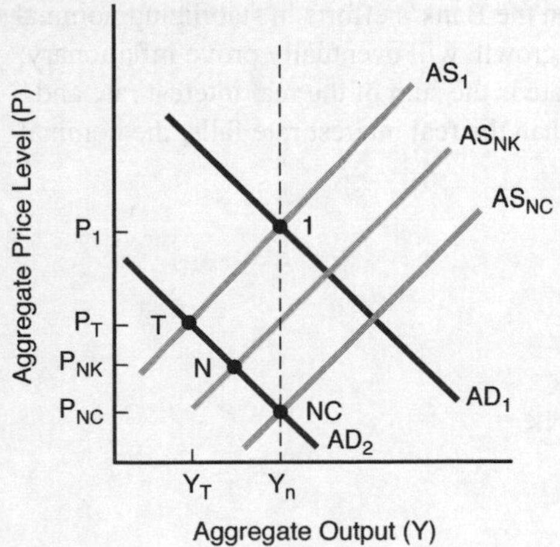

Figure 27A

Exercise 2

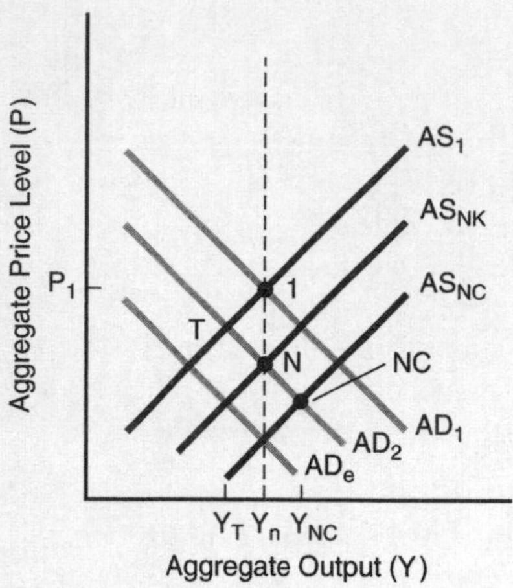

Figure 27B

In the new classical model, the aggregate supply curve shifts out to AS_{NC} (where output would equal Y_n if the realized aggregate demand curve were AD_e). The economy goes to point NC, at which point aggregate output has risen to Y_{NC}. Aggregate output does not fall but rather rises.

In the new Keynesian model, the aggregate supply curve shifts out by less than in the new classical model. As drawn, the aggregate supply curve shifts to AS_{NK} and the economy is at point N with the level of output unchanged. Thus aggregate output need not fall. However, the new Keynesian aggregate supply curve can lie above or below the AS_{NK} drawn in the figure, and output could fall as well as rise in the new Keynesian model.

In the traditional model, the aggregate supply curve does not shift, so the economy ends up at point T. Only the traditional model gives the unequivocal result that output falls from the contractionary policy (to Y_T).
This example illustrates that in either the new classical or new Keynesian model a contractionary policy does not necessarily lead to a decline in output and can even lead to a rise in output if the policy is less contractionary than expected.

Exercise 3

The Bank of Canada will buy securities, but if expectations are rational, then the Bank's efforts in stabilizing nominal interest rates will be hampered. People realizing that higher rates of money growth will eventually prove inflationary, will bid up nominal interest rates further. (Recall that the nominal interest rate is the sum of the real interest rate and the expected rate of inflation, so that if inflation expectations rise by more than the real interest rate falls, the nominal rate rises.)

Exercise 4

1. NC
2. NC
3. K
4. M, NC
5. NC
6. NC, NK
7. NK
8. K, M, NK

Exercise 5

1. NC, NK
2. NK
3. T
4. NK, NC
5. T
6. NC

Exercise 6

In the traditional model, your announcement will not affect the aggregate supply curve; expectations about the Bank's policy will not affect the outcome. In the new classical model, your announcement will shift up the aggregate supply curve if it is believed and so the Bank's policy will not be as expansionary as the governor of the Bank hopes. The governor would prefer that you keep quiet about his intentions. The new Keynesian model leads to a similar conclusion as the new classical model. The Bank's policy will not be as expansionary as the governor hopes; again, he would prefer you to keep quiet. However, the announced policy is likely to be more expansionary in the new Keynesian model than in the new classical model. If no one believes you when you make your announcement, then the aggregate supply curve will not shift even in the new classical or new Keynesian model.

Exercise 7

Part A. The main advantage is to reduce undesirable fluctuations in output. If the public has rational expectations, then they will form expectations about policy based upon their best "guess" as to what the Bank of Canada will do. If the Bank signals more clearly what it intends to do, then the Bank has a much better idea what the public policy expectations are. Therefore, the Bank will be more likely to match those expectations, and unintended output fluctuations will be reduced.

Part B. The advantage is to achieve a faster drop in the price level without a significant drop in output. If the public has rational expectations, and if the Bank of Canada is credible, then the public will expect a lower price level. When the Bank actually delivers the lower price level, public expectations will be met, and there will be no drop in output.

Exercise 8

A. Traditional Model

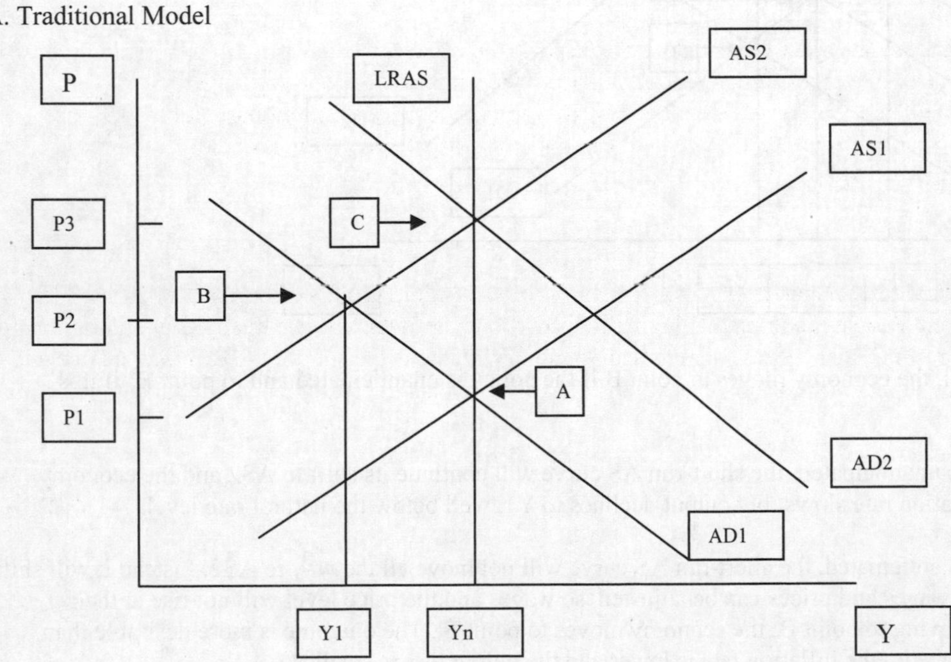

In the traditional model, the economy moves to point B whether the anti-inflation policy is anticipated or not. As the economy moves to point B, the inflation rate slows down because the price level increases only to P2 rather than to P3. The reduction in inflation has not been without cost: output has declined to Y1, which is well below the natural rate level.

B. The New Classical Model – Graph is same as that in part A).

In the new classical model, the economy moves to point B if the policy is unanticipated and to point A if it is anticipated.

If the anti-inflation policy is anticipated, it will occur without any output loss. In other words, the aggregate demand curve will remain at AD1, but because this is expected, wages and prices can be adjusted so that they will not rise, and the short-run aggregate supply curve will remain at AS1 instead of moving to AS2. The economy will remain at point A and aggregate output will remain at the natural rate level while inflation is stopped because the price level is unchanged.

If the anti-inflation policy is unanticipated, the AD curve remains at AD1, but the short-run AS curve continues its shift to AS2. The outcome of the unanticipated anti-inflation policy is a movement of the economy to point B. Although the inflation rate slows down in this case, it is not entirely eliminated. In addition, aggregate output falls below Yn.

C. New Keynesian Model

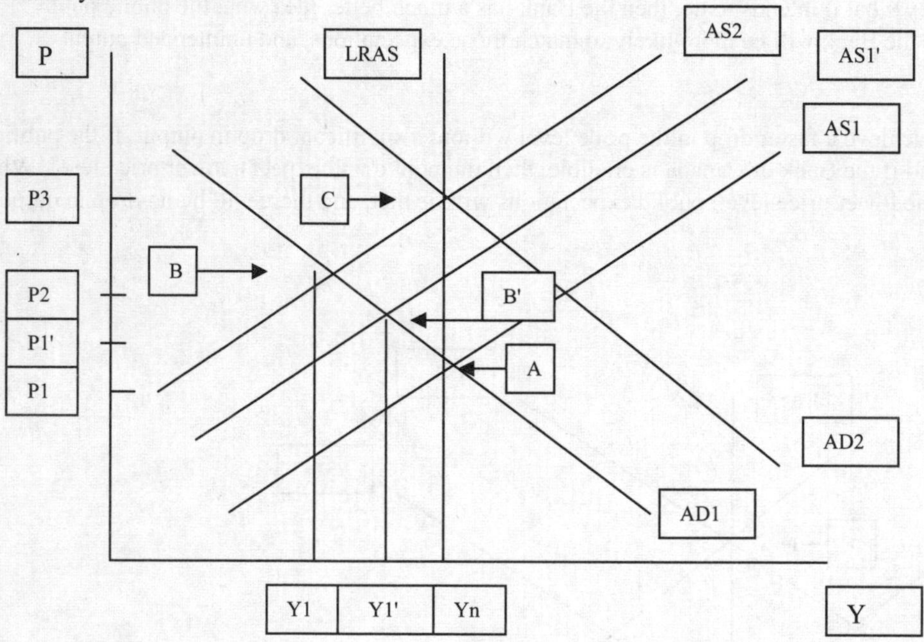

In the new Keynesian model, the economy moves to point B if the policy is unanticipated and to point B' if it is anticipated.

If the anti-inflation policy is unanticipated, the short-run AS curve will continue its shift to AS2 and the economy moves to point Y1. The inflation rate slows, but output declines to Y1, well below the natural rate level.

If the anti-inflation policy is anticipated, the short-run AS curve will not move all the way to AS2. Instead it will shift only to AS1' because some wages and prices can be adjusted, so wages and the price level will not rise at their previous rates. Instead of moving to point B, the economy moves to point B'. The outcome is more desirable than when the policy is unanticipated – the inflation rate is lower and the output loss is smaller.

D. According to the new classical and the new Keynesian model, for the anti-inflation policy to be successful in reducing inflation at the lowest output cost, the public must believe (expect) that it will be implemented. A successful anti-inflation policy must be credible.